MASTER OF NONE

Other titles by J. E. Morpurgo include:

American Excursion
The Birth of the U.S.A. (with R. B. Nye)
The Growth of the U.S.A. (with R. B. Nye)
The Road to Athens
Venice (with Martin Hürlimann)
Barnes Wallis: A Biography
Their Majesties' Royall Colledge
Treason at West Point
Allen Lane: King Penguin
Verses, Humorous and Post-Humorous
Christ's Hospital: An Introductory History

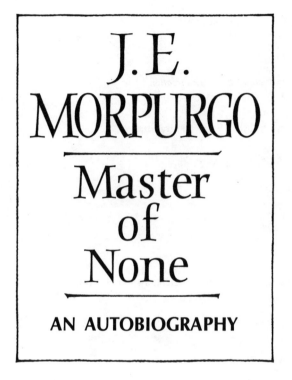

J.E. MORPURGO

Master of None

AN AUTOBIOGRAPHY

First published in Great Britain in 1990 by
Carcanet Press Limited
208-212 Corn Exchange Buildings
Manchester M4 3BQ

British Library Cataloguing in Publication Data
Morpurgo, J. E. (Jack Eric) *1918–*
   Master of none.
   1. Prose in English, 1945– Biographies
   I. Title
   828'.91408

   ISBN 0-85635-884-3

The publisher acknowledges financial assistance from
the Arts Council of Great Britain

Set in 10½pt Bembo by Koinonia Limited, Manchester
Printed and bound in England by SRP Ltd, Exeter

For Kippe

Contents

Poor Jack, farewell! I could
have better spared a better man.

Henry IV Part I

1

Tuppence to Piccadilly

I begin with humiliation, with a jar of home-made jam shattered on an asphalt-path and my flooding tears, unquenchable and publicly-shaming, at just that moment when I had thought to turn from apron-tied babyhood into superb and independent boyhood.

The mind at the business of remembering resists the decencies of chronology; there could be other beginnings, and almost all that force themselves on my memory's eye are both brighter and more consequential than this recollection of petty disaster.

Today as clearly as fifty years back I see the soiled brown leather of the armchair in which I sat when first I went to be taught by David Roberts. Then it was that my mind's life began. Then it was that I was freed from the drilled conventions that are generally imposed upon the bright but lazy child. Then it was that curiosity, imagination and intellect were brought together and given force and utility. Ever after, on into my adult years and even into my senescence, David's 'Why?' and 'Where is your authority?' have echoed and re-echoed in my ears.

I look back at myself standing before a mumbling Registrar in a shabby Registry Office, my pose of immaculate assurance for once shaken and my habitual decibel-laden voice for once quietened by surprise – almost by horror – at the vows that I was rehearsing, but I all unaware that even forty years later this mean ceremony which tied me to a girl of rare gentleness but unshakeable sureness that came to her as much from her own spiritual strength as from firm foundations in a family which for several generations had enjoyed an international reputation in the arts, would remain with me as representing the wisest decision that ever I made.

I stand at the rail of the ship that took me on my first lunatic excursion to North America. There began my professional career. From that moment I took on the pleasures and responsibilities of emotional dual-nationality. There was set the pattern for a life which has taken me to all the continents and set me down, a frequent visitor but seldom a foreigner, in many countries.

April 13, 1940? Should that date, the day when I was commissioned, be the first in my history? Certainly it was prelude to one of the most extraor-dinary of the many strange metamorphoses I have experienced, for there was (and is) little in my nature that made it conceivable that I would manage as a soldier, and nothing whatsoever to support a forecast that as soldier I would be tolerably successful or that I would come to look upon the Army with pride and affection.

Any one of these circumstances – and there are many more – I could with justice set down as my opening line, as signpost to the way I have passed – touched sometimes by tragedy and often by disappointment, never so sensationally successful as some predicted when I was in mid-course, but not without influence in many countries and on many people – a life that has been in sum wondrously contented because it has been so varied and because I have been held from despair and the consequences of immediate disaster by the care of family and friends.

Yet from all the possibilities, instinct demands that I choose as starting-point that trivial-seeming accident on a September afternoon in 1929 and leave all other beginnings to follow after, each to take its place – not necessarily according to the severe rule of chronology – as a theme in a composition which is, I hope, even after seventy years, still susceptible to novel variations.

On that day in 1929, as men but recently millionaires prepared to hurl themselves from skyscraper-windows, I entered upon a rich inheritance which has sustained me ever since. I became a Blue, a Scholar of Christ's Hospital, a Housey boy, a C.H. boy.

The news of this sensational change in my status, from child in a London elementary school to heir to Campion, Peele, Coleridge, Lamb and Leigh Hunt, had come to me one morning early that summer. Then, from his little podium in the Hall of Canonbury Road School, the Head Master read out to the whole school the results of the Junior County Examination set by the London County Council. I was arrogantly confident that I would pass into a grammar school but the list of successful candidates was short and so it was that I did not notice that the alphabetical order had not included an M before Mr Fox set down his paper, took off his glasses and, his beard made royal by pride, proclaimed in a voice unusually rich, 'And, most magnificent achievement of all: Morpurgo, a Scholarship to Christ's Hospital, only our second such in sixty years, the first since William Henry Portwood in 1916.'

That Bill Portwood was my godfather added to my excitement, and because over the years I had come to know a little of his enthusiasm for Housie (the affectionate noun always spelt this way; the adjective Housey), I was immediately certain that I was destined for the best school in the world, but the euphoria that came with triumph and anticipation was made up of a kaleidoscopic and contradictory series of glimpses granted me from Bill's happy reminiscences, by my reading of Elia's two mutually-contradictory essays, and by my devotion to *The Magnet* and *The Gem*.

For my golden addition to its Honours Board the Canonbury Road School was given a whole-holiday and it must have been as token of gratitude for this rare benison rather than from any nice appreciation of its cause that my schoolfellows carried me home on their shoulders, though whence they discovered this custom, so alien to the mores of Islington, I cannot tell. They did not read *The Magnet* or *The Gem*.

The approval of my elders was more sophisticated but no less effusive. My sisters knew that out of all London but a very few were selected for Christ's Hospital. My father, once he had survived the shock of hearing on his office-telephone 'Jack's in hospital', had the full measure of my success brought to him when, the news having climbed the hierarchical ladder of the Motor Union Insurance Company, he was summoned to receive congratulations from the Managing Director, a personage whom in all his twenty-five years service my father had never met, but himself an Old Blue. Bill Portwood preened himself as if it was his godfatherly care that had brought me to this worldly confirmation. Even the clergy at St Mary's looked upon me with a fresh eye: I was no longer the precocious child of energetic parishioners; I was about to become an equal.

It was Prebendary Hinde, that stalwart opponent of the 1928 Prayer Book, who first demonstrated to me this shift in the pattern of relationships. He invited me to tea. I had never before been inside the Vicarage, never before been alone with a man whose photograph appeared in national newspapers, never before been waited upon by a butler, yet I had not been five minutes in the Vicarage study before I realized that the great man was no less nervous than the small boy lost in a huge armchair, whom I watched with as much detachment as if he, Jack-bound-for-glory, was an actor on the stage at Sadler's Wells.

The Vicar talked too much, changed topics too abruptly, moved uneasily around the room, showed me the same Cambridge college-group twice and offered me fruit-cake three times after I had refused to eat any more. Then, as if suddenly deciding that he must act, he gathered his courage around him, pulled an upright chair to within inches of my knees and stared into my eyes. 'Jack, my dear boy, you are going away to school. There you will face temptation.'

Temptation, in the language of St Mary's, was just another word for drink. I was a member of the Band of Hope, three years earlier I had signed the Pledge, I had won medals for reciting prohibitionist verses, and for almost as long as I could remember I had spent at least one evening a week belting out 'choruses' – 'Fling out the life-line' and 'Washed in the Blood of the Lamb' – reading the words from brashly-coloured lantern-slides, but even at that age I could not believe that Prebendary Hinde was warning me that Christ's Hospital might sweep me to perdition on a flood of beer and port-and-lemon, nor credit that his embarrassment was created by knowledge – not given to me or to Bill Portwood – that Christ's Hospital was built around a public-house. There must be in his mind some more sinister vice and I thought I knew what it was, though I had understood but dimly the hints dropped by my comparatively sophisticated sisters. It

must be this mysterious, unspecified sin which the Vicar found it so difficult to name, this temptation that made him lower his habitually powerful
voice.

Suddenly he stood and then, his voice now unhesitating and strident,
his conviction as firm as anything that I had heard from him as, beside
William Joynson-Hicks and my father, he stood at Highbury Corner
denouncing the papistical impertinence of the 1928 Prayer book: 'My dear
boy, you are going away to school. They will insist that you bow to the
altar.'

He walked behind my chair and put his hands on my head as if to confirm my membership in his Church, the only church that he would recognize: 'My boy, when you speak to your God, stand up straight, and keep
your thumbs down the seams of your trousers.'

From all this attention and adulation I grew blasé. At about the time
when I had taken the Junior County Examination, I had been entered also
for a Foundation Scholarship at the local grammar school and for an exhibition at a small independent day-school in Hampstead. Both results
arrived on the same day – a week or so after the Christ's Hospital
announcement. I hardly bothered to open the envelopes; Bill Portwood
had taught me too well that if Christ's Hospital would have me, any other
school would clamour for my presence. Time has not reduced the force of
his lesson; even today honesty and arrogance combine to convince me that
he was right.

Though with the years I have come to acquire some considerable
knowledge of the methods of entry into C.H., there are questions that I
have never dared to ask the authorities for fear that the answers might
cause nightmares about what might have been. Was the announcement at
Canonbury Road School premature? Had I, in fact, won a Scholarship?
Was the oral examination that followed no more than a means whereby
Christ's Hospital establishes some measure for placing us in forms, or were
there present on that occasion some boys who had ben shown the Holy
Grail and then had it snatched from their grasping hands?

This much I have learnt: customarily the Orals were held in the pan-
elled Council Chamber of the Christ's Hospital Counting House in the
City of London, almost within blood-spurting distance of Tower Hill. In
1929 the 'Office' was being redecorated and so we were summoned to
Syon College on the Embankment.

My fears about that occasion are all retrospective but my memories are
clear and, if the details are enlarged and sharpened by what I came to know
later about my three inquisitors, still the reconstruction inspires nothing
but awe.

Facing me at the centre of a long shining table was William Hamilton
Fyfe, Head Master of Christ's Hospital, formerly Fellow of Merton
College, Oxford, subsequently Principal of Queen's University, Kingston,
Ontario, Principal and Vice-Chancellor of Aberdeen University and my

friend and mentor to the end of his days. On his right sat H. L. Price, a mathematician, whose inability to pronounce an *r* made him almost as notable among us as his great skill at all games and whose fame is secure in the history-books as the only man who scored a try in a Rugby Football International before any member of the opposing side had touched the ball. On Fyfe's left, the Senior History Master, A. C. W. Edwards, servant of Christ's Hospital for sixty years, whose teaching methods were 'progressive' before ever the word entered the pedagogic vocabulary, a man who stayed somehow in his profession always in advance of the current avant-garde.

I was quizzed about my home, my hobbies and my aspirations. I answered all questions well enough, I suppose, though I wish that I could boast for myself the hero's part in Willy Fyfe's favourite story. Sadly I must admit that it was some other Cockney child who, on being asked by Fyfe 'Why do you want to go to a boarding-school?' replied without pause 'Better 'eadmaster, sir', thereby justifying his racial inheritance, his place at Christ's Hospital and the gloss which Fyfe added whenever he told the story: 'I wish I could remember his name. I am sure that by now he is an ambassador.'

If there were in truth any doubts about my 'Scholarship' then Teddy Edwards had been suborned by the gods to remove them. Cunning in the examination-process beyond my years, I subverted one question to make of my answer a pompous and precocious little lecture on my hero, the Emperor Napoleon. Teddy Edwards, never unkind but frequently mischievous, rounded on me: 'But do you know anything of the history of the place where you live?' Two weeks earlier I had been to a 'Pageant of Islington' at the library in the Holloway Road. Even the harshest of examiners could not have failed a boy who talked of Dame Alice Owen, Sir Hugh Myddleton and the brothers Wesley. No Christ's Hospital interviewer could reject an eleven-year-old boy who was familiar with Charles Lamb and his fellow-Blue, George Dyer, *amicus redivivus*. My examining trio was both kindly and of Christ's Hospital. I had survived the ordeal-by-quiz, whatever its purpose.

The first hours of my first day as a Blue were anti-climactic, even disappointing.

Such was the sense of occasion that we had a taxi to take us to Great Tower Street and so widespread the knowledge of my glory that several neighbours broke with their custom of curtain-fluttering and actually came out to their doorsteps to wave us off. My mother was with us, tight-gloved and tight-lipped.

The Christ's Hospital Counting House was still in the hands of the decorators. We sat in a draughty waiting-room among used paint-pots and builder's ladders, from time to time attempting conversation with other scrubbed parents and shined boys. It was not so very different from

Canonbury Road except – and this hideous truth I realized with a sadness that shattered the glory of the Summer – that these other children were just as bright as me; I was no longer a prodigy, just one terrified child, frightened of showing his fear, convinced that he was unique only in that he had fear to hide. We waited, it seemed for hours, and then at last some lordly official asked to see our health-certificates, issued us with free railway tickets and gave us house-labels to tie to our cases. I was to be in Coleridge B. I looked around the room. Lamb A, Barnes B, Thornton A: there was no other boy present destined for Coleridge B. My attitude to my companions changed. Now, it seemed to me, these were old friends and I was to be taken from them, hurled out alone into the desert of Coleridge B.

On to London Bridge Station. The School, all but new boys, had gone back the day before and so the train journey was a continuation of the awkwardness at the Counting House, all of us gathering into a community founded upon apprehension, and I miserably aware that even this communion must so be decimated.

Everything was unreal. It was as if I were acting in a play in which I was invisible to the other characters and unheard by the audience. When at last I met my first established schoolfellow I did not catch his name. This was my 'nurse', the boy who was to guide me through my first weeks. He it was who, with the experience of a year or so of seniority, was to coach me in our complex customs. His first duty was to extricate me from my parents and march me off to the Wardrobe. There he crammed me into my first pair of knee-breeches and then (and in the fledgling weeks thereafter) it was he who taught me how to dress in Housey clothes. He it was who persuaded me that the long yellow stockings must be folded neatly below the knee and not pulled thigh-wards as their length seemed to demand, he who showed me how to fix my bands whilst I attempted the contortion of watching what was going on just below my chin: neck-band safety-pinned to the centre of the back of the shirt-collar, another safety-pin ready and open in the place of an ordinary mortal's collar-stud, band-ends set to mathematical exactitude, starched linen gripped in dry mouth; close the front-pin and, when the long blue coat is on and done up, in theory if not in novitiate practice, the two cravat-like bands will drop central to a line extended upwards from the seven silver buttons – one large and six small – that bear the likeness of Edward the Sixth, our Founder King. He it was who set my girdle (never a 'belt', though the Lower School version was little different from the leather strap which, but a few minutes earlier, had held up my grey flannel shorts).

Encased in unyielding cloth and spiritually mummified by disbelief that this puppet-figure could be me, I was returned by my nurse to my parents. My father's eye glistened with pride, my mother's with anguish and I was ashamed for both of them, certain that they would indulge in some silly demonstration that would be reported to my fellows and so damn me throughout the eternity of schooldays that lay ahead of me. I shivered as my father asked my 'nurse' for his name. 'McRae, sir.' Nobody ever called my father 'sir'; I was embarrassed for him and suddenly I wanted my parents to go. They did not belong in all this spaciousness. They could not match the blatant dignity that surrounded us, already even the elegance of my new uniform set me in another world; I belonged with McRae, not with them, felt lonely in their presence and bereft when McRae disappeared.

For some time we wandered, aimlessly and speaking very little. All the buildings were cathedral-size but which was which I did not know and I would not let my father enquire.

Although the great clock chimed out each quarter of an hour (a sound which still sometimes rings through my dreams with Greenwich precision), there was much consulting of watches. Then suddenly we discovered ourselves in front of the Coleridge Block. We walked straight through the centre-door (something I would not do again until I was a Grecian and Captain of my House) marched through the building and out on to the Coleridge Asphalt. I prayed for hasty and unobserved goodbyes. The past was ended and the short uncomfortable present. Now I could begin my future.

I watched as my parents walked off down the long straight path towards the station. My father's back was stern with determination not to turn for one last wave. My mother, her dumpy figure wrapped for once in a new coat, stumbled along beside him and I knew even then that she was bewildered. She had not been able to share the euphoria that had gripped my father, my sisters and me since first we heard the news of my 'Scholarship'; for her there was nothing for pride and even a little for shame in driving an eleven-year-old out of the security of his family. She could not comprehend the strange power of Englishness which had suddenly overpowered her husband and son, quelling their habitual demonstrativeness so that neither had shown any emotion at this unnatural parting.

They were almost out of sight when the jar of home-made jam which my mother had given me slipped through my fingers and smashed, a hideous, embarrassing mess, upon the asphalt.

I began to sob.

That moment of paradox, when the elation of discovering my new inheritance was broken by the realization that I could not shake off entirely my childhood dependence, I take then as the beginning of my story. Were the character I am attempting to describe someone not myself, were I seeking to produce from documentary evidence the biography of a stranger, I would begin most probably on that April night in 1918 when Zeppelins raided London for the last time and I was born in Tottenham, Middlesex, the youngest child and only son of a Cockney insurance-clerk and his Dutch wife. But I stand unashamedly by my conviction that without Christ's Hospital there would have been no story to write – and leave the psychologists and the zealous egalitarians to make what they will of the statement.

Christ's Hospital wrought a miracle for me as for so many of its sons and daughters. Yet, when compared with the intake of the more conventionally-inspired public-schools, or even with the population of the grammar and comprehensive schools, we were (and are) a heterogeneous collection with no educational or sociological unity other than lack of parental wealth. Among my Christ's Hospital friends of all school generations are some who came from what might be called public-school families, some who in the words of one of my predecessors at school, a friend of my later years, John Middleton Murry, came from 'the black-coated proletariat . . . the spiritual waifs of modern industrial society', and some whose home-roots were settled in the slime of big-city slums.

Almost I belonged with Murry's group. My father, like his, was a clerk. My home, like his, was in the inner, meaner suburbs of London. Yet there was in my family history a touch of the extravagant which gave me advantages that I must recognize.

So it is that I must go back beyond September 1929, and beyond April 1918, to my father's esoteric boyhood and young manhood. His roaming youth, his rare but largely unused gift for languages and his thwarted versatility explain in part how it came about that a Londoner of Londoners married a Dutch girl and as often as not spoke Dutch at home, but explain also how it was that a man who never earned more than ten pounds a week somehow contrived to give to his children a love of the theatre, some admittedly uncritical enthusiasm for opera, a highly-selective but by no means English-centred knowledge of history, a zest for sport as well as for the things of the mind and the spirit, and – for my future most important of all – a view of the far horizon.

I must go back, too, to my mother's lovable but unintellectual acceptance of the tenets of the Evangelical Wing of the Church of England, which took us all to the severe altar of St Mary's Islington, the high church of the Low Church group in the Anglican Communion, where we gathered to ourselves the sonorities of the Authorised Version and The Book of Common Prayer, where when young we came under the powerful and stern influence of Prebendary Hinde and after him under the kindlier but still severe aegis of John Marshall Hewitt, and through him came to accept as friends his curates, two of them later archbishops, Donald Coggan of Canterbury and Hugh Gough of Melbourne.

My father was energetic, even prodigal, in his determination to hold us from the meanness of vision that was then common in the streets of North London. For me he sacrificed his one free Saturday morning each month and, savouring the pretence that he was winning a trick in his match with the General Ombibus Company by using his season-ticket on this extra occasion, he took me 'Up West' to the National Gallery, or into the City to St Paul's Cathedral. Even despite our indigence, sometimes we went holidaying to Belgium or Holland, in those days extraordinary adventures for a lower-middle-class family that were made possible, I am convinced, only because my father's fluency in French, Flemish and Dutch allowed him to seek out for us cheap lodgings. He had a mind littered with historical gossip, with delicious trivia such as must have driven a formally-trained hist-orian to despair, and what he did not know he invented, but the stream of anecdotes that poured out from him as we stood on the battlefield at Waterloo or walked through the sinister rooms of the Gevangepoort in The Hague were all that could be desired by a small boy whose mind was delirious with curiosity about the past. Still today, when I stand worshipping at the high altar of the Rijksmuseum, Rembrandt's *Night Watch*, I hear my father's voice as he describes for me the life-history of every member of Captain Cocq's company, even the little girl in the golden dress, and I wish that I could bring back to memory his interpolations on the biography of the artist, whom he never failed to call, with nicely-conceited pedantry, Rembrandt Harmentsoon van Rijn, for they were few of them canonical but all of them revelations. One sentence from my father's Rijksmuseum monologue stays with me. Each time, as we turned away from the *Night Watch*, he said something in Dutch and then, for me, translated it into English: 'If you use what you know already, then in time you may come to understand those mysteries which now exercise your mind.' It was twenty years and more before I discovered that the words were not his own; they are from Rembrandt Harmentsoon van Rijn.

These foreign excursions were rare. For holidays in most years we could afford no more than a week in a Buckinghamshire farmhouse or in a fisherman's cottage at Leigh-on-Sea. Yet all the year my mother worked as volunteer for the Children's Country Holiday Fund, organizing days and weeks in the country for the slum children of Islington. And Islington in the 1920s was grim with slums, rat-ridden, thief-infested tenements full of out-of-work fathers, slatternly mothers and shoeless children.

Almost my first memory is of my mother's charity. It must have been in the summer of 1922 that men came to repave the St Paul's Road outside our house. There was that year a heatwave and even then I realized the discomfort the men were suffering and sensed, perhaps, something of their humiliation. Only four years earlier, these had been the heroes who held the skies from falling on civilization and the tattered khaki that they wore as they hacked at the roadway was all that remained of the glamour that had won them kisses in Armentières, the glory of successful Crusaders as they marched behind Allenby into Jerusalem, and the frenzied approval of their compatriots on Armistice Night.

Three or four times a day I was sent out with cups of tea for the workmen and I must have become something of a mascot, for they allowed me to sit with them while they drank and they taught me the songs of the trenches and the desert. Those songs remained with me, and when I myself became a soldier, I bettered all my mess-companions with verse after verse, quaintly-bowdlerized, of 'Three German Officers crossed the Rhine' or 'When this ruddy War is over'. Even later, when Joan Littlewood brought *Oh What a Lovely War* to the London stage, it was not the Western Front that I saw but the St Paul's Road, and the adult tears that I could not hold back were shed not for a history that was mine only by way of folk-memory, nor yet for my more recently acquired burden of tragedy, but for a group of navvies digging in an Islington street – and above all for Captain Halton.

Halton stood out from his companions, not because of any palpable seniority nor yet because he had an extra ribbon, blue and white, in front of the other ribbons which, like all the navvies, he wore defiantly on his khaki tunic, but because he had a strange accent. I soon discovered that he was a Canadian, though for all I knew being a Canadian was like having scarlet fever. Halton was invited in and became a frequent visitor. He would take off his boots, scrub himself in the scullery, eat at our table, and then for hours on end, he talked with my father. Although they became close friends there was no agreement between them. Sometimes they called a halt to discord and spoke of Vimy Ridge, of Loos and of Poperinghe – this I loved – but most of the time my father went on and on about how all would come right when Ramsay Mac won power and Halton punctuated these lectures with protests that the Conservatives must soon bring back to Britain dignity, sense and prosperity.

I was not sufficiently sophisticated to relish paradox. Despite their intimacy, my father, the ardent Socialist, never failed to address his friend as *Captain* Halton and we, the children of a 'businessman', were never allowed to refer to the navvy without granting him the full dignity of his military title – 'only one rank below Major Attlee'. But for me the most sensational discovery was that Halton's children called him by his Christian name.

Looking back, I love my mother for her charity but I doubt if it served me well. She respected those she helped; I came soon to look down upon them; my early and entirely undisciplined greed for literary association identified my mother as the Lady Bountiful of Victorian novelettes and us as a genteel but impoverished family maintaining, despite our restricted circumstances, a decent benevolence towards our inferiors. The illusion, though sensationally inappropriate, was supported by accidents in our manner of living that were both physical and social. Our house in St Paul's Road had what I then took to be a large garden; all the houses on our side of the street had similar gardens. Behind the houses that faced us there ran the North London Railway – that mysterious but most convenient of lines, a link between London's northern and southern suburbs and between us and our relatives in Richmond. When five years old I still envied our neighbours across the street their view of the trains; already when I was seven I had come to recognize the consequence if not the cause of proximity to a railway: the houses on that side of the street were meaner, more dilapidated, broken up into tenements and filled with men, women and children who spoke a Cockney dialect that was forbidden to me.

It was when I was seven that we moved to Canonbury Square. As yet I could not appreciate the remnants of Georgian elegance which, after the Second World War, were to be used as the basis for a restoration that was to make this one of the most expensive addresses in Central London, the focus of covetousness above all for the more successful practitioners of the arts, but already at seven I could not miss the overtones of respect shown, even by my schoolteachers, to a boy who lived in Canonbury Square, a whole world if only a hundred yards away from Fagin's Kitchen in Canonbury Dwellings.

By the late 1920s the Canonbury Renaissance had begun and in the decade before the War the advance-guard moved, marching ahead of that post-war regiment of intellectuals which included George Orwell, Basil Spens, Walter Allen and my favourite broadcasting-colleague, Lionel Hale. There was, for example, at Number 25, only four doors away from us, a 'distinguished writer' – so distinguished that I cannot remember his name. Whenever he saw me in Christ's Hospital uniform, he stopped me for talk, once he lent me two books 'one by a schoolfellow of yours, Edmund Blunden, and one by a schoolfellow of mine, Percy Bysshe Shelley'.

But Old Etonians and their kind, even Old Etonian authors, were still uncommon in Islington whereas, whether in St Paul's Road or Canonbury Square, there was a substantial difference between our way of life and the way of life of many of our neighbours, a difference that set us above most of them in the unspecified but clearly understood hierarchy. We were poor but I was always well-clothed and well-fed. From time to time (as now I can guess, when my maternal grandmother lived with us and shared the household expenses) we had a maid, always some stunted Welsh child. My elder sister was at grammar school. Of us only my father had even a trace of Cockney in his voice. My mother dispensed charity; my Canonbury Road schoolfellows received it. We went regularly to the Wells (ninepence a gallery-seat, or sixpence 'late doors'), in those glorious days when the theatre put on opera, ballet and Shakespeare week-about. (Rich among my earlier memories, as much for the fact that we paid all of one-and-sixpence a seat as for the magic of the performance and its conse-quence – I heard 'voices' for weeks after – is that evening when we, all five of us, went to the Regent Theatre opposite King's Cross Station to see Sybil Thorndike play St Joan.) Theatre-going, books in the house, some knowledge of foreign places that had not been gathered in the esoteric experience of war, and the circumstance that none among our immediate acquaintances, except the clergy at St Mary's and our doctors, were in any obvious way our social superiors, made us in Islington middle-class.

True, in London we seldom moved outside the society of Islington and never with any confidence. True too that, even within Islington, we had no contact with the prosperous businessmen who owned the palaces on either side of Highbury New Park, who employed butlers, chauffeurs, and one of them still, when I was eight years old, a coachman. Kensington, Chelsea and Hampstead were as far beyond us as Balmoral, and Balmoral was not as close to Heaven as Compton Wynyates, the home of our landlord, the Marquess of Northampton, to which we were taken, once a year in charabanc-loads, for tea – outside the house. The inhabitants of such places we regarded, not as upper-class and therefore superior, but as upper-class and therefore incomprehensible.

So it was that until I was eleven, when I went to Christ's Hospital, I was to my own way of thinking, and to a considerable extent also by the acclaim of my contemporaries, undeniably of high social status. Then, as I inherited a world of tradition and the privilege of the centuries, so also did I gather to myself for the first time some sense of *egalité*.

At Canonbury Road School I was cosseted as much for the sake of my parents as for my own infant precocity. When I took a note to school seeking to be excused some activity, my case was accepted without question and the note passed round the class, so that all might profit by inspecting my father's impeccable copper-plate. When the school governors made their visitations, I was invariably chosen to recite. I was top in everything and I gathered to myself as prizes a small collection of children's books which I never opened, because I suspected them of being far less interesting than the books owned by my father and sisters. To this day I have not read *Naju of the Nile*, though I see that it was presented to me in 1928 by the London County Council for being 'First in General Excellence' (a strange concept), but the second-hand copy of the two-volume *Life of Napoleon* by John Holland Rose given to me as a birthday present in that same year contains my marginalia and a heavy underlining in red crayon of the epigraph, a quotation from the Emperor's last instructions to the King of Rome: 'Let my son often read and reflect on history; this is the only true philosophy.'

I do not think that I delude myself when I say that my elementary school-companions did not resent my successes and at the time – as in the years that have followed on those rare occasions when I have met a Canonbury Road contemporary – I was treated with friendliness and with that strange amalgam of respect and pity which those who can see and handle the results of their labours reserve for their fellows whose work is less practical and more mysterious.

There was much that was vicious in the English social system of the 1920s but I doubt that its failings were in truth those for which it has been castigated by succeeding generations. Too many were hideously disadvantaged; children came barefoot to school, unemployed Welsh miners sang in the Upper Street, old soldiers begged outside the Essex Road Underground Station, but despite the General Strike and the Jarrow March – at least in an area such as Islington where the social mix was the rich (very few of them), the poor, the very poor and the desperate – there was little evidence of the covetousness which has soured English life since the Second War. Though our aspirations must now seem mean, even as children at an elementary school we were aware of the possibility of social mobility. By way of the Shoreditch Technical School, Barnsbury Central or the Islington Continuation School some would become craftsmen; some, by way of the Grammar and County Schools, Clerical Class civil servants – or even teachers. Pitman's and Clark's were the route to a job in an office; Cossor's, we were told, paid good wages for factory-hands; the Services were still recruiting – occasionally – and life in the Royal Navy was immeasurably superior to existence in Canonbury Dwellings or Halton Mansions.

It was one of the contradictions of the time (and infuriating to my father, a devout Fabian) that throughout the 1920s our ward returned a Conservative to Parliament. It was typical of the neighbourliness which survived that many from our street, both Conservative and Labour voters, joined together and allied themselves with the police to hurl back forcefully the Communist and Fascist thugs from the next ward who had the impertinence to extend their Redshirt *versus* Blackshirt battles into our neighbourhood.

At Canonbury Road School I was the bright boy, the scholar, but I was hideously incompetent with chisel and hammer and though, because of my father's care, I was not as clumsy in the playground as were my few academic rivals, it was clear that I would never acquire the athletic prowess that forecast for one or two among us a career with the Arsenal or at Lords. Even though I outshone them all in the classroom and in the company of adults, I was too timid to venture alone into a shop and I was terrified of the dark. This fallibility was known to my schoolfellows. I was never teased about it; indeed the more kindly of my class-mates would find some excuse to walk me home on winter evenings or to go with me to the shabby little front-room shop opposite the school to spend our halfpennies on snakes, miggies and glarnies.

I cannot deny that school-life at Canonbury Road was for me generally and almost unnaturally easy. The many privileges that I enjoyed should have made me into an unbearable little prig, and perhaps I was. All that I can plead in my own defence was that I was rich in enthusiasm and curiosity, and to this I must add that the staff of Canonbury Road School worked almost as zealously as my family to encourage in me these antidotes to priggishness. More important: that staff tried just as hard to offer some enrichment to all their pupils.

There is a belief, widely-held and lovingly fostered by the educational press and by politicians of the Left, that the reform of our primary schools is a recent development brought to us by grace of the Welfare State. As counter to this myth I can offer only the evidence of my six years at one North London elementary school. It may be that Canonbury Road was unique; I do not know; but this I do know, that sixty years ago Canonbury Road School was launched upon experiments which, in all but the superficialities of classroom discipline, would make many of the vaunted advances of recent years look no more adventurous than the efforts of a Victorian dame-school.

The building – it stands still, unaltered and even now in use as a primary school – was already a slum but in it we learnt French, by the direct method. Hubert Welch, an excellent musician who was also the organist and choir-master at St Mary's, taught us to read music well enough so that we could follow the simple line of a Stanford sea-shanty, and by statement and quotation on a tinny piano, persuaded us that Bach, Beethoven and Brahms are Music, with an upper-case M. We wrote and edited our own school-magazine, hideous in violet ink and blotchily reproduced on the school 'jelly', but for us infinitely satisfying because it carried our own verses, our own short stories and our own sporting-journalism: accounts of the game between Arsenal Reserves and Tottenham Hotspur Reserves, and even a description of the Boat Race.

Matches between the Gunners and the Spurs caused me agonies of divided loyalty, for I had been born within shouting distance of White Hart Lane and lived within cheering-range of Highbury. As for the Boat Race, for what reason I do not know I supported Cambridge, wept unashamedly when Oxford won, I think in 1923, and took to myself the glory of that long run of Cambridge triumphs which saw me through my Islington school-days. I doubt that I knew what a university was; none of my family and very few of my acquaintances had progressed that far up the educational ladder, though before I left Canonbury Road my sister Bess was at Teacher Training College. My schoolfellows were just as ignorant and no less partisan; for weeks before the Boat Race we wore our favourite's colours and bought Oxford and Cambridge gob-stoppers, sucking off layers of dark and light blue sugar and inspecting the last remnant of the sweet before it disintegrated, in the belief that its colour would forecast the winner of the Race.

From Canonbury Road we went out on local-history projects, and we were shepherded on school journeys to Middlesbrough and to the Yorkshire Dales.

Without in any way understanding what was being done to us, we, most of us children of the bedraggled streets around Highbury Corner, were drilled into a passable imitation of the patterns used in schools of a kind that none of our parents and, I suspect, few of our teachers had ever seen. We were formed into houses and, unprotestingly and indeed with pride, we wore school-caps and ties in our house-colours. The school badge was a symbolic representation of Canonbury Towers, that mixture of Tudor and Edwardian red-brick which seems to rise accidentally from the surrounding houses just behind Canonbury Square, to this day one of the least-known of London's historic buildings, and the setting for an obscure Gothic novel that not one of my erudite literary acquaintances has read. The four houses were named after Islington notables. Clio loves a coincidence; I was in Compton House, so-called after the family name of our landlord the Marquess of Northampton and my future was to be much affected by the activities of one of his distinguished ancestors, the soldier-turned-bishop of London, a benefactor of Christ's Hospital and author of its sonorous Graces, a founding-father and first Chancellor of the College of William and Mary in Virginia.

Another coincidence, less remote in consequence and more nearly understood by me even in childhood, occurred during that school journey to Middlesbrough. I loathed almost every moment of those two weeks. I was separated from my family for the first time. Touring factories bored me, the sight of cascading molten-metal horrified me and the smell of chemicals brought me the shame of vomiting in public, I was too small to enjoy the daunting walks through the Cleveland hill-country which seemed to be our only respite from technological indoctrination. But, on the day before we returned to London we were invited to tea in the gardens of Grey Towers, the home of Sir Arthur Dorman, joint-founder of the great Tees-side engineering firm Dorman Long.

How the invitation was contrived I cannot recall or imagine, but I do remember that my first sight of Sir Arthur was a devastating disappointment. I had never before seen a knight and he was ordinary, no Lancelot or Galahad, not a Raleigh, a Drake or a John Moore, just an untidy old man in dirty grey flannels, a patched tweed jacket and a shabby panama-hat; less impressive than my father in his carefully-pressed city suit, bowler-hat, carrying always his silver-topped walking stick; far, far less awesome than Prebendary Hinde in his severe clerical frock-coat and shovel-hat. But when, I suppose in a desperate effort to bridge the conversational gap between a sixty-year-old industrialist and a group of Cockney children, Sir Arthur announced that he too had once been a schoolboy in London, at Christ's Hospital in Newgate Street, the excitement of association overcame my shyness and I blurted out 'My godfather was at Christ's Hospital'.

In a more sophisticated society, an attempt such as this to identify with the great man must have brought down upon me the rancour of contemporaries but it was part of the miracle wrought by those not-so-simple schoolteachers that they had instilled in their charges not envy for those who had succeeded but pride in their success. The school's honours-board was prominently displayed, with the names of those who had won scholarships to Owen's, to Holloway and Highbury County Schools, the names of our three Military Medallists and our one D.C.M., our two Middlesex cricketers and our three Arsenal footballers, but only Bill, in his bluecoat and white bands, had his photograph on show in the School Hall. My relationship to Bill was well-known and made me something of a hero by association, as if I had been Joe Hulme's cousin or Charlie Buchan's nephew. Had I kept silent in the garden of Grey Towers one of my schoolfellows would have spoken up in my place. As it was my piping boast won for me a personally-conducted tour of Sir Arthur's treasures and the stupendous gift of half-a-crown.

Because of Bill I was dutifully delighted by the faded photographs of Sir Arthur as a Blue. Though I did not understand what my host meant when he pointed to a model of Sydney Harbour Bridge saying 'That's ours', I knew that this was the moment which would be the dramatic centre in the account of my visit that I would give to my waiting companions.

I have not seen Grey Towers since that day in 1928. It is more than likely a Victorian monstrosity of the kind that successful industrialists built around all Northern cities, but, though I had toured the Tower of London, Hampton Court, the Huis ten Boos and, of course, Canonbury Towers, these were to me history-book palaces inhabited only by the ghosts of history-book men and women. A man lived in Grey Towers, a man who called me Jack, a man who was almost a relation, and this man took me into rooms for which he had names that for the most part I had never before heard used in the context of ordinary domestic life. 'The library. . .', it was nothing like so grand as the building in Holloway Road but it was personal, and I grasped the difference and knew envy. All these books belonged to Sir Arthur and would not have to go back after a fort-night or else be the cause of a penny fine. 'My study. . . ; Prebendary Hinde had a study but at that time I had never seen inside it. 'My dressing-room. . .', but where was the theatre? Or was it the place for dressing-up? Perhaps this was where the Knight kept his armour.

There was nothing mean-spirited and certainly nothing servile in Canonbury Road's aping of a public school. Looking back through years that have brought me some knowledge of educational institutions in many countries, I can see that the experiment was doomed and perhaps even misguided, that the loyalties engendered in us were pathetically out of place in a society scrabbling for survival, but even now I cannot find it in me to condemn the efforts of our teachers as either retrogressive or laugh-able.

Later, but not so very much later, when I came to be a member of a truly privileged school community, I was quick to appreciate that the Islington copy lacked several important elements. At Canonbury Road we were taught to respect academic excellence and there was, within the limits presented by equipment, some opportunity for achieving excellence and winning respect by effort other than academic. We had both competition and sociability. But all attempts to create for us a continuity of community were bound to be artificial and thus only minimally successful. The school had no evident past, except in so far as it was represented by its grimy building. Compton, Spencer and Paget were not one with us as Campion and Peele, Lamb and Coleridge, Murry and Blunden were part of the life and being of a Housey boy. We learnt about them but we did not recog-nize their lives in our own; indeed we knew that they would always be foreigners to our world. When, on occasion, some old boy came visiting from his secondary school he was to a few of us an inspiration but to all of us a stranger, no longer a member of our intimate society and scarcely to be accepted as one who had ever formed part of that society; he had discarded his past and came to us as an emissary from a distant and uncomprehended country. Because the school had no continuing past it had no future. Even for the present, school was for most of us (and even in a sense for me, who enjoyed the privilege of a family which was both prepared and competent to be interested in my school hours) a place where we abandoned our real life and our genuine traditions for the make-believe of a social structure imposed upon us by our teachers.

In one other facet of school life − simpler but not unimportant − the staff failed to complete the copy they wished to engineer: there was little sporting activity. Our teachers tried, but the environment, the time-table, and, I suspect, the social ethos, were against them.

Like many another London borough, Islington was well-supplied with open spaces. Closest of all to the school were the two gardens in Canonbury Square, divided spatially one from another only by the main road and its tramlines, but spiritually, socially and even physically, as unlike as the Celestial City and the Slough of Despond. On one side all was sunlight, well-ordered displays of flowers, their cheerful colours challenging the drabness of Canonbury Road, on the other darkness, padded earth and stunted, unfulfilled bushes. But neither the one side nor the other was large enough for organized games. Also, not far away, there was Highbury Fields, but the Fields, its tennis courts and open-air swimming-pool were by some *lex non scripta* the province of the bourgeois citizens of Highbury New Park, of Compton Terrace and of the mysterious gated cantonment, John Betjeman's own Aberdeen Park:

> Geranium-beds for the lawn, Venetian blinds for the sun.
> A separate tradesman's entrance, straw in the mews behind,
> Just in the four-mile radius where hackney carriages run,
> Solid Italianate houses for the solid commercial mind.

Not so very far away there was Finsbury Park, a green barrier between the shambling, bustling, dingy Seven Sisters Road and the trim prosperity up towards Palmers Green and Southgate. In the other direction there was Clissold Park with its mangy zoo and for me, through my father's introduction, stern echoes of the great Victorian preacher, Charles Haddon Spurgeon and, far more welcome, associations also with the young Edgar Allan Poe. To these two parks we were taken, occasionally, from school to play cricket on a grass square or football between real goal-posts but these expeditions were voluntary excursions on Saturday mornings. Generally, such team-games as were arranged for us or by us set in motion spontaneously were confined to the school's asphalt playground. Cricket was customarily single-wicket, the bowler's crease marked by a jacket on the ground and the stumps by chalked-lines on the school wall close to the gritty water-taps, though on more pompous occasions, for inter-house matches, two wickets, made to the appropriate size out of blocks of wood were set up, like enlarged book-ends, in the centre of the playground. For our games of soccer, at one end we marked a chalk goal on the brick wall of the noxious outside lavatory and, at the other, we signalled the limits of the goal by hanging coats from the railings.

There was for most of us a difference in kind and not merely a difference in skill between our sports in the playground and the sports that we watched and followed with the aid of cigarette-cards and the back-pages of our fathers' newspapers. What in the playground we called cricket and football were no more than formally-modified versions of the shuffling, shrieking, ball-bouncing tactics that was usual when we were all gathered together out of school. Save for the gifted few, who could dance their way out of the glum streets on to the sporting-pages and so on to ownership of a pub or a corner-shop (but not yet, as did their successors, into the Savoy Grill or the Royal Enclosure), it was not our birthright to be participants. We were by nature spectators. Every other week I went with my father to watch Arsenal Reserves and at Highbury on those Saturday afternoons, even in the brutally impoverished 1920s, I met my schoolfellows with their fathers. (First-team games were too expensive for any of us.)

Cricket at that time did not interest me. Later, many years later, I was to come to love cricket almost as I loved Rugby football and poetry, and to have my passion enhanced because I was allowed to share it with cricket's poet-laureate, Edmund Blunden. In old age, with but one eye and that disastrously dimmed, paradoxically I take more pleasure in cricket well-played than in any other relaxation unless it be the music of Mozart – or the sight of a good-looking girl. But at the age of ten I cared little for cricket, perhaps because my father cared less, but more probably because when watching cricket, that most beautiful of all team-games, some recognition of innate cowardice denied to me what is, for the small boy as spectator, the magic of imagining himself as hero.

Cricket is not only the loneliest of all team-games it is also the most implacable. A mistake made in either code of football can be redeemed by subsequent effort; on the cricket-field a catch dropped is irrevocable, a partner run-out is gone for ever and forever furious. Swift though I was in the class-room and in the company of adults shamefully competent, I went still in terror of revealing myself as fool in public. Nowhere is it easier to turn shambling idiot than on the cricket-field and nowhere is idiocy more public.

'A man in his time. . .' Even as a child I did not lack the capacity to perform. Then and ever after, for me as I suppose for all men and all women, some of my acts were honest but polished projections of my real self, some contrived to please either my audience or myself, but as a child I relished only those parts in which I excelled. Christ's Hospital gave me much. It taught me to refine what was genuine and to suspect what rang untrue in my projection of the personality I thought myself to be. But not the least of the gifts that I owe to Housie was the blessing of confidence. (My enemies and the enemies of Christ's Hospital describe it as the customary arrogance of Blues!) With confidence I was able to perfect those roles which, already at Canonbury Road, I had played with zest. Academically, I became more critical and more self-critical. At Canonbury Road my infant efforts at verse and short stories had been so extravagantly successful with my mentors that I had come dangerously close to thinking myself a literary prodigy. At Christ's Hospital, where scribbling was as much part of the tradition as punting a rugger ball, where there was Sydney Carter two years above me and Keith Douglas two below, no brash effort could suffice. I began to write again, with enthusiasm unabated but now with consideration and some sensitivity. On stage, in the Dining Hall pulpit or standing at the lectern in Chapel, I was unashamedly florid; no need to hold back my undeniably rich voice, no need to restrain my Heaven-granted capacity for sight-reading. And, almost to my surprise (surprise that is with me to this day), I discovered in myself a new talent: I could dive with some elegance.

Whether the sustained performance of my final year at C.H. was pose or representation of the real me I must leave to the verdict of my contemporaries. I know, even now, that but for the influence of Christ's Hospital, I could not have held, as House Captain, my stance as leader-king, as firm but just and kindly demagogue, and I know that it was to some extent fashioned – if with embellishments – upon the models of my predecessors, but I like to think that this was truly what I had become.

Yet if Christ's Hospital encouraged me to go where my talents lay, and in that process made those talents glister whereas without its benevolent influence they would have shone only as fool's gold, it gave to me a blessing even more comforting: it trained me to the pleasures of playing supporting roles, taught me that there is nothing for shame and much for satisfaction in being second-best. So it was that at C.H. I bustled round Rugby pitches. I shot at the rifle-range. I hit my way about the Fives Courts with abundant energy and sufficient skill to give my more competent partners their chance at the winning shot. I enjoyed myself and it was, I believe, not my successes, not my starring parts, but this generous training in the art of the bit-player which prepared me for the most surprising role of my life – and that little more than a walk-on part – as the unflappable, thoughtful, efficient but utterly unheroic Army officer; just as it was that preparation which, many years later, has made it possible for me to sustain over several decades a much more difficult performance, as lead in a self-dramatized version of *The Light that Failed*. But, though I had a good eye and safe hands, earned my House colours when I was only fifteen and once played a supporting role to much applause (5 not out in 76 minutes while, at the other end, Peter McRae won the Cup for Coleridge B), because I dared not risk playing Fool in public not even C.H. could teach me to enjoy being cast as cricketer. It was not until three years after I left school when, having through all that time suffered from cricket-starvation in North America, I determined to recover my Englishness by joining a club far too good for my pretensions, that I found a mode for acting my way out of my timidity.

Then it was that, determined to shine before my watching American fiancée, who knew nothing and cared less for the game and thought a run a ladder in a silk stocking, but knew a great deal and cared greatly for applause, I settled for the languid elegance, for an imitation of Peter McRae's well-remembered grace (by that time Peter was scoring centuries for Somerset). Enthralled by the manner of my performance, I had no time for fear. In my debutant game I hit my first half century and took three catches and in that too-brief summer of 1939, which for my generation carries in recollection something of the same sweet but tragic finality with which our predecessors recalled 1914, I topped the batting-averages.

I never again played cricket regularly, though once, during a break from battle, triumph even more glorious came my way on a cricket-field. I hit Hedley Verity out of the ground at the Maadi Club near Cairo. (He had me next ball but the consolation and the trophy I keep still amongst my prized possessions: a letter from Blunden commending my feat, 'Better to strike Verity to the boundary than to write *Undertones of War*'.) Not infrequently since 1939 I have made myself a public fool but I have never given a damn. That, beyond all else, has made bearable a public life; that, no less than the confidence of publishers, family and friends, has made possible the constant exposure of self to criticism, abuse and ridicule which, at least by his own accounting, is the fate of a writer.

Back before the War, before North America, before Christ's Hospital, a decade or more before my maiden half-century, I kept myself as often as I could from the wood-block wickets and the erratic bounce of an old tennis-ball.

Neither at Canonbury Road nor since did I learn any liking for soccer, unless it be watched with my father. In the playground, once I had shaken off the timorousness natural to an only boy, I performed adequately but my one moment of glamour was followed by remorse that still scars my conscience. When I arrive before St Peter I will have to confess that the only goal I ever scored for Compton House went between the hanging-jackets from my hand. St David, who must be the patron-saint of the nobler footballing sect, may intercede for me, I have at times given some useful service to those he holds in care, but he too may discharge me to the lowest Circle when he recalls that the only try I scored for my Canadian university (and that the winning try) came after I had knocked-on, and my road to Hell is certain if he has it on record that in my very last game of Rugby Football I broke the leg of a Welsh Trial Cap before ever he had touched the ball.

We were children of the Great War and we knew it. My first memory is of my father's tunic rough against my cheek as he bent to kiss me; it must have been early in 1920, when he came home to be demobilized. (Because of his utility as linguist he was held by the Army long beyond his term, an experience which I was to share a quarter-of-a-century later, though for reasons very different.)

Also among my earlier memories is the sight and sound of guns being towed along the St Paul's Road; a troop, a battery, a regiment: I do not know, nor why they were there, but, four years old, excited and curious, I followed the guns to their Assembly point in Highbury Fields and was discovered there by my sister, Julia, eight years my senior, who, happening by on her way from school, caught sight of me guzzling boiled sweets given to me by a bombardier. (Julia called him a corporal and I knew no better until I was twenty-one.)

This was my first and only contact with the Royal Regiment until that day in 1939 when I blurted out 'the Artillery' as reply to a member of the Newcastle Officer Selection Board who had asked, with appropriately heavy professional humour, 'And which arm do you intend to honour with your service?' Precognitive conditioning? Perhaps, but I prefer the reason for my unconsidered choice that I have given ever since: I saw no cause to walk if I could arrange to be driven.

My father had experienced much but suffered less than many in the war-years, yet he could not forget and was determined that I would grow up remembering what I had never known. In my childhood I did not once hear a fairy-story and the only nursery-rhymes I knew before I went to school were taught me by my mother, in Dutch, but from my father, with a considerable repertoire of music-hall songs (which he sang always off-key), I gleaned a rich if chaotic anthology of tales about battles. The Siege of Troy, the Siege of Calais, the retreat from Moscow, Waterloo, the Silver Fleet: my father knew them all and all he re-fought for me. Before I was seven years old I was more familiar with Napoleon, Hector, William the Silent, Drake and van Tromp than I was with the doctor next door. But most of all my father talked to me about his own wars. Mafeking, Spion Kop, Ypres, Jutland and Cambrai were all entered in my vocabulary and, because my father's view of the past was never parochial or partisan, I knew as much about Ludendorf as about Haig, as much about Buller as about Botha and, for reasons precious to him, rather more about Smuts than about any other general from any army at any period in history. He was no dispassionate, study-reared historian. He had seen wars and seen men die, and the soldiers who fell at Agincourt or at Zutphen were to him as real as the friends who had been cut down by a sniper's bullet on the African veldt or dismembered by a whizz-bang at Arras. Born a Londoner of a long line of Londoners, educated partly in England and partly in Holland, he had been for much of his young manhood a South African.

His devotion to Holland and to South Africa remained with him; yet despite these early alien loyalties and despite his fiery denunciation of the British political hierarchy, he was punctilious, for himself and for me, in all overt demonstrations of duty to Britain. For hours on end we would wait by the kerbside for a glimpse of the King and Queen. The only time I knew my father lose his temper in public was when someone laughed in the middle of the Two Minutes Silence. The only times I saw him close to tears in public was at the sounding of the 'Last Post'.

None of my immediate family had been killed in the War. True, my Aunt Susan had lost a fiancé at Gallipoli but her hysterical outbursts each Armistice Day struck me, even in childhood, as a prime example of her zest for histrionics. My father carried the loss of friends always with him and, as he himself said often. 'a private grief is worth a public ceremony'.

Almost every year before I went away to school he took me with him to the Armistice Day Service on Islington Green. I felt the solemnity of these occasions – now in memory indistinguishable one from another – but for me they were as thrilling as the Changing of the Guard.

First, at home, what my father called the Sergeant-Major's Parade. He shined his shoes and, for once, mine also, polished his medals and pinned poppies to our coats. Then we walked along Upper Street, gathering ourselves into a throng of men, women and children, all be-poppied, some – even of the children – wearing medals.

Though there were more women and children, the crowd at the Green was not so very different from the crowd at the Arsenal. Almost it was festive: a Salvation Army band playing some of the tunes lifted from the Devil's repertoire; applause for our MP major, more applause for a platoon of Territorials from our own Middlesex Regiment, the Diehards; cheers for Old Bill, a London General Omnibus Company bus which had carried troops in Flanders (already by the mid-1920s the bus looked quaint, a relic from a distant past), and the loudest cheer of all for its driver as he clambered down from the open cab, his heavy leather overcoat bouncing metal.

Solemnity set in with the procession of clergy: Roman Catholics, Unitarians, Methodists, Baptists, Salvationists, Jewish, with our own Prebendary Hinde at their head, the medals on his cassock and the CF on his stole proving to me that he was not, after all, the Third Person in the Trinity made incarnate but a man, a soldier who, like my father, had trudged through the mud of Flanders.

Then, from far down the Upper Street, military music and the sound of marching men. They came, it seemed to me hundreds upon hundreds of them, all in their best clothes, all wearing caps or bowler-hats, all bearing chest-fuls of medals, and they marched as well as my favourite Guardsmen. Some I recognized: the muffin-and-crumpet man, the little Jewish shopkeeper (I was frightened of him when I was sent on a Sunday to his shop to pick up some errand forgotten from yesterday's shopping at Williams Brothers, but now I knew him as hero), the chimney-sweep, his face for once pink and closely-shaven, and in line-of-four with him, our doctors, father and son, and the undertaker, wearing that same ludicrous hat, just like Winston Churchill's, that began as a topper and finished as a bowler, which he always wore to funerals. There were women too; their presence amazed me, but they marched as erect as the men and medals shone from their dark coats.

The voice that called halt I knew at once. Those were the gruff tones of Mr Marker, the teacher at Canonbury Road we called Stumpy, because he limped, a man infamous among us for his quick temper and quick heavy hand.

A few prayers, a hymn – 'Our shelter from the stormy blast', the Deity to me an enormous tin-helmet perched above His world – and then a clock in the distance striking the hour, its chimes somehow on this day more solemn, more deliberate, than on any other day in the year. The Silence and 'Last Post', played by a Boys Brigade bugler, even in its false notes, poignant.

I had my eye on Mr Marker. He stood steadfastly at attention, his hat pressed to his chest, solitary, closest of all to the Memorial. There were tears dropping on to his black overcoat. I felt ashamed, not for his public grief but because I disliked him. Next to me I could feel my father shaking as he tried to hold back sobs. I dared not look at his face.

As the bugler sounded 'Reveille' my father whispered, 'Look at Mr Marker. That first medal, it's the Distinguished Service Order'.

This was no longer the most unpopular of our teachers. Here was a man to be measured almost with Boy Cornwall and Captain Ball.

Such demonstrative closeness to the tragedy and heroism of war, which was reared in me by my father and which I believe to be generally incomprehensible to latter-day generations, was commonly held by my schoolfellows at Canonbury Road. There was on the wall of the school-hall a shelf carrying a vase and a glass case and in the glass case a leather-bound book. Fresh flowers filled the vase for most of the school-year but in the first two weeks of November their place was taken by poppies from Earl Haig's Factory. On the day before Armistice Day the whole school – even the girls from upstairs and the infants from the floor below – crammed into the Hall. 'O God our help in ages past': just as at the Islington Memorial; then the book was taken out of its case and the headmaster read out the names of men, once boys at Canonbury Road, who had gone to war and not come back – an obscenely long list – and some of the older children denied their advancing maturity by offering up sobs for a brother or a father, almost forgotten except on this one day in the year.

My father would never allow me to pass Lutyens' Cenotaph in Whitehall, even on the top of a bus, without raising my cap. 'They did it for your future': he must have repeated those words a thousand times and today, when that austere monument with its afterthought salute to my contemporaries has become for me intensely personal, its unmanning simplicity cue to a mental roll-call of companions – John Horn, Peter McRae,

Basil Hewitt, John Maxwell, Donald Price, Ragbhir Singh, the list almost the sum of my youth – still, whenever I walk past the Cenotaph, it is not so much sorrow that I feel as a sense of guilt that I have no cap to raise to those who 'did it for my future'.

There is a lack of logic which I have never been able to resolve about the domiciliary position of my maternal and paternal families and about our knowledge of the two groups. Despite our Italian name, my father, like his ancestors for several generations, was Cockney-born. He had ten brothers and sisters, yet in all my life I have never met one uncle or aunt from his side of the family, not one cousin, nor indeed any of his relations except a fiercely-corseted, henna-haired old lady who insisted that I call her 'Grandma' though, even as a child, I knew that she was not my father's mother, and later came to understand that she was not his father's wife by any reckoning except the wildest courtesy. My mother's family, on the other hand, though they all spoke some Dutch – the younger members less fluently than any except my maternal grandmother, an Englishwoman who had married a Dutchman – by the time that I was aware of family were all settled in London, all much involved in English life and all much visited by us. There was the successful black sheep, my Uncle Edward, who lived in style with 'aunts' who changed yearly, who had a chauffeur to drive his Essex and who, calling once in Canonbury Square by chance on my birthday, accepted with ill-grace my grandmother's broad hint and hurled at me a screwed-up five pound note – the first and, until I was eighteen, the last example that I was to see of those gloriously-engraved predecessors to the shabby proclamation of scant riches that is today common currency. Annie, his discarded wife, lived in Richmond and her son Leslie was the one male member of the family who was for a while my close companion. Aunt Adèle was deaf, dumb and terrifying. My mother's sister Ann lived in uncharted North-West London and was somehow a little outside the circle but her younger sister, Susan, lived with us until she married. She was entirely British, very much the flapper and, in my earliest recollections, set apart because she was said to be still mourning that fiancé killed in Mesopotamia, a romantic privilege in which I shared because I had my middle name, Eric, from the dead hero. As soon as Dean Farrar came my way I lost any sense of pleasure in the association and found it difficult to forgive Aunt Susan for persisting in her folly by marrying eventually another man called Eric.

Despite our closeness to my mother's family, I knew and know nothing about the causes that brought them all from Holland to England. Their Dutch background I have never been able to reconstruct and I have no authority except the coincidence of name, and one remark made by my fable-creating father, for claiming blood-relationship with the Dutch painter B. C. Koekoeks, but if ancestry can be inferred from the professional habit of later generations then it is safe to assume that, hidden in the

Dutch past, there must have been some mainspring of artistic energy. It came out again, if in a somewhat twisted style, in my Uncle Edward, whose temporary ladies were all actresses and who was said to have garnered his fortune, even this early in the age of the moving-picture, by dreaming-up the idea of making short dramatic films which admitted only in their last few frames their true purpose as advertisements. It was revealed by my Aunt Susan's near-professional singing-voice. And it seems beyond coincidence that, in my generation, each of the families produced at least one aspirant to a career in the theatre. When I was a child we were certain that the most successful would be Cousin Juliette, the cousin that I knew least of them all though her face and magnificent hair was familiar to everyone in Britain as the face and hair of the Amami Girl ('Friday night's Amami night'). She played the lead in one of the road companies touring *No, No Nanette* then married her manager, disappeared from the stage, from the Amami advertisements, and from my life. Eventually the laurels for theatrical success fell to the youngest of all, my favourite cousin, Cousin Betty. Like me Betty won her way from a London elementary school to one of the most distinguished schools in the country, the North London Collegiate. Thence with the aid of that great teacher of dancing, Phyllis Bedells, she entered the Sadlers Wells Ballet and before she married an American and went off to live on Long Island, she had achieved the well-nigh impossible double of dancing as a ballerina and, a few months later, acting as a lead at the Birmingham Repertory Theatre. Forty years on she is Professor of Dance at an American university, a fine choreographer and still my favourite.

Although I had no association with my father's family and very little knowledge of its past I can guess what it was that brought together my father and my mother. When they met in Tottenham in 1904, he must have been the only Englishman for miles around who spoke fluent Dutch.

At about the same time that my mother's family moved from Holland to England, my father had been taken the other way by his parents. He was then twelve or thirteen years old and his family more prosperous than by later evidence seemed possible. He was sent for a while to the Gymnasium in Amsterdam and there sat desk-by-desk with at least two of Holland's future Prime Ministers. Above all other people the Dutch have the gift of tongues. Although my father's stay at the Gymnasium was short, before he was fifteen he had added French and German to his well-nigh native Dutch and London-native English. Later he was to boast that he could read a newspaper in any Western European language. I remember him learning Spanish while recuperating from double pneumonia. He was then fifty but it was not the last language he collected. During the Second World War, then almost seventy years old, suddenly he decided to learn Russian.

When he was sixteen my father's family broke up. Just as in 1493 the Pope divided the world between the Portuguese and the Spaniards, so now the Morpurgos organized their own segmentation. One brother went to the United States, one to Canada, one to Brazil, others for all I know to the North and South Poles. My father took South Africa as his portion.

That was not a happy time to arrive in South Africa. Tension between the Afrikaners and the British was high, was turned to fever-point by the Jameson Raid, and in 1899 to war, even so, it was a time of high excitement and this was some compensation for a youth who saw fabulous wealth being gathered in all round him, but who seemed incapable of bringing even the tiniest speck of gold-dust into his own pockets.

My father moved far up-country and there tried his hand, not very successfully, at running a country-store. His customers were all Afrikaners, his fluent Dutch and the unEnglish sound of his name hid from them his British origins and in time hid my father from the British Army. When war came, I suspect from a feeling that here at last was the great adventure he sought and certainly with no political conviction beyond a sense of neighbourly responsibility, he joined a Boer Commando. He was then eighteen years old.

My father's Boer War experience enlarged with the years and with retelling. It is a development not unusual with soldiers' tales (the key to Henry the Fifth's Agincourt speech is in the words 'remember, with advantages'). When a child I enjoyed my father's stories and accepted each elaboration as no more than a delightful after-thought, but by the end of my school-days, when there had been drilled into me an historian's professional scepticism and when I had learnt to recognize that of all forms of evidence the first person singular is the least reliable, I dismissed as fables all the more extravagant episodes in his accounts of his Boer War service.

There was, for example, the Smuts story. This was in two parts, separated by a quarter-of-a-century in my father's life. In the first chapter of the gospel according to my father, he had ridden commando alongside Jan Smuts. The sequel told how in the 1920s and 1930s, when Britain's one-time enemy had become a much respected Imperial statesman, whenever Slim Jannie was in London he invited my father, his Boer War companion, to take coffee with him at South Africa House. Almost, I was prepared to accept the first part of the tale, though I found it difficult to imagine my father on a horse, the more so because, in this like most adolescents, I could not bring myself to believe that he had ever been anything but elderly, balding, dressed neatly in a shiny blue suit with stiff collar and bowler-hat but, as I grew out of adolescence and into some knowledge of the world, the second part of the tale I dismissed out-of-hand. Generals, great statesmen, men who were praised in the *Morning Post* and attacked in the *New Statesman*, did not bother themselves with insurance-clerks.

Until one day in 1937. I was back home for a few weeks from my transatlantic adventure and for once alone in the house. (By that time we had moved from the elegant shabbiness of Canonbury Square to the bourgeois hideousness of Cockfosters.) The telephone rang; I answered and when a girl's voice asked for Mister Morpurgo, partly because it was a girl's voice and partly because I assumed that all enquiries for a Mister Morpurgo must be for me, I accepted the call. I listened with growing apprehension but no enhanced comprehension as a series of clicks and mumbles at the other end of the line transferred my attention through an ascending hierarchy, then finally, understanding, awe and from me an unspoken apology to my father: 'General Smuts' Private Secretary wishes to convey to Mr Morpurgo an invitation to drink coffee with the General next Thursday.'

Once only did I see my father on a horse. I knew immediately, not from instinct but from hard-won experience under the tutelage of a Havildar-major, that this was a man who had at one time ridden a horse as easily and as unthinkingly as for forty years he had ridden an office chair. He was then almost seventy years old and wearing the very clothes which, for so long, had made me doubt the historicity of his tales. For the first time I saw behind the disguise. Youth was his reality; youth and adventure; age but a shadow cast by unfulfilled promise.

Adventure there had been, and in full measure, in his young days. A few months before the end of the Boer War he was taken prisoner by the British. Not once did he let slip that he could speak or understand one word of English. It is for me an uncanny thought that had he confessed to a birthplace within sound of Bow Bells, I would not have existed.

It perplexes me still that, with such excitements behind him, my father was willing to spend the next fifty years – with but one enforced interruption when he was pressed into Kitchener's Army – peaceably if not always contentedly in drab London suburbs. Yet the *beau sabreur* turned insurance clerk never lacked resource. When my mother was close to delivering their third child, he was in the trenches. An ACI caught his attention seeking liaison personnel for service with the Portuguese. My father informed his Commanding Officer that his knowledge of the language of our new and gallant allies, the Port and Geese, was somewhat rusty but could be polished by intensive study. Granted six weeks' leave, he learnt Portuguese from a primer, added an interpreter's allowance to his pay, and was on hand for my arrival.

For his last Boer War escapade my father waited almost forty years. The Boers had scant hierarchical organization in their army; in the Great War my father had risen to the rank of corporal in the Northants Regiment. Utterly free of servility, he had nevertheless untrammelled ambition for me and so it was that his pleasure when I was commissioned outweighed the fear that gripped him whenever he recalled the life-expectancy statistics of First World War subalterns. On the day that I put up my first pip I came home from Larkhill dressed, as never again in all my seven years' service, as if ready to pose for an *Illustrated London News* photograph *circa* July 1914: field boots, riding breeches, shiny Sam Browne, floppy cap by Fultons of Woolwich, fawn tie, leather-bound swagger-stick and one kid glove in my gloved left hand. My father surveyed me with more care and far more apparent pride than had Field Marshal Ironside that morning at the Passing Out Parade of 122 Officer Cadet Training Regiment, Royal Artillery. I must be displayed to our neighbours and, as he was called for an Air Raid Wardens' parade to be inspected by 'some dugout colonel', I was sent on ahead to pirouette in the Saloon Bar of the better of our two pubs. That early in the War uniforms were still novelties in a suburban bar, for my unwarranted exploits with the socially self-satisfied cricket-club and for my exquisitely unsuburban fiancée I was well-known to many in the bar, and so it was that, when at last my father arrived, he found me surrounded by middle-aged men, all intent upon buying me drinks – as tribute, I suspect, to their own distant pasts as second lieutenants. I looked over the heads of my eager hosts at my father in his ARP dungarees and in that moment felt closer to him than I had for years. He had something he must tell me, that I knew, some glory to pass on that for once was his own and not vicariously enjoyed through my triumphs. I shook off the gratification of adulation and free drinks. Now it was I who would listen, I who would buy the drinks.

He brushed aside my invitation. His tale was bursting to be told. His eyes shone and his finger shook as he jabbed it towards the four medal-ribbons on his chest. Pip, Squeak and Wilfred: these I knew, the indicators of service in the Great War, but the first ribbon I had not studied and did not recognize.

'I told him. I told the old dugout.' His voice rocked with delight and he took on a guttural accent, Dutch or Afrikaans, such as invariably overlaid his Cockney when he was excited.

'There we all were, drawn up for inspection by this *verdommte rooneck* colonel. He comes up to me and he points to this. . . "What have we here, my man?" "This is the South African War Medal, sir." He points at his own flabby chest. "How can that be? This, next to my OBE (Military), is the South African War Medal." "The South African War Medal from the other side", say I and this time I don't say sir. "You can't wear that on a British uniform." A British uniform! These plumber's overalls! "Can I not?" I says, calm-like but pointed. "Should we not enquire first of General Jan Smuts?"'

From my father I inherited a zest for travel; in his case, after his early days, satisfied largely by the courtesy of the public library; in mine, creator of the varied back-cloths against which my life has been acted out. He passed on to me his love of history, though I am by no means certain that I have not reduced its covenant; becoming a professional historian and the process of academizing and making mercenary the search for the past too often dims the eyes, so that they miss that glint of gold which promised treasure to his untutored and unsophisticated vision. From my father, or else from my imagined theatrical forebears, I have taken on a quick ear so that I find it not difficult to pick up a few phrases from those languages which from time to time have formed my aural environment, but even the languages which I claim to speak fluently I speak freed from the discipline of grammar and most certainly I have not inherited my father's gift of tongues. Nor have I held to his Fabianism, though because of him and because of his hatred for the Blackshirts who bullied their way through Islington in my boyhood, I came sooner than most of my contemporaries to fear of Fascism and, for longer than most, I have held to the frightening conviction that Fascism has not yet been exorcized. I shall not inherit the earth, for I did not inherit my father's meekness.

Of tangible possessions all that I had from my father was £365, his life's savings, and the engraved gold watch presented to him when he retired from the Motor Union.

His dreams he kept to himself. Yet I know that as he walked with my mother to the Christ's Hospital Station, leaving me alone with my shattered jam-jar, my fears and my bewilderment, he was weaving the most exciting of all his dreams: that his son would enjoy what to him had been denied, a life unshackled by ordinariness.

2

Fortunate Bluecoat Boy

No less than any Smith or Marjoribanks I am proud of my surname. More than any Smith and just as much as any Marjoribanks I resent the imputation that all who share it must necessarily be my siblings. There are Morpurgos everywhere. There was a Morpurgo a hero of the Croatian Liberation Movement, a Morpurgo who held the majority share-holding in the Lloyd Triestino Shipping Company, there is another who sits at an Oxford High Table and yet another who has but recently come to prominence as a singer. When I was a school-boy, for the enhancement of my status with my peers, I boasted cousinage with that Baron de Morpurgo who, with di Stefano, made up Italy's first pair in the Davis Cup. In almost every city that I have visited anywhere in the world I have found Morpurgos in the telephone directory (there were at one time six in London's, and not one related even remotely to any of the others). I have met Jewish Morpurgos, a Morpurgo a Papal Count and, in Canada, an Anglican Canon Morpurgo. For thirty-five years I have corresponded (and in recent times have become happily intimate) with that Henry von Morpurgo who is a prominent Californian. Even longer ago, when on leave in Cairo, I was handsomely entertained by Nelson Morpurgo, an advocate in the International Court, an Italian who published poetry in French and spoke impeccable English. Not one of these is my kin. I need accept no responsibility for that Mr Morpurgo who figures in a novel by Rebecca West, nor for another, a steely-eyed Intelligence-director who is immaculate in the spy-stories of William Garner. Alas, I can boast no part in the antique shops blazoning my name to London's Wigmore Street and Amsterdam's Rokin, or any right to use the Morpurgo armorial bearings proclaimed in the *Almanach de Gotha*. The only Morpurgos who are truly mine are my mislaid uncles and cousins, my children, the girls who have taken on our name, my grandchildren and, *mirabile dictu*, my great-grand-daughter. Morpurgo was long ago derived from *Marburger,* the man of Marburg. It is no more likely that I am related to any other Morpurgo than that Norman Chester is cousin to any other 'man of Chester' or Alvin York to any other 'man of York'.

It remains, however, that because for all its simplicity, the name strikes strangely upon Anglo-Saxon ears – and how strangely I could demonstrate by listing the variant spellings and pronunciations to which it is subjected –

I am forever being confused with some other Morpurgo, and my denial of relationship seems never quite to convince.

The Library Catalogue of my own American college lists with my books several volumes by an Italian poet, Giovanni Morpurgo and here, as in my first just-missed encounter with the greatest of my literary contemporaries, confusion is made more confusing by my plebeian but rare Christian name. I was baptised Jack but when so addressed, rather than enter into debate, I answer to the name John, if with a sense of grievance.

Not long after the War the Cresset Press accepted my first full-length book. I was summoned to the flat of the firm's literary adviser to discuss the typescript. As yet unsophisticated in the ways of the world of letters, amazed and elated by my success, and much in awe of a man whose Nonesuch edition of John Donne I had treasured for years, I could not fathom why it was that, as we went page-by-page through my *American Excursion*, John Hayward rocked in his wheel-chair. I hoped and believed that there was wit in the book but Hayward's braying would have flattered Patrick Campbell or Chauncy de Pauw. Daring rebuke I questioned the cause.

'Tom heard you were coming and left in haste.'

Such was my innocence that I stuttered 'Tom who?'

Hayward looked at me as at one who queried the identity of the owner of New Hall, Stratford-upon-Avon. 'You know this address, 19 Carlyle Mansions, Cheyne Walk.' It was an accusation, not a question. 'Why then, Thomas Stearns Eliot, of course. You have plagued him with your verses these last fifteen years.'

Time was to come, and not so long thereafter, when I had many dealings with Eliot, me as publisher's editor and he the head keeper of Britain's leading poetic stable. Time was to come, but a decade thereafter, when I was not infrequently in his company. That he was habitually austere is well-known and I found him none other, his social manner, like his appearance, more appropriate to the banker that once he had been than to the poet he had become. But I do not believe that it was my sensitized imagination which convinced me that whenever he became aware of my presence he turned furtive, Monte Cristo looking for a way out of the Chateau d'If. It may have been because he feared that I would thrust a sheaf of verses under his Brahmin nose. And it may have been because he never gave me the chance to convince him that it had been some other poetaster Morpurgo (and he a genuine John and no relation) who had burdened him with novice poetry that it was not until after I had attended his Memorial Service that I recovered the expansive admiration for Eliot's work which, in late boyhood, had encouraged me to batter my uncomprehending juniors and my indignant housemaster with passages from *The Waste Land* and 'The Hollow Men', as illegal substitutes for the chapters from the Scriptures which I should have read at Duty each night in the

House day-room.

Or maybe it was just that I detest cats and abominate cat-worshippers.

Not so very long after the publication of *American Excursion* I became myself a talent-spotter for Cresset. I do not claim that I was Hayward's heir; there are in each publishing generation high priests whose consecration depends as much – and often more – upon their percipience as upon their own literary powers. Of such before my time were Edward Garnett and Richard le Gallienne and, in my early days, Daniel George, John Lehmann and John Hayward. Of these three, Daniel George was the most charitable, Lehmann the most influential and Hayward the most awesome. But for Cresset I plucked a few orchids that Hayward might not have noticed from his archiepiscopal throne in Carlyle Mansions. Jack Plumb, whom already I had gathered in for Penguin, I took to Cresset for his elegant biography of Robert Walpole. For my friend Tom Jarman I contrived a commission which harvested his classic *Landmarks in the History of Education,* and from another friend, Douglas Grant, but recently translated from Royal Marine to Edinburgh lecturer, I discovered the book which, of all for which I can claim any responsibility, gives me most pride for its quality, and most sorrow for its too-hasty disappearance from public fame. Grant's *Fuel of the Fire* I hold to be, with Keith Douglas's *Alamein to Zem-Zem,* the nearest that any soldier-writer of my war came to the sensitivity of our predecessor fighter-artists, the authors of *Memoirs of an Infantry Officer* and *Undertones of War.*

I took such benefit as might come to my literary judgement from Cresset to Christopher's, or rather, I had conferred upon me the duty of dining on two or three evenings each week with the remarkable but lonely old man who had founded the firm and who remained its sole proprietor. Bertram Christian was also a Christ's Hospital product, though his schooldays ante-dated mine by some forty years. Rare among Blues, in his generation or mine, for few of us could afford to waste time eating dinners and waiting for briefs, he had been called to the Bar, but, after a year or so in chambers, he joined *The Times* and served as war-correspondent in several of those obscure but bloody Balkan campaigns which preceded the Great War. Then he turned publisher and was, as I remember it, the first President of the Publishers Association.

Christian had known everyone who mattered in the world of letters and most who mattered in politics. His table-talk was littered with allusions which I was expected to catch. 'GBS told me . . .'; 'I could have had Arnold but he wanted too much for that hotel nonsense . . . ; 'Good-looking lass that secretary-mistress of the Welsh Wizard, much too good for him. You knew her brother, I suppose'. (P. J. Stephenson, the brother of Frances, eventually Lady Lloyd George, was the first Old Blue killed in the Great War!) 'Jack and Kitty used to sit on that rug pouring out their many troubles.' (Never, before or since, have I heard anyone else call Katherine Mansfield by a diminutive.) Sometimes, half-way through an excellent dinner, he would tire of his monologue and my company. Then he rang the bell and in came his formidable Miss Adams, who seemed never to go home. 'Sammy,' he would say 'put on your dancing-pumps', and off they went to the Gargoyle. But sometimes his conscience dictated that he give me some instruction in the science of publishing. (I was one in a long line of apprentice-advisers. Many became prominent in the Trade and we sustained for some years a dining-club called the Early Christians.) On one such occasion he, whose list was heavy with school text-books and stolid footnoted scholarship and who in all his years as a publisher had not produced one title on the arts, decided that the time had come to educate me in the commercial techniques appropriate to publishing books on ballet and theatre. 'When we decide to commission a ballet-book', he pontificated, 'I beg of you, insist that the prospective author compiles his index before ever he writes a word of the text.'

Christian got up from the table, opened a second bottle of superb claret, then, his eyes suddenly brisk with mischief, he almost impaled me on the jabbing corkscrew. 'No bad advice, that, my boy, for you when you come to write your memoirs. Guard your patience. Keep back that immortal prose. Leave the scratching of conscience to John Newman and the impenetrable philosophy to Samuel Taylor Coleridge. Consider the bookshop browsers and the reviewers in the cheaper press. Sit for days with sheets of paper before you, write down the name of every famous or infamous person with whom in all your life you have spent even five minutes; use that list of names-to-be-dropped as framework for your *oeuvre*. You will make your publisher happy and leave behind you a rich widow.'

Long and hard experience on both sides of the editorial desk has convinced me that this counsel was shrewd. The circumstances of a vagabond and varied career have allowed me such diversity of acquaintance that I need but a little more capacity for exaggeration than is available to me to permit me to enter into that persuasive index the names of almost every leading writer of my times, British, American, Canadian, Australian, New Zealander and Indian, several French and German authors, many eminent actors and actresses, generals, politicians, scientists, surgeons and one or two notorious crooks. I have started my index, sensibly enough, with 'Blunden, Edmund', and 'Eliot, T. S.' I am myself a quarter of a sentence in Field Marshal Slim's *Unofficial History*, General Hertzog, the President of Israel, was my chairman when I lectured in Tel Aviv, it would not be scandalously extravagant were I to write into the index 'Philip, Prince', there would be cause, if perhaps also *lèse-majesté*, were I to precede it with 'Nixon, Richard'. And because for thirteen years I was responsible for the conjoined festival of my favourite arts, literature and cricket, the annual match between Authors and Publishers, and as in our times almost every Test cricketer has qualified to represent the Authors – if too often only with ghostly sponsorship – so would it be no burden upon my conscience were I to insinuate into my index the names of many cricketing heroes.

Indeed two, 'Constantine, Learie' and 'Jardine, Douglas' could be admitted by right of friendship.

Presented, as I am, with such lavish potential, it is with regret that I reject Christian's canny counsel and commit myself to summoning back to mind only those, be they world-famous or obscure, my most generous friends or my most perfervid enemies, who, by their personality and activity have helped to plot the course which has brought me at last to recording my memoirs.

Not only in my seven years as school-boy but in the many decades which have followed, Christ's Hospital has figured hugely in my life. Christ's Hospital must figure hugely in my memoirs.

'A Christ's Hospital boy's friends at school', wrote Charles Lamb, 'are his friends for life'. Even Elia told but part of the story and, because its character as a continuous and continuing community forms part of the justification of the boast which comes so readily, and so often, to the lips and pens of men and women of C.H., that the Foundation is *sui generis*, the Blues who will appear in my pages are not all of them my school-contemporaries, not even my contemporaries in the larger sense that they have been alive in my lifetime. As almost every literary Blue, I have been much influenced by my C.H. literary predecessors and it is a sense of fraternity stretching back far beyond awareness of 'the old familiar faces' which has given me amity not only with Keith Douglas, Murry, Blunden, but also with Peele and, above all others, with the noble trio Coleridge, Lamb and Leigh Hunt, of a kind that the acquired gloss of critical sophistication could never confer.

It is, however, those three, the brightest ornaments in Christ's Hospital's Golden Generation, who are more daunting to any who follow after them in writing about C.H. Others, from David Baker in the sixteenth century to Murry, Blunden, Youngman Carter and Michael Swan have contributed to Christ's Hospital's effulgent anthology of reminiscence, tribute and gratitude for 'the great benefits received in this place'. There could be no shame in following their example. But to venture where three of the greatest autobiographers of all time had led? That was daunting and to attempt it demanded bravado, even brashness.

I was conscious of this potent inhibition already when I was twelve years old and it was then that I decided to slip the challenge of these unassailable precursors by transposing into fiction my account of life at Housie.

It was not C.H. which made inevitable my choice of a career in letters; that I had settled for me when I was seven years old and Hubert Welch read to the whole Canonbury Road Junior School my story about the Martians. To the very first question asked of me when I crept into the Coleridge B Day-room after watching my parents vanishing from my life down the Centre Path, I answered 'I'm going to be an author'. (That question, a commonplace from adult to child, 'What will you be when you grow up?') was asked with abundant kindliness but from a great height, physical and metaphysical, by the House Captain, John Knight. His answer, 'Then you will starve', showed more than ordinary perspicacity. It did not foretell that in the years to come we would be colleagues in the commerce of books or that he would stand by me, kindly as ever and courageous in his loyalty, during the most difficult and lonely crisis of my book-world career, as I attempted to thwart the chicanery and treachery which led eventually to my resignation as Director-General of the National Book League.)

It was towards the end of my second year at C.H. that I decided that Coleridge, Lamb and all the rest were too strong for me. Christ's Hospital must have a novel, something which, for all their marvellous powers, not one of them had provided.

Long ago, in 1770, a wit published *The Fortunate Blue-coat Boy*, but though there is in this novel much on C.H. life as then it was lived, and though it is sometimes listed as the first of all school-stories, 'Orphanotrophian's' work is a morality-tale turned upside-down, a success-story in which the hero's prime qualification is his ability to cuckold Aldermen – perhaps not the greatest of lessons taught by Christ's Hospital. Mark Twain gave us the last pages of *The Prince and the Pauper* and showed himself in those passages a little closer to understanding English history than at any other time in his literary career, for in them he did recognize that the greatest honour that Henry the Eighth's son could confer on the poor lad who had temporarily taken his place was to make Tom Canty Treasurer of his Foundation, but *The Prince and the Pauper* is even less a book about Christ's Hospital than *The Connecticut Yankee* is a book about Camelot.

In my own lifetime there have been two novels which the *cognoscenti* can locate in Christ's Hospital. R. C. Woodthorp was a master at the school just before my school-days and before he wrote *The Public School Murder*. To any Blue of the Fyfe era the identity of the author of *Sweet is the Breath of Morn* is but thinly disguised by the pseudonym Mary Hamilton. With a little assistance from some a few years my senior, I could put real-life names to every character in *The Public School Murder*, the heroine and, despite certain amazing amendments to his personality, the hero of *Sweet is the Breath of Morn* are as obvious as if they had been permitted the names by which they were known to the Registrar-General. But Woodthorp wrote about a murder which happened to take place in a school, and Mary Hamilton a love-story for which a school is mere background. By changing the name of the school, both deprived themselves of all possibility that they could place emphasis where I would have it: on the grandeur and uniqueness of Christ's Hospital tradition. When I was thirteen the field was still clear and so it remains.

Already in 1931 Christ's Hospital had wrought for me its wondrous alchemy. Those early tremors of bewilderment, set off by the vastness of the estate, the hugeness of the buildings, the complexities of custom and the esoteric language, had disappeared after a term or two and I had settled down to be what I was to remain for the next six years, a contented schoolboy.

In adult years I have repeated this assertion, on occasion to disbelieving coevals who knew not Housie and even, more than once, before a microphone, and it has marked me forever as an outcast from the pale of intellectual society where unhappiness at school is a qualification for acceptance almost as imperative as an unsuccessful marriage. (A placid family life has been another bar sinister on my intellectual escutcheon.) Even so and even now I do not withdraw the statement, unfashionable cliché though it may be, that my school-days were as happy as any in a life that has not often been miserable. At thirteen, when I had been promoted from Lower School to Upper, from Junior to Senior Dormitory, from narrow girdle to 'broadie' – complete with the one item of school uniform which we paid for ourselves: an ornamented silver buckle bought from Sir John Bennett's in Cheapside – I was plush with the delights of possession and determined to share my enthusiasm with the uninformed.

I had discarded the caricatures of school-life presented each week to all who could pay twopence for *The Magnet* or *The Gem*. I had outgrown by two years *The Bending of the Twig*, *Jeremy at Crale* and *David Blaize*. Such books, I accepted, were not without verisimilitude but the truth that they told was prosaic, for the enthrallment of readers their authors depended upon an injection of fable compounded of last-minute, match-winning tries, broken bounds and stupendous beatings – a formula that was both inappropriate to my experience and superfluous to my intentions.

That school-story I planned with care. Of that first version nothing was ever written except a synopsis and a lexicon ('swob = fag; flab = butter, crug = bread; kiff = tea, coffee or cocoa . . .'), but my bewildered parents and my easily-impressed sisters heard most of the tale, told as a serial – with increasing skill and decreasing hyperbole – instalment by instalment on the first day of each holiday.

My determination to keep my written work honest and accurate – insofar as honesty and accuracy could be made consistent with the identity of my hero – soon came into conflict with my unquenchable sentimentality. Those novelists whom I then regarded as my competitors did not have, as did I, the advantages provided by our dramatic traditions, both spiritual and physical. I pitied them their monotonous procession of comfortable middle-class boys going the road that their fathers and their grandfathers had gone, by way of Cock House matches and school feasts. It was poor stuff when set alongside our magical capacity to make aristocrats out of boys from the slums of London. I pitied them their drab grey suits or Eton collars. How could such compete with our Tudor dress? But what they had, which I had not, was the benediction of chronology. So that I might accept that blessing for myself my dream-novel slipped time and took my hero back more than two decades. Already I had produced a dramatisation of Ernest Raymond's *Tell England*, had committed it to paper and had it performed one Christmas holiday in the basement of our Canonbury Square house by a cast that included my cousin Betty, two Housey boys who were also neighbours, and the ten-year old sister of one of them. (Betty and the two boys learnt nothing from this ordeal, for later all three became professional actors. As for the sister; it would not surprise me if I discovered her prominent among the leaders of Women's Lib for we made the privilege of acting with us contingent upon her accepting the part of a small boy who was thrashed ceremoniously at the beginning of each act.) As I wrote it in my mind, my novel was Ernest Raymond transposed from St Paul's to Christ's Hospital.

At that time – as for many years to come – I had no knowledge of the critical theory voiced with such firmness by E. M. Forster, that in 'the losing battle that the plot fights with the characters, it often takes a cowardly revenge . . ., so that 'nearly all novels are feeble at the end'. Had the notion been put before me, I would have dismissed it as ridiculous for not only did all those novels which were then my favourite reading – *The Tale of Two Cities, Tess of the D'Urbervilles* and *Les Miserables* – have high-pitched and inevitable endings, but so also did my own fiction. Indeed, it was the final chapter that I devised first, for beyond all else this was clear-written on the pages of my imagination. The scene varied according to my mood; Jutland, the skies above Flanders, or the burnt sands of Mesopotamia; but the event was certain: the death of my hero only a few months after he had delivered the finest English Oration in the history of Christ's Hospital and then resigned his Oxford Scholarship to fight for King and Country. That it was an Oxford scholarship which was sacrificed was a concession to the discipline of fiction, a bold attempt to avoid accusing myself of writing premonitory autobiography. In truth even now, when both universities had become for me real places inhabited by characters I actually knew and not beyond the reach of my own ambition, I still clung to my elementary school loyalty to Cambridge.

I was no more than fourteen years old when I received the laying-on of hands which confirmed me as a candidate for the priesthood of letters. Already in my first term I had repeated to my housemaster the intention that I had confessed to John Knight. Leonard Dale was one of that remarkable band of schoolmasters which Dr Upcott had selected to release Christ's Hospital from the dignified claustrophobia of Newgate Street, close to the heart of the City of London, and to give to it the freedom of rural spaciousness, to preserve its antique traditions even whilst fashioning from them the most up-to-date and forward-looking of British educational institutions.

A man genuinely terrifying in the classroom (or so I am told by those who went to him for Latin – an ordeal I was spared) and much given to mock-fierceness on the touch-line, Lenny was the most generous of housemasters, and kindly, even gentle, with small boys whose hands bore still the stigmata of their mother's apron-strings. On Sunday afternoons, if it was fine, he would take us – most of us children whose little knowledge of nature had been gleaned in city parks – on walks through the lush Wealden countryside; if wet, he gathered us in his study and there encouraged us with cocoa and buns to act out plays of our own devising. Some murmur of congratulation on one of my Sunday afternoon dramas wrung from me the confession that when my time came to choose a profession, I would be a writer. Lenny grunted, smiled and said nothing but when he retired at the end of my first year (Fyfe left at the same time and we knew that the end of the world had come), he must have passed on this amazing information to his successor, for almost immediately Hector Buck made me free of his own bookshelves, and soon he was pointing me to the books by his favourite writer, his favourite man, his friend since the two had been schoolboys, on the other side of the Block in Coleridge A.

One Saturday afternoon, just as I was changing for rugger, I was summoned to Buckie's study. There, almost lost in two enormous armchairs , sat two men, Buckie and another no bigger than he, a bird-like individual notable at first only for his bright eyes, gentle but sad.

There was no introduction, only Buckie's high-pitched barking laugh, the punctuation-mark inset into so much of his conversation and for me, with the chimes of the Housey clock, punctuation to so many of my adult dreams. 'This boy says he's going to be a writer.' And, from deep in the other chair a soft, almost squeaky voice. 'If that be so, then we must find ways to help him.'

And so Edmund Blunden did. He helped me for the next forty years, as he helped so many others, often to his own disadvantage. Some have questioned his capacity as poet; I doubt their critical percipience. Some have reservations about his authority as biographer and literary chronicler; they are men for whom I have little regard. A handful (but only a handful) of crass illiterates even dare to undervalue *Undertones of War* ; they are 'damned from here to Eternity'. I came myself to know Edmund's fallibility, his poor head for beer and his too-eager response to any attractive girl, but if before me some vile creature were to impugn Edmund's generosity to his fellow-writers however humble, I would strike the villain dead.

At sixteen I was still determined to write the Housey novel but I had much else to occupy my time. I was a House Monitor, an energetic if not notably skilful games-player, an argumentative member of the Debating Society, I played lead roles in Block plays, acting in a style fashioned after Matheson Lang, I wrote sardonic verses for *The Outlook*, the school literary magazine, (which was at about that time beginning to publish drawings and amazingly mature poems, over the initials RCD or the pseudonym Raps, by Keith Douglas) and I wrote long and deliberately literary letters to my several attractive but manifestly unliterary girl-friends. Yet somehow I managed to prepare elaborate notes for the novel and some fifty or sixty pages of manuscript.

Sentimentality, even sentiment, were banished. So too was the social concern which under the influence of a subscription to the *New Statesman* had coloured an interim version begun the previous year. Now I held it as my lofty opinion that salvation comes only to the intellectual élite and, though my setting was still ostensibly Christ's Hospital, this was a Housie that no Blue would recognize.

I calculated cheerfully that, when published, my novel would run to a thousand pages but – by that time I had discovered James Joyce – the action I confined to one day in the Summer Term. Already cynical about public taste, though homosexuality was comparatively rare among my contemporaries, I considered it incumbent upon me to encourage sales by including a love affair between the Senior Grecian and his swob; and, much more congenial to my decidedly heterosexual taste and just as rich in commercial potential, a rape – I had also discovered William Faulkner. If there had ever been rape within the Ring Fence it had been successfully hidden from my inquisitive eyes but I had discarded my recently-acquired historian's conscience for the freedom of a fantasist. However, I did abandon my original intention to have the Chaplain (in reality a sad, unvirile man known to us all as 'the Wet Smack') ravish a Classics master's handsome fiancée (for whom I and several of my friends harboured dishonourable intentions) and set myself to compromise instead the cricket-coach (in truth blameless as St Benedict) and Dolly, one of our housemaids, who had long since been both effectively and consentingly compromised in a box-room, if, as I could but regret, not by me.

The novel I abandoned, almost definitively, as I entered my last year. My dignity would no longer permit me the frivolity of fiction. I was House Captain, a History Grecian, a First Parting Grecian, a School Monitor, and other influences had taken over my mental processes. I had fallen, an eager victim, to the spell of David Roberts and, if to a lesser degree still to some considerable extent, the complementary and supplementary magic of Troops Hornsby. My mind thus fashioned by two of the most stimulating teachers it has ever been my good fortune to meet, my immediate role was set, and my destiny. Still I would be a writer, but a writer true to the discipline of history.

Even so, when eventually, and not so many years later, I launched into a professional career it was as a writer of fiction that I made my debut.

There was nothing else for it; the Western Desert, the Gothic Line, the streets of Piraeus were not convenient for the writing of travel books, history, biography or literary criticism. Fifty and more years on I have returned occasionally to the genre but as, one after another, the periodicals which have been in the habit of accepting my short stories vanish from the market-place, professional shrewdness demands that I go back to the last at which I had worked, not without some little success, for so long. Still, sometimes when I tire of the trades I know, I play once again with the novel. There are, buried somewhere in a box with other disappointed trifles, a completed typescript on nonsense literature, proposed, contracted and approved by a publisher who promptly turned bankrupt; a chapter or so of a travel-book on Holland, which became instead a paragraph or so in my *Road to Athens*; an extensive synopsis for a biography of William Cobbett, which became instead an edition of his American writings; even the first draft of a scrupulously-researched book which is grandchild to my school-boy novels. Christ's Hospital is still there, but a C.H. I never saw, Newgate Street *circa* 1770. And in this, my last dream-novel, Newgate Street is no more than preface; all else is set in the America I know only by way of regular excursions of imagination, the America of Jefferson, George Wythe and, above all, John Paul Jones, and even so know to be mine as surely as I know that Williamsburg, be it in 1788 or 1985, has been my second home since 1937.

There were among my contemporaries at C.H. two whose tastes and skills could have qualified them to step firmly where I but set my toes.

Michael Swan published only one novel in his tragically short career but, had he so chosen and had he lived long enough, he could have given to Christ's Hospital, not a school-story in the out-moded manner, but a fiction much more subtle and much more significant than anything that Ivor Brown dedicated to Fettes or Hugh Walpole to King's, Canterbury (or was his Crale his other *alma mater*, Durham School?), and in no sense embarrassing to our sensitivities, as must be Thomas Hughes's contribution to Rugby's reputation by *Tom Brown's Schooldays*. Swan's rare empathy with Henry James demonstrates his qualifications for, like Henry James the American in Britain, most Old Blues carry with them both the burdens and the benefits of expatriation; they come as aliens out of deprivation to claim citizenship that is not theirs by right of birth.

Parenthetically: it was Swan who offered in print the opinion that it was he (of Coleridge A House), Blunden (also of Coleridge A) and me (of Coleridge B) who of all professional literary critics were the most likely to comprehend the greatness of Samuel Taylor Coleridge, for we alone among critics had first learnt to honour his name by howling it from a muddy touch-line.

That Arthur Thompson became a novelist at all reflects no credit on me. Indeed he set himself to that career in direct opposition to my declared wisdom. At school we shared the guilt of hours wasted in the Library rocking benches in dry-land rowing-matches across the polished floor by methods and according to rules devised by the two of us. No glory shines on me from his superb, artful and unorthodox spin-bowling or from his DSO won with the Burma Rifles. Soon after the War, Arthur came to me for advice. He was then a public relations officer with a large industry and, with no literary credentials whatsoever. This well-paid security he planned to abandon for the hazards of full-time authorship. My articles, short stories and poems had been published in some of the most prestigious journals and in several countries. I was heard regularly on radio. Most significant of all as conferring upon me the right to pontificate, I was at Penguin, comfortably settled in one of Britain's most influential editorial chairs. I listened patiently to Arthur's ambitions and then delivered myself of my unctuous and infallible verdict: 'Hold on to what you have and, if write you must, write on Sundays.'

Arthur nodded, smiled and let me pay the bill for lunch. In the next twenty years, as Francis Clifford, he wrote many novels of which Graham Greene would not be ashamed and at least two, *The Naked Runner* and *Amigo, Amigo*, which are even now winning from critics, as from their publication they won from readers both in Britain and America, acceptance as notable contributions to the record of English fiction. During all our years of continued friendship, even when, through prodigious circulation, translation-rights and the sale of novels to Hollywood, Arthur was forced into tax-exile in Ireland, he had the grace never to remind me of our lunch at the Reform Club.

Arthur's tastes were for outlandish settings, his genius in portraying anti-heroes, but he had a gift for characterization and atmosphere, a sensitive conscience and a refined ability to conceal polemical purpose behind plot and action. These attributes, coupled with his loyalty to the Foundation, must have made him from my generation – and perhaps from all generations so far – the likeliest candidate for authorship of the Christ's Hospital school-story.

Michael Swan and Arthur Thompson are, alas, both dead. Somewhere perhaps even now, a younger Blue, or an older, is scribbling away at a novel that will offer all that I would wish. If so he has my blessing. He will not have me as competitor.

In 1952, as Christ's Hospital prepared for its Quatercentenary, sixty-five of what Fyfe called his 'inky Blues' – writers, journalists, publishers, broadcasters, publicists – dined together in London under the chairmanship of Fyfe, himself no mean writer and a superb performer before a microphone. Our purpose was to discuss the contribution that we, all members of what has been over the centuries the Hospital's premier profession, would make to the celebrations.

From that dinner came two proposals. The first, that we stage a broadcast, we sold without difficulty to the BBC; not surprisingly for at that time the Head of Administration at Broadcasting House, the Senior Announcer and the Senior Talks Producer were all Old Blues and we could offer the Corporation as panel several broadcasters well-known and generally well-liked by the listening public: Fyfe himself, Frank Phillips, Graham Hutton, and (the author of this autobiography) one of the team of that most popular series 'Transatlantic Quiz' who was also the seemingly-permanent chairman of the weekly programme 'Behind the News'. Most persuasive of all to the planners, we could produce for them one performer they could not otherwise afford to contract, the film-star heart-throb of the day, Michael Wilding.

The programme never went out on the air, not because we talked too little but because, encouraged by the flowing lunch provided by the BBC's Head of Administration, we talked too much. Thomas Radley, another Old Blue, was a skilful director but not even he could cut to thirty minutes two-and-a-half hours of rambling reminiscence.

We talked too much, all of us except Wilding. Fyfe as Chairman, who knew all that there was to know about attracting an audience, knew therefore that it was Wilding's voice beyond all others that the public wished to hear. Desperate to bring him into the conversation, Fyfe posed a simple question. 'Michael, tell us, when at school did you have any particular ambition which since has been either fulfilled or thwarted?' Wilding pondered, it seemed for minutes, then slowly, hesitantly, he delivered his reply: 'I wanted a green Rolls Royce; now I have two.'

The second notion came to glorious success; it even made money; we would produce a book in which every facet of Christ's Hospital in its first four hundred years would be described in the prose and verse of 'sons of the House'.

The editorial duties were remitted to Blunden, to me, to Philip Youngman Carter and to Eric Bennett; the design of the volume to Max Martyn, Production Director of the distinguished publishing-house, Hamish Hamilton. Ashley Havinden, who designed among other things the typography for the Milk Marketing Board, would prepare the wrapper. Business matters were left to Henry Durant, head of Britain's Gallup Poll; publicity to John Hackett, Managing Director of one of London's leading advertising agents.

This Committee met frequently, and often bibulously, for we had at our disposal some of London's plushest expense-accounts, but it worked hard. The *Book* appeared on time and was reviewed widely and ecstatically. There were Old Blue critics on most of the leading papers; the rapturous notice in the *Times Literary Supplement* was written (of course anonymously) by the junior member of the Editorial Committee.

The Christ's Hospital Book sold eight thousand copies in two editions. There are only five thousand living Old Blues!

I have that volume before me now, and the list of contributors dazzles. Coleridge, Lamb and Leigh Hunt, of course, George Peele, David Baker, St Edmund Campion (these last two, both recusants, strange alumni of Edward the Sixth's determinedly Protestant foundation), Thomas Barnes, the Editor who put thunder into the voice of *The Times*, George Dyer, Elia's *amicus redivivus*, T. S. Surr, who is said to have killed Georgina, Duchess of Devonshire by featuring her as central character in one of his novels, and, from this century, Murry, Blunden, Graham Hutton, Constant Lambert, Youngman Carter, Michael Swan, Keith Douglas, Sydney Carter, Percy Young and many more.

As now I write I dream that, when Christ's Hospital approaches its fifth century, another Committee of Blues will find at least some small part of

Master of None worthy of publication in *The Second Christ's Hospital Book.*

For me, as I suspect for most Blues, Christ's Hospital changed my scale of social relationships. We were part of a blatantly hierarchical society but our standing within that hierarchy was in no way related to family status. Whether 'the son of a convicted burglar or the orphan of a bishop' (Fyfe's words) we were all poor. There was, it is true, some communal pressure which soon erased from new boys any trace of a local accent but the handsome uniformity of Housey uniform saved us from any awareness of the comparatives that can exist even within the generalization of poverty. We had our active snobberies (and many who are not of our number complain, with justice, that we carry them with us throughout our lives) but they sprang from our certainty that Christ's Hospital is not as other schools, that no parent could buy for his son a place among us, that no County Council could direct the Foundation to accept its nominees, that from wheresoever we came, with whatever advantages or disadvantages, we were, like Lord Mansfield's escaped slave, 'all equal before the laws' – of Christ's Hospital.

At Canonbury Road I, the prize pupil, the darling of the teachers, had looked upon the staff with benevolence but with little respect. I knew that I needed their tutelage but I knew too that the limitations on what they had to offer me were many and severe. Of them all, only Hubert Welch won from me any affection. The masters at C.H. I could not patronize, not even in my most private thoughts, for these were great men. Yet perhaps the most sensational of the many surprises that came to me in the years after my initiation was the discovery that so many of these giants were both human and humane.

C.H. has always welcomed change. In some ways the school as I knew it when a boy was hardly recognisable as the same institution which had prospered and suffered under the great flogging Upper Grammar Master, Coleridge's 'educer of the intellect', 'old Jimmy Bowyer'.

The school of my youth was kindlier, its domestic organization less restrictive and its educational philosophy far more catholic. Paradoxically, it had become far more like the great public schools so fervently despised by Coleridge, Lamb and Leigh Hunt. Since my schooldays C.H. has changed again. The lack of privacy – a disability which we in my generation shared with our eighteenth-century school-fellows – has been overcome. Vanished too is that fierce system of superannuation which, for us as for Coleridge's contemporaries, thrust from the school at a comparatively tender age all but the few destined for university scholarships, and vanished with it – but whisper it not at Horsham – something of the lordliness of the Grecians who, in Coleridge's day as in mine, like the Cabots and the Lowells of Boston, spoke only to each other, or to God, the Senior Grecian. And, the most sensational of all metamorphoses, greater even than the move from London to Sussex, after three centuries of separation C.H. re-united its Girls' School with its Boys' School. ('Re-united', it will be noted; I detest the customarily-used word 'merger' – it smells of a take-over.)

When, in 1902, C.H. moved from Newgate Street to West Horsham it acquired spaciousness such as few other schools can boast: the green, cloistered Quadrangle, the wide, tree-lined Avenue, the vast playing fields proclaim a promise of continuity with the richness of the Sussex Weald and distant views of both South and North Downs extend the spiritual landscape, so that the whole countryside seems to belong to Christ's Hospital and Christ's Hospital to be the pivot of England. The architects had risen to their opportunities and had transcended the inhibitions and conventions of their time. Not even the most partisan commentator could describe their creation as beautiful; the lingering curse of Victorian Gothic was still upon them; but they built generously, with dignity and with care for light, in a manner that must have surprised many of their *fin-de-siècle* contemporaries.

There were more subtle changes such as must have been noticed only by that first generation of Sussex Blues that knew also Newgate Street – and by historians. With the move, Houses took the place of the Newgate Street Wards, housemasters took over from Dames the care of the boys in their out-of-class hours and even the aristocrats, the Grecians, who in London had scarcely deigned to speak either to younger boys or to 'mere ushers', began to play their part in the running of the school and its houses.

But, as I see it now and as, even in my schooldays I perceived dimly, the most significant consequence that followed upon the great events of 1902 was that it left us still with some survivors from that galaxy and, in every sense of the word, new young men which the first Horsham Head Master, Dr Upcott, had gathered round him to carry forward noble traditions and to meld them with the novelties of the twentieth century.

It was our remarkable good fortune that Fyfe surpassed even Upcott's undoubted genius as discoverer and supporter of schoolmasterly talent.

By 1929 only a few were left from that group of bright young men whom Upcott had enlisted in 1902 to engineer change in C.H. without destroying its essential character. By strict accounting, A. C. W. Edwards was not of that founding generation; he had joined the staff two years after the Great Migration; but he was the most enduring and one of the finest of Upcott's many fine apprentices.

In one capacity or another Teddy remained at Christ's Hospital for sixty years and, according to the cliché of those times, he became the Mr Chips of Christ's Hospital. The analogy is absurd and, had James Hilton written his saccharine novel when, in 1930, I first went to Teddy for History, already I would have recognized it as such. Fantastically good-looking, alert, erect, wearing always well-cut country clothes at a time when schoolmasters affected frayed tweed jackets and baggy grey trousers, his eyes and his lessons twinkled. His wit he varied to suit the age and the tastes of his audience; simple prep-school humour for the lower forms ('William the Kinkering Kong') and, for the blasé History Grecian, comment upon historical characters that was as sardonic and almost as advanced as their own sophisticated essays.

Like so many of his C.H. colleagues in all disciplines, he had caught the infection of the heuristic method from the Science School – the method which Christ's Hospital had pioneered already in the last years in Newgate Street. He did not teach History, he taught us to seek it out for ourselves. Already on the Lower Erasmus (the Fourth Form of other schools) we were using documents. When he came to introduce us to the workings of Parliament, he had us shift our desks so that the classroom became a fair representation of the Chamber, and to this day I can never read of John Hampden without remembering with pride my speech on Ship Money delivered, at the age of thirteen, in the Edward Parliament.

Teddy I admired and respected; Leonard Dale (who had served since 1902) I loved. A dapper little man with a bull-like voice, a schoolmaster reared in the stern conventions of Victorian England, nevertheless his care for bewildered new boys transcended both the capacity and the inclination of most fathers. We were sad when the end of our first term removed from us the privilege of participation in those Sunday afternoon drama sessions, but still we were qualified to assist at his Saturday night entertainments when we huddled around him, blankets over our pyjamaed shoulders, listening to his heavily theatrical readings from the adventures of the French-Canadian trapper, Jules Verbaux. (Who was Verbaux and what is his book? For sixty years I have sought him out.)

In his one year as my housemaster, Lenny went far towards fixing the destinies of my life. He encouraged competitiveness but versatility he honoured above all else. The boys who did best with him were not the great athletes or the profound scholars; what he wanted from his charges was effort at anything and at everything. His motto, he would say, was 'have a go' – he put it in Latin but not even my most erudite classical colleagues can reconstruct for me the Latin tag which I have long-since forgotten. In that one year he set me on a road with many turnings, on a career which has been more remarkable for the many things at which I have 'had a go' than for notable success in any one field, and if for this I bless him and offer for myself no apologies, even so I am forced to admit that he imbued me immediately with a devotion to his methods which was to make me in the last years of my school career something of a reactionary.

The exercise of our severe superannuation system had left me at the beginning of that last year in Coleridge B the sole survivor of Lenny's regime and, as I saw it, the sole caretaker of a tradition that stretched back to 1902. Hector Buck, Dale's successor, was himself an Old Blue and as tender as any man could be towards all Housey customs. It is not the least among the many examples of his extraordinary patience that, when I came to be his House Captain, he tolerated my conservative objections to all innovations (except those I had myself dreamed up). Only on my very last day did he allow himself a momentary rebuke. 'At last!' he said as he shook my hand. 'Now there is no one left to remind me how things were done

in Mr Dale's day. Now, after six years, at last I can have my own House.'
Through fifty years Buckie remained too charitable to remind me of my
youthful arrogance and too generous to resent my unshakeable conviction
that I was and remain 'one of Lenny's boys'.

As Dale in one year gained my lifelong devotion so also, and again in
only one year, did William Hamilton Fyfe. Fyfe was the head and the
inspiration of a new breed of schoolmasters who were most of them still
young men when I was a new boy. He was Head Master for only eleven
years but his influence was phenomenal and not only on Christ's Hospital.
Late in his life he was dined-out by no less than forty headmasters, all of
whom had been either on the staff or boys at C.H. during his short
regime. He was vital, far-sighted, always courteous and kindly even to the
humblest boy in the School, a wit who never allowed his quick humour to
deteriorate into sarcasm (the favoured vice of school-masters). He was
thought to be a Socialist as was his famous journalist brother. For almost
thirty years I was tempted to ask him if this was true but, though I came to
know him well enough to have him, with Lady Fyfe, as occasional week-
end guests in our home I never found courage to put the question direct. I
suspect that he was in truth a radical in politics as he was a progressive in
his educational theory and mode of administration, but that he would not
have accepted without protest the erosion of competition in society or in
education which we have suffered since 1945.

The quality of schoolmaster or don is often best measured by the quantity of anecdotes told about them by their pupils. There is a rich collection
of stories about James Boyer, the best (not strictly an anecdote but in
themselves an anthology of implied anecdote) the three variants of one sore
epitaph produced by his three most famous pupils: Lamb's, 'Old Jimmy
Boyer is dead at last . . . lay thy animosity against Jimmy in the grave. Do
not *entail* it on thy posterity', by Coleridge's 'Poor J.B.! – may all his faults
be forgiven; and may he be wafted to bliss by little cherub boys, all head
and wings, with no bottoms to reproach his sublunary infirmities', and by
Leigh Hunt's 'It was lucky that the cherubim who took him to Heaven
were nothing but faces and wings, or he would infallibly have flogged
them by the way'.

Fyfe, himself a master of anecdote, is the hero of innumerable revealing
stories from which selection is made whenever two Old Blues of his era
are gathered together.

In this utterly unlike Boyer, and even in his own era a rare schoolmaster, Fyfe rejected corporal punishment as unbefitting to his own dignity
and to the dignity of his boys. Once – and it is said only once in all his
years as Head Master – he did beat a boy. The efficient chastisement over,
he dismissed the offender with the remark 'Now your housemaster cannot
demand that I expel you.'

The Fyfes employed as governess to their daughter a notably glamorous
French girl. One boy, more venturesome than his equally lascivious peers,

thought to satisfy his lubricity by glimpsing her in her *déshabillé*. He was but half-way up a drainpipe at the back of the Head Master's house when Willy walked through his garden. He looked up, called out 'My dear boy, that's the wrong drainpipe. That leads to my dressing-room window', and passed on into the house.

When, in the Spring of 1930 the news broke that we were to lose Fyfe to Canada, the whole community was thrust into a condition which can be compared only to bereavement.

So it came about that after only one year at school I lost the two men who had made easy for me the transition from being the favoured prodigy of a slum school into an ordinary, contented but not particularly privileged member of an extraordinary and indubitably privileged community.

The successors to Dale and Fyfe were on trial before an implacable court of schoolboys. For me Hector Buck came out of that trial triumphant. At first I looked upon him with suspicion and a touch of patronising charity, but soon I came to accept him as a tolerable and by no means insignificant heir to a genius, and in the lifetime of experience which took me from my twelfth birthday to my eighteenth, I learnt for Buckie both affection and admiration.

It was no fault of the Foundation, if much to my discredit, that in my first years at Housie I allowed my pleasure in the School and my growing sophistication to separate me from my mother. I loved her and even at times I admired her but, because she could not understand or share my enthusiasms, I could not respect her.

During the summer holiday of 1934 my mother was taken into the Middlesex Hospital. On the last day of that vacation I went to visit her and I see still in conscience a look which at the time I did not comprehend, but which I have seen since in the eyes of many wounded in battle and in the eyes of my sister Julia when she too was close to death, that grave, unquestioning, consolatory look which, more than words, speaks farewell. I went back to Housie and, in the grandeur of my first year as a Grecian and first also as a House Monitor, almost forgot my mother's pain.

One night some six weeks later I was troubled by dreams, an affliction at that time rare in my experience. I must speak Dutch – and not a word of the language could I muster. Next morning after breakfast I was summoned to Buckie's study. I knew the news before he broke it but I could not have foreseen the manner of its telling. 'Jack', he said, and not even Buckie had ever before called me by my Christian name, 'Jack, your mother died in the night. Weep if you will but better drink this sherry. Here is a ticket for Victoria and here a few books for the journey. Come back in your own good time.'

On that day, as through all that was left of my school-days as in the many years of friendship which followed, Buckie's attitude to me was more gracious than I deserved. Even that last-day rebuke was followed by his barked signal of affection. Among my treasures I hold a collection of letters from Buckie. Written over almost fifty years, the most recent – which came to me only a few weeks before he died – is in a hand as clear and as elegant as the earliest, and all between. The first, as all that followed after, is gossipy, witty, spiced with bawdiness and fashioned in a literary style as exquisite as his calligraphy. Each and every letter makes evident the depth of his devotion to Housie. Over each and every letter there hangs the shadow of grief: for his boys killed in the War and, darkest shadow of all, for the loss of Peter McRae, my 'nurse' and friend, Buckie's friend and, in a strange way for housemaster and pupil, his hero.

For Fyfe's successor I had in my school-days scant respect and no affection. I was told that Oswald Flecker was a fine classical scholar but I am no classicist. I knew him to be an admirable administrator but for me, as for many of us, the most obvious consequence was change in time-honoured and Fyfe-condoned customs. I thought him arrogant and – most heinous of all – disdainful and, perhaps, unaware of the unique character of C.H. Even then I appreciated that Oswald merited a headship of a great public-school but that, in my opinion, youthful but austere, was no qualification for a Head Master of Christ's Hospital. 'Oswald wanted Eton,' I said to my fellow First Partings on the Dais, as we discussed the Head over liver-and-bacon, 'aspired to Eton, deserves Winchester and thinks of Housie as a consolation-prize.' In my last years at school my haughty disapproval was ridiculously compounded by a circumstance for which he was in no way responsible. Oswald was the brother – a much younger brother – of James Elroy Flecker, a poet whom I had dismissed as a worthless romantic. 'Marie Corelli in clumsy verse'.

For years after I left school I persisted with an unspoken and inactive feud with Oswald and I noted, with the satisfaction of one who sees his opinion justified, as black marks against him, every new offence. I hold still to the view that, because it surrendered C.H. to serve as inviolable shield against the enemies of Independent Schools, his high-profiled Chairmanship of the Headmasters' Conference was a mistake. I shall never forgive him for his malodorous treatment of Blunden. But time, experience and some little enhancement of my capacity for charity and for self-knowledge have reversed the harsh verdict I handed down when young. In its place I offer admiration, reluctant but unfeigned. Now I know that in his twenty-four years as Head Master Flecker worked strenuously and successfully for the good of the Foundation.

I have seen many other headmasters, by no means all of them at C.H., and I know that, of all those I have observed from close range, few were Oswald's equals. I recognize that for schoolboys of my generation there could be no satisfactory successor to Fyfe. I see, too, that though I had cause for resenting his vehement opposition to my errant choice of a future in a foreign university when I might have moved on to his beloved Oxford, much of the Flecker-phobia, which in my year as First Parting Grecian I demonstrated by polishing my not inconsiderable talent for riling him, I took on too readily from Buckie, whose virulence for the Head Master was seldom silent.

And – now it must be told – since the day when she had walked into the C.H. Chapel to be his bride, I had been just a little in love with Pippa Flecker.

The character of C.H. as I knew it in my schooldays owed much to the brilliance of Fyfe's appointments. Some I never knew well but even as a schoolboy I saw them for what they were, originals, dedicated men who did not accept that teaching ended when they left the classroom. Roy Macklin, for example, who stays in my memory as much for his velvet jackets and brilliant ties (this in 1930!) as for his odd, knees-outstretched manner of riding a bicycle but whose principal contribution to my schooldays, and perhaps to my whole life, was one chance remark made when I was fifteen: 'Never stop writing poetry if you want to be a writer of prose'; Derek Macnutt, later famous far beyond the Ring Fence in his pseudonymous personality as Ximenes, the crossword-master of *The Observer*; Bill Kirby, whose ferocious reputation as a teacher of Biology persuaded me to take Divinity in School Certificate but whose general unorthodoxy of appearance and manner, together with the affection in which he was held by some of my closer friends, convinced me that Christ's Hospital loves its eccentrics. Some taught me on the way up the school. George Newberry strove valiantly to make me bullish about economics; David Temple, a member of the great ecclesiastical and pedagogical family and, I am sure, in all that family the untidiest, who taught me English in the Middle School and, against all the regulations, encouraged me also in the one athletic pastime in which I was above the average by daring me to practise my highdiving from the girders in the roof of the swimming baths.

There were other men who never taught me who were my friends even whilst I was at school. The age-gap between a schoolboy and his masters is not susceptible to arithmetic. At eleven, a twenty-two-year-old is Methuselah. Even at eighteen, despite the C.H. tradition which holds a Grecian to be the equal of the twelve Apostles, it is not easy to accept young masters as members of one's own generation. Even now, when I list the masters of my time whom still I number among my friends, I shy away from awareness of my own advanced age and comfort myself with the thought that teaching at Housie must induce longevity. It is only in moments of shattering realism that I am prepared to admit that Gordon van Praagh, Arthur Humphrey and Arthur Rider are only a few years my senior.

One who never taught me in the classroom and who, in my schooldays and in the years thereafter, I could never claim as friend in any social sense, was nevertheless for me, as for many of my contemporaries, a powerful and enduring influence. As Director of Music, C. S. Lang inherited from the centuries a tradition of musical excellence which eventually he in his turn passed on, much enriched, to successor–directors. His labours and theirs have given to Christ's Hospital in this century a record in composition, performance, music administration and music scholarship unequalled by any other school and which is, in the Christ's Hospital story, surpassed only by the school's contribution to literature. Names support my boast – many of them names of men who were among my adult acquaintances: A. K. Holland (whose fine little book on Purcell I put into Penguins), Constant Lambert, William Glock, John Hunt, Percy Young, Ivor Keys, Colin Davis, Wilfred Brown and Andrew Porter. Yet the proof of the achievement of Lang and his fellow–directors is not the glittering list nor yet the unchanging excellence of the Chapel Choir and the Band. More revealing is the informed passion for music of men, once boys at C.H., who have made their careers in other fields; Bernard Levin, for example, is wonderfully provocative and mischievous on most topics and ency-clopaedic on all, but when he writes or talks on music the sharp edge is blunted by enthusiasm. Brian Magee, so often Levin's companion on the centre-pages of *The Times*, handles philosophy as a professional and politics – as a politician. Some other philosophy dons might achieve a respectable book on Wagner, but surely no other politician.

Even so, it is not either the professionals or these highly professional amateurs that stand as memorial to Lang, his predecessors and successor, not even the odd circumstance that our only judge was once Assistant Conductor of the Liverpool Philharmonic, nor yet the fact that even I have on occasion dared an essay on Tudor music. Far more significant is the part that music has played in the lives of hundreds of seemingly unmu-sical and certainly unprofessional Blues. This is the proof of education as it should be.

Lang was a composer in the Stanford vein, already a little out-of-date when I was at school. His settings of hymns, sea-shanties and canticles are easy to sing and easier to bellow; they are not great works of art; but, as Henry Wood brought excellent performances of fine music to a vast audi-ence, so did Lang bring music to our community.

I have heard great symphony orchestras in many parts of the world and I have watched most of the leading conductors of the last half-century, yet no musical experience is as fresh in my memory as the first time I saw Lang rehearsing the London Symphony Orchestra in Big School one summer morning in 1930. Dvorak's *New World Symphony* may be, to those with superior taste, a musical cliché; to me it will always be a reminder of reve-lation. Lang, his jacket off, bright blue shirt and red braces deliberately and dramatically revealed to convince us, the whole school and yet a volunteer audience, that music-making even at its highest level is hard work but not pompous; the logic of the symphony interrupted by his rebuking baton, by amiable arguments between the leader and the conductor, and by interpo-lations never scored by the composer but impertinently introduced by the bassoon. And, almost as clear in my remembering mind, the full perfor-mance on the afternoon of that same day when even I, the musical novice, was able to appreciate the wholeness that had been wrought from the chaos of the morning.

In my later school years, visits from the LSO brought pleasures that were not entirely musical.

Between the morning rehearsal and the afternoon concert we played asphalt-cricket against a team from the Orchestra. There was for me, as I listened to the miraculous opening bars of Tchaikovsky's Violin Concerto, a satisfying sharpening of aesthetic pleasure when I recognized the soloist as the man I had caught first-ball from Tom Miller's bowling only an hour before.

There were also in the audience at those afternoon concerts girls from neighbouring schools, and, already by the time I was fifteen, looking at girls was among my hobbies almost as exciting as listening to music.

Those annual visits of the LSO were the grandest occasions of the Lang-inspired musical calendar but the calendar was full and rich. Early in my school career, a young Old Blue was scheduled to give us a concert of songs. We waited for him, more or less patiently, when we were told that he was substituting as a soloist in 'Hiawatha' at the Albert Hall. Later, without musical accompaniment, the voice of Frank Phillips became familiar to millions as the voice of the Senior Announcer at the BBC.

Fachiri and Daranyi came twice during my last year and I earned the envy of my peers when they accepted an invitation to tea in my tiny study; envy which was directed also against my swob, who had the dubious privilege of making and serving the tea and the horror implicit in using a bone-china tea-service borrowed for the occasion from the Coleridge Matron.

The frivolous sound of the tinkling of tea-cups interrupts recollection of the sonorities of grand musical performances and great performers, yet there is logic that is by no means lunatic in continuing the equation of influence by way of C. S. Lang to that same Coleridge Matron, Violet Dearden. Lang magicked musicianship into all of us, his artifice was deliberate and his purposes grandiose but he was for me a remote wizard; I doubt that I spoke to him more than six times in six years; Violet Dearden I saw and talked with almost every day of my school life, in my last two years often for several hours at a time. By the custom of the place she had no hierarchical right to influence our lives; most matrons were shabby, anonymous creatures, heirs to the Dames of Newgate Street, but heirs who had been deprived of the disciplinary prerogatives that were invested in those awesome females, their most obvious duties to supervise the domestic staff, to inspect the smaller boys for rashes or dirty necks and to hand out clean clothes to all. I doubt that Violet Dearden had aspirations to influence her charges but for me and several others she, like Lang, extended the conventional boundaries of schooling and made of it education. Both of them presented us with examples of something which I can only describe by using the word 'elegance'. That word is out-moded and the concept now generally despised but growing awareness that there were processes of personal enrichment that could not be garnered in the class-room, on the playing-fields – or even in Chapel – was the measure of my increasing alienation from my North London background.

It is possible – and indeed likely – that my contented recollection of Violet Dearden's casual tutelage opens her to the accusation that she was a snob who found in me a willing pupil. If so, the fault is in my exposition and not in her teaching. True, she had very little use for most of her colleagues and was not slow to let us know that she despised their dowdiness, their clucking gossip and the complacency with which they accepted the ambiguity of their status suspended somewhere between the Senior Common Room and the domestic staff. But it was not her distaste for other matrons which affected us. We saw her as a civilized, older and quintessentially female friend. Always immaculately groomed, even when she wore the navy-blue dress which was virtually a uniform for the matrons, she presented to us a stylishness of which the rest of the matrons would have been both incapable and fearful. More than most women of my acquaintance (or for that matter most men), she had a great capacity for listening – a gift much-honoured by boys in their later teens – and few inhibitions about what it was she heard. In my last years I talked to her as freely about sex as about football, as readily about politics as about the problems of the House. Her only reaction to my more outrageous statement was a quizzically-raised eyebrow. Her enthusiasm for bridge and golf I could not share, though because at that time even playing golf was regarded as somehow outrageous behaviour in a matron, and playing golf with senior boys positively scandalous, her golf I looked upon with pride and used it in argument with the more perspicacious among my contemporaries (who needed no persuasion) to demonstrate our good fortune in having as our matron a lively and very modern woman.

In the House even those who did not know Violet Dearden as well as I were fond of her. She was always on the touch-line at important School and House rugger-matches. She was unsparing in the time she gave to preparing costumes for House-plays. Above all, she did not fuss and respected our code.

As with Pippa Flecker, as indeed in 1936 with any good-looking woman who came my way, smiled at me and treated me as equal, so was I more than a little in love with Violet Dearden. Now, but not then, I suspect that she knew it, was neither shocked nor scornful but instead dealt with what could have become an embarrassing situation by enter-taining for my inspection girls more appropriate to my years. Why else did she invite me so often to tea when the only other guest was a buxom, blonde and twenty-year-old nurse from 'the Sicker', who was identifiable to my fellow Grecians as the object of my more florid contributions to *The Outlook*.

The autobiographer sees his life through the wrong end of a telescope. Consequence is to him more compelling than sequence. Thus it is that

already in this narrative I have come close to the end of my schooldays
without ever considering my schoolboy middle-age. There is in truth little
from that time, the years between my thirteenth and my sixteenth birth-
days, that merits recording. I progressed up the School, unremarkable and
generally unremarked, active and contented, my only notable idiosyncrasy
my determination to make my way towards the nobility of Grecian status
on the Modern Side – an example of obstinacy which set me apart from all
others competent in the Arts and from the severe custom of the time
which had all such as me construing Latin and translating Greek.

Then at sixteen I found myself at the feet of two men, Troops Hornsby
and David Roberts, and under their miraculous tutelage I was changed, my
school career enlivened and with it, indeed, the whole course of my life.
Both men were originals, both set about blasting me out of the slit-trench
of convention in which I had hidden for five years.

I cannot write of Troops and of David only in terms of my last years at
Housie, for they remained my friends and even my mentors for the rest of
their lives, Troops for almost fifty years, David for twenty. In David's case
friendship was soon extended to include his wife and mine and, after his
death and to this day, continues to include in the amity his children and
mine.

Almost forty years after I left school – and Troops by that time the
grand panjandrum of New Zealand education – when my wife and I first
visited New Zealand, every door we wished to enter opened for us. In the
intervening years we had met but twice, and then briefly, but every month
there came a letter, scrawled on one of those fragile air-letter forms which,
on being opened, seem always to be bisected in the middle of a paragraph.
Once deciphered (and that process often engaged three or four crypto-
graphers for hours on end), these letters were enthralling. Troops wrote, as
he talked, somehow out of the side of his mouth, sardonically, pungently.
He commented on books, passed on scabrous gossip about politicians,
schoolmasters, his fellow headmasters, he lamented the decline of Britain,
the follies of the United States. He offered canny criticism of my most
recent work and always warmth, always encouragement.

Troops (so called for his mode of addressing both rugger teams and
English sets: 'Come on, troops') arrived at C.H. in only my second or
third year, as a learner straight down from Oxford, but I saw little of him
until I became a Grecian. Then his skill and his enthusiasm soon overcame
the resentment I felt at being placed by Flecker in Hornsby's set, the
Second English Set, instead of Macklin's First Set with all the other History
Grecians – and I the winner of the Deputy Grecians' English Prize!

This vicious aberration put Troops on his mettle and he put me on
mine. His criticisms of my essays were at once ferocious and heartening, at
once ruthless and yet flattering. He treated my efforts as if he was a distinguished literary critic and I a young author who could be helped to distinction by dispassionate advice and passionate stimulation. I might have

profited from his comments even more than I did had he not written them in a hand that was almost beyond communication. Perhaps once in every three submissions, I dared to ask him to decode his cryptograms and then the comfortable paradox of his attitude to his pupils, at once acerbic and generous, was emphasized by the contradiction between his pungency of voice and his self-mocking, self-deprecating smile.

By the Easter Term of 1936 it was common knowledge among all the Grecians – and not a little resented by some – that Hornsby had betted with Macklin that I would win the Lamb Essay Medal. I hope that Troops collected on his bet.

Of David Roberts it is difficult for me to write without entering upon hyperbole, but I know that my admiration and affection for him is shared by all who profited from his tutelage and friendship. There is a sensible C.H. convention which ordains that no memorial may be raised even to the noblest of Housey's servants until that servant has been dead for twenty years. When the time came to commemorate David, subscriptions came in from all over the world, from ambassadors, bishops, headmasters, professors, tycoons, all 'David's boys', and with the cheques, letters rich with grateful reminiscence. Much to our relief, Peggy Roberts refused to allow the customary honouring plaque ('how David would have laughed had he thought he would be memorialized in stone'); instead she chose, for David, for us and for C.H. a painting by a modern artist. On the day of the presentation we had on exhibition in the School Library some two hundred books written by his one-time pupils (perhaps the most eloquent of all memorials to his genius), and a hundred of 'David's boys' gathered for the appropriately informal ceremony.

As I looked at the chosen painting, my mind went back to those many days in 1935 and 1936 when I came to the door of his study – the setting he thought more suitable than any classroom for his sessions with his History Grecians – there to have my eye caught by some strategically-placed addition to his arcane collection – a Henry Moore drawing, perhaps – and I remembered how, just as he had intended, in that moment my eagerness to discuss the historic implications of the virginity of the first Queen Elizabeth or the significance of the 'Augmentation of the Indies' vanished, and I found myself – again as he had intended – launched on a critical assessment of the painter's art.

According to the time table, David taught History to the History Grecians. He taught it brilliantly, yet I cannot remember even one hour when he lectured at us in a classroom. The many hours each week which we devoted to our own specialist subject we spent in the Library, in our own studies or in his, each of us working at his own chosen topic, offering our esoteric views of the past to each other and to David, disputing his deliberately provocative interpolations, reading, reading more and producing essay after essay for his firm but encouraging comment and for the sharp criticism of the rest of the group.

This mode and method was so exhilarating, and the personality of our tutor so rich, that not a few of 'David's boys' found that their years as History Grecians were in the short run disadvantageous. They won their open awards at Oxford or Cambridge but, once up at the university, discovered that college tutors were dim and dreary when compared to David and that reading History at the university was, for those who had come first to serious study of the subject under David, a pedestrian exercise. They survived, most of them with good degrees, and the memorial to a great teacher is the persisting devotion to his subject of so many of those he once taught. Five of David's boys became professors in British universities; a record which might make him smile, for he had no great respect for academic hierarchies and considered it to be a trifling addition to his responsibility (and one not difficult to fulfil, given that we were all possessed of some wit) that he should teach us how to bamboozle Examination Boards and Chair Committees. He would take more pride, I suspect, from that considerable bibliography of historical and creative works by former History Grecians.

My own initial response to David's unorthodoxy was to refuse to follow him where most of his pupils went, into the study of Medieval History. My preference was for the Tudors and Stuarts.

David accepted this inconvenient aberration with his customary amused grace but neither he nor I could foresee the influence that his eccentric decision would exercise in that part of my subsequent career which, by the most generous terms, can be described as academic or scholarly.

My second demonstration of nonconformity was to have even greater and more general consequence but for that wildness David cannot be held in any way responsible. Not David, not Buckie, not Troops, not even Flecker, but only some lunatic and almost unidentifiable compulsion persuaded me to go abroad after leaving Christ's Hospital.

The amiability and adult skills of Fyfe, Buckie, Teddy, Troops and David were not universal in the adult part of our community There were some who made little impact outside the classroom, several who, even before a blackboard, were pedestrian, and one, but only one, whose pleasure in making a direct impact was exercised without restraint. He left us, none too soon, to be headmaster of some obscure institution; for a while we prayed for the children in his Dotheboys Hall, then we excised him from Christ's Hospital mythology.

There were some who were condemned by us, not for any sins of commission but because their enthusiasms, though proper and benevolent, brought to the surface our deeply-held prejudices. These we treated with disdain and thus it was that, when my junior housemaster rebuked me for maintaining Coleridge B's antique tradition, a poor showing in all activities involving cross-country running or the OTC, I rounded on him with words of pompous impertinence: 'But, sir, you have been in this house but six weeks, I six years.'

For no good reason Colin Healey forgave me, and in later years in Australia he has been my ever-generous host.

3

In my Joyful School-days

At the time, I was quick to explain away my decision to turn from the course plotted for me by my status and by precedent. It was, I insisted, some whisper in the blood made audible by my father's tales of his youthful emigration which persuaded me to chase my destiny into strange lands. Even in the years that have followed, I have allowed this pleasantly idealized variant of the truth to stifle recollection of all those other and more potent influences which, in 1936, thrust me out into the unknown and unpredictable.

I was not born to be a pioneer. I neither relished nor coveted 'The slow progress, the scant fire, the axe, the saddle-back, / The beauty of all adventurers and daring persons.' Seven years, the nights passed sleeping on wooden boards, the mornings prefaced by cold baths and the days spent exposed to the brisk winds of the Weald had but enhanced my dedication to the sybaritic. Others among my school-fellows – and even some who were, by the measure of our mentors 'university material' – were bound for Malayan rubber plantations, for the gold mines of South Africa, or for the Indian Police, but such intrepidity was beyond me. I refused to sit for Oxbridge and would not deign to accept the second-best which was sometimes reluctantly allowed to a Grecian: a place at the University of London. I would go abroad but I would go abroad to a university.

My proposition was eccentric, not only to Christ's Hospital but also to me, for I was then – as I remain – essentially conservative, held firmly to my roots and comfortable in convention. I loved England and the England that I loved was compounded of familiar and romantic images, many of them superficial but to me the symbols of continuing stability: cricket on a village green, formal dinners, Grace before Meat, the unchanged and unchangeable formulae of military display.

In none of this have I been much altered by the years. True, I held almost for a lifetime some dedication to the Liberal Party, but this for me is in no sense out-of-key with my innate conservatism; regular association with friendly ghosts, with Cobbett, Lamb and Leigh Hunt, has confirmed my conviction that in England radicalism is itself a tradition.

My churchmanship, such as it is, is founded upon devotion to the familiar. Old and well-known hymns I bellow, usually off-key but always with pleasure and without reference to the text. Amendments to

Cranmer's liturgy I resent. Let any upstart read a lesson from some new fangled unlovely translation and my whisper will be heard rehearsing the only words I accept as Holy Writ, the words of the King James Bible. (In this I follow the excellent example of that American girl who rejected the *American Revised* with the simple but unanswerable comment that what was good enough for St Paul was good enough for her.)

Even as literary critic I have marched always several paces behind the avant-garde. Old friends like old shoes are most comfortable to my feet.

This pusillanimity in the face of change was in me already when I was eighteen, but then, as ever after, there were working upon my habitual conformity two mischievously antagonistic forces: I can never refuse an invitation to travel and I am incapable of rejecting any chance to make for myself a new career.

The first of these influences I can in truth mark to my father's example, and it was certainly his awareness of the blame that could be set upon him for my seemingly ludicrous refusal to become Oxonian or Cantab which kept him silent when I announced my determination to go abroad.

The second was assuredly no fault of his for he too suffered like paradox. Despite his pride in his boyhood adventures, for me he could imagine no future more marvellous than that I complete the miracle of my education by moving on to Oxford or to Cambridge – and thence into 'a good safe job' in the Higher Civil Service.

For the most part, it was not the compulsion of heritage but youthful pig-headedness which propelled me across the Atlantic. Once I had announced my intention, that which I had intended as no more than tentative became inescapable and irrevocable because, with the solitary exception of my father, all who had any influence over me were against it.

Flecker, once my obduracy had convinced him that I would never be a Brackenbury Scholar of Balliol (nor even an Exhibitioner at his own college, Brasenose), would have me a merchant banker. I spurned Oswald's benevolence and thus mislaid my only chance of becoming a millionaire.

Hector Buck, who agreed with Flecker on nothing else and who bellowed his disagreement frequently and with lurid adjectival support from his open study-window into the air between Coleridge and the Head Master's house, nevertheless could not conceive as possible that a Grecian, his own House Captain, would condemn himself to a life-sentence served among aborigines.

My contemporaries looked upon me as upon one who had settled for damnation at just that moment when St Peter held open for him the Gates of Heaven.

Even David Roberts, by insistent and probing question if not by opposition, made my course inevitable. Unlike Flecker, David was confident that the University Scholarship which, in those days before Local Education Authority grants, I must have if I was to go to Oxford or to

Cambridge, would be mine almost by divine right. He offered to go to battle with Flecker to gain for me another year at school so that together we could ensure my divinity. This was my chance to retreat with honour, but not even for David would I lower my colours. For Trinity, Cambridge, David's choice for me, I substituted the Sorbonne. His response was mild, and, as always, set in the form of a question: 'How fluent is your French?'

David's questions, like surgeons' scalpels, cut deftly and with certainty through intellectual bombast or scholastic hesitancy but there was always compassion for his victims, compassion and benevolent mischief. On this occasion – his head cocked more even than usual to one side so that it seemed to rest upon his shoulder, his smile close to burgeoning into laughter, the handkerchief taken from his sleeve fluttering like a semaphore-flag – the question had no question-mark. We both knew the answer. And then the laugh exploded to another question-framed statement. He had read my mind before ever I said the word he expected. 'Heidelberg? You're quick with a sabre, are you?'

So, with the gates of the French and German universities closed to me by David's wisdom, as surely as were the gates of Oxford, Cambridge and London by my obstinacy, the possibilities were reduced but clarified. I would go abroad; I would go to a university; I would go to a university abroad; I must go to a university in an English-speaking country.

It was no small part of David's rare genius – and it is sure testimony to his gentleness – that, though he revelled in the battles with us, and delighted in victory, he never left us humiliated. We had minds of our own; he saw it as his duty to enlarge them, to sharpen our faculties, to persuade us into adding the force of logic and the weight of knowledge to our prejudices and whims, but he neither wished nor attempted to recreate us in his own image. (That being said, I confess that when eventually and almost by chance I became a professor, having had no pedagogic training whatsoever, such little success as came my way was mine because I did all that was in my power to model my methods on those of David Roberts.)

In triumph he was always generous. With but two sentences and a twinkle he had routed me, and I his most argumentative acolyte. At that moment he could have pressed me towards Trinity, Cambridge, and I would have gone, eagerly and with purpose firm. Instead he asked one more question. Just one word: 'Canada?'

It was not I but David who bearded Flecker, and not I nor Flecker but David who wrote to Fyfe. I must have a scholarship.

Fyfe wrote back from Kingston, Ontario. 'Let the boy try the Anglo-Canadian Education Committee, but don't send him to me at Queen's; it would be too much like staying at home.'

I tried, succeeded, was accepted as a Sophomore at the University of New Brunswick; and Christ's Hospital allowed me a grant from its Exhibition Fund and the money for my fare, second class and one-way, from London to Fredericton.

This achievement, when compared with the triumphs of my peers at once eccentric and unsensational, erased in me all hesitancy. I had argued with David and made him into an ally. I settled to revelling in my aristocratic condition as a First Parting Grecian and House Captain of Coleridge B.

Confidence I had never lacked; now I indulged in a deliberate and not unsuccessful attempt to model myself after the pattern which I imagined Coleridge had recognized in his schoolfellow Thomas Middleton, 'a scholar and a gentleman in his 'teens'. I fancied myself as urbane among my contemporaries, gentle and yet firm with my juniors, easy but courteous with those I regarded as elderly (anyone over twenty-five). Younger masters I treated to studied indifference, and in this was no better and no worse than most of my equals or most of our predecessors as First Parting Grecians. We held steadfastly to their example, an example enshrined in the tale of Cyril Burt – by 1936 the philosopher-king of English pedagogy and fifty years later its most reviled fraud. Burt, so ran our legend, when himself a First Parting and on being mildly rebuked by a senior master for using a door which authority had decreed to be reserved for masters, had replied with what was in our social custom infallible logic. 'But, sir, a few moments back I saw Mr Smith enter thereby, and he's a mere usher.'

Those were for me glittering months. Not everything went well but nothing was disastrous. I could not recover for Coleridge B the sporting glories which had been ours two years earlier; we had no Peter McRae. Then we had won everything and then in every winning team I had played a part, humble but energetic. (That last wicket stand with Peter which won us the Cricket Cup; the frantic pass which allowed him to drop a goal in an Homeric rugger semi-final and so took us to an easy victory in the Final; fourth place in the Four which won the Fives Cup and, glory of glories, first string to Peter's Number Two in the team which began for us a run of victories in the Diving Cup.) But, by machiavellian process I calculated us again into first place in the Diving Cup – and even persuaded Buckie, who reviled all swimming as blasphemy against the gods of cricket, onto the balcony of the Baths to watch our triumph.

In other sports, Rugby football, cricket, shooting, fives, our teams, all captained by me, performed no more than creditably but it was only in the steeplechase (from which I myself was a total abstainer, preferring instead to launch myself into a career on radio by serving as commentator over the broadcast-system set up by Bill Kirby and his signallers) and in all competitions organized by the OTC that Coleridge B came handsomely last.

Encouraged by Buckie in the myth, so handsomely fashioned by tradition, that it was the House Captain and not the House Master who ran the House, I settled myself into a pose of magisterial omnipotence, remote but kindly, austere but flecked with touches of amiable eccentricity.

In Dining Hall I abandoned my mask of austerity. Here, among my few peers, my fellow First Parting Grecians, I was bonhomous, by my standard (and, still I suspect, by theirs) witty, scabrous, the prime source for gossip. We took our meals in state, sitting together on the Dais. Even our food was not as that of other boys; ours was the same as that served in the Masters' Common Room. We were waited upon by a maid and not for us 'kiff' (an extraordinary concoction in a huge tin-can of tea – or was it coffee? – sugar and milk of a noxious kind such as never again passed my lips until I tasted Army *char* brewed on a Benghazi burner). We had our tea from tea-pots, the sugar-bowl and the milk-jug on the table before us. We drank from tea-cups; the rest of the School from kiff-bowls (held always in two fingers of one hand). And we talked: our conversation deliberately sophisticated whether it was of Proust, Wagner or the alleged misdoings of some notably pudacious master's wife.

As House Captain I had three swobs – one more than my predecessors, two more than was allowed to house captains or monitors in other houses – their duties to clean my shoes, to make my bed, to run my bath, to take messages to other First Partings, to serve tea in my study when I entertained; often my fellow Grecians and on occasion some distinguished visitor to the School: Barnes Wallis, for example, (this, my second meeting with a man who would become a valued friend and the subject of one of my most successful books); George Bell, the Bishop of Chichester (whose high-pitched voice had reduced to farce the solemnity of my Confirmation), and, at one and the same time, Nelly D'Aranyi and Adila Fachiri (the occasion for my youthful quip 'Here is proof that it is possible to get two galleons into a pint-pot').

That two of the Coleridge B small fry (one, Tony Tighe, my swob, since risen to be Signal Officer-in-Chief, and the other, John Gayner, in time an eminent engineer) remain to this day my friends is evidence to their abiding charity and perhaps, just a little, to the success of my pose as dictator always benevolent.

I was then, as I have been ever since, unshakeably and even virulently heterosexual. (In later years my friendship for John Gayner, which has long-since bridged the chasm between House Captain and 'squit', has been not a little strengthened because even my dim eyes are sharpened to delight when I see his wife, Wyn, across the table from me at a meeting of the Council of Christ's Hospital.) I had several girl-friends in Islington and Cockfosters; after the Grecians' exchange of Speech Day visits with the monitresses of our Girls' School, a girl-friend at Hertford (and she the Mayoress of Stepney!) and there was that busty Infirmary nurse in whose dishonour I wrote gently erotic pieces utterly out of character with the sardonic verses which ordinarily I contributed to *The Outlook* and unrecognisable as the work of that same sharp critic who reviewed films for *The Blue*. But for that conventional school-magazine, even when writing the termly House Note, I refrained from convention ('Congratulations to Maxwell and Andrews on winning House Rugger colours') and set myself instead to demonstrating, by deliberate and generally overblown literary artifice, that I was destined to be a man of letters.

The months that carried me towards the Leaving Service were dream-like; never placid and never traumatic but after that manner in dreaming which I have always enjoyed, the sort of dream which, when interrupted, creates resentment. There were periods of refreshing contentment inter-spersed by high-pitched excitements or comic episodes, and all with *ego* as hero.

There was but one shattering, nightmarish interpolation: my father's marriage to Alice, a harmless woman whose only public faults were dull-ness and rampant snobbery, whom nevertheless from the day when I saw their wedding as imminent, I cast as wicked stepmother. In reality she was easily, and generally, terrified, by my sharp tongue, by my sister Julia's histrionics and by my sister Bess's schoolmarmish austereness. Bess and Julia joined me in a conspiracy of contempt which became virulent and open dislike when Alice announced that it was not *comme il faut* for a boy to stand as best-man to his own father.

In the five years that were left to her, I doubt that I spoke civilly to Alice more than three or four times but she exercised on me a profound if perverse influence. It was not she who moved us from the flaked elegance of Canonbury Square to the open but semi-detached dreariness of Cockfosters; that move had been engineered, unsuccessfully, for the bene-fit of my mother's health; but I set the blame upon Alice. This china-duck suburbia was, by my accounting, her natural habitat. Then, as ever after, I knew terror amounting to mania that I might be forced to live in a suburb. From that terror came the circumstance that in later years I have lived always in houses that shrieked prosperity which has never been truly mine.

Housie was the dream and Housie was the wondrous reality. I acted in House plays; of course playing only leads. I drank sherry each night with Violet Dearden. I talked, and generally without interruption. Hours passed in David's study, relishing his interrogations and revelling in amiable debates with my fellow-Grecians, kept me alive to the excitement of history.

Once during all that year, once only indeed in all the years that we were friends, did I see David nervous: when he brought to us – as I have said ever since for our approval – his new fiancée. Peggy was younger than some of his Grecians; she remains in spirit younger than any of us.

In the Summer Term, my last at school, I had two sensational triumphs, and both were made all the more glorious because they were wrought, as I thought, against Oswald's predictions and, as I suspected, contrary to his wishes. I won both the Lamb Essay Medal and the Chapel Reading Prize. Both competitions were judged by external examiners. Winning the Lamb Medal placed me in a distinguished line which included Cyril Burt (so proud of this achievement that he listed it with his many honorary degrees in *Who's Who*), Middleton Murry (who, as now do I, gives to this grandeur several paragraphs in his autobiography), Blunden and, after me, Keith Douglas.

The topic for the essay was not announced until all Grecians of all kinds, even Engineers, were sitting at desks in the Library. Our efforts were pseudonymous and, as salute to my hero, I chose the pen name Cumberback. Troops won his bet and I a handsome silver medal, according to Murry 'the finest of Wyon's designs'.

The Chapel Reading Prize added a privilege even more public. Speech Day at Christ's Hospital is unlike similar occasions at most other schools and much more resplendent. The Lord Mayor attends and with him all his acolytes, the Masters of City Livery Companies, the Monitresses from the Girls' School, visitors, distinguished and undistinguished by the hundred, and (a rare concession in my school-days) the parents of Leaving Grecians. First: a Service, superb music superbly given, the bellowing of the Foundation Hymn, the Bidding Prayer for Christ's Hospital, and one Lesson, taken from the 44th Chapter of Ecclesiasticus. Next: Dinner Parade. Though we marched into Hall to the music of our band on every week-day in the school year, on this day the Parade is more ceremonious because the Lord Mayor doffs his cocked hat in response to the salute of each house as it marches past. There follows lunch in Hall for all the visitors, but of 'the Foundation's children' only the First Parting Grecians and the Monitresses – and wine at our table. Then, the Speeches; and in Big School our uniqueness among schools most blatant; not for us a headmaster's speech, like a Managing Director's Annual Report, but the English Oration given by the Senior Grecian – without benefit of text or notes and as much as twenty minutes long, and a reply, often shambling and shameful by comparison with the youthful oratory which had preceded it, from the Lord Mayor.

Other than the Senior Grecian, only one of us plays a solo part: the winner of the Chapel Reading Prize. So it was I who strode the length of the Chapel, mounted the steps of the lectern and read that magnificent passage beginning 'Let us now praise famous men'.

Decades later, after hearing the same lesson, The Worshipful the Treasurer (who had been a boy in *my* congregation) said to me, 'Today, for the first time, the reader matched the standard set by you in 1936'. The value of the compliment is not a little reduced because Angus Ross repeated it every year.

Prize Giving is at C.H. a domestic affair, shorn of the panoply which we give to so many other occasions but already fifty years ago School policy was liberal. Not for us leather-bound, crested copies of Bede's *Anglo-Saxon Chronicle* or Palgrave's *Golden Treasury*; instead all prizes were given monetary value and the winner freedom to make his own selection. Such indeed was the liberal-mindedness of our seniors that there were among the eighty or so books I acquired on that day in 1936 Joyce's *Ulysses* and Faulkner's *Sanctuary*. I give no credence to the tale which Tony Tighe has put about ever since, that my prizes were so many that I ordered him to accompany me to the platform to act as porter, but I can hear still, and still with pleasure, the roar from the Coleridge B claque as I collected the Coleridge Trophy awarded to the House winning the most prizes.

On that Prize Day in 1936 I gathered to myself also the Master Mariners Prize. What I had done to earn it I did not discover until forty years had passed and then the revelation stirred my conscience, for it was as if in youth I had committed incest, murdered my mother or pawned the Hospital silver. Can it have been possible that at eighteen my acting fooled even Flecker? By the rubric, the Prize must be given to one:

> selected by the Head Master for cheerful submission to superiors, self-respect and independence, outstanding character and exemplary behaviour, kindness and protection to the weak, readiness to forgive offence, desire to conciliate the differences of others, and above all fearless devotion to duty and unflinching truthfulness.

'Conscience has a thousand tongues.' Nine hundred and ninety-nine offer gratitude and apology to Flecker's shade – the one thousandth still whispers that I know where his shade is to be found.

Prize Giving over, there followed on the last night of my school-days another essentially dramatic occasion, but this, the Leaving Service, the most dramatic and the most poignant of all Housie ceremonies.

With the rest of the School and all the Staff as audience, the hundred or so who were destined next day for the world beyond the Ring Fence lined the Chapel aisle in Indian file and in reverse order of seniority. One by one we were summoned forward to receive leather-bound, crested Bibles, the Grecians (as if their arrogance required for them more spiritual compensation) also a leather-bound and crested Prayer Book.

Next morning, reduced to ordinariness by a city suit, I walked down the Centre Path and, for the last time, boarded the Special Train. Colin Chivers was with me, as he had been seven years earlier on that other seminal journey into the unknown from London Bridge to Christ's Hospital, his eyes behind his glasses for once unwinking. Metaphorically and often actually he has stayed by me ever since, indulgent to my foibles, ready with support in my times of stress, eager with applause for my petty triumphs.

I was no longer a Housey boy but I was still, as I would remain for all my days, a Blue. It takes more than a Bible, more than a Special Train, more than a city suit as was mine, at the insistence and expense of my father (who had in all his life never owned one custom-built garment) crafted by a well-known City tailor, more even than the width of the oceans, to divorce 'a child of the Hospital' from the sodality.

4

Hoops of Steel

Often in the last half-century I have been bruised by offence more vicious by far than that I had imagined from Colin Healey, my innocent and well-meaning junior housemaster, and not infrequently, with justice to quicken my wits and sharpen my tongue, I have given back a verbal blow that has silenced even the most belligerent opponent. On one occasion when I wished to strike the offender to the heart with the poisoned arrow of my rebuke, however, I was so choked by indignation at the enormity of what I had heard that I could not speak.

The only Blue at the dinner-table, I had listened, it seemed for hours, as a brutish politician poured out his bilious and cliché-ridden diatribe against Independent Schools. Our host, thinking presumably to calm the perfervid egalitarian by offering concession and sweet reason, broke in on the ranting monologue and said, 'All the objections that you have raised against most of the public schools, against Eton, Rugby and Winchester, may have some validity, but surely even you cannot level such accusation against Christ's Hospital.'

The aggressor set down the knife which he had been waving menacingly as if he wished to use it to cut the throats of every parent who dared to send a child to a public school, every master and every mistress who had ever taught 'the spoiled brats of the rich', every boy, girl, man and woman who had ever been educated in one of those 'nation-divisive, socially abhorrent bastions of aristocratic pretensions'. He ground his teeth, smirked at me, pondered a moment then growled: 'Christ's Hospital? Christ's Hospital I despise and fear more than I despise Eton or fear Winchester. Eton and Winchester merely perpetuate privilege; Christ's Hospital creates it.'

Animus so vicious is armour-plated against reason. But there is also in that miserable politician's sour aphorism just that flicker of truth which confounds even the most spirited counsel for the defence. The rest is, therefore, silence; or so it would be were it not that the exercise of autobiography, if it has purpose at all beyond the gratification of narcissistic impulses, imposes on the autobiographer the duty to seek out from memory those influences, be they historical, sociological, institutional or individual, which by his accounting have made him what he thinks himself to be, to rediscover those potencies, be they beneficial or malign, which have significance beyond the petty circumstances of his own life.

While I cannot deny that for me – as for all its sons and daughters – Christ's Hospital did create privilege, still I insist that by my advantage none other has been harmed and not a few just a little assisted, advanced or comforted.

I profited because in my school-days, in addition to a sturdy classroom training, I was urged towards recognition of civilisation and humaneness.

I profited because throughout my adult life C.H. has made accessible to me a worldwide connection, a range of contacts wider and more diverse than any of the other springs of friendship from which I have benefitted.

To this advantage instants stand as useful illustration; they fall far short of record entire.

Strangers to Australia, my wife and I were made immediately other than alien by the open door to the Sydney home of Henry Lathwell and to the Melbourne home of Robin Paul (Henry and Robin both hitherto unknown to me and both my senior by several years). Tourist in New Zealand, at every bus-stop we were greeted by an Old Blue, but not one with a face remembered from my years at school. We flew in to Delhi Airport. There we stood, battered by noise, overwhelmed by strange odours, bemused by the seemingly aimless bustle which is peculiar to the Sub Continent, and suddenly all became secure and well-nigh familiar for there, towering above the crowd, was a welcoming committee of one, the huge and hugely comforting figure of Alan Everest, my junior by many years and never before known to me. Once in New York I was hauled from my hotel bedroom by an elderly stranger who had learnt of my presence in the city from a paragraph in the *New Yorker*. Out we went to the far pole of Flatbush, there to dine and there to drink the Housey Toast (he for the first time in thirty years) in the company of our unexpected host and his bewildered American wife.

In one sense only can I concede that the advantages which have come to me from C.H. have in them something of that quality which the ignorant and the envious castigate as the old-school-tie syndrome, in this sense alone have I profited as much practically as emotionally. Because I settled eventually into a professional world which is virtually a C.H. colony, I have had throughout my working life the ease of two-fold association – as fellow professionals and as fellow Blues – with many writers, editors, publishers and broadcasters. Hutton, Christian, Murry: all helped me at that time when, already in my thirties, already married and already with two children but with behind me only a few published short stories, some published poems and the ability to write an operation order or to bring down troop-fire on an advancing tank, I decided that I would keep my family by my pen. Thomas Radley was for many years my patron-producer at the BBC; he it was who settled me into the most exhausting, the most frivolous and certainly the most lucrative of all my varied broadcasting commitments, the year-long run next to the computer-memory Denis

Brogan in 'Transatlantic Quiz'. When I was in mid-career, Pip Youngman Carter, as editor of *The Tatler*, added handsomely to my bank-balance and some amazing entries to my bibliography by allowing me space for essays entirely out of character with almost all else in his glossy recorder of Britain's glossiest socialites. Above all other Blues (as already I have made obvious) as mentor, guide and friend I number Edmund Blunden. From the first time when I heard it in Buckie's study until his death forty years later, Edmund never forgot the promise that he had made to assist me on my literary way.

Such is the inequality of the rewards offered to artists that I was for years more affluent than Edmund, but my affection for him is to this day touched with awe.

I see him now, nervous and earnest as he was when I had him once on the field captaining a side that included no fewer than six Test cricketers in the annual festival of his twin gods, Cricket and Literature. Memory recaptures him, back on leave from his Hong Kong Chair, marching down the drive towards our Hertfordshire home, impervious to the rest of the world as he concentrated on conversation with my ten-year-old son after they had been together foraging the bookstalls in Faringdon Road. With a privileged few, I share ownership in another rare picture of Edmund, his CBE and his MC safety-pinned, most unsafely, to his greening dinner-jacket, as he drank pints of beer in a City pub which we had made our rendezvous before going on to the gilded grandeur, the vintage-soaked pomposity of the Mansion House for the Christ's Hospital Quatercentennial Banquet. From that evening, and from many another, I catch sentences, hesitantly, even stammeringly, delivered and yet brilliantly compelling, from his talk on some obscure literary personality of the distant past, more often than not a Blue or else someone who for neighbourliness and character was measured by him as worthy of benediction – 'He should have been one of us' – I remember how, by quotation and praise, Edmund made the honoured obscurity more memorable than achievement should allow. From that evening too, and from many another, there echo still Edmund's paeans to one who in truth I knew far better than he, and it is Edmund's talk even more than my own recall which for me makes Peter McRae's batting even more elegant than it was on Big Side or at Taunton.

There have been many others who, by the arithmetic of intimacy and the balance-sheet of affection, seem to be more obvious as candidates for extended attention.

Sydney Carter, for example, I have known for more years than I knew Edmund. I have played no role in that part of Sydney's work which has made him 'the grand-daddy of English folk-poetry', a writer favoured by millions who know not Coleridge, Shelley or Blunden – a poet without honour in the anthologies whose verses, above all for his 'Lord of the Dance', are nevertheless familiar to church congregations, to radio and television audiences all over the English-speaking world, but I have heard him through all the many hesitancies of faith, the many crises of confidence, that have possessed him over forty years. (Was there ever a credo more aptly titled than Sydney's *The Rock of Doubt*?) As was seldom possible with Edmund, I have been at times in a small way an agent in Sydney's career. I persuaded him to produce his edition of Walton's *Lives*: this as much to prove to him as to establish in the world's opinion the truth that Sydney is in scholarship as skilful as he is in versifying. At one time, early in our careers, between us we wrote regularly almost entire issues of *Books of the Month*, reviewing with the same alacrity works on subjects on which we were utterly without authority – cooking, water-sports or economics, – as we gave to those on which we had some little right to claim expertise – books of verse, literary criticism, histories and biographies – and pouncing with even greater delight upon ponderous academic volumes of all kinds, not because we could match the footnoted scholarship of the authors but because the exorbitant price on the dust-jackets promised handsome resale value at Clarke-Hall's off Fleet Street. For a while Sydney worked with me at the National Book League. To me he addressed some of his brilliant light verse.

> (Faber and Faber have a thing to crow about
> In T. S. Eliot whose poetry you know about,
> That'd be a thing to make a movie-show about,
> I'm waiting for the film to come.)

In a sense that Edmund never was, Sydney is a family friend. He was my best man and godfather to Mark, my youngest son.

Pip was also a family friend. With him, as with both Edmund and Sydney, our friendship had its roots in our C.H. heritage and with him, as with Edmund but not with Sydney, it was strengthened by our mutually-held pride in membership of the close and closed community of soldiers. With Pip it was enlarged to take in also his wife, Margery Allingham, and her sister Joyce.

Many pitied Pip, as some pitied Joyce, for living always in Marge's substantial shadow. Others despised him, as none could ever despise Joyce; to these, his detractors, he was Fedallah in a Saville Row suit who, casting no shadow himself, even so by his satanic presence blacked out the genial lights of Tolleshunt D'Arcy and made for Marge a domestic Hell. I, who saw them often together and not infrequently apart, could never ignore the ambiguities in their relationship. Pip's amorality was notorious, Marge's care for him almost maternal. It was as if she looked upon him as an adopted son, amazed and delighted by her possession of such a marvellous boy, amazed and dismayed by his many delinquencies. Yet the affection between them was patent and so also was the professional respect. Pip strove for her success and Marge never attempted to hide how much that success owed to Pip's advice and shrewd criticism. He was, she said, more than a counsellor; he was her collaborator.

Even of those who did not find Pip despicable there were many who thought him formidable. His uninhibited prejudices, his forthrightness, the sharp edge of his humour, even the monocle which sometimes he affected in place of his Albert Campion horn-rimmed spectacles, raised barriers between him and all but the very few he had selected for friendship. Even his versatility – he was soldier, artist, novelist, theatre-critic, editor, country gentleman and man-about-town – was cause for awe. So also was his almost foppish elegance.

I first met Pip in 1941 in Baghdad, he sitting at a desk to which he had been posted from the Western Desert by a Military Secretary wise enough to appreciate that as Editor of Army newspapers he would aid the war-effort more effectively than ever he had done when, already by military standards elderly, he had roamed the Western Desert, a determined and courageous Service Corps captain. Already on that day of our first meeting I noticed that his capacity for gin was as enormous as his zest for work, that his enthusiasm for a tightly-encased female bottom was as quick as his appreciation for a well-turned phrase, but from that day, too, I recall my sense of shame for the contrast between my sweat-laden, sand-encrusted, Officers' Shop khaki-drill and his immaculate, even resplendent dress, as fresh and well-cut as if every twenty-four hours there came to him, on a magic-carpet from Savile Row to Baghdad, a new uniform.

Arrogant Pip could be, and often was, but never with those he had admitted to amity; to us he was gentle and generous. Himself a great talker, like many of his kind he was also a ready listener and for him listening did not suffice. His knowledge, his worldliness and his many opportunities for patronage: all were at our disposal. Fortunately I never let him down; friends who disappointed him forthwith and unequivocally he cast as enemies.

Almost immediately after the War, Pip invited me to his Essex home, to one of those now-fabled Summer Parties (deservedly capitalized) which, once a year, he and Marge gave (assisted only by Marge's sister Joyce and by Chrissie, maid to the Allingham parents and still today Joyce's companion). For twelve hours D'Arcy House, with its lovely gardens, was filled with authors, artists, editors, publishers, actors, all drinking champagne and (because the party was set deliberately to coincide with a country fair) the D'Arcy House Meadow bristled with the eminent, the almost-eminent and the would-be-eminent shooting at plastic ducks for plastic prizes, riding roundabout horses and shying wooden balls at coconuts.

I had enjoyed my first Margery Allingham when I was still at Canonbury Road and even through my last years at C.H., when my taste was extravagantly intellectualized and my critical perception was deliberately inimical to reading for pleasure, I had retained sufficient wisdom to recognize that, for her craftsmanship, for her characterization and for her brilliance in handling atmosphere, she merited something more flattering than the place customarily accorded her as, with Agatha Christie and Dorothy L. Sayers, one of the three *grandes dames* of English detective-fiction, that she was a novelist, perhaps even a major novelist, not just a writer of crime stories. As soon as it was published, Bess had sent to me Marge's only non-fiction work, *The Oaken Heart*, that warm evocation of life in an Essex village in the year of alarms when war was imminent and the year which followed when war was only too real. That book I had read in the Desert. My copy I lent to another Old Blue, who presumably took it with him at the end of his parachute when he dropped into Leros: he never returned it.

Since those days I have read every novel and every short story Marge published. My respect and affection for her work has never wavered and I hold it as one of the truly worthwhile achievements of my life that, long after her death, I have played a major part in bringing her work to the attention of a vast and world-wide audience.

Marge's popularity never vanished entirely but somehow after she died it was allowed to dim. In 1983, at her sister's request, I took over as a *quasi* literary executor. With Joyce and with my American friend, John Robling (formerly a Vice President of *Encyclopaedia Britannica* and before that an officer in the American equivalent of the National Book League), I have worked for Marge ceaselessly and, I can but boast, with success. With one exception, all of her novels have been brought back into print on both sides of the Atlantic; twenty-three are now available in German translations and many are available in other languages; *The Oaken Heart* has been reissued (by Julia Thorgood, who is also at work on a life of Marge); so also, in collections, are most of her short stories. There have been, at our instigation, many Allingham adaptations on radio and, after a sequence of efforts in itself worthy of a novel, at last we contrived our greatest triumph: the appearance of Campion on television-screens in Britain and America and, we have reason to hope, in many other countries, set there by the brilliant, successful – and surely the most amiable – of producers, John Hawkesworth, of *Upstairs, Downstairs* fame.

Wherever they are now, I am convinced that Marge and Pip are now raising gin-and-tonics to us and convinced too that, because in their lifetimes they suffered in like manner, they forgive our abject failure to overcome the habitual Anglophobia of the French.

Marge and Pip would be grateful but both would take even more satisfaction from my enduring memory of their genius as hosts.

I hold, forever, in happy recall, the little bar which in D'Arcy House they reserved for the entertainment of their closest friends. Marge, an undeniably large lady, plays the role which pleased her most, her stance, her dress, even her hair-style set deliberately to make her look like twin-sister to Toulouse-Lautrec's barmaid, Pip, an arrant male chauvinist, lord of the manor and master of the house, on the other side of the bar.

The walls of that bar, 'the Half Nelson', were crammed with Christ's

Hospital memorabilia and Marge cherished them as much as did Pip. Like my own wife, like Ruth Hook (wife of our only bishop), Elaine Barr (wife of our only judge), like Peggy Lathwell and indeed like many another – Marjorie Ross, Ann Riches (both wives of Treasurers), Liesl Gale, Win Gaynor, Ann Grant, Anne Oliver – who have married into the fraternity, Marge thought of herself as almost a Blue. Many of these friends of my mature years have worked as hard as their husbands to further the purposes of the Foundation; it was Marge's intention that eventually some considerable proportion of the proceeds of her years of strenuous professional labours would go to Christ's Hospital. No less than Pip she would be gratified could she know that, because of the Allingham Renaissance engineered in recent years by Joyce, by John Robling and by me, the benefit to C.H. is likely to be much richer than ever she could have dreamed.

Others of the C.H. community have been my intimates – and several my benefactors – throughout my adult life. The Right Reverend Ross Hook as my friend, my fellow History Grecian and my companion on the Dais in the Dining Hall and even then dignified by the spectral mitre which, in its mundane but no less resplendent form he would wear as, successively Bishop of Grantham, Bishop of Bradford and Chief of Staff to the Archbishop of Canterbury. If on the Day of Judgement Ross has difficulty in persuading St Peter to pass me through the Pearly Gates, I am confident that there are others from the fraternity who will support his advocacy, that he can call upon two diplomats, His Excellency Sir Donald Hobson and His Excellency Colin Brant and a distinguished lawyer, His Honour Judge Barr, to serve as his juniors. I flatter myself that The Worshipful the Treasurer Angus Ross will speak up for me, as will the Worshipful the Treasurer Ted Kenney (Ted almost certainly in Latin, which will confuse a simple Galilean fisherman).

'Come back to memory', wrote Charles Lamb in the more astringent of his two essays on Christ's Hospital, and on those words he discarded the persona he had affected as Coleridge, his schoolfellow and closest friend, abandoned all sharpness and allowed himself to be swept on, as if on a flood of delighted reminiscence, into a torrent of tributes to the 'playmates . . . and companions of his joyful schooldays'.

So it would be with me were I to accept the urging of Lamb's cue and, because I would be bound to include Blues of school-generations other than my own, and even were I to exclude all who have appeared previously in these pages, however cursorily, my roll-call of memory would justify my enlargement of that other quotation from Lamb, 'a Christ's Hospital boy's friends at school are his friends for life.' John Gale, Ken Oliver, Norman Ilett. . . .

Max Martyn demands more than the anonymity of four dots. My oldest friend, my loyal colleague and most frequent drinking-companion in the years when I was in the National Book League, Max was one of the finest book-designers in Britain and it was he who contrived the blessedly elegant appearance, and so contributed hugely to the commercial success of that rarely successful act of piety, *The Christ's Hospital Book*. His abrupt expulsion from the publishing firm, Hamish Hamilton, reflects no credit on that house or on the Book Trade at large. Max remains, as he was when twelve years old, the most cheerful grouser of my acquaintance – and still my friend.

So too does my affection for Ian Shaw – next only to my grandson Stuart my youngest C.H. friend – persuade me that his name cannot be left in the obscurity of implication. Admitted to C.H. on my Presentation, Ian advanced to captain several of the School's first teams and, as a Grecian, to follow me, after a gap of forty years, as House Captain of Coleridge B, but it is not only for the glory that his schoolboy eminence reflected on me that I need no summons to bring him to memory, but rather because he (and eventually also his wife Yianoulla) has warmed me with loving-kind-ness that transcends by far gratitude for the favour which once I did him by making him a Blue.

John Gillham, Roy Salisbury, Henry Lathwell, Robin Paul, Charles Gibbins, Cyril Harvey, Fred Grant. . . so the list could run on, advancing towards infinity, but I am sensitive to the perplexity inflicted upon readers by the fluttering of unfamiliar names in Lamb's two C.H. essays and in the equivalent C.H. passages in Leigh Hunt's *Autobiography* – the burden of exegesical footnote I have borne as editor both of Elia and Leontius – and so I leave my personal galaxy of Blues still incompletely mapped.

Native cunning, much sharpened by many years passed on the bastard side of an editor's desk, should encourage me to exaggerate the extent of my association with the most notable member of my generation at C.H. but, though I knew him slightly at school and thereafter was with him sev-eral times in the Middle East, I cannot with integrity name Keith Douglas as friend nor yet dishonour him in my record of rancid enemies.

At school we were separated by the almost unbridgeable chasm created by the fact that he was two years my junior and in another house. When the Army brought our paths together we raised our glasses in salute to our mutually adored mentors, David Roberts and Edmund Blunden, talked about Rugby football or the latest ENSA show and did not once mention literature, the War or any intimate feelings.

There was between us some coolness and for that I must shoulder most of the blame. I was by no means unique in thinking Keith arrogant, but I did my not inadequate best to out-play him at his own game. I was envi-ous of his genius and I resented the ease with which he had usurped my status as the most likely of all our school generation to make his way suc-cessfully in the world of letters. But I dare the hint that Keith was a little envious of me for at that time his work had appeared only in Cairo; it was I who was the honoured professional – two of my short stories and one poem had been published in London!

I castigate myself for my grudging manner when I was with Keith, but take some consolation from the fact that I was never grudging in my admiration for his writing. At school I was among the first to appreciate that we had among us a rare talent. Long before Ted Hughes and other influential critics dragged Keith's poetry out of the near-oblivion into which it had been thrust because most of his finest poems – and *Alamein to Zem-Zem* – had been published by the shrewd but notoriously shambolic Poetry London, already in 1946 I was impertinently irate with that wisest and most benevolent of editors, John Lehmann, when he spurned my suggestion that I write for him an essay on Keith Douglas. He spurned it not because he questioned my capacity (Lehmann was at that time flatteringly receptive to my efforts) but because he questioned the validity of my prophecy that the time would come when Keith Douglas would be hailed as the poet-laureate of the Second War. In 1947 I proclaimed that same message from lecture-platforms all over the United States and ever since, in print, on the radio and from lecterns, I have insisted that Keith's early death dealt a blow to English literature in our times no less vicious, and in its consequences no less disastrous, than were the deaths of Sorley, Rosenberg and Owen in the preceding generation.

So, at the last, not as response to literary historians and Ph.D. candidates who for forty years have clamoured for my intimate reminiscence, but because his poetry has inspired me to continuous advocacy, after all I list Keith Douglas, a man who cared as little for me as I for him, among the Blues who have affected my life.

Long after Keith died, I read for the first time a letter to him from Blunden. 'We have had', wrote Edmund, 'some pretty good poets, Peele, Coleridge, Lamb, Hunt, but the line must be extended and I think you can do it.' To that clarion call, Keith Douglas responded nobly.

There is, however, yet one more of my Housey friends, who, though he was my companion for all too brief a time, in all my days has seldom been out of my mind and who, therefore, in an account of my life must emerge as more than just a name.

As did I, so did John Horn enter Coleridge B in September 1929 but as he had been for two years in the Preparatory School and was consequently sophisticated in Housey custom, it was not until I too had shed my neophyte nervousness that we were mutually fitted to be friends. He was, however, of all the boys in the Junior Dormitory, the most remarkable. He stood (literally) head and shoulders above all the Juniors.

How tall John was at the age of eleven I do not remember. I do know that before he was fourteen he was the tallest boy in the House and that before he left, still not seventeen years old, because he had added another eight-and-a-half inches, the authorities were forced to have built for him a special bed, though a bed as all of ours, with wooden planks in the place of the customary springs.

John's height was the only characteristic which made him notable to the School at large. He was no athlete; even playing rugger, when his size should have helped him to glory and when his phenomenal reach should have made him uniquely useful in the line-out, he was almost sensationally inadequately inhibited not by timidity but by innate gentleness. He did not achieve a 'red bather' (the skimpy loin-cloth, bought for ninepence from the Tuck Shop, worn by all who could go head-first into the water and swim five lengths of the Baths) until three years after all his co-evals. He must have played cricket – Buckie would have insisted – but I do not remember that he was ever in any House eleven. Nor was he a scholar, a musician, a debater, an enthusiastic actor or one of the *literati*: his interests lay rather in bird-watching – and talking.

It must have been his talk (and the fact that in those early days he had a seemingly inexhaustible supply of tuck sent to him from home) which first attracted me to John. As time went on, as still in that one year immediately before the War when we were so often together, it was his talk, witty, sensitive, perspicacious but never malicious, which made time with John unforgettable.

Although he was inept in all those activities which customarily win for a schoolboy the respect of his peers and immediate seniors, John was universally popular. It could have been because he was so gentle, so patently without malevolence, that he was liked by all, but adult percipience encourages me to believe that it was even more his courage which won from us all admiration and affection. He carried his great height with self-mocking dignity and he fought valiantly against all the disadvantages forced upon him by his ineptitude.

Already in our first Summer Term we had evidence of his bravery. At one of the 'Cubs' Comp.' tests set by Lenny Dale to measure the versatility, the ability to 'have a go' of all the new boys, we were set to go into the water, head-first or feet-first, from the top diving-board, John, by that time the only non-swimmer of us all. He stood for minutes, his head among the rafters, white and shaking, whilst we, his friends but his rivals for the Cub's Comp. prize (for the first four a 'gut', a gargantuan tea in the Tuck Shop) stood, watching and shouting encouragement and – proof also that there was much that was gentle in the ethos of C.H. – while John Knight and all the other monitors swam about in the deep end waiting to catch him. Then he smiled, pinched his nose between thumb and finger, and jumped.

My friendship with John grew and deepened during our five years together in Coleridge B so that, in the light of our contrasting enthusiasms, ambitions and skills perhaps surprisingly, we had become virtually inseparable – what later, when I had gathered to myself Army slang, I might have called 'muckers' – and were as such recognized by all and when John was superannuated I was bereft – until I found other 'muckers' among my fellow First Parting Grecians.

My friendship with John was intensified by the coincidence that his family home was close to mine. We continued our 'muckerdom' in the vacations. In his home or in mine we talked for hours on end, in time with lubrication from a bottle of South African sherry bought for two shillings and ninepence from the Victoria Wine Store. (In John's home, even when at seventeen I had reached my full height, close to six feet, I was a Lilliputian in a family of Gullivers; his father was almost as tall as John, his younger brother, Frank, not so very much shorter and even his mother and his sister Lois, both of them remarkably beautiful women, were at least two inches taller than me.) Together we went to the Schoolboys Exhibition, to plays, operas and concerts. Together we courted local girls. Each Christmas (with Basil Hewitt as our only colleague) we toured Pensioners' Clubs, acting sketches and singing popular songs and invariably we won our audience, not by the brilliance of our sketches – most of them written by me – and certainly not by our singing voices, but, initially at least, because we began every performance with an irresistibly funny charade. Even before curtain-up John poked his head above the front-drop we had constructed by hanging two blankets from a string across the front of the stage; chords on a piano, pull wide the curtain and there, not, as the audience had expected, a boy standing on a chair, but John, all six foot eight and a half inches of him.

As so many C.H. boys who did not go on to university or into the Services on leaving school, John was sent to work in an office. He loathed the City so tried his hand as master in a preparatory school. He loathed the school and his colleagues and took to selling vacuum-cleaners, a chore he found even more distasteful than clerking or teaching. By the time that I came back from America, though his accounts of his various misadventures were deliciously comical, he was close to desperation. For hour after hour we discussed his future; it was I who suggested farming and, when he had brightened at the possibility but insisted that he must first study his chosen profession, it was I who urged him to seek from C.H. financial support for three years at Macdonald Agricultural College in Canada.

In August 1939 I saw him off on the boat-train. He had just become engaged to a pretty, intelligent, charming (but not very tall) girl and his parting-words to me were a reminder that I must be available to be his best-man when he came back to England, a qualified farmer. I never saw him again. When he did return home I was already in the Army in India and he not a farmer but an officer in the Princess Patricia's Canadian Light Infantry. He was killed in Italy, as later I discovered not more than twenty miles from where I was on that very day.

Because Basil Hewitt has already twice entered into this narrative, because in school-holidays the three of us spent so much time together, because I had vowed that if ever I married I would have two best-men and by reason of the hideous coincidence that Basil also was killed, in Italy, on the same day as John and not so very far away from where I was at the time, Basil must have his place, and this place, in my record. He was not a Blue, but had Edmund Blunden known him he would have paid him his greatest compliment: 'he should have been one of us'.

I saw him first in the Vicarage pew at St Marys sitting next to his sister and looking at her disapprovingly as she gobbled the sweets lined up for her next to hymn-books and prayer-books to keep her quiet during her father's fiery Ulsterman's sermons. My parents, perhaps conscious of the fact that there were in the congregation few children who had much in common with a twelve-year-old from an expensive prep. school, invited him to tea. At first he was shy but once we began to play Pit he took off his neat jacket, loosened his striped tie and bellowed, 'Wheat, Wheat, Wheat', 'Barley, Barley, Barley' in a voice that drowned even the roaring of the Morpurgos.

He was never again shy, with me or any of us.

My sister Julia, who did not often fall victim to the obvious, nevertheless insisted on calling us the Three Musketeers – 'all for one, one for all' – and there was in the analogy enough of the apposite to justify the cliché with John, of course, as the giant Porthos, me, for my strenuously assured refinement, as Aramis and Basil as the cadet D'Artagnan.

Basil's parents would have been more readily contented had he cast himself for the part of Aramis, providing always that the call to the priesthood did not come from 'the Bishop of Rome', but he knew and I knew that could never be. His pugnacity and his seemingly paradoxical courtliness made him inevitably our D'Artganan and there is much in the Irish which condones the assertion that they are the Gascons of the British Isles.

In war-time the news of the deaths of friends came to those of us who were serving abroad only after many months and then often accidentally or casually. So it was that I was informed of the death of Peter McRae by a chance, and devastatingly matter-of-fact, remark dropped by a schoolfellow in a Casualty Clearing Station in Italy. It was not until a year later than I learned the details which, after the War, were made public in Lord Moran's book *On Courage*: how Peter, a naval surgeon aboard a destroyer on an Arctic convoy, had saved the lives of many of the crew of his torpedoed ship, had himself climbed aboard the raft on which he had placed them and then had dived off (I am sure gracefully) with the characteristic last words 'This place is disgustingly overcrowded'. So it was that I heard that John had been killed from a Canadian, himself an officer in the Princess Pat's and our guest in the Brigade H.Q. Mess in a rest-area somewhere close to the Gothic Line, whose table-talk was filled with admiring and affectionate reminiscence of the gentle, courageous and English giant, 'Tiny' Horn.

At about that same time I received two letters from Bess, written five weeks apart but delivered on the same day. The first told me that Basil had been awarded the Military Cross, the second that, as had been four of his uncles who served in the Enniskillings in the First War, he had been killed in action.

That I had been deprived forever of John and Basil, the two I had assumed would be my companions for the rest of my days, left me desolate. If I survived – which at that time seemed unlikely – I must live out my life in isolation. True, in those idyllic pre-War days in Islington now so precious in my memory, the Three Musketeers, like those of Dumas, had at times numbered four but Moyra, Basil's younger sister, was no D'Artagnan, By our lofty standards an infant she had often thrust herself into our company and, almost as often, she had been summarily ejected. I remembered her as a pert and pretty child and I remembered also that the advice on how best to deal with his sister which John and I had frequently given to Basil was in no way influenced by Willy Fyfe's aversion to corporeal correction.

5

Bluenoses and Magnolia

Four weeks after I emerged from the idyll of my last year at C.H., I was aboard a small Atlantic liner, a second class passenger looking down haughtily on the steerage scum, bound for Montreal, Fredericton, for the University of New Brunswick, for at least three years away from all that was familiar – and it could be for a lifetime as exile in Canada.

What I could not then perceive was that my eccentricity and obstinacy would mark me forever as in some senses an outsider to all the societies in which I was to move, never entirely a North American and yet never securely British. By entering simultaneously my adulthood and my career as wanderer, I cut at the stem which linked me to my childhood. Not the Army, not my subsequent intimate involvement with Christ's Hospital affairs, not even my latter-day centrality to British literary life could ever mend completely that broken line. To this day I remain, in Britain or in America, in some senses a stranger, an observer, sometimes burdened and often blessed by prejudices gleaned on the other side of the Atlantic.

What I did discover almost immediately after my arrival in Fredericton was that I had settled myself in Hell without hope of redemption, that I was alone among aboriginals. Nothing in my background, not the eager curiosity of my family and certainly not the richness of C.H., had prepared me for the stolid company of the Forestry and Engineering students of UNB. When compared to Fredericton, Cockfosters was as ancient Athens, Canonbury Square as elegant as Regency Bath and C.H. the slopes of Parnassus.

There was open to me no alternative but endurance. Deprived of the physical, spiritual and intellectual spaciousness to which, in the previous seven years, I had grown accustomed, I found solace in contempt and resentment. The meanness of the University buildings scattered around the hillside campus, the surliness of my fellows and, in the lecture halls, drab pedantry: these I compared with all that I had surrendered. The contrast was valid but exaggerated by my loneliness. I found compensation for my loss in arrogance, and arrogance made my isolation entire.

I looked for New Brunswick's past, for a tradition complementary to the glories that had been for so long my property. I found only pink teas (why 'pink' I have never discovered) given by descendants, bluenose-in-air, of United Empire Loyalists, and stiff receptions at which I was presented to His Majesty's representative, a prosperous local grocer whose lieu-tenant-gubernatorial nose dripped on to my obligatory white silk gloves.

I longed for friendship and, by my patent condemnation for all that I saw, won for me only animosity. As substitute for the easy companionship of the First Parting Grecians' table, the most that I contrived was an ado-lescent affair with Muriel, a sharp-faced, parsimoniously-busted but warm-hearted nurse, five years my senior, the daughter of a general practitioner and he the most prestigious in Fredericton because his pedigree was infall-ibly UEL.

Even the catharsis of the football field was soon denied me. At my first attempt I was marshalled into the University rugby-squad. I loathed the ice-hardened, stone-littered playing fields of the Maritimes but to my amazement and, at the outset, to the raucous delight of the coach, I found myself to be generally more competent than any of the other burlier aspi-rants, my feet more lethargic but my mind more nimble than theirs. The conceit in which I then cloaked myself helped a little, for there is nothing so useful to the footballer as arrogance, but my technique was more sophis-ticated and my footballing mind – sharpened by sound training and by rec-ollection of Peter McRae's brilliance – much shrewder. At my debut in a university match – and playing at scrum half, a position which at school I would not have dared – I gained for myself the only applause that ever came my way at UNB by winning the match with a blind side try. Thereafter but consequently I brought down upon myself the profane abuse of the coach because, like Eric Linklater's Juan in similar circum-stances, I had ignored his touch-line instructions.

It was that same coach who, by his insistence that I practise for three hours in every day during the season and by his frequently repeated sump-tuary code ('No smokes, no booze, no women!') drove me from the foot-ball field. I would not live by his orders; I dropped myself just in time to avoid the ignominy of dismissal.

In the years before I went to Canada I had found in precedent sturdy support for my juvenile ambition to become a man of letters. New Brunswickers annexed to themselves much that, by their accounting, was worthy in Canadian literary tradition. I strove to follow where their pride led and in all that unhappy year this was my one effort untainted by preju-dice, but well-founded criticism shamed all my good intentions. The maunderings of Charles G. D. Roberts and of his brother Theodore could not make up for the loss of Coleridge and Lamb. Their cousin, Bliss Carman, the only one of the three whose name I had known before com-ing to Fredericton and the only one of the three whom today I might salute as almost a true poet, I had discarded three years earlier, at about the same time that I had rejected Swinburne as too cloying for a palate that favoured the astringent.

A moment staunched, then forth again.
Ah, not alone you climb the steep
To set your loving burden down
Against the mighty knees of sleep.

I would be a writer but I had condemned myself to be a Canadian. With such forbears and exemplars as these there was no such thing as Canadian literature. *Ergo*, I would never be a writer.

No one in Fredericton told me – perhaps no one in Fredericton was aware-that there was elsewhere in Canada, even at that very moment when I was deciding that as I must stay in Canada I must abandon hope and settle for the law or commerce, a liveliness in letters unequalled at any period in the nation's history. Decades later, I was to become a self-appointed advocate, arguing the merits of Canadian poetry before the deaf and blind jury of British critics; in the New Brunswick which I took to be Canada I found no literature more substantial than the society column in the *Fredericton Gleaner* and no feeling for literature more lively than the professorial weary whine: 'John Keats was born in London, England, in 1795. His first volume was published in 1817. . . He died in Rome at 11pm on 23 February 1821.'

I was not a countryman and, despite much travail on my behalf by my wife and by Blunden, I have stayed, unflinching, in the company of my beloved Elia preferring a view of Fleet Street to the distant prospect of Skiddaw, but I had acquired some warmth of feeling for the soft, green richness of the Sussex Weald. Muriel and her father strove hard to arouse in me similar affection for the New Brunswick landscape but it remained for me, as it was for William Cobbett, by 150 years my predecessor as a reluctant Maritimer and as an obstinate and arrogantly British interloper, 'One great heap of rocks'- so Cobbett described the Maritimes-'covered by fir trees.' And, as then I saw those provinces, covered also, for months without let, by a blanket of grey ice. This was Swindon-in-the-Slush.

Like Forster's Dr Aziz I have two distinct faculties of memory, the one enduring, the other conveniently ephemeral. Habitually my recall of places is of the first kind; set me down in Asmara or Basrah and still I could find my way without benefit of street map; send me to Dijon, to Helena or to Santiago and I will walk the streets as surely as any native; but the grime of misery obscures my picture of Fredericton. Effort most determined brings back only confused recollection, a disordered anthology of miserly streets with here and there a blurred memory of some house, grander than the rest and yet failing even in its attempt to be pretentious. I know, but I cannot make my knowledge pictorial, that there was a pompous Provincial Office Building (and, this I do remember, its staff changed with the fortunes of the political parties after each election). Main Street I can just see, straggling its shoddy way from the ponderosity of the Legislative Building through a fringe of cheap and cheaply constructed stores to the Windsor

Hotel. The St John River I recall, its waters hidden beneath sempiternal ice.

Here I was imprisoned and, it seemed, for life. A ticket-of-leave man with the football team or the debate squad, I went for a day or so in Sackville, St John, or Moncton, but when compared to these three, Fredericton was Paris-in-the-Maritimes! Once I went into Nova Scotia, to Halifax. I had been told to expect a metropolis but I saw nothing through the fog.

For my first Christmas away from home, I escaped the Fifth Circle and discovered Paradise. New York, not then declined into seediness nor made terrifying by reports of muggings, was at that time the obvious refuge for a disconsolate exile from London, a theatrical and musical capital city, its streets filled, as London's, with bustle, its stores resplendent, its art galleries magnificent. The art galleries I walked by the hour, for most of them were free. In Macy's, Gimbel's and Lord and Taylor's I admired, coveted but did not buy. My meagre savings I spent on the cheapest seats at the Met., at Carnegie Hall and on 'standing room' at the Martin Beck Theatre for a wallow in home-sickness at a performance of *The Gondoliers*. Delirious with my assumed cloak of sophistication – and with her charms – I spent much of my time with a dancer from the Rockettes, introduced to me by the hospitable Welsh couple who had invited me to New York and, with her as companion, I engraved in my memory that most fabulous city-scope, the view of New York City from the Jersey side.

Back to Boston by bus and then, because I had missed the boat to St John and had no money left, I was forced to hitch-hike through New England, spending one night truly in prison as the well-fed guest of the sympathetic and kindly policemen of Bangor, Maine.

The memory of those euphoric weeks in New York made all the more intense my despair when I returned to Fredericton. 'No greater grief than to remember days / Of joy, when misery is at hand.' There was in Fredericton not one person to whom in my disconsolate state I could turn for comfort... not even Muriel, who considered Fredericton no mean substitute for Montreal, the only other city she knew. My pride would not permit that I write back to England, or to Willy Fyfe in Kingston, to confess that obstinacy had trapped me into irredeemable error. I must spare my family the pain of helplessness. David and Willy had dared so much in support of my foolishness that I could not bring myself to burden them with the knowledge that their aid had made folly into failure. Flecker would crow; or so at that time I thought, though years later I discovered that he, and certainly Pippa, had read something of the truth between the lines of my consistently smug letters.

There was, however, after New York, a faint glimmer of light in the gloom. The Harries, the couple with whom I had stayed in Hackensack, New Jersey, were new friends; they knew nothing of my previous glory, nothing of the glittering future that I, and a few of my seniors, had prophesied for me. With them I was not shackled by the inhibition which held me from revealing my unhappiness to my father, to David or to the Fleckers. To them I poured out my sorrows and their response was immediate and practical. I was discontented at UNB; why not try an American university? Leslie had friends and business acquaintances who were alumni of Brown, Princeton, Harvard, Virginia, Columbia, Amherst, Dartmouth... he would see to it that I met them all.

Brought up to be familiar with the implacability of Oxford and Cambridge I had never heard of the custom, commonplace in North America as in medieval Europe, whereby a student migrates from one university to another. I lunched at the Harvard Club, I drank with young graduates of almost every Ivy League college, not one showed any surprise when, hesitantly, I proposed transferring myself from an obscure university in the frozen wastes of Canada to his own glamorous *alma mater*, not one recognized as obstacle the fact that I must have a scholarship to see me through the next years.

I was not convinced. I could not credit that any great academic institution would offer both place and funds to one who had proved himself inadequate or that such benevolence could be prompted by no more than a letter of application and a supporting reference from an alumnus, not yet out of his twenties, who had spent no more than a couple of hours in my company.

I had suffered humiliation sufficient for a lifetime. Rather than risk the battering to pride that must come with rejection I concluded that I must stay where I was, my discontent perpetual.

The strength to dare a snub I gathered to myself in the Rockefeller Center on my last day in New York. Leslie Harries had a friend who had a friend who was a neighbour of an official of some sort working for John D. Rockefeller. That official agreed to see me (I wish I could remember his name so that I could commend him in my prayers). Waiting in his plush outer-office, I read in the *National Geographic Magazine* Dr Goodwin's article on the restoration of Williamsburg. The brashness of the coloured illustrations did not faze me. Dr Goodwin wrote of Jefferson, Monroe and Marshall at William and Mary; these surely were true and adequate substitutes for Coleridge, Lamb and all the rest of my mislaid ancestors. As St Paul on the road to Damascus this was revelation, this the way my life must go. . . if only. . . But the 'if only' was daunting.

Rockefeller's acolyte listened patiently to my stammering and abject autobiography. I did not so much as mention Williamsburg. Then, as if in the voice of the Holy Ghost, he confirmed my vocation, 'William and Mary! No doubt of it William and Mary's the place for you.' He gave me a cigarette, a cup of coffee, a few leaflets and the name of the Dean.

Back in Fredericton I wrote to Williamsburg. Back came the customary application form and with it a courteous letter, amazingly encouraging but for one damning sentence. My application must be supported by references from senior faculty members of institutions I had attended previously. David, of course: he would stand by me, but surely not one of the drearies at UNB. Gambling on a long-shot, because he hardly knew me, I wrote in the name of the President.

When at last another letter arrived from Williamsburg at first I dared not open it. Throughout a long hour listening to a lecture on John Dewey and another hour in the geology laboratory, I fingered the envelope in my pocket. Then I walked a mile out of town. I would have no New Brunswicker catch me in tears. I was offered a place, a small scholarship and, if I chose to accept it as supplement, a part-time job in the College Library.

Years later I saw those references. David's was warm, as I had known it would be; the other did not surprise me for by the time I read it I was myself an experienced employer accustomed to writing references and I recognized the President's as just such a reference as I wrote when I wanted to be rid of an awkward employee. There was in it nothing derogatory and yet nothing that could be construed as praise: a record, no more, of my unfailingly good academic progress, a mention of my part in debating, acting and Rugby Football.

Because now I could predict a terminus, almost I tolerated what remained to be served of my prison-sentence but I left New Brunswick with not one sigh and, though I have been frequently across the border in Maine, not a hundred miles from Fredericton, I have never returned. With Egypt, the Province stays rare among the many parts of the world that I have visited in that it does not tempt me to recidivism.

I have but one reason to be thankful for my time in New Brunswick: there I learnt to ski. On the slopes, as nowhere else near Fredericton, the snow was white and, in the exhilaration of the downward rush as never at any other time in that hideous year, I lost all consciousness of the futility of my existence.

And from my recollections of that year, most of them blurred by remembered discontent, there remains just one picture which, because even at the time it presented to me the impression, surprising but welcome, that there was after all empathy between my immediate companions and those from whom I was separated by the Atlantic and because it was brushed with undeniably genuine sentiment, stays with me to this day, still vivid and emotive.

The evening of 11 December 1936 opened with farce. That afternoon Muriel and I had been to the cinema to see Charles Laughton as Rembrandt and at dinner with her parents I attempted to emulate Laughton's feat of picking up a glass and drinking without benefit of hands. An exquisite Waterford glass shattered between my teeth, wine, glass and blood spattered the Persian carpet and I must have been expelled forever from that house had it not been that more shattering events were thought to be imminent.

My wounds expeditiously dressed by a doctor and a nurse, we waited for hours, such little conversation as there was tense and stilted, then the voice came over the wireless, the voice, high and hesitant of the man I had seen fingering his tie nervously as he sat on the Dais in Dining Hall next to Willy Fyfe, the voice of the King.

I looked across the room. Muriel's dignified, undemonstrative father was sobbing, tears were running down the crevasses in his face and falling, as sharp as rain-drops on the polished wood of the sitting-room floor.

In my first book, with two chapters of diatribe, I took sweet revenge for my misery at UNB. Although I did not once name the University, the City or the Province I must have made the cap fit neatly for I am told that my *American Excursion* is locked away in the University Library safe with other obscene books, *Justine, Fanny Hill* and, if I judge aright the University authorities, *Little Women* and *The Secret Garden*.

In 1936, with New Brunswick, I included in my litany of distaste all the rest of the Dominion. In truth I had seen almost nothing of Canada. From the deck of the liner that had brought me from England I had glimpsed Quebec City, noble on its heights. My romantic spirit still untarnished by disappointment, there the eye of my imagination had seen those two young heroes, Montcalm and Wolfe, pacing together on the eve of the battle that brought death to both and, in death, an eternal place in Canadian mythology. Landed at Montreal, I had had just enough time to buy myself a beer before catching the train that carried me through the night, through the Province of Quebec, and through the North of Maine to Fredericton. Of all else outside New Brunswick I knew only Halifax, almost lost in the fog.

In the years still to come I learnt much of Canada and with knowledge came affection. Toronto I now number among my favourite cities, its energy I find always inspiring, its artistic athleticism forever stimulating, its cosmopolitanism exciting. Montreal, for all that it is burdened by racial tension, I have come to admire. Vancouver, placed exquisitely between the sea and the magnificent backdrop of the mountains, is a setting *non-pareil* in North America. Time, and I hope, enhanced tolerance, has taught me to forgive the tawdry paradox of gilt-encrusted church-domes and slums which line the St Lawrence as it flows through French Canada and in Trois Rivières, walking hand-in-hand with the ghosts of *seigneurs* and *habitants*, I have lost, for hours on end, both my fervent Protestantism and my chauvinism. Once I spent three days in Winnipeg, and was not displeased.

To Canada, and to Claude Bissell, my cherished friend and the most persuasive of all spokesmen for Canadian culture, I apologise for my youthful disdain. That in youth I convinced myself that all Canadians were as Maritimers, if some misplaced in other Provinces, is, I fear, beyond forgiveness. All that I plead in mitigation is that I was transformed from 'calumniator' into affectionate admirer before ever I had experience in provinces outside the Atlantic Provinces.

One dark night in 1944 I stood at a road-side near Catania and watched as a Canadian Scottish regiment moved into action. Above the clumsy, clattering noise of carrier-trucks I caught the sound of pibroch. In that moment, for the first time, I gathered some pride from the fact that I had been, for one year, almost a Canadian.

There is, then, for me some shame, still lingering, for my distaste for Canada and the Canadians but that I missed, through no fault of mine, all knowledge of Canadian literature brings no shame but only regret.

Already at eighteen, I diagnosed as the most virulent of the many causes for my disaffection the effects of submersion in a provincial morass. None in Fredericton advised me to look for an antidote outwith the boundaries of New Brunswick, none told me that there were elsewhere in Canada leaders worth following, men such as Brookes Clavion and Massey, still by the leisurely measure of statecraft young, who were even then struggling to drag Canada out of the colonial mists into the light of nationhood. None informed me that, at the very moment when I was deciding that, as I had sentenced myself to a life-sentence in New Brunswick I must abandon all hope of a career as writer and must serve out my endless term with hard labour as lawyer or banker, there were at work in Montreal, Ottawa and Toronto many spirit-surgeons, and most of them young, busily engaged with sharp scalpels cutting for the tumour of mediocrity which threatened the literature of the Dominion.

> Oh Canada, oh Canada, oh can
> A day go by without new authors springing
> To paint the native maple, and to plan
> More ways to set the self same welkin ringing.

Frank Scott's 'The Canadian Authors Meet', to this day the sharpest and wittiest of all comments on the emptiness and folly of Canadian chauvinism, had been written ten years before I arrived in Fredericton. I can but assume that it had not yet reached New Brunswick. Almost another ten years would pass before I read even one line by Frank or by A. J. M. Smith, his brilliant confrère in the art of chopping down 'the blasted pine':

> Is there no Katharsis
> But 'song' for this dull
> Pain, that every Saul of Tarsus
> Must pour himself into a Paul?

Even more years would go by before I woke to the fact that Canada possesses a rarely rich anthology of self-mocking verse, or appreciated how much the nation owes to its poets for its liberation from provincialism.

By pedantic exercise almost worthy of those drearies who taught me at UNB, I can exonerate UNB for the gap in my Canadian education which left me for years ignorant of the work of E. J. Pratt (who later I discovered to have been, at that time and in Montreal and Toronto, the centres of Canadian civilization, the most honoured of all 'Canadian' poets), for Ned was born in Newfoundland and Newfoundland was not yet part of the Dominion, but I excoriate the University and the Province for leaving me innocent of all knowledge of Frank Scott, Art Smith and A. M. Klein.

I slipped out of UNB and New Brunswick unmourned by all (except, perhaps, for a few weeks by Muriel) and unmourning. After a few weeks touring Britain with the UNB Debate Team, a brief stay in Cockfosters and several week-ends in the family home of George Leigh-Mallory, the man who had tried to climb Everest because it was there, again with a generous grant from Christ's Hospital I sailed westwards once more, but this time 'steerage'.

David's farewell words were set, as ever, in the form of a question: 'But where on God's good earth is Williamsburg?'

Had my second invasion of North America been as ignominious as my first there would have been no future for me in the United States, no hope of making my way in Canada and shame must have kept me forever an exile from Britain. I would have been forced to emigrate to Borneo, the Antarctic or the land where the bong-tree grows. But as I took ship for New York, I experienced no flutterings of apprehension. Reprieved from the Roberts brothers, from the United Empire Loyalists and from pink teas, my mind was filled with optimistic anticipation.

Later, much later, when I was well-established as a pundit on all things American, there were moments when I questioned the wisdom of my youthful choice of William and Mary, Williamsburg and Virginia. The College, so I told myself, was atypical; Williamsburg, *grâce à* Rockefeller an eighteenth-century town, and the Commonwealth still in many respects as it had been before the War between the States, for its esoteric traditions and arcane prejudices, virtually a nation to itself. Might I not have fortified my understanding of America and Americans had I entered one of the great Midwestern state universities? Would I have made undeniable my oft-respected boast that in the United States I was never quite an alien, had I gone to live on Main Street in one of those small towns on the Prairies or in the Rockies? (By the time I asked myself those questions I had been Visiting Professor at Michigan State College, I had visited almost every state in the Union. I knew towns – villages by English standards – like Darby, Montana and Hereford, Texas, even I had spent a night in Aberdeen, South Dakota!)

Doubts of this order have assailed me but rarely. For most of half-a-century I have been proud to be an anomaly, an unquestionably and generally unquestioning, patriotic Britisher who none the less takes to himself the dignity of proclaiming with Robert E. Lee 'Virginia is my nation', I see now that the very atypicality of the American scene evident in the College and in Williamsburg gave to me an early advantage, a sharpening of perception in observing America, which most of my fellow British commentators on the United States have never attained. At William and Mary I was settled at a junction, at the very point where British and American traditions meet. In the College and in that sparkling, elegant little city I found American history alive just where it is coincident with British history. Yet there was all around me enough that was so transparently foreign to my experience, a sufficiency of pressure from Americanism, to alert me to the difference between my origins, my background, my inherited prejudices, and the mores of the United States. Elsewhere I might have remained forever a foreigner, here I was a close relation returned to the family. As did my college friends, so did I look out on the rest of the United States as one whose forebears had made the United States possible, whose ancestors had fashioned its virtues, its foibles and must be held responsible for its shortcomings.

I was not blessed with the gift of prophecy. I could not then predict that the College would seize a grip on my loyalty as secure and as lasting as any that I have ever experienced,unless it be the hold on my affection exercised by Christ's Hospital. I could not foretell that the College and Williamsburg would build for me a reservoir of friendship sufficient for a lifetime, so that I would come to claim Williamsburg as my second home. I would not have credited it had some genie whispered that I was destined to be the College's official historian and by the College festooned with honours. At that time, coming to William and Mary after a year at UNB where I had been not once into the home of a faculty member and where only twice had the President spoken to me (once, infuriatingly, calling me John), I would have screeched scepticism had that same genie assured me that in time I would number among my intimates almost every President of William and Mary from the then resident in the President's House, that great and noble Virginian John Stewart Bryan, to Tom Graves.

All this was beyond my anticipation but even without the advantage of a crystal-ball something in the tone of the letters which came to me from Williamsburg to addresses in Fredericton, Banff in Alberta, London and Minehead assured me of the warmth of welcome awaiting me.

Arrived in New York, I spent an uncommitting and hilarious evening with my Rockette, the night with the Harries and early next morning went to Pennsylvania Station to meet the first of my new fellow-students. ('You may care to travel south with friends', Dean Hoke had written.)

Nick Woodbridge greeted me as if we had grown up together. The train was not yet under the Hudson before I was Jack to a half-dozen of his companions. Progressively, at Philadelphia, Wilmington their number doubled. After Washington DC we had a carriage to ourselves. After Richmond the train was a William and Mary colony. By that time Nick was lost to me, somewhere at the other end of the carriage, but I, surrounded by extraordinarily pretty girls, was utterly content. Then, as ever after, I was convinced that, for girls, William and Mary recognizes no qualification for admission more compelling than pulchritude, unless it be pulchritude and elegance combined.

Some prescient sense demanded of me that I attempt to register for life-time recall my first impression of Tidewater but, though I fancy that I saw then through the windows of the train a glorious pattern of greens, reds and browns, I cannot be certain that this vision of loveliness, this cherished spectacle of Tidewater in the early Fall, became part of my visual anthology on that first journey. Since that day I have looked upon it over and over again,and since that day the picture has become undeniably my property.

What I do remember as unique to my experience was the clatter of amiable inquisition within the carriage. Where was my home? Why William and Mary? Did I act? Did I fence, play tennis? What would be my major? Would I seek to be initiated into a fraternity? (I did not then catch the awesome significance in the seemingly slight modification in the quality of this question.)

This barrage of kindly questions was interspersed with gossip, bartered across me which even so, in a fashion that included me as a familiar, ignored my incomprehension and rejected the necessity for exegesis. Professor Blank had decamped with a sophomore co-ed. (Already before Baltimore I had become accustomed to America's generous and all-embracing use of the title 'Professor'). Roger Child had flunked for the third time. He was returning to try again. He was not coming back; he had taken a job as organist in a movie-house in Vermont. Nick had given his fraternity-pin to May Fielder.

Arrived at Williamsburg, bursting with pleasure and with beer, I hauled my baggage out of the train and stood, for a few moments bewildered, timorous and, even in the mêlée, for the first time bereft. Then above the clatter I heard a voice, already familiar; Nick shouting 'Come on, quick or these bastards'll take all the taxis.'

Within minutes Nick had settled me in a dormitory. 'I'm next door. If you want anything just yell through the wall. When we get the fraternity-house fixed up I'll be moving out of here – probably next week. Then I'll have the brethren pledge you, and you can move in with us.' No question, no hesitation; a statement of firm intent.

I floundered through the unfamiliar waters of Registration. History was my first choice, that was obvious and I signed for as many courses in American history as the rubric allowed. English came a close second; I set myself down for American Literature and for a subject, Creative Writing, which, until that day I had not known to be appropriate for academic instruction. Beyond that I had no ideas but the regulations demanded that I find a third option. Economics? Too many statistics, I had suffered enough from the dreary sociologists at UNB. Education? Politics? As I turned the pages of the catalogue, under the heading Philosophy I glimpsed the name

William James. I was at that time addicted to the novels of Henry James; I might as well learn something of his brother. I enrolled and surprisingly was accepted for a seminar in Modern Philosophy.

So it was that, on my third day at William and Mary, I sat in my room with a pristine copy of *The Selected Essays of William James* open before me. At the end of an hour all that I had achieved was puzzlement that any grown man could waste his intellectual energy on the problem of chasing a squirrel round a tree, and the conviction that Philosophy was not for me.

A fusillade of obscenities erupted in the corridor and the door exploded against the inner wall of my room.

At once relieved to be liberated from bemused concentration and apprehensive lest this be preface to sadistic hazing of the kind that was UNB's customary welcome to newcomers, I stood erect, my gaze unflinchingly fixed on a point appropriate to my height.

I stared into an empty corridor.

Lowering my eyes I saw, first, a hat and then a grinning face, dark and powerful.

That first impression of Tim, his hat as halo, was to be repeated a thousand times over fifty years. The hat might change. Sometimes it was a yachting-cap of a kind that no one but Tim has worn since the days of Edward the Seventh. Often in later years it was a bowler, on a distinguished Washington lawyer, a trustee of the National Geographic, an anomaly, on any American well-nigh unpatriotic and, even had it been worn by a City of London merchant-banker, because it was made on a mould never blessed by Lock's, an eccentricity. But always there was a hat and always Tim wore it on the back of his head.

Tim stood, his arm imperiously outstretched, Chorus silencing the groundlings, then he bellowed in a voice that must have roused from their graves the dead in Bruton Churchyard half-a-mile away: 'Jack, you Limey bastard, dump that crap, get off your arse and come with me to the corner Greeks.' A pause and, as if the information was supererogatory, as if I and all others from Maine to Florida, from Chesapeake Bay to the Golden Gate, must know his identity, he added 'Tim. . . Tim Hanson. . . Arthur B. Hanson.'

There were in those early days other meetings which presaged consequence, both immediate and long-term, but none carried portent as rich or as enduring as this, my first encounter with Tim Hanson. The moat of the Atlantic has made our association erratic. In fifty years Tim has written to me perhaps three times, for six of the seven years that followed my graduation, my business with Mussolini and Hitler, Tim's with Hirohito, was all-consuming, so that in 1945 neither of us knew if the other had survived the War. There is almost nothing on which we are in accord except our devotion to William and Mary. Tim thinks of me (more accurately: Tim talks of me) as a Limey Red, I recognize him as Genghis Khan re-incarnate, as Hitler with an American accent. In my Transatlantic persona I favour the Democrats; Tim's Republicanism is so rock-ribbed that I fancy he looks upon Ronald Reagan as a weak-kneed liberal. Poetry and music, the arts which keep me close to sanity, Tim does not disdain; for him they scarcely exist. I regard his passion for ocean-yachting as the folly of a perennial juvenile who resents the fact that Columbus was at sea five hundred years before he took the helm. Yet I am one of the very few men whom Tim deigns to accept as almost an equal and, for my part, in my friendship for Tim I find consolation absolute and entire for the fact that I never had a brother.

Within weeks of our first meeting, Tim and I had forged an alliance, unholy but effective, to shatter the calm of the campus. We were both versatile, both articulate, easy and even garrulous talkers, both capable of thinking on our feet and neither of us timid before our seniors or our contemporaries. From his father Tim had inherited political agility, I was rich in juvenile cunning. He had useful contacts everywhere, I the advantage that my Englishness served as excuse even for eccentricity or impertinence. Above all else valuable to the success of our ventures; we were both untiring.

Together we forced several novelties upon the campus but of them all the one which gave us most satisfaction, then and ever after, was the Backdrop Club.

In my first semester I made my debut with the William and Mary Theater as, of all unlikely roles, Chief Justice of the United States in *First Lady*. I enjoyed myself and enjoyed above all the acclaim which followed. Tim too had tried the Theater but his histrionic skills were more evident away from the footlights; he would have played Macbeth as a Washington wheeler-dealer, Coriolanus as a Tammany ward-boss. Both of us chafed under the bonds of direction, both of us resented the pseudo-professionalism of the Theater, its academic seriousness and its dedication to vocational training. We wanted something more spontaneous, more light-hearted, more obviously by and for students and we had before us the model of Harvard's Hasty Pudding Club.

The Backdrop Club was our creation, Tim's and mine, but we were fortunate in our collaborators. Bill Green, later I believe a successful New York stockbroker, was our Irving Berlin. We discovered a co-ed Busby Berkeley. With two other co-eds I wrote the book and the lyrics. I directed the show, Tim was business manager. Faced with President Bryan's insistence that we put up a considerable guarantee, in a matter of hours Tim unearthed an angel. Wise beyond our years, from the outset we agreed that we must make it appear that membership of the Backdrop Club, participation in its shows however humble, even a seat at its performance was a privilege not easily acquired. And it worked. We had two or three contestants for all the leads, girls ('gym-shorts *de rigueur*') flocked in for chorus-line auditions (conducted, of course, by Tim and by me).

For the first sight of *Spring Cleaning* we insisted that no one be admitted to Phi Beta Kappa Hall who was not dressed appropriately in tuxedo or evening dress. Tim had set up in the lobby a microphone and, in the auditorium, loudspeakers. As the notabilia arrived – President Bryan, the Deans, the Professor of Theatre Arts, the Mayor of Williamsburg – each was brought to the microphone for interview. I came from back-stage to pass to the waiting audience our ambitions for the Backdrop Club.

Spring Cleaning was a dazzling success. Station WRNL in Richmond invited us to broadcast a shorter version which, again of course, I wrote and introduced over the air and if there was in all this any dissension between Tim and me it was only over which of us would play the lion too. The Backdrop Club exists still, though it no longer dares originality.

President Bryan was one among many who sent us warm messages of congratulation,but it was for *Spring Cleaning* that I earned from him a rebuke, mild in tone and yet unique in all the years when he was, first, my President, then my patron and at the last my close friend.

Late in rehearsals we had decided that, as is the convention in musical comedy, we needed a rumbustious chorus to break the run of moon-and-blue solos and knock-about duets, something of bluster to set against the bright little imitations of Noel Coward which had been my major contribution to the libretto. Standing by Bill Green as he fingered the piano-keys, I scribbled a political campaign-song. I intended no more than that metre and rhyme be set to the rub-a-dub-dub rhythms of the tune that emerged from Bill's explorations. Most certainly I did not seek to blaspheme but blasphemy it was to Bryan and to many in the audience, for what I brought forth to be yelled as finale to the Student Government election scene was a series of verses mocking Roosevelt and the New Deal.

On the morning after the first performance, bleary-eyed from night-long celebration, I staggered to a class in the Wren Building. On the steps I walked into the President. He put his hand on my shoulder, looked down at me from his great height and said, his one clear eye sorrowful: 'My, my, sir. Here in Williamsburg, the cult of elephant-worship propagated by a British high priest! My ancestors are rotating in their graves.'

I would have understood as much had he addressed me in Sanskrit and, almost, he explained. 'You a Britisher and you seemingly a Republican. This, sir, is the lion's den, not every Daniel escapes the lion's claws. But you'll learn, sir, you'll learn.' He patted my back, turned away and as he walked off called over his shoulder: 'A moment, Jack, dear boy. Is there space in your calendar for tea with me at the President's House this very afternoon?'

Virginia was still then the heart of the Solid South, Bryan a firm supporter and a friend of FDR. As if the fates were set upon preparing me for my future,within weeks of my arrival in Williamsburg I was tossed into the cauldron of Republicanism. Tim took me to stay with his family in Bethesda, Maryland.

Since that, my first visit to 1801 Old Georgetown in Bethesda,

Maryland, a large rambling house surrounded by pigeon-lofts, residence for the birds which Elisha Hanson pretended to prefer to human beings, I have been allowed to regard as home several Hanson houses. Already in my student days I would appear, unheralded save perhaps by a casual telephone-call, and there was my room ready for me. And so it has been ever since. But in all houses presided over by Tim, he who questions the Virgin birth will be readily forgiven, he who doubts that the United States Marine Corps is the noblest, bravest and best-disciplined fighting-force in the world will be abused and never again invited, but he who dares to deny that the Republican Party has a God-given right to rule the United States – and all the rest of the universe – will be hurled through the window. Yet I, a man who never keeps silent his conviction that if all the armies of the world were drawn up on parade there would be, at the Right of the Line, the Royal Regiment of Artillery, and who makes plain that America and all the Continents would be better served if there was always a Democrat in the White House, I am welcomed time and time again, a member of the family, into the Hanson household. It is a miracle more remarkable than the Immaculate Conception.

I learnt much of American politics at 1801 Old Georgetown. For all my flickering doubts, it was no mean part of the comforting flattery paid to me that nothing was ever explained to me nor was I ever made to think myself an eavesdropper. Taking their cue from the Hansons, the Congressmen, newspaper editors, journalists who were frequent visitors in that household accepted me as a member of the family and, therefore, a Republican.

Beatrice, Tim's mother, was one of the most beautiful women it has ever been my good fortune to meet. (Tim took his looks from his father.) She was also generous and gentle. (From her Tim took that rare capacity for caring which he strives to hide under bluster and aggression.) Elisha Hanson, as Tim after him, was one of the most distinguished lawyers in a city choked with legal distinction, a blunt, raucous despot who did not suffer even wise men gladly if they opposed him but, somewhere behind his tough shell, there was a benevolent, warm-hearted man fighting to be set free.

'Lish welcomed me as his son's friend and so was persistently rude to me. Bea accepted me as a son, indeed very soon she announced herself to all her friends and to all mine as 'Jack's American mother', and consequently allowed me to use her shamelessly.

There was in the Hanson household, in addition to Tim, Bea and Lish, yet another who, by accepting that I was of the family, conferred upon me the blessing of dual citizenship that I have enjoyed from that day to this. Aunt Elizabeth, who could have served as stand-in for Hattie McDaniel or as *alter ego* for William Faulkner's Dilsey, ruled supreme in the kitchen, bullied Tim, his brothers, Bea and even 'Lish. Soon she came to bullying me also. 'Master Jack, that shirt of yours is a disgrace. Take it off at once; now, I tell you. I'll wash it and iron it. Here's one of Mr 'Lish's for you to wear.'

At the time when first the Hansons made their home mine,I was utterly unaccustomed to the kind of society, influential, scheming and well-heeled, which I met in Bethesda and at their beach-house at St Mary City. Thinking back, I see it as the noblest of the gifts then granted me that not once was I made conscious of the fact that,had I withdrawn every penny from my account in the Peninsula Bank, I would not have been able to pay Aunt Elizabeth's wages for a month.

At that time Bea and, I think, 'Lish were planning for Tim a dynastic marriage that would unite two of the great houses of the National Geographic Society. Tim played up dutifully. . . when he was at home. Bea had similar plans for me: I was to be matched with her god-daughter, the largely beautiful daughter of a Commissioner of the District of Columbia, already a horsewoman of note, and at that time a student at one of those expensive finishing-schools which help to shatter all belief in America as a classless society. Almost Bea succeeded. Show-jumping apart, Ann and I had much in common. I would be a writer, Ann was determined upon a career in journalism (an ambition which she fulfilled amply as columnist on the *Washington Post*). When eventually I graduated from William and Mary, because I had no parents on hand to admire me in my new academic robes, Bea insisted that she be present at the Commencement Exercises, and Ann with her. Bea gave parties in my honour, bought for me the obligatory orchid to pin to Ann's dress before we went off to the June Ball in the Summer Garden and lent me her car to drive Ann to my last fraternity party on the beach at Yorktown.

A week or so later, on the beach at St Mary City, I told Ann that I had decided to allow her to be my wife, but on the condition that she abandon her horses. Wisely, she settled for the horses and, for my consolation, gave me a volume of the poems of Edna St Vincent Millay.

> The fabric of my faithful love
> No power shall dim or ravel
> Whilst I stay here. . . but oh, my dear,
> If I should ever travel!

Tim, like me a transfer from another college, was already a member of a fraternity not represented at William and Mary. As Nick Woodbridge had promised, a week after my arrival in Williamsburg I was immediately pledged to Sigma Phi Epsilon.

From the first I found risible the shabby rituals of Greek-letter fraternities, the secret handshakes, the cabalistic insignia, the specious oaths, and in maturity I could but deplore their vicious social exclusivity. It was, therefore, yet another example of the generosity of the gods that I was pledged to SPE, by measure of bank-balance the poorer fraternity on the campus but in terms of worldly wisdom and influence the richest, for most of my fraternity-brothers cared as little as did I for the sub-Masonic trappings. Close to bankruptcy we took advantage of Williamsburg's burgeoning tourist-industry, rid ourselves of our lavish house to an entrepreneur eager to lure some of the thousands of visitors away from Williamsburg's one luxury hotel, and colonized the smallest and most dilapidated college dormitory. Infrequently, and only when some sophomoric geriatric arrived from SPE Headquarters to rebuke us for our indolence, we allowed ourselves to be embarrassed into an hour of mumbo-jumbo. Generally we lived together in a state of congenial squalor, the reality of fraternal feeling made evident not by any bogus forms but by our eagerness to borrow each other's ties, jackets, girl-friends, and by our willingness to support the aspirations of all and every one of us.

Nick was ambitious to serve as Student President; every fraternity-brother canvassed energetically in his cause. Dan played football; we were all on the bleachers to cheer him on. Bobby had designs on a lusciously-built co-ed freshman; evening after evening I ran interference on her notably zealous and watchful 'older sister'. Because it offered to me magnificent opportunity to travel the States at the expense of the College, I worked my way into the Debate team. I chafed under the rigid direction of the professional Debate coach, a man almost as influential as the football coach and even more dreary, but tours into New England, to Chicago and to Georgia justified my persistence. I became something of an expert on the National Labour Relations Board and as additional reward was entered automatically as a candidate for the individual Debate Cup.

The final was rather more a popularity contest than a public-speaking competition for,though independent assessors offered opinions, the ultimate verdict was left to the audience. And I had SPE; even more propitious, I could count on the votes of all whom my fraternity-brothers could conscript.

On the night of the competition there in the front rows were all my fraternity-brothers (most of whom had never before attended a debate), all their girl-friends, a few non-fraternity men and women lured into my claque by our promise to support them in some other venture, Tim – and Tim's blackmail victims.

The logic of my most formidable opponent was devastated by Gil Crandall and Pat Kelly. Gil, it seemed, was suffering from St Vitus Dance brought on by the threat of a punch-line, Pat's imitation of Camille lasted just as long as my rival was at the podium. For all the less likely contestants my supporters maintained an air of unendurable boredom and a threatening silence but when I spoke they laughed uproariously at all my contrived witticisms, nodding approvingly – and dramatically – as I elaborated my arguments and, as I finished my carefully-rehearsed 'impromptu' peroration,the applause was no less thunderous than it would have been had I scored the winning touchdown in the Homecoming game against the University of Richmond. Even the assessors were cowed out of independence.

After a few months of fraternity life, of energetic alliance in chicanery with Tim, of cheerful conversation with Pat Kelly (who, though she was fourth-generation Irish still believed that Oliver Cromwell was the Devil incarnate, but somehow excepted me from her generalized assumption that all Britishers regard Drogheda as the noblest of all our battle-honours), and of even more hours in the company of Beverly Boone (whose charm and delectable physique seemed to deny her claim to be a direct descendant of the obstreperous and rough-hewn Daniel), I lost all sense of being an observer, an anthropologist looking in on the strange customs of some remote tribe. I had gone native. I had become in almost every respect an American student.

I had no wish to become formally an American citizen and there remained one inhibition which denied to me the possibility of making entire my social and intellectual naturalization. Contented though I was with my American existence, I could not close my eyes to the storm-clouds lowering over Europe.

Unless it was Tim (and he, after Pearl Harbour, the most bellicose and the most dramatically belligerent), not one of my companions was isolationist; they merely shrugged off Hitler, Mussolini and Franco as of no significance to the United States,and all the horrifying portents – the invasion of Abyssinia, the Spanish Civil War, the Anschluss – they shrugged off as the follies of the inhabitants of some remote planet.

When, in bull-sessions lasting often long into the night, we discussed politics and society, it was our intimate world we were putting to rights, a world which did not include Europe. I tried, and tried desperately, to match their comforting complacency but, with increasing ferocity as 1937 turned to 1938, the hideous magnetism of events on the other side of the Atlantic pulled me homewards.

At that very moment there had opened up before me the possibility that I could extend my idyllic existence into the distant future, even that I might ensure that it would never end. It was suggested to me that, after graduation, I could move on to take a Ph.D. at Princeton, Harvard or Johns Hopkins and so qualify myself for an academic career in the United States; but every letter from home and every copy of the *Times Overseas Edition* splintered such cosy dreams. At school and at UNB I had resented compulsory membership in the Officers Training Corps, at William and Mary I was still, if hesitantly. a pacifist, but before ever I took my degree I knew that I could no longer hide myself against my Britishness in the convenient bunker of my newly-discovered Americanism.

There were even then only twenty-four hours in every day and, scrabbling back over the years to recover the arithmetic of time,I find it difficult to measure how it was that I found hours or the energy sufficient to justify the promise of academic advancement. I was often away from Williamsburg, travelling with the College Debate Team to New York, into New England or out to the Middle West, weekending with the Hansons or the families of one or the other of my fraternity-brothers. I wrote for the College newspaper and for the Backdrop Club. One of my essays published in the College Library magazine – significantly called *The Royalist* – by courtesy of Blunden opened up for me a friendship-by-correspondence with Siegfried Sassoon. When I was in town and not obliged to earn my keep as an assistant in the Library, most week-day evenings I passed either studying the glories of Virginia's night-sky under Beverly's eager tutelage from a porch in Sorority Court, or gossiping with the brethren in Taliaferro Hall, our commandeered fraternity-house. (I called it then, as I call it still, in proper Virginian fashion, *Tulliver* Hall.)

It follows that it was not my diligence which allowed me to emerge from college with some academic distinction. C.H. had grounded me well in my two 'majors', History and English; I had a capacity for fast reading and a retentive memory, both given to me, I suppose, by God; and some cunning, the gift no doubt of the Devil, for returning what I had read or heard in a fashion which simulated originality. Most of the credit for my quasi-scholarly successes I credit to the Fates who, at William and Mary as at C.H., set me down under the tutelage of rarely gifted teachers.

Jim Miller I place next only to David Roberts in my pantheon of preceptors. When I was his student, and even by my nineteen-year-old measure, a comparatively young man and still sensitive to the inspiration of Alfred North Whitehead, Jim was charitable to almost everything except sloppy thinking. His wit, his undeniable authority and, for my conversion most persuasive of all, his capacity for communicating to students his excitement for the subject, soon lured me out of my spontaneous aversion to Philosophy. He cossetted me into some comprehension of the processes of Logic, instilled in me some understanding of Santayana, Bergson, Peirce, Bradley and Russell, and he even had me enthusiastically chasing after William James as James chased his squirrel. He failed to persuade me that John Dewey did not deserve election to my short-list of the most boring writers of all time, but it was typical of Jim that for him disagreement with his opinions was no sin if well argued. For my pages-long diatribe against Dewey he gave me the highest mark that ever I earned as a student, an A plus.

In the sense that I needed no persuasion to make me interested in literature, Mel Jones's task was easier than Jim's, but I owe a huge debt to Mel, another scintillating teacher, for introducing me to the art of Emily Dickinson, Wallace Stevens, Robert Frost, William Carlos Williams and – a particular favourite of his, as of mine ever after though now of few others – Edwin Arlington Robinson. By so doing he conferred on me the privilege of adopting these riches as an integral part of my own heritage. Mel it was, too, who in his Creative Writing class encouraged me to attempt a novel, a book which, with more prescience than originality, I called *Bright Beginning*. Fortunately it never found a publisher but even so taught me (and presumably Mel also) much about its author.

Before I went to my first history lecture in the Marshall-Wythe Building, I could have written all that I knew of American history on two sides of a sheet of paper and even so would have filled more space than most of my British contemporaries, or for that matter most of their successors. At Canonbury Road I had been informed that George Washington never told a lie, a morality-tale which even then I suspected and which later I discovered to be sensationally mendacious. With most of my countrymen (as indeed with many Americans) I believed that the Pilgrim Fathers were the first English settlers in North America. My father spoke sometimes of President Wilson and General Pershing and more often of Peter Stuyvesant. My childhood admiration for Bonaparte had parenthetically revealed to me that the Americans entered the Napoleonic Wars 'on the wrong side'. At C.H. I had been prepared for School Certificate with sufficient thoroughness to allow me to provide five-line answers to questions about Abraham Lincoln and the Alabama Incident. But I knew little of Jefferson or Robert E. Lee, I doubt that I was aware that John Marshall was Chief Justice and I am certain that I had never heard of George Wythe. Even so I had come to William and Mary in part because I wished to discover America's past. I was eager to know more – and my eagerness was handsomely rewarded.

I cannot elevate Richard Lee Morton to the status of scintillating teacher. His lectures were delivered in a monotone, the only release for his listeners admiration and wonderment at his perverse capacity to read from notes placed the wrong way round on his table, first line towards the audience, last line towards him. But his expertise was undeniable (his *History of Virginia* is the most exhaustive study of the story of the Commonwealth, as the book by Parke Rouse, my amiable companion and friend in later years, is the liveliest) and, for all the dry manner in which it was vouchsafed, I was enthralled by his unbridled partisanship. From Dick Morton I learnt never to commit the blasphemy of writing of 'the recent unpleasantness', the Civil War. In conversation, as in the 1930s still for many Southerners, it was still 'The War' *tout court*, as if in all history there had been no other conflict, but on paper he allowed only 'the War between the States'.

His care for this seemingly prejudiced pedanticism, as all else that involved him in defence of the Southern cause, he argued with solemn, scrupulously scholarly supporting evidence, and without once changing the timbre of his voice or lifting his eyes from those strangely misplaced notes. One sensed rather than heard or saw the hurt deep within him when he spoke of Sherman's March through Georgia, of carpet-baggers and Reconstruction, the disdain that came close to being hatred when he mentioned Ulysses S. Grant or Abraham Lincoln.

Sixty years and more after Appomatox, Dick Morton remained a Confederate patriot and from him I gleaned a new galaxy of heroes – J. E. B. Stuart, Longstreet, Calhoun, Judah Benjamin – at his instigation I too became a Johnny Reb and, as none knows better than Russ Nye, my much-loved and much-respected collaborator in the *Penguin History of the United States*, I have never been entirely reconstructed. 'Forgit? Hell!'

My classroom-acquired knowledge of the War between the States was made vivid because Gil Crandall owned a yellow Packard tourer. Gil, a Marylander but no copper-head, shared my zest for battles without bullets. Often and always to the delight of the other inhabitants of Taliaferro, he would cease strumming at his guitar and drive off with me to the scene of some ancient engagement.

This part of Virginia is the Belgium of America; several of the fiercest campaigns in America's two domestic wars have been fought within driving distance of Williamsburg. If time was short we went to Yorktown.and there Gil stood by patiently whilst, defiantly proud even in defeat, I paid homage at Fusilier Redoubt. More often we drove to the outskirts of Richmond, to the quiet green countryside which had been drenched with the last blood of the Confederacy.

The awareness of immediacy and of intimacy with the American past that is inevitable to any resident of Williamsburg erased such doubts as once had plagued me about my choice of William and Mary. In that great historic triangle, Tidewater, Virginia, which had staged so many of the most sensational scenes in the national drama, I was no longer an onlooker. I could never take centre-stage,and the theatre itself had lost the influence which for so long it had exercised in American life, but here I was a player in crowd-scenes and so close to the great actors of days gone by that it was impossible for me to accept that they were all long-since dead, their acting done.

With Beverly or Pat – and with John Smith, John Rolfe and his tragic child-wife, Pocahontas – I picnicked on the grass by the old church at Jamestown.

With my fraternity-brothers I went often to Yorktown. We went to swim and, on the rare occasions when we could muster the cash, to eat Chesapeake Bay oysters and lobster at Nick's. Even had I wished to ignore Yorktown's ghosts, my companions never allowed me to forget that this was the place where the world turned upside down, the scene of Cornwallis's surrender.

Under the instruction, amiable, casual but superbly informed, of Jim Cogar, the Curator of Colonial Williamsburg, I learnt to flesh out the ghosts I welcomed, to dress them as they had dressed themselves, to surround them with furniture, silver, glass, pictures, appropriate to their times, to allow them to behave according to a code of etiquette foreign to the twentieth-century.

Jim's course, a judicious amalgam of instruction and informed tourism,based substantially on Williamsburg and nearby plantations, was open only to the very few students who had gained consistently high marks in other History courses. Reared in another and quite different process I was never comfortable in the American system of almost continuous tests but I had not lost my cunning, I could still fool examiners and I was admitted to the select band.

Visitors from Europe, and most blatantly visitors from Britain, have not spared Williamsburg their criticism. They find pathetic, or risible, even somehow blasphemous, this attempt to bring back to life a long-dead city.

Even I, after a few weeks no longer a visitor but a proud resident, could not so far submerge my Englishness when I watched the O'Hallorans from Boston and the Finnegans from Chicago as they stood awestruck, gaping at the British flag flapping its braggart proclamation of empire over the Capitol. Brisk with condescension. I followed the moms and dads as they shepherded their brats down the Duke of Gloucester Street to the greasy spoon called by its Greek proprietor The Colonial Restaurant, 'specializing in American and Chinese foods', and I could not always hold back a bark of derision at the sight of some sweaty tourists, exhausted by so much antique culture, dropping a coin into Steve Sacalis's juke-box to bring forth some noise that would drown all memory of an exquisite harpsichord heard but an hour before in the Governor's Palace.

Though not then, nor indeed ever after, could I rid myself entirely of my patronizing airs, I soon acquired understanding and with understanding came abiding affection. Williamsburg, when I first saw it, was virtually unique in the United States yet it is not untypical for, a shrine which is even so a commercial enterprise, the product of meticulous scholarship which is nevertheless a highly popular holiday resort, an overtly eighteenth century city equipped with central-heating and air-conditioning, it demonstrates the peculiarly American capacity for qualifying contradiction. The will to make paradox acceptable and useful is intrinsic to the American spirit. Why else would a nation which worships modernity hold as the Thirty-Nine Articles of its people's faith a 200-year-old constitution?

Europeans, accustomed to stumbling over their past round every street-corner, may find the Restoration incomprehensible, even laughable. Americans need Williamsburg, for this is the living symbol of national continuity, the outward and visible sign of association with the men who created the United States. And so it was for me: as I came to know and to understand Williamsburg so did my enhanced empathy bring me closer to knowing and understanding America, past and present. But my acquisition of spiritual· and intellectual dual-citizenship would have had no practical consequence had not my duties in the Library, defined by one of my fellow library assistants as 'replacing books and displacing necking couples' brought me also into the orbit of Dr Swem.

Unlike most of my College mentors, Earl Greg Swem was, even by the stern measure of the reference-books, truly an old man. Born in 1870, the year of Robert E. Lee's death, he was an Iowan, a shameful fact he rarely mentioned. Married to a Virginian, before ever he moved from being an Assistant Librarian of Congress to the post of Librarian at William and Mary he had made obvious his dedication to his State by matrimony.

Already he was better informed than any Virginian-born about the minutiae of Virginia's colonial past and – because Virginians are habitually besotted with family history, a more difficult achievement – already he was an
acknowledged expert in Virginian genealogy.

Swem's mode of scholarship – its ripest fruit the guide to Virginian historical magazines known to historians, simply and deservedly, as *Swem's
Index* – was polar and close to being antithetical to the mode in which I
had been reared. He did not positively deny, though I sensed he found suspect, the notion of history as an art but for him it was a technology,
research an end in itself, no detail too trivial to be recorded, his vocation to
amass evidence. Interpretation, the pronouncing of verdict, he left to men
less sedulous than he.

Yet it was apprenticeship to this gentle master which reduced my aversion to stern, footnoted scholarship, and it was he who endowed me with
such limited skills as are mine in the techniques of the craft which already I
had decided to serve.

Parenthetically, it was also Swem who made me familiar with hundreds
of men and women, obscure or even unknown to most historians, who
had lived, worked and died in seventeenth and eighteenth century
America.

Whenever I was on duty in the Library he would stop by my desk, to
tell me of a new discovery, to demonstrate bibliographical processes or to
set for me, as diversion from my prescribed and more mundane responsibilities, some small research task.

These advantages which Swem conferred on me were to have considerable significance for my career but none was as immediately seminal as the
part he played in ensuring that I could have a career of any sort.

He had accepted, with gracious resignation, my refusal to acquire
American academic respectability in the North but when, at the beginning
of my last semester, I announced that I must go back to England and
remove the barrier to English preferment which I had erected when I
turned away from Oxford, Cambridge or London, immediately and with
zest he set himself to supporting my intention.

Evening after evening we studied British university catalogues. I estimated that I had before me two years before I must decide between going
to Wormwood Scrubs as a conscientious objector or seeking some foreign
field to make forever England (an estimate which events proved exaggerated), so we agreed that I apply to Durham, at that time the only British university which allowed a student to advance to the dignity of a doctorate in
less than three years. Swem would not only support my application, he
would also see to it that I had equally enthusiastic support from Morton
and Cogar, but he recommended that I try to add to my sparse credentials
the prize given by the Society of the Cincinnati for the best contribution
to original historical research by an undergraduate.

The topic he chose for me was,not surprisingly, 'Christ's Hospital and the Virginia Colony'. When it was announced that I had won the Society of the Cincinnati Medal, his pride in my success was so extravagant that he did not wait to discover that no other student had entered the competition. Instead he hurried off to initiate a charitable conspiracy with President Bryan.

When I called at the President's Office to collect my prize, Bryan greeted me with the comment that this was the best joke of the year, that the only 'redcoat' (his word) in the College be given a medal donated by heirs of officers in the Continental Army and bearing the name and arms of the Society funded by Washington in a ludicrous and futile attempt to foist upon republican America some kind of hereditary aristocracy. He then handed me the Medal ('Sir, I must read your essay, I surely must. And, my dear Jack, I am content that it will not be the last of your works that all of us here will be pleasured to read'), handed me the cheque for one hundred dollars which went with the Medal, then told me that the College had awarded to me a research fellowship with only one proviso; that I undertake in Britain any devilling asked for by Dr Swem.

The Medal gratified me and the Fellowship made feasible my plans for the next two years. (It was not until much later than I discovered that my stipend was paid out of President Bryan's pocket.) But the hundred dollars made me ecstatic.

From the President's Office I returned to Taliaferro, wrote a letter to the Clerk begging continued support from Christ's Hospital's Advancement-in-Life Fund, then went down-town and booked my passage back to England.

When, on my last day in Williamsburg, I went to thank Dr Swem for all that he had done for me and for all that he was still doing, he put his arm round me and said, 'Someday, my boy, you will write the history of our College.'

Alas, though he lived on into the 1960s he was dead too soon to see Elijah's mantle round the shoulders of Elisha.

6

All with Smiling Faces

In the last half-century I have travelled on all the continents, but not once since 1940 have I dared return to Newcastle.

There is no logic in my craven sensibility. I have been back time and time again to Hexham, Alnwick, Durham, to many of the places which first I saw with Jane, and never have I suffered more than a dutiful flicker of sorrow for vanished delights. Though since the War I have walked the Champs-Elysées and the Place des Vosges a hundred times, seldom have I given more than nonchalant thought to the past, to those spring days of 1939 when I walked this way with Jane on my arm and all our future before us. Even when, on my way to some conference at UNESCO, I have passed the hotel with the grandiloqent name, the Grand Hotel au Lion d'Or et des Maréchaux de Saxe et de Suffren, I have glanced up at its grubby windows, remarked to myself that this is a seedy pension fit only for impoverished students but not often has it occurred to me that in the weeks I spent behind those grimy lace-curtains – unwashed it would appear since 1939 – I was myself the epitome of impoverished student and impetuous lover. All these promotings to misery I ignore or spurn with no great effort. In London on Waterloo Station I suffer a moment of reminiscent pain when I pass the bench, unmoved in fifty years, where Jane and I said *au revoir* for the last time but it is only Newcastle, the very name, the very thought of Newcastle, which turns me coward to memory.

Reason would have it otherwise. In that year before I discovered that life can in truth end with a bang and a whimper, I was marvellously content in Newcastle and there, for the first time in my life – indeed for the only time in my first twenty-six – I was truly a private person, liberated from regime and free to turn a deaf ear to calls for communal activity, pleasant or disturbing, which had engulfed me as a child in a family, at school and at college – as subsequently in the Army. But it is not this rare and glorious independence which I remember when I think of Tyneside; Newcastle spells Jane – by parentage American, by birth Nicaraguan; by education Spanish, Portuguese and, reluctantly, British; by choice and prejudice vehemently *Parisienne* – and Jane loathed Newcastle and despised all Geordies.

More than a half-century has passed since last I saw Jane and forty-seven since she shrugged me out of her life. It was in 1970 when, somewhere on a Florida road between Jacksonville and St Augustine, her sister broke to me the news – already long out-of-date – of Jane's tragic, horrific and inexplicable death, and it was 1973 when I stood for hours in a steamy Puerto Rican airport waiting, in vain, for the sequel which I hoped would offer me some consolation. All is ancient history, yet the wound inflicted by Jane's treachery has never been healed, not even by the balm of a wondrously contented marriage, and still today as I write of Newcastle pain flares, with pain, resentment – and the pangs of frustration of a narrator who must tell a tale without an ending.

I spent the last day of August 1938 with James Morison at his exquisite house close to Hadrian's Wall. Professor of History at King's College, Newcastle – at that time the huge bedraggled tail which wagged the tiny elegant puppy, the Durham Colleges – at a time when an American degree was in Britain worthless, Professor Morison had accepted as appropriate preface to a Ph.D. my bachelor's degree from William and Mary (the first given to an Englishman since the Revolution); my Society of the Cincinnati Medal; my virtually assured election (also as the first Englishman) to the Founding Chapter of that élite American academic-honours society, Phi Beta Kappa; and the enthusiastic references from my College tutors. Although he was a sterling authority on the history of British India, even at our first meeting he confessed with ready candour that he knew nothing about Colonial America and it was only his Scottish education which gave him his right to supervise a thesis provisionally, ponderously and all-embracingly entitled 'The Influence of English and Scottish Schools and Universities on Education in the Early Virginia Colony'. He promised to bring in adjunct-supervisors, Winstanley for one, the Vice-Master of Trinity, Cambridge, who also knew little of the 'early Virginia Colony' but whose knowledge of seventeenth and eighteenth century education was profound. Together, with their aid, he assured me, somehow we would muddle our way to my doctorate.

It was Morison who won for me some additional and very welcome funds by arranging that I act as crammer for a few struggling First Year students, and in the months that followed, when I was his pupil and for a while his humble colleague, he treated me to many courtesies and with unfailing patience which, now when apology is without value, I repaid only with fecklessness and disdain. I was too much taken up with the delights of my newly-acquired independence to accept the disciplines of yet another regime and, not so very long after that day at Corbridge, and for the rest of the academic year, there was Jane.

But, on 1 September 1938, as I travelled the short journey from Corbridge to Newcastle, my mind was filled with the optimism he had induced. War might come; what of it? Still the year ahead would be the most fascinating, the most creative year of my life and the prelude to a career as a scholar.

I walked out on to the forecourt of Newcastle Station and into nemesis. The darkling sky denied the hour and the season, the scene belied the year. This was a provincial and impoverished version of Mayhew's Victorian London. Slowly, as if even the sky, November in September, was reluctant to empty itself on to such drabness, rain fell on to shambling, grim-faced men and women. The buildings, the people, the one bus, even the rain: all were grey.

Was it for this that I had quit the sparkling, red-brick Georgian elegance of Williamsburg, for this that I had denied myself Harvard Square or Nassau Hall? I counted the money in my wallet. I could not afford to buy my way out of doom with a return-ticket to London. I squared my shoulders, picked up my two suitcases and marched out to become a Geordie.

Within weeks I wished for myself no other fate. Before ever I fell in love with Jane I had fallen in love with Newcastle, with the surrounding country and the magnificent beaches of Durham and Northumberland and, most of all, with my freedom.

I had found for myself two rooms close to the Elswick Road, in one of the humbler districts. My landlady fitted neither of the caricatures commonly associated with university landladies; she was neither a she-dragon nor a nymphomaniac. An intelligent, quiet-spoken and attractive woman in her early thirties, at the time when I was Mrs Johnson's lodger for me her most endearing qualities were her competence as a cook and her tact. Only when she thought I was not eating enough and once, when she introduced me to a pretty and talented cousin, did she venture any interference in my life. For the rest she did not raise an eyebrow when, unannounced, I brought back friends, male or female; instead, for them all, even for Maggie, the pudacious red-head I had met on my first venture into the Union, she prepared sandwiches, plates piled high at sixpence a head; and she asked no questions when I disappeared for days at a time. Had she enquired, I fear I would have given the response with which I was then justifying to myself my frequent absences from Newcastle, that I was off to consult Winstanley, and would not have added the more compelling reason, that Ross Hook, Harry McQuade, Colin Chivers and Bernard Taylor were all still up at Cambridge.

Then in came Jane and out went Maggie, Mrs Johnson's charming cousin, Professor Morison, the pioneers of Virginian education, and, for a while, even my fellow-Grecians.

There was at that time in Newcastle a small colony of Americans, most of its members associated in one way or another with the manufacture of soap, and my ambiguous status as an Englishman with an American degree brought me many invitations to parties in their homes. On the evening which was to prove for me so seismic there were twenty of us, all but me American and all young.

We had been together at least an hour when the door opened and there was Jane.

She stood surveying the room, an aristocrat deigning a brief association with the plebs, then stepped forward, her hand outstretched to greet our hostess. All the girls in the room were well-dressed but suddenly all looked shabby. It was not that her frock was elegant – not I, nor I suspect anyone else in the room, could tell that it had been made in Paris (as later I discovered by an inexpensive *modiste* round the corner from the rue José-Maria de Heredia) – but rather that she wore it with the confidence of one who knew that on her even a coal-heaver's sack would look elegant. And she was beautiful: a fine figure, admirably displayed, good legs, large grey eyes and immaculately groomed hair.

The effect on me was immediate and sensational. My mind told me that I should resent her extravagant sophistication and hide myself from her haughtiness. Every instinct informed me that this was the girl for me.

Later that same evening I described Jane in a letter to my sister Bess: 'She moved proudly [I wrote, without quotation-marks or acknowledgement to Max Beerbohm] to the incessant movement of a paean, aye! of a paean that was always *crescendo*.' I was no Duke of Dorset, both too timid and too strong a swimmer to drown myself in her honour, but this vision of Jane as Zuleika Dobson come to Newcastle was by no means extravagant. Only once in all the years that have followed have I experienced that same strange amalgam of exhilaration and determination which was mine when first I saw Jane; only once, seven years later in a Hertfordshire sitting-room, has the first sight of a girl persuaded me to vow that, however loaded the odds against me, I would not permit this loveliness to escape into a world in which I was not king.

The effect on the party was immediately disastrous. Conviviality vanished. We stood around, all, presumably as was I, groping for some topic of conversation which would not bring down upon us the silent disdain of this intruder from another world. In an attempt to revivify her party, our hostess asked Jane to sing for us. She pretended to none of that reluctance which comes conventionally from those who, without notice, are asked to entertain their fellow-guests. Instead, unaccompanied, and in a superb and obviously well-trained voice, she sang *fado* and, after acknowledging with the only smile that so far she had granted to the company, Carmen's most provocative song. I was appropriately provoked but all that *tu-toiement* was not addressed to me or to anyone else in the room; Jane was singing for an audience at the Opéra Comique and when she finished, her hand on the piano-top, she looked round the room as if to say 'How can I waste my talents on a bunch of hicks from a soap-factory?'

Somebody proposed a sing-song. The engineer whose services as accompanist Jane had previously rejected, took his place on the piano-stool and for the first time I noticed a blemish on her highly-polished armour. She did not know the 'Stein Song', 'Anchors Aweigh' or any of the American college songs or English and American folk-songs we bellowed.

Every man in the room except me had his arm round a girl's waist but none dared attempt such familiarity with Jane. My moment had come, I put my arm round Jane's shoulders. She did not remove it, indeed she made no sign that she had even noticed my presence and when, because no one else knew the words, I sang 'Bladon Races' almost as a solo to an accompaniment of la-la-las from all the rest save Jane, I moved my arm to round her waist, still she remained stiffly unresponsive.

I left that evening so put down by her coolness and so besotted that it was not until I was back in my Croftsway rooms that I realized that all that I knew about her was that her Christian name was Jane and that she was the daughter of the American Consul.

Next morning I had lost not a whit of my determination, had gained no composure but I had recovered my wits. I fossicked the Consul's name and initials out of the switchboard-operator at the Consulate, looked him up in the directory and rang his private number.

Twice my call was answered by a maid. The first time she told me that Miss Jane was not yet up, the second time, her voice exasperated out of all pretence to service in Mayfair, in an accent that revealed Gateshead, she said 'Hinny, I said it, didn't I? Jane's gone to Bainbridge's with her ma. She won't be back for at least an hour.'

She had told me nothing of the sort but I watched the clock for precisely sixty minutes then called again. Jane answered: I gave my name and asked fatuously if she had enjoyed the party.

She did not reply but at least she knew who I was. 'Oh, you're the boy with the wandering fingers, the one with the lovely speaking-voice, the one who shouldn't be allowed to sing, not even in his bath.'

I would not be put off. 'Will you dine with me tonight?' I asked. That line I had prepared; 'dine with me' was my London and New York for her Paris; but I was not prepared for her response, 'Of course not, why should I?' and I answered with a schoolboy's *tu quoque*: 'Why in the Hell shouldn't you?'

She retreated, just a little. 'I'm only home for a few weeks. My parents would be terribly hurt if I went out two nights running. Give me your phone-number and I'll call you if something can be arranged.'

Down went my pride to the bottom of the pit. I had to admit that I was ringing from a call-box, that there was, 'as yet', no telephone in my apartment.

'Hold on a minute.' I heard voices and strained to catch what was being said, then Jane spoke again. 'Do you play bridge?'

Pride plummeted into an abyss but I did my best. 'Poker, but not bridge, I fear.'

'Never fear.' She giggled; I believe it was the only time that ever I heard Jane giggle; 'nor do I. My parents would play every night if Daddy didn't have so many official engagements, Come to dinner, seven o'clock. They can play, we'll talk.'

Before I went home that evening, I was certain that I had found the real

Jane. There was no denying that this girl was elegant but she was also warm, intelligent and unusually well-read in four languages. I did not immediately suspect that her musical knowledge had severe limits, that she knew more of Bizet and Massenet than of Beethoven or Brahms, that she had never heard of Vaughan Williams or Constant Lambert, and that she preferred Chopin and Cesar Franck to Elgar or even my beloved Mozart. As yet I did not notice her manic Francophilia; I was enthralled by her eagerness to hear me tell of my adventures in America – her native land which she had not seen since she was six years old – and flattered out of any doubts that this was the girl I must marry. The girl I had met the night before, I decided, was a self-created artefact, an anthology of poses put on to disguise the feeling of isolation from her contemporaries, sparked off by her advanced physical and intellectual maturity (she was not yet eighteen), her travels and by her talent; isolation that, at times, because she had shared few of the experiences common to her co-evals, she herself interpreted as inadequacy. I can but add that I never again saw the Jane of the party.

In the next few weeks we were together for a large part of every day. We went to the cinema and I discovered that, as did I, she detested Nelson Eddy and Jeanette Macdonald and, as did I, adored Madeleine Carroll. She read Shelley and, more often, Villon to me; I read Wilfred Owen to her and, more often, my own verses. My two new friends, Raghbir Singh Rao and Kumar Singh Chaudhiri thought her a princess, and so did I. We were both so certain that we must make a future together that, at Jane's suggestion, I bought a set of golf-clubs so that when she was off in Paris I could court her father's approval. (I won his affections more easily than I won playing golf against him.)

Forgetful of the excuse she had given for refusing my first invitation to dine, she announced to her parents that she was leaving Newcastle a few days earlier than had been planned so that she could go with me to Cockfosters. My father fell in love with her, my sisters approved, only Alice was cool and Alice's flagrant dislike proved to me, and to Bess and Julia, that I was right about Jane.

I brought Basil and John to meet her. They acclaimed her as our Anne of Austria. I took her to see David and Peg Roberts, Marshall and Evadne Hewitt, the Leigh-Mallorys, my Aunt Susan and my Cousin Betty. She passed all inspections though I suspected some reservation in Betty's approval. Jane took me to Crosby Hall, to her older sister, Pat. I passed muster. I wrote to Bryan and to Swem.

Jane went back to Paris and a week or so later I followed 'to spend a few days delving through manuscripts in the Bibliothèque Nationale'.

At Christmas 1938, the last of peace, we announced our engagement to our unsurprised but surprisingly delighted families.

At about the same time I renounced irrevocably all thought of conscientious objection. I did not admit even to Jane that this coincidence of seminal decisions was not touched by 'the majestic hand of chance'. Jane, I knew, would be of little use as a prison-visitor, that Aucassin, Lancelot, Petrarch, Dante. . . all the great lovers of fable, fiction and fact, would have looked ridiculous wearing broad arrows – and so would I.

A letter from Dr Swem jerked me back to my academic responsibilities but not to my thesis. He reminded me of the many times we had talked about Lord Dunmore, the last and most reviled Royal Governor of Virginia and of how, in the tempestuous days immediately before the Revolution, Dunmore had done as many Imperial shoguns, before and after; he had moved to assuage disaffection by bringing from England to the seething colony his wife and children.

That much, said Swem, was verifiable from the archives, but there was no evidence for the sequel: that Dunmore had entered his two sons, along-side the sons of the men who spoke loudest against their King, into the College of William and Mary. What Swem wanted from me was that I follow where many eminent scholars had failed and see if I could establish this tale as either fact or fable.

Perhaps because, despite Swem's tuition, I was still unsophisticated in research methodology, perhaps because I was so much taken up with Jane, but more likely because I was indolent, I did not go the way of my learned predecessors, to the Public Record Office, the British Museum and the National Library of Scotland. Instead I consulted *Who's Who* and wrote to the then Lord Dunmore.

Back came his reply, courteous but doubtful. All his ancestors, back almost to Adam, had been Etonians.

I consulted Eton. In all halves of the relevant period the Royal Governor had paid fees for his sons. And the Dunmores are Scots!

I was about to pass this disappointing news to Swem when a letter arrived from Dunmore's son and heir, Lord Fincastle, which gave me hope: at some time, somewhere in the family papers, he had seen a refer-ence to William and Mary. If I would meet him at their London residence, he would give me the freedom of the Murray family archives.

On the night before the appointed day Jane arrived from Paris for one of her now-frequent visits to Cockfosters. She begged to go with me to Cadogan Gardens and, when I suggested that she would find boring an hours-long scrabble through dusty, and almost certainly worthless, docu-ments she took my justifiable opinion as cue for one of those bouts of sulks, tantamount to fits of depression, which sometimes and inexplicably overcame her. Finally, however, she conceded that she would travel with me to town, spend the day browsing in the Charing Cross Road book-shops and meet me for tea in the Strand Corner House.

Dressed in my one good suit, as I thought appropriate for a meeting with a viscount and perhaps with an earl and a countess, as the clock struck eleven I arrived at the Dunmore house. The door was opened by Fincastle himself. He hurried me up to the family muniment-room, a musty loft filled with the dust and debris of all the centuries, pointed to a dozen cardboard-boxes and four or five antique trunks, told me to help myself and went off to his club.

I tipped the contents of a box onto a moth-eaten Persian rug, squatted on the floor and began my inspection: butchers' bills from 1924, an invitation to a Society wedding (August 1914!), a card for the Monte Carlo Casino, the programme of a Nellie Melba concert and, the first but still dim signal of hope, some eighteenth century marriage-contracts. The second box yielded much of the same kind and one nugget: a small bundle of letters, tied together with a frayed shoe-lace, from the nineteenth century banker-poet, Samuel Rogers. More detritus in the next two boxes and then, a sensation, a letter in a hand I thought I recognized.

I was right: here was George Washington, writing in 1775 'to His Excellency the Governor at his Palace in Williamsburg from Mount Vernon', and offering to have his private coach meet Lady Dunmore and her children when their ship docked.

Within two hours I had piled up on the rug signed and often holograph letters from every English monarch from James I to Edward VII; letters from the Maréchal de Saxe, from the Indian agent, Sir William Johnson and, as I thought, the richest find of all; letters from both sides in the 'Forty-five, from two Murray boys judiciously placed, the one as aide-de-camp to the Butcher Cumberland, the other, also as aide, to the Young Pretender.

I was tempted to read what I had found but I plodded on. I unroped the trunks. Every one was crammed with yellowing papers, all unsorted, and every one yielded something of interest but of no great significance; more invitations, more bills, the eighteenth century account-books of the Murray Highland estates, an early marriage contract. I was close to deciding that I had found all that I would find – and more than enough to justify a few hours prospecting – when I came upon the richest jewel of all: five more holograph letters of George Washington, again tied together with a shoe-lace.

Ecstatic, I read the letters; to the best of my knowledge, at least two of them and perhaps all had not been reproduced in the definitive edition of Washington's correspondence.

I had to share this momentous discovery with someone. Clutching the Washington papers, I stumbled down the ladder from the loft. An elderly gentleman was in the front hall. He had just set down the telephone and without so much as asking who he was or introducing myself I thrust the Washington letters under his nose. 'Look at these, sir.'

It was then that Lord Dunmore proved himself worthy of the Victoria Cross he had won long ago on the North West Frontier. He took the bundle from me, put on his glasses, glanced at the signatures, then looked at his watch and said, 'Two o'clock and you've had no lunch. Come into the dining-room. I'll have my wife cut you a sandwich. You could do with a glass of claret, I'm sure of it.'

As, suddenly aware of my dishevelled state and of my brashness, I ate the sandwich and drank what I was sure was an excellent wine, Lord Dunmore read through each of the letters then passed it to his wife for her to read. Finally he stacked the letters neatly, pushed them across to me and asked, 'Anything else up there of any use to you?'

Some unsuspected streak of honesty forced me to say that six Washington letters alone would bring a small fortune in the sale-room. He would have none of it, for all the malice those damned Colonials had visited on his ancestor he had always liked Americans. The family papers were not much good to anybody stuck up there in the loft. Would my College like to have the whole litter-heap as some kind of permanent loan? He turned to his wife, 'Permanent loan! Silly phrase, isn't it?' then back to me to ask if I could possibly come back next day to collect the papers. 'You'll need a taxi, perhaps even a van.' Lady Dunmore added that next day she would give me a proper lunch.

I left Cadogan Gardens, found a post office and wrote out a cablegram. The clerk was already counting the words – and it was the longest cable that ever I have sent – when an artful sprite whispered in my ear. I asked to have the form back and changed the name and addressee from Swem to Bryan.

There was something else I must do and suddenly I felt sick. For the first time in months, for hours on end I had not once thought of Jane.

I took a taxi to the Corner House. Jane sat huddled, several empty coffee cups and a book on the table in front of her. She was close to tears and they were not the tears of anger which I expected for keeping her waiting for almost two hours. There was I, she moaned, off furthering my career, off on some fascinating exploit, while she had nothing better to do than forage through bookshops. She pushed her book across the table. It was David Garnett's *Pocahontas*. 'I bought it for you. You might as well have it. Look what happened to her, an American girl married to an Englishman and doomed to live in this godforsaken country. Is that going to be my fate? What about my career? You don't give a damn about me. Let's call the whole thing off.'

I tried to pierce her misery with the news of my miraculous good fortune but she appeared not to be listening. Then suddenly she straightened, smiled, reached for my hand and said, 'I'm sorry, darling, I'm just a little depressed and this place doesn't help. If I've got it right, what you're trying to tell me, it's wonderful.'

All the way to the end of the Piccadilly Line she plied me with questions about my discovery and, as we were walking out of Cockfosters Station, she announced that she had been struck by a brilliant idea. We could go to Williamsburg for our honeymoon, taking the Dunmore Papers with us.

Bryan's reply arrived next morning – the longest telegram that ever I have received. He would come to London to take the chair at a banquet to be given at the Ritz Hotel in honour of the Dunmores on one of three dates. I was to make all the arrangements. There followed a list of some forty names I must invite. It began as I remember with 'American Ambassador Lady Astor' and included at the appropriate point in the scrupulously alphabetical order 'Jane Playter' and ended with the words 'and of course anyone else you think to ask'.

I had never before entered the Ritz, not even through the trade entrance, but a kindly and tactful banqueting manager guided me through the protocol. 'We can arrange, sir, to have invitations engraved for you' – with only the slightest emphasis on the word 'engraved' – and my confidence that all would go well was not shaken until three nights before the banquet, when Jane and I were dining with Bryan – at the Dorchester – he informed me casually that he intended to call on me to give 'our distinguished guests a brief account of the treasure that is now in our care'.

On the afternoon of the banquet, Moyses Stevens delivered to our Cockfosters home an orchid and with it a card 'For Jane, from her elderly admirer John Stewart Bryan'.

That evening a friend drove the two of us and my sisters to Piccadilly. He stopped the car at the corner of Albemarle Street, Bess and Julia got out and from the far side of Arlington Street they watched as we made our way to triumph, Jane as ever *soignée* and me, for once almost worthy of her elegance in tails ordered for me from his London tailor and paid for by President Bryan.

I had not answered the question posed by Swem (later it was established that the Murray boys were indeed enrolled in the College), but I had achieved something much grander. With the acquisition of the Dunmore Papers I had justified my College Fellowship. Letters from Swem, Cogar, others in Williamsburg and press comment from both sides of the Atlantic supported my assumption that this was as my future would always be. Jane too, warmed by the approval she had won from that distinguished gathering for her *chic*, poise, beauty and intelligence, and exhilarated by public attention, appeared to have been cured of her tendency to temperamental outbursts.

Euphoric with success, publicity and with each other, we scarce noticed the rumblings of the impending storm. Even when Bryan arranged to take the Washington letters back with him to Virginia and added that, if war came, I must put all that remained in my bank vault, it did not occur to us that he was doing more than guarding against an unlikely threat. (Eight years would pass before I stood on a New York quayside, trying desperately to explain the contents of a twenty-five-pounder ammunition box to a bemused Irish customs-officer.)

The first eight months of 1939 had been for me so filled with activity and delight that I had given little thought to making purposeful the consequences of my renunciation of pacifism. I had made two half-hearted attempts to join the part-time Services. I went to inspect an RAF

Volunteer Reserve squadron in Hertfordshire and I looked in on the RNVR in Newcastle. I did not like the look of the Squadron Leader and the Lieutenant-Commander did not like me. If war came, so be it, others would take care of my future.

Early in the morning of 1 September Jane and I drove to Newcastle. By midnight we were back in London, summoned at the insistence of Nancy Astor, whose hand I had shaken at the Dunmore banquet, to prepare myself for duties with the American Section of the embryonic Ministry of Information. At eleven o'clock on 3 September, for the second time in my life – the first at my mother's funeral – I saw my father in tears and three days later I wrote two indifferently bad poems, a long letter to John Horn in Canada, a curt note of self-dismissal from a post for which I had not as yet been briefed and, without warning to my family or Jane, went off to enlist.

When I did tell Jane that I had the King's shilling in my pocket she showed no surprise, and even my insistence that this sensational change in my circumstances and prospects must force us to postpone our marriage, she dismissed with infuriating nonchalance. I said that I would almost certainly be dead within the year and that the annual pension for a private soldier's widow would not keep her in cami-knickers and so we must wait to marry until the War was over. She replied that this was a *non sequitur*, which I could not dispute, that if I insisted on getting myself killed she might as well get something out of my idiocy and that if we married soon, say the next day, she would have the benefit of marriage allowance for a whole year before she began to draw her widow's pension. At all events, she added as if that ended all discussion, they could not be stupid enough to keep me for long in the ranks, I would be commissioned and soon I would be a captain, perhaps even a major.

It seemed that the authority accepted as valid at least part of her premise; with expedition such as never again I experienced from the War Office, I was summoned to appear before an Officers Selection Board – in Newcastle. On the road North, over the shrieked protests of my much-abused fiancée and the metallic clangour of my much-abused 1932 Lanchester, I changed tack. England would be bombed, I told Jane, and more than likely invaded. I wanted her in sanctuary until the War was won and we could embark upon our idyllic *après la guerre*. She must return to the States. Her answer was ready: she had committed herself to becoming British, so she must suffer all the adversity and enjoy all the triumphs that war would bring to her adopted countrymen.

The Selection Board was remarkably generous. Despite my brazen, if unpremeditated explanation of my choice of arm in the Service – that I did not like walking – I was told that I had been accepted as a candidate for a commission in the Royal Artillery.

There followed anti-climax but not peace.

I heard nothing from the War Office for a month, but every day and all of every day Jane argued, cajoled, wheedled, even she threatened: if I would not concede an immediate wedding she would throw in her hand and either go back to France or into a convent.

The thought of Jane in Paris disturbed me; I could imagine the effect she would have on lascivious officers on leave from the B.E.F.; but the alternative ultimatum was more menacing. I could not imagine Jane as a nun but whenever she was depressed she considered taking instruction and she knew, as I knew, that Catholicism would raise between us an insurmountable barrier.

When at last I received my first posting, to 122 Officers Training Regiment, Royal Artillery, Jane was joined by a formidable ally, her mother. Wilfully discarding all knowledge of the life-expectancy statistics of second lieutenants in war-time, Jessie Playter argued that my future was now assured, and that Jane and I, so patently in love and so obviously suited to each other, should seize what little we could of happiness, a commodity rare in war-time.

I turned to Jane's father for assurance but he remained diplomatically neutral.

Still I was adamant, still I preened myself on the nobility of my self-denial and still, with images stolen from First War poets ('Oh, what made fatuous sunbeams toil to break earth's sleep at all'), I gave as my reason my prediction, confident and morbid, that I would be killed in action. In truth, since the day of my enlistment I had been confident that I would survive the War (I knew no such certainty from the first time I heard a shot fired to the last) but the premonition which still gripped me, though less dramatic, perhaps more honourable if less likely to persuade, was, even so, telling as argument against marriage. I was convinced that I would be severely wounded, maimed, emasculated or blinded. ('Does it matter? – losing your sight?/ There's such splendid work for the blind. . .') I wanted to spare Jane the trauma, because for a life-time inescapable more painful than widowhood, of being shackled to a half-husband.

I went to Salisbury Plain almost glad to be for a while out of range of the continuous bombardment of pleas, promises and protests fired at me by Jane and Jessie Playter.

In the years that followed, I was told not infrequently by senior officers that they were advising others more senior that my eclectic education made me notably useful for liaison work with United States forces. Only once in all my service – when drivers from the U.S. Fifth Army came from the far side of Italy to fill their water-trucks at the vermouth factory we had captured – did I come close to Americans. Had the Army been less adept in forcing square pegs into round holes, I might have been spared a deal of discomfort and not a little danger.

There was no danger at Larkhill, except the ever-present menace of RTU (Returned to Unit), but through all the War, not even in desert sandstorms or the mud, snow and rain of Italy, was I ever again as uncomfortable as I was in the hastily-constructed camp 'next to Stonehenge'.

There was never a winter as harsh as that first of the War. God, we decided, was on the side of the Axis and so was the War Office. When it did not rain it snowed. For the first five weeks we had no uniforms but sloshed around the camp on paths without duck-boards wearing dungarees and gum-boots. We learnt gun-drill, and eventually gunnery, on Great War eighteen-pounders. The stoves in the huts gave off so little heat that it was possible to sit on them with impunity.

When for the first time we were given passes, I went into Salisbury to a cinema and, so exhausted was I after three weeks of torture, of unaccustomed physical and mental exercise, and so enervated by the warmth that I slept through three showings of the feature-film.

Jane came to Cockfosters to share my first week-end leave. She was more loving than ever and surprisingly indulgent to my black mood, surprisingly sympathetic to my exhausted state. She made but one brief and gentle attempt to persuade me to change my mind and then handed me a letter from her father. She watched me as I read and I sensed that she knew the tenor of its contents. The decision must be ours, wrote Harold Playter, but the Embassy had informed him that space could be made for the families of Foreign Service officers on a ship sailing for New York in two weeks time and, as if giving me one last cause for procrastination, 'Jessie refuses to leave me'.

I dropped the letter to the floor and turned to Jane. She held herself erect as Queen Mary, but her eyes were blank and her face ashen. This, I thought, is how she will look when she is old and, as if she had read my thoughts, she forced a smile, shrugged and said: 'This damn war won't last forever and we're both young.'

So we came to that bench on Waterloo Station.

Jane was gone, I could not forget her but I could no longer see her. I was left to fight alone my battle against isolation and the drudgery and discomfort of Larkhill.

I engaged in my first skirmish on Boxing Day 1939, dancing all evening to Carroll Gibbons with a girl from the FANY, that band of high-toned young women who looked down their aristocratic noses at the plebeian ATS. Her titillating manner, her expensive gown, her good looks: none of these attributes could make me see her as a stand-in for Jane, not even when my receptivity and her friendliness had been fuelled by a generous supply of champagne poured into us by our host, Robert Graves's brother Charles, not even when she told me, as she did with ever-increasing fervour as the evening and our acquaintance progressed, that she owned a coal-mine in Wales.

On that evening I wore, not my rough, shapeless battle-dress, but the evening-dress tailored for me in Savile Row by courtesy of President Bryan. Most of the men on the Savoy dance-floor were similarly dressed, in tails and white tie, which is evidence, if such be needed, of the phoniness of the Phoney War.

On the last night of the year, a night colder even than any I had suffered in Fredericton, I returned to the Plain. Determined to dull my misery I hurled myself into the life of the OCTU. I edited the Camp magazine, wrote lyrics for a review put on by the cadets, went to every show at the Garrison Theatre and to every party to which I could get myself invited. I discovered that I could still enjoy myself and, most surprising discovery of all, that I was beginning to enjoy the training and that I was most nearly contented when applying my mind to the nicely mathematical problems of gunnery. And, as if the elements were susceptible to my spiritual condition, the weather improved.

I wrote daily to Jane, long adoring letters and I suspect that if those letters could now be read in chronological order they would show a steady confidence. For me, RTU was no longer a possibility.

I looked forward to the Passing-Out Parade.

In five months we had been taught to command men and guns in action but in that early Spring of 1940 there was no action anywhere, not so very many trained men and damnably few guns and when I looked forward it was to years in Britain, or perhaps just across the Channel in France, serving as some kind of war-time imitation of a peace-time soldier.

The shame and the glory of Dunkirk and – for me of significance both more immediate and more terrifying – of St Valèry, erased all possibility of pacific ease, but those heroic disasters strengthened the prognosis that I would be based in Britain for a long time to come. Like every man in the Army, I appreciated that we had neither the men nor the equipment to recover the Continent. Optimists predicted 1943 as the year for the assault on Hitler's Europe, realists 1945 or even 1946. I saw myself perhaps taking part in forays, but I had no doubt that, from these away-matches, I would return always to my home-ground. Until that September night when we heard the code-word Cromwell not I nor, I suspect, many of my colleagues were fully convinced that the Germans would invade Britain. Military and political logic demanded it, we talked of invasion, we trained to meet it, as best we could we guarded against it, but complacency induced by nine centuries of island virginity convinced us that rape was improbable.

This sense of existence in limbo, in a time that was neither peace nor war, was intensified when I was posted to 128 (Highland) Field Regiment.

The Regiment was, demonstrably and deservedly, proud of the parenthesis in its title. At the time when I joined, in Montrose on the east coast of Scotland, the strength was still largely composed of Clydesiders and most of the officers had known each other, not merely from evenings together in the drill-hall but as neighbours or as bankers, lawyers, teachers in Glasgow or Greenock. For them service in Montrose was an extended version of participation in the annual Territorial camp with only one sensational difference, and that only for the married men, of whom there were many: when they came off-duty their wives were waiting for them.

We were set to defend a considerable stretch of indefensible Scottish coast-line and, after the fall of France, I spent night after night staring out to sea with such befuddling intensity that several times I saw coming over the horizon the German invasion-fleet and each time I was discomforted by the thought that I could call upon as counter to a landing only a hand-ful of Gunner-riflemen (as already I knew, a contradiction in terms) and two Great War 4.5 howitzers, so utterly devoid of precision that they would have been incapable of landing one round on the *Graf Spee*, even if her captain had obliged by anchoring her two hundred yards offshore. Occasionally we went out on exercises, but we were short of transport – when, after a flurry of postings-out, I was given temporary command of a troop, I was compelled to drive up to my Observation Post in a 1934 Lancia tourer – we were short of fuel, and well-nigh starved of practice-ammunition.

There were, however, compensations. We were billeted in private homes or boarding-houses, we were allowed much free time and Montrose seemed to be unusually well supplied with pretty girls.

I spent most of my spare time either in the bar of the hotel, where sev-eral of the married couples were billeted, or in the temporary home of Arthur and Helen Stobo, Glaswegians who forgave me for being English even before the rest of my officer-colleagues had decided unanimously that Sassenach is not a social disease. I was happy in the Regiment, I liked almost all my fellow-officers, I was encouraged by the readiness with which the men of my troop accepted me as their commander, and I was rendered almost speechless by surprise and delight when the Battery Commander told me that he had recommended that my appointment be confirmed. A captaincy already! Jane was a more efficient prophet than she or I had dared to believe. Given promotion at this rate I could indeed expect a majority before the end of the War. Even so I was disturbed by the unreality of my life; I had not abandoned pacifism just to hide myself away in Scottish military suburbs; and my discontent was turned almost to despair by constant association with contentedly married and comfortably housed couples.

I might have reconciled myself to my state had not Jane's letters revealed, at first by implication but ever more often by overt statement, that she was floundering in a depression. For reasons that she did not explain, she had given up all thought of career in opera and, for reasons that I found inexplicable, she had enrolled in a small liberal-arts college. At first the news of this development made me smile; I could imagine the effect that Jane's poise, her linguistic agility and her Paris frocks would have on a gaggle of Californian hicks fresh out of high-school; and I was not above a sadistic smirk when hints in her letters conjured up images of Jane's elegance at the wrong end of a sorority-sisters paddle; but when, at last, complaint became plea, when she begged of me to find some way to bring her back to Britain, and to marriage, I knew that I must act.

I discussed my problem with the Stobos and with my fellow subalterns; all agreed that I should try. I went to my Battery Commander; he said that his wife was with him in Montrose, so were the wives of several troop commanders, that he could see no reason why I should not enjoy like comfort but that I must ask the CO. Harold Playter's response to my request that he use his official status to further my intentions for his daughter was unexpectedly encouraging; he too had wakened to awareness of Jane's depression, he would write to the Embassy to see if it was possible to find for her a passage back to Britain. But I did not approach the CO. He sent for me.

Colonel Campbell was by general agreement a terror. In the years between the Wars he had built for himself a *persona* which fitted precisely to a conventional civilian's caricature of a certain type of Regular Army officer; steely eyes, steely hair, clipped moustache and clipped voice. On the gun-park and on exercises he was appropriately abrupt and often, as we thought, unreasonable, and when I appeared in his office I feared that I had been summoned to account for my habit of taking my troop out on exercises which invariably took in some church or country-house I wanted to see.

My expectations seemed to be justified. He opened the conversation by giving it as his opinion that I must know more Scottish kirks than any Scotsman, but then he smiled – or it could have been a scowl – and added that he had heard from my Battery Commander that I was thinking of applying for permission to marry and so, though by now she must be an expert on gun-drill it could not be that girl – 'Anita, isn't it?' – who lured Don Troop so often into the forecourt of a castle. Then he smiled again, and this time I was sure that the smile was benevolent, explained at some length and without bowdlerisation, that good order and military discipline was better served by arranging for his officers to have their wives close by and waiting for them in bed, for them to come from military to matrimonial duty rather than leaving them free to disrupt good relations with the civvy population by getting local girls 'in the club'. An American, wasn't she? this little bit of fluff of mine. There was no accounting for taste and he could do nothing to help her across the Atlantic, but I had his blessing and if I managed her re-migration I would have his permission. And when I thanked him, saluted and prepared to leave his office, he asked, with his eyes as near as he could manage to a twinkle, if I thought I could support a wife – 'one of those expensive American wives' – on a captain's pay and marriage-allowance.

The Regiment was moved northwards, – first to Tain and then to *ultima thule*, to a tented camp five miles from John O'Groats.

Events in another world, the Battle of Britain and the first raids on London, were abruptly revealed to me as portents of menace that must soon overtake all Britain when a lone German raider emptied his guns over a Rugby pitch which, but seconds before, had held for me no threat more sinister than the tackling of my opposing centre three-quarter. As I cowered in a ditch pretending to myself that it was sweat drying on my shorts and jersey and not fear that made me shiver, I began to question if it was either wise or charitable to attempt to rescue Jane from the indignities and miseries of her California college.

Harold Playter wrote that he had received 'a curt, sniffy and stuffy response' (his words) to his request. It was, according to the Embassy, inconceivable that a return-passage could be found for a nineteen-year-old girl who had but recently filled one of the few vacancies available to 'non-essential personnel' on a ship going westwards, just because she was 'eager to be married' (the words of the Third Secretary, as quoted to me by Jane's father).

I had lost my beloved Don Troop; Arthur Stobo's battery was camped a dozen miles from Wester Watten; Helen Stobo had gone back to Glasgow; I would not see Jane for five, six, ten years; I was bored with everlasting map-reading exercises and it rained all of every day. I volunteered for service in India.

With unflattering eagerness, the new Colonel endorsed my application and when I went to say good-bye he gave me some profound advice: if I did not own mess-kit I must be sure to take out with me a dinner-jacket, riding-boots and, if I owned such elegancies, also tails and white ties. 'Of course', he added, 'visiting-cards you can have engraved in any cantonment.'

Two days before Christmas I reported to the Depot, bringing with me a cabin-trunk, two suitcases, a bedding-roll, a kit-bag and an ammunition-box full of books. I was equipped for war but I was not spiritually prepared for my first experience of a fire-raid.

On Boxing Day the detachment of 'Gunner Replacement Subalterns' entrained at Woolwich Station and was dragged out of London through sulphurous tunnels and over tracks unknown to peace-time travellers. For the next four years and five months – despite the fact that five weeks later, in Durban, I heard that though the Cathedral had been ringed by burning buildings, St Paul's had been spared – the image of London which remained with me was of St Paul's in flames.

H.M.T. Ormonde, a former Orient liner, had been hurriedly adapted to serve as a troop-ship. In her holds the conversion crews had erected tier upon tier of bunks, mess-halls and sanitary facilities supposedly sufficient for two thousand Other Ranks. They had not touched the First and Cabin Class accommodation, which remained exactly as it was when *Ormonde* had plied the route to Australia. All officers were shown to their quarters – not more than three to a cabin – by white-jacketed stewards who were quick to inform us, with leers, that part of the First Class had been reserved for forty Army nurses.

We were anchored off the Tail of the Bank for four days but the bars were open: gin at 3*d*, whisky at 6*d* a tot. Shore leave was forbidden us; but after more than a year in the Service I was expert in dodging inhibiting regulations. I volunteered to be Ship's Entertainment Officer, predicting that the duties would allow me to escape for all the long voyage ahead of us boredom and the most tiresome duties, Orderly Officer and Officer i/c Anti-Aircraft Detail, and immediately would give me reason and right to go ashore, ostensibly to collect 'comforts' and sports equipment, but actually to dine with my Cousin Betty, who was in Glasgow dancing the lead-role in a pantomime ballet.

My position close to the Ship's Adjutant also gave me prior warning of the arrival of the nurses. This spiced information I shared with Ronnie Whytock, a friend from 128 (Highland) Field, and we were at the head of the gang-plank when the nurses came aboard.

It was not a stimulating sight. Some of the QA's looked old enough to have served at Scutari under Miss Nightingale, most would not have inspired lust in a blind man on a desert island, a handful were possible. Ronnie studied them, dredged from folk-memory the Great War ribaldry 'Officers' remounts', then he changed his mind, decided that even that was unjustified compliment, sighed and grumbled 'Fit only for the knacker's yard'. But there were two who earned full marks from the inspectors, a little blonde and a tall girl with shining black hair, big bright eyes and a figure that denied the repressive authority of a QA's uniform. Ronnie whispered that he was by a year my senior, that he would have the blonde. I conceded his right with alacrity and the tall girl looked from one to the other of us as if, had the Matron not been close by, she would have said 'Bloody lechers!'

Ormonde set course due north. The thermometer dropped below zero as we hugged the coast of Gréenland. Then, as we were told, a hundred miles from the United States we turned south and, close to New Jersey, east and suddenly we were in the Tropics.

At night the heat in our blacked-out cabins was unbearable (and on the troops' decks a fair reconstruction of Dante's Inferno) but on deck it was balmy, few officers and very few nurses slept below, some seemed not to sleep at all.

I was enjoying this cruise at His Majesty's expense. Perhaps on the premise that there is more safety in singularity than in numbers, Pat, the dark girl, an Irish nurse from the London Hospital, had allowed herself to be attached, firmly and demonstrably, to me. I was busy arranging concerts, race-meetings, table-tennis competitions, auditioning and preparing to direct an Old Time Music Hall (with Pat in my tails as Burlington Bertie) and productions of Richard Hughes's one-act play *The Man Born to be Hanged* and Noel Coward's *Red Peppers*. I paid little heed when it was rumoured that, somewhere out of sight, two ships in the convoy had been torpedoed. I was engrossed in preparations for Crossing the Line.

It was essential, we were told by a ship's officer, that we pay tribute to

King Neptune by tossing a virgin into the pool. When I asked the Entertainment Committee to name qualified candidates, all the members sat silent for minutes. Then someone suggested the acidulated Matron-in-Charge but immediately an objection was raised: she was rumoured to be sharing a cabin with the Colonel i/c Troops. I offered Pat as a worthy sacrifice. My colleagues looked sceptical but it was Pat who was our votive offering.

Six days out of Cape Town, salt-water leaked into the fresh-water tanks; it was our patriotic duty to drink beer at breakfast. The beer was free but it was also plebeian; officers from Yeomanry regiments paid five shillings for a jug of Black Velvet.

The convoy came into close order. Swimming, deck- and cabin-games gave way temporarily to a new pastime: watching the excited gyrations of the South African destroyer that had been sent out to escort us.

We anchored off Cape Town early one sparkling morning in February. The view was a glorious cliché, surprising only because it fulfilled with such precision the expectations of a life-time. Table Mountain looked like a table, the soft white clouds like a fine linen tablecloth just about to be spread.

The first ship in the convoy up-anchored and sailed into harbour, followed by a second, a third and a fourth. *Ormonde* was next in line and we were silent, made tense, overcome by that conflict of expectation and sadness which is usual when the close community of a long sea-voyage is about to be shattered. I indulged in a bout of what I can only describe as prescient excitement. I was about to set foot in the country which, romantic fervour out-playing historical accuracy, I claimed as the land of my father.

The ship's engines throbbed. *Ormonde* turned and sailed out to sea.

We were not told, but within an hour we all knew that the four ships detached at Cape Town were going on to Singapore. Yet another hour, and again without announcement, we all knew that we were bound for Durban.

We landed and immediately we were kidnapped. In that moment when we came ashore cars queued at the dockside, their occupants eager to take us to their houses, to their clubs, to the beach or for drives into the country. I had been ashore twice, and each time for twelve or fourteen hours, before I could free myself to call on a South African, a friend from a pre-War Atlantic voyage.

Pat and I slipped the clutching hands of South African hosts and hostesses and went for lunch to one of the best of the many hotels that ringed Durban's fabulous shore-line.

First, we took baths; fresh water a luxury after weeks of bathing in sticky salted liquid; then we ate splendidly and drank too much. I asked for the bill. The grinning Goan waiter told me that it had been paid 'by the gentleman who just left that table in the corner'.

I am, by instinct and by choice, a collector and, for me as for many of my kind, ever eager to show off my latest acquisition to all who can be persuaded to look. I had just that one friend in Durban and Henry Miller had been shown, and had admired dutifully, three of my pre-war prizes, the Mayoress of Stepney, Beridge Leigh-Mallory and Jane. Now I was determined to increase his respect for me as connoisseur and so it was that my constancy to Pat throughout those five memorable days in Durban must stand – *mea culpa, mea maxima culpa* – as memorial to my conceit, and to her generosity.

On our last night in Durban Pat and I went to the beach. We swam in the moonlit sea, dried on my best uniform-shirt, warmed ourselves with a bottle of Van der Hum and then, made tipsy by the moon and the sickly liqueur, we talked our way towards the dawn.

Or rather, I talked and Pat listened. I had not forgotten Jane and Pat knew, for I had told her so a dozen times, that I was determined to marry my American fiancée as soon as I was done with soldiering. *Ergo*, I would never propose to Pat and at all events, though I flattered myself that she was no less happy in our companionship than was I, she had no wish to be married to me. (I added a rationalization in appallingly bad taste; she was a devout Catholic and so would never consent to marriage with a rabidly Protestant agnostic.) But I had come to depend on Pat's company, I relished her quick wit, her independent mind – and her good looks. Such ambiguities as there were, and there were many, could all be set to the account of 'this bloody War'.

Pat nodded, and thereafter was as vocal as was I in continuing the process of rationalization.

Already in Scotland I had been aware of the suspension of reality brought about by the circumstances of war. Now, for the first time but not for the last, I was conscious of the suspension of chronology. Like so many of our contemporaries Pat and I talked frequently of the cheerful days before the War and, even more often, of that wondrous future when we would be out of uniform, at home – and safe – but the only time which was truly ours was the time between peace and peace. It was this, the implacability of the immediate, I reasoned, rather than inherent wickedness which allowed so many of us to justify amorality and this which explained the profundity of many war-time relationships: they were not ephemeral because they were outwith time.

Reason, scrupulous but ineffectual, gave way to *non sequitur*. Neither of us thought of marriage and yet I reverted to that argument against matrimony which I had used so often with Jane: I would be dead before the year was out.

Pat turned on her side, nodded sympathetically and mumbled 'Me too, probably.'

I stared at her. In all my reading, from Homer to Wilfred Owen, the privilege of death in battle had been granted exclusively to men.

I shook myself. 'Nonsense,' I snapped, 'you'll live to be Matron of some gigantic hospital, Gorgon to the shaking probationers and to the consultants that "unconquered virgin" who "freezes her foes to congealed stone".'

Neither of us could know that for once I had read the entrails correctly; Milton was not numbered among Pat's familiars but she caught two words. '"Unconquered virgin!"', she grumbled, 'but you tossed me into the pool when we crossed the Equator.'

Flippancy made impossible further earnest debate. We swam again, dried ourselves on Pat's frock, finished the Van der Hum and went back to the ship.

As *Ormonde* sailed past the end of the harbour-wall, we saw a lone figure, a middle-aged woman holding a Union Jack. Her voice rang out clearly across the water as she sang 'Auld Lang Syne'. It was the last that I ever saw of the land of my father.

Nine weeks after we had left the Clyde we entered Bombay Harbour. The Army, suddenly impatient for the service of its roving subalterns, had sent a Gunner Staff Officer out on the pilot-launch to organize our postings. He asked for volunteers skilled in horsemanship. A half-dozen Yeomanry officers leapt forward but I, who had never ridden anything more mettlesome than a beach-donkey, was posted to Rawalpindi, to the one horsed-regiment left to the British Army in India.

I moved out from lounge to the ship's rail and glowered out at the mysterious East. The coolies shrieking at each other as they hauled trunks and kit-bags out of baggage-holds were scrawny little men as unlike Duleep, Patandi or my Newcastle friends Raggie and Chaudhri as apes are to gods. All that I could see of Bombay was a few ponderous Victorian buildings emerging out of a huddle of hovels and tin sheds. A sour, gangrenous smell assaulted my nostrils. So this was the Gateway to India! All the enthralling images gathered in years of reading vanished in five minutes. And this was the gateway to my future, a future burdened by shame, just because I could not manage a horse, a future in a Regular regiment! I was full of gloom.

Ronnie joined me, as effervescent as I was flat. Since Munich he had been fired by just one ambition, 'to get at those bloody Huns', and now that, like me, he had been assigned to a Regular unit, surely it would not be long before he could fulfil his bloodthirsty aspiration. (In Iraq on V.E. Day Ronnie committed suicide. He had not heard a shot fired in anger.)

Pat came up. She had been ordered to a hospital in Lahore. Perhaps we could suborn the Railway Transport Officer and travel up together on the Bombay Mail.

My dire prognosis of life with a Regular regiment was proved to be miserably accurate by my first months in Rawalpindi. Most of the senior officers had been with the Army in India for years, many even of the more junior were Assam tea-wallahs turned soldier for the duration. I was uneasy with them, I resented their dedication to the conventions of the cantonment, I detested the Wimbledon-in-the-Orient pretensions of their wives and in my mind I excoriated them all, men and women, for what I thought to be their disdain for the people and culture of the Sub-Continent.

Before the Regiment left India for the Middle East, I was given cause to doubt the validity of my contempt and in Iraq and Iran I came to admire the unshakable coolness of the Regulars, their dedication and their care for the men under their command but by then it was too late for me to throw off my cloak of superiority.

Later I served often with Regulars and, for the last two years of the War often in harsh and dangerous circumstances, I worked day and night close to one of them, I discovered humility and both admiration and affection. These men stood tall among their contemporaries and none taller than my Brigadier, Chippy Block. But in my first Regular regiment I remained always an outsider, a critic and therefore criticized, suspicious and consequently suspect.

The Warrant Officers, NCOs and Gunners were, almost all of them, Regulars and many of them with long service in India. I watched them as they swaggered round Rawalpindi and marked their crudely arrogant attitude to 'the wogs' and 'the chi-chis' as even more despicable than the aloofness of their superiors. Even in India I did not question their military efficiency, and in the Middle East I had ample occasion to admire their resilience and their gallantry, but respect never progressed to affection and I never achieved with them the easy relationship which the temporary Gunners or Don Troop had allowed to their palpably temporary officer in those months in Scotland.

There was, however, even in those first months in India rich compensation for disaffection. An Army Command Instruction, a troopship and a railway-warrant had wafted me back in time to the India of the Queen-Empress. In the months which bracketed my twenty-third birthday I saw the Raj as it had been when Kipling worked in Lahore on the *Civil and Military Gazette*. Even the very things I disliked most – the senseless distribution of *engraved* visiting-cards, the cringing servility of the shopkeepers, the heartiness and unabashed exclusiveness of the Club and the silly pomposities of the *memsahibs* – were essential to the experience of living in an anachronism. By the time I returned, in the spring of 1942, the Japanese had bombed Pearl Harbour, India was a theatre-of-war – and the country was full of Americans – and India had been hurled into the twentieth century.

At 'Chastity Mansions', the bungalow which I shared with two other subalterns, we paid, in addition to our three bearers, a whole Trades Union Congress of servants; gardeners, watchmen, sanitary men; and on the not infrequent occasions when we put on a party, we added to their number a supplementary work-force of cousins, brothers and aged uncles.

The terror that had consumed me in the *Ormonde*'s lounge off Bombay proved to be unfounded for the Regiment was in the process of being mechanized. Nevertheless, the horses were still with us and must be groomed, paraded and exercised. I learnt to ride under the callous but effective tutelage of a havildar-major and, in a matter of weeks, I had acquired some competence and inordinate confidence. Also – a rare achievement in one of my generation – I became adept at driving a pair-in-hand and even, on two or three occasions, I took over the brake and six-horse team owned by the Mess.

My criticism of the society in which, whether I liked it or not, I was entrenched was neither so informed or so determined that I could reject the privileges granted me by membership; I was sufficiently sybaritic and, I hope, insufficiently priggish to allow myself to refuse its manifold delights. I swam, drank Gibsons at the Club before Sunday curry-tiffin, I watched cricket, polo and show-jumping on the *maidan*, went for excursions into the Murree Hills and danced the night out at the Club or the Mess. But I was troubled: this, I thought, was not the real India, and I tried to compensate for my assumption of the practices and mores of an officer of the Raj by frequent and, as eventually I discovered, unnecessarily secretive reconnaissance of the bazaars, the temples and the crowded, bustling and smelly streets of Rawalpindi City, by visits to Choudhri in his Punjab village, and, as often as we could arrange it, with Pat as companion, by essays into India's past, to Taxila or to the Shalimar Gardens.

Ten years later, when I was Managing Editor of a small publishing-house with offices over a greengrocer's shop in a shabby alley-way mislaid among the elegancies of St James's, I talked often of my India with a colleague, our accountant, who, like me, had served for part of the War in India. I was impressed by his sympathetic understanding for both the Indians and the British in India and, listening to him as we drank our beers and ate our ploughman's lunches, I concluded that my own comprehension might have been sharpened had I, as he, been posted to the Indian Army and not to what was called 'the British element'. At times he spoke of writing a novel about India but so did almost everyone in publishing dream of writing a novel about something. To my amazement the novel appeared. The book was *Johnny Sahib* and the accountant Paul Scott, eventually the author of *The Raj Quartet* and *Staying On*.

Later still, I returned often to the Sub-Continent, carrying with me in my pocket the keys to UNESCO's coffers and working closely with Indians and Pakistanis and travelling widely in India, Pakistan, Ceylon and even Burma. It was only then that knowledge enriched what had hitherto been instinctive love for India, the love of a boy for some glamorous screen-beauty, but it was also then that I realized that my peregrinations in the war years had endowed me with the capacity to comprehend something about India which would remain forever unrecognized or mysterious to latter-day Englishness. In 1941 I had seen the British in India and the Indians as two distinct societies, in part dependent on each other, often in conflict, on occasion strangely empathetic. Twenty years on I understood that history is immutable and cannot be erased, that British and Indian traditions were for so long intertwined that, whatever the change in social and political circumstance, there remained still integral to the character of India and Indians, Pakistan and Pakistanis, some trace of Britishness that was immediately identifiable to a time-voyager from the days of the Raj.

'East is East and West is West. . .' is a cliché, an over-used quotation, but it is also a quotation that is consistently abused because, taken out-of-context, it is twisted to imply meaning antithetical to Kipling's intention. Read on:

> But there is neither East nor West
> Border, nor Breed, nor Birth
> When two strong men stand face to face, 'tho
> They come from the ends of the earth.

I began my _amour_ with India in 1941, long before I began to understand her complex nature. Neither my enthrallment with this magical land, nor all my absorbing curiosity with her perversities, with those blatant contradictions of beauty and squalor, abundant riches and shameful poverty, could make me forget that I had another love, almost as complex and no less perverse, and she thousands of miles away in California.

There was fighting in North Africa, at sea and in the air, but we fired our guns only at dummy targets on the ranges at Nowshera. I lived a life as near to luxury as I had ever known, many of my fellow-officers had their wives with them. This was war more phony than anything we had known in the winter of 1939 and the spring of 1940. I began to ponder the chances of bringing Jane to India.

I might have done nothing to make my lunatic dream come true had not Jane seized the initiative. I had bullied her out of England, she wrote, by threatening her with German bombs. That was a ploy that could not be repeated. By my own hand and in a 'dream' letter I had made it abundantly clear that Rawalpindi presented no threat to life as powerful as crossing a road in Pomona. She had enquired and had been told that booking a berth to India was no great problem; she would borrow the passage-money from an uncle. Playing at being a memsahib would be great fun – and what clothes should she bring?

It was the most decisive and the shortest letter that ever I received from Jane even with the postscript: 'And if I stay in Pomona I surely will be killed, if not by a car then by boredom. Or else I'll kill myself just to have something exciting to do.'

My interview with the CO was a reprise, not of my interview nine months earlier with Colonel Campbell, but of that meeting long ago in Prebendary Hinde's study in St Mary's Vicarage. I scarcely knew Colonel Scott-Watson, he was not the kind of commanding officer who wastes conversation on subalterns, but he had a reputation for decisiveness. Yet, when I put to him my request for permission to marry he seemed confused, even embarrassed. He fingered his tie, shuffled his papers, licked his moustache, glared at me, smiled at me, patted his hair and then, his mind made up, he pushed himself up, walked round the desk and put his arm round my shoulders. 'Sorry old chap, can't advise it. No, don't protest; no objections to an American girl; good for you. But you'll be wasting your time and hers if you encourage her. Mustn't say more.'!

That night my bearer told me that the Regiment was ordered to Iraq.

7

Gone for a Soldier

Most of the little I know about the campaigns in which I served I have learnt from historians who were still playing with toy-soldiers when I was demobilized. There are among my Army contemporaries some whose memory for the minutiae of battle is precise and infallible, who can recall the exact time of Zero Hour for the crossing of the Sangro, and the name of the subaltern who led the point-platoon when we broke into the Gothic Line. In my school-days for my own amusement I drew detailed sketch-maps of Wellington's manoeuvres at Ciudad Rodrigo and in my student-years, with Gil Crandall as crammer, I qualified myself to go back in time to serve on the staff of Robert E. Lee; in the post-War decades I have written much on ancient battles, on 'Cornwallis's country dance' through Virginia, on Saratoga and Yorktown, and have even contrived from the records a comprehensible and, I hope, accurate record of 617 Squadron's attack on the Ruhr Dams. Nevertheless, from that war which was truly my war, for esoteric reasons, only two campaigns, 'the Great Persian War' and the Greek Civil War, stay with me, remembered in precise detail and as a recoverable narrative. I do not forget – 'Look down and swear by the green of the Spring that you'll never forget' – but that which I remember is not, as in the histories, precisely ordered: a withdrawal here, there a decisive charge, elsewhere some fatuous and fatal error, all reduced to a conflict of shaded or stippled rectangles, the head of an arrow as frugal demonstration of a hundred lost lives. I remember lines of tracer bright against a night sky, the agony of wet feet as I sloshed up to Tac HQ 'somewhere in Italy', the sweet, syrupy taste of Army tea. And I remember the progression of tension, part exhilaration, part terror and part no more than professional curiosity, as I came back into the line after some brief respite; 'Now I'm in range of their heavies, now their mediums can get me, now their field-guns. . .' I remember the eyes of a boy as he pleaded with me to rescind the order sending him out yet again on patrol. I do not remember his name but I do not forget his words. 'If you don't call it off that'll be the end of me' and, even forty years on, I cannot cleanse my mind of the horror of shared premonition that was mine as I shrugged him off, nor shall I ever rid the ear of my conscience of the crash of an exploding land-mine, which threw me off my feet and the boy into eternity.

The soldier at war understands little of strategy, of the movements of corps or divisions, his only concern for logistics is that there should be for his use a sufficiency of food, ammunition, fuel and cigarettes. He is locked into a picture which is framed by the limits of his vision – at most into the limits of his field-glasses – and even that picture vanishes from mind and memory in the moment when he is moved and a new picture takes the place of the old.

In the years between 1941 and 1945, the years when I was truly a fighting-soldier, the events of the day were represented by chinagraph lines on cellophane-covered maps, here, marked in blue, our own troops and there, in red, the enemy. Each map was for its moment more real to me than the sound of tanks, the whine of shells or the clatter of machine-guns; come tomorrow: and the chinagraph lines were erased as easily from my mind as from my map.

The War is seldom for long out of my thoughts. Dates, places, the identification of formations and objectives, all elude me, but not a day goes by and few nights without some sudden and vivid illumination of memory, seemingly unprompted by the world around me. The flash of a gun lights up the marbled grouping of its crew, their names long-since obliterated or never known but their sculpted poses as clear and as certain today as they were forty and more years ago. I hear the tube-train rush of shells overhead, a sound once as familiar and as commonplace as is today the clacking of a typewriter in the next room. I glimpse faces, identifiable but in recall unidentified, held, like portraits in a group-photograph, in the light of a hurricane-lamp as I pull aside a blanket hanging across a broken doorframe. My eyes, for twenty years now the playground of teams of ophthalmic surgeons, are momentarily sharpened to acute night-vision and my stomach lurches as I note the white tapes that mark my way through a minefield and there, at the periphery of sight, his hand reaching for a tape as if he were a drowning swimmer clutching for a life-line, I see a bloated figure in grey. And, in recall almost as pleasurable as it was when first I looked, I catch sight of the tight-skirted rumps of WAACs as they skitter across the terrace of Shepherd's Hotel.

A hundred glimpses come to me daily but consequential recollection eludes me and even the assistance of historians cannot bring entire order to my own service-record.

Memory manufactures its own prophylactics against mental disturbance and thus it is that when I come as recidivist to my own past, to that time before I was allowed a kind of military fulfilment serving with Brigadier Block, I recall, most comfortably and in most detail, those episodes when I was liberated from the routine of battery-shoots and barrage-tables and from the boredom of waiting for action; the weeks, for example, when I was sent as instructor-in-gunnery to the Iraq Royal Military College, those other weeks when, during the abortive Aegean campaign, I was on a Greek island; and, scarcely less hazardous for they were close to mutiny, my time, again as an instructor, with the Congolese troops of the Belgian Army. But the first of my exotic adventures beyond the limits of modern war, my foray among the Arabs of North-West Iraq, is by far the most memorable and in memory the most enjoyable.

The Regiment had been rushed from India to join the small force set to put down Rasheed Ali, but his rebellion was already over when we reached Baghdad. For weeks we loitered, and sweltered. Even at night the thermometer stood at ninety degrees. Temporary release from boredom was granted me because German victories in the Caucasus stirred Tenth Army HQ in Baghdad to the probability that soon we might be forced to defend Iraq. Someone must be sent to plot potential gun-sites in the uncharted area of the country close to the Turkish and Persian borders.

I was ecstatic. I was no hero, I did not resent the postponement of battle, but I found debilitating idleness in the scorching sun and I was growing restless, increasingly discontented with my uncertain status. Now for a few weeks I would have my own independent command, now I was off, the first time to do a job that was genuinely significant to the conduct of the War.

At the head of my tiny expeditionary force – one other officer, one sergeant, my batman, two despatch riders and twelve gunners – I drove to Mosul; all the way on a tarmac road. There I dined with Freya Stark, the Arabist and explorer. I listened enthralled to every word she said, but I thought her too frail and too old to be out there on the edge of nothingness. (Then so frail and then so old that she is still alive when I write these words – and a friend of my son and daughter-in-law!)

In my early boyhood I had often taken to myself a character stolen from some other man's fiction. I did not just imagine myself to be Richard Hannay, for hours at a time I was Richard Hannay. In war-time I found it convenient and comforting to reverse that childish habit, to dismiss my fears and tribulations by convincing myself that I was not me but someone nobler, braver, more talented, more competent, but as a young adult I turned for my adopted persona generally to facts rather than fiction; I was Wilfrith Elstob holding off the last great German offensive in March 1918, or I was Stonewall Jackson or, more often, I was Rupert Brooke. That evening in Mosul, Freya Stark talked about the part played by the Arabs in the Great War. I forgot that in my last year at school I had turned my sophisticated wrath on the blushless, blush-making prose of the *The Mint*, forgot too that my sturdy heterosexuality disqualified me for the part. I knew who I was; this was my country and I was T. E. Lawrence.

Thirty or forty miles out of Mosul something happened to Lieutenant Morpurgo RA that could not have happened to Colonel Lawrence. I lost my way in the desert. I could enter a strong plea in mitigation; a sandstorm had blown up, my sun-compass was valueless if I could not sight the sun and the antique maps I had been given were as useful as might have been one of those plans of the London Underground one saw on every

tube station. Instead I brushed the sand off my goggles and my cravat and
led the convoy in the general direction of a line of low hills that I had seen
in the distance before the sand-devils started their diabolic pirouetting. I
was confident that Tel Afar, the village I had chosen as base, was somewhere beyond those hills.

I drove up a goat-track, turned a bend between two steep cliffs and
there, spread out before me, I saw the valley. I had been starved of greenery since my last summer in England and, after the sun-baked monotony of
the last weeks, the excoriation by sand of the last hours, this was Shangri-
la, the grass greener, the trees shadier, the flowers more plentiful and more
beautiful than any that I had ever seen.

A few hundred yards ahead I saw two figures. I studied them through
my binoculars all the while rehearsing in my mind the gestures I would use
to explain my predicament. Then , suddenly, it occurred to me that both
wore uniform and that one was looking straight back at me – through
binoculars.

I yelled to my driver to turn the truck and as we bumped back as fast as
we could manage on a goat-track I did not need to tell the rest of the convoy to follow my example.

Even now I cannot be sure that those men were dressed in a uniform
that I had never before seen, nor can I claim with undeniable authority
that I led an invasion of Persia when that country was still a neutral.

I groped our way to Tel Afar and selected a camp-site a few hundred
yards outside the village. A crowd gathered, the dogs barked, the children
shrieked and the men jerked their rifles up and down in what I hoped was
a welcoming ritual. Two men elbowed through the audience, one small,
Turkish-looking and dressed in a dark city-suit, the other a tall, dignified
Arab in flowing robes. The small man approached me, his hand outstretched. 'Good evening', he said, 'Welcome to Tel Afar. I am the
schoolmaster. This is Ibrahim, the brother of the Rais.' His English accent
was immaculate. 'You are the Officer?' he gave it a capital O. I nodded
and shook his hand. 'Mohammud Youssis Said Abdulla El Said Wahab,
Rais Tel Afar requests the pleasure of your company.' For all its courteous
formality it was more order than invitation.

Obedient to precepts handed down to me from Western movies, I
ostentatiously handed my revolver to my batman, whispered a few words
to my second-in-command and set off for the village on the arm of the
Rais's brother, the schoolmaster a step behind us and after him twenty
armed men, thirty children and ten dogs.

I was taken to a large house, the only brick-building in Tel Afar. The
head-men sat on benches round the walls of the central hall, gathered as if
for Parliament – or for a trial. The Rais, a huge, handsome, bearded man,
exquisitely-robed, rose from a battered leather club-armchair at the end of
the room, smiled and intoned the magnificent Arabic greeting, '*Salaam
aleikum*'. His hand moved from head, to heart, to hearth.I summoned the

whole of my Arabic vocabulary and all my histrionic skill: '*Aleikum Salaam*', in tones suitably fervent and warm.

The headmen grinned. Behind me the schoolmaster clucked 'good-good-good' and the Rais stepped forward, took my hand in both of his and for my little Arabic returned his little English: 'Good morning. Good afternoon. Good night.'

Then, in all friendliness, the struggle began. From the Rais: a torrent of Arabic and a flurry of gestures, from the parliamentarians: many affirmative nods and from the schoolmaster: 'Here, here.' I waited for translation and as each phrase came to me I tried to answer, courteously but firmly. Why did I insult the Rais by camping outside his village, famed as it was for hospitality? A party of seventeen? There was room in Tel Afar for one hundred and seventy honoured guests. A cook-house? Why cook for ourselves; were not the women of Tel Afar renowned throughout Arabia for the delicacy of their cuisine? (The schoolmaster actually used the word 'cuisine'!) Food? there was no shortage of food in Tel Afar; sheep, eggs, dates, melons, goat's milk, we had but to command and all were ours.

Defeated, I rationalized my acceptance by taking on once more my Lawrence cloak. This was for the furtherance of my purpose to bring the Arabs, wholehearted, to the British cause. I made but one condition: my men would cook their own rations. (It would not have been the Arabs but my own gunners who would have murdered me had I ordered them to eat Arab food!)

For three weeks we lived, happily and comfortably, in Tel Afar, the Other Ranks behaving impeccably. The British soldier is a born diplomat and I doubt that it needed my threat of a firing-party to keep them from so much as looking at a woman. By the time we left, despite the language barrier, each of them was accepted as a member of the household in which he had been billeted. We two officers were accommodated in a surprisingly modern guest-house next to the residence of the Rais.

The Rais made easy our military responsibilities. He detailed villagers to serve as guides, he lent me a horse, furnished with Arab saddle and woven stirrups, and, with Ibrahim as companion, I rode over country that no truck (and no gun-tower) could have managed, making sketch-maps, locating potential defensive-positions – eating in the surrounding hamlets innumerable feasts of dates, figs, melons and roasted sheep. At each feast I was honoured with the prized delicacy, the sheep's eyes.

Every evening five of us gathered at the Rais's table, the Rais, his brother, the schoolmaster and two junior Gunner officers. We talked for hours on end, of the War, of life in England and Iraq, of religion and politics. The talk never limped, nor was it ever reduced to the fatuity which so often comes from conversation through an interpreter. For its liveliness the wit, the intelligence, the curiosity and, more than all else, the sparkling personality of our host was responsible.

At dinner on our last night, for some reason I mentioned T. E.

Lawrence. The response that came to me by way of the schoolmaster was so surprising that I thought that, for once, the interpreter had been fallible. 'Did you say, sir,' I asked, 'that it was last month that you saw Lawrence?'

The Rais bridled. For the only time in the weeks that I was with him I feared he was about to lose his temper. 'Last month, of course, last month. Do you doubt that I can recognize Lawrence Pasha, I who when a boy rode side-by-side with him? I saw him last month in the bazaar.'

I remembered how, in 1935, the news of the death of Lawrence had struck me as a blasphemy, a denial of the immortality of the gods. I could not hold back the next and obvious question: 'Did you speak to him?'

'Of course I did not address him; if Lawrence Pasha wishes converse with me he will ask for it'. Then, as if explaining the mysteries of life to an unsophisticated child, he continued, counting off on his fingers the items in his proposition. 'Your people are in trouble. My people are in trouble. Lawrence is a great leader of your people. Lawrence is a great leader of my people. Whenever the Arabs and the British face danger, Lawrence Pasha is there waiting: waiting to lead our two peoples in glorious alliance against our common enemies.'

There was much ceremony on the day when we left Tel Afar. The Rais initiated me as a blood-brother to all in the village and presented me with an Arab head-dress. Some dim recollection of early reading informed me that in Arab countries a gift given demands a gift returned. I asked the schoolmaster to explain that we had with us nothing worthy of so great a chief. Was there anything among our humble possessions that we could give to him? Even as the words were being translated I wanted to call them back, for I saw in the Rais's eye a glint of covetousness and I feared that he was about to ask for a rifle or a motor-cycle.

The Rais surveyed his feet while the schoolmaster passed his request. 'The Rais begs that you do him the honour of leaving with him as memento to undying friendship your tobacco-pipe.'

The whole village turned out to see us off, even the women, their eyes above their *yashmaks* brisk with curiosity. Mohammed Youssis Said Abdulla El Said Wahab stood upright a yard or so in front of his headmen. I shouted the order to mount and, as we passed the Rais, another order: '15th Field Regiment, Royal Artillery. Eyes Left!' Erect in the open cab of the truck, thumb over the centre of my right eye, palm outstretched and knuckles rigid against an Arab head-dress, I saluted.

The Rais added three inches to his six-foot-three. With as much dignity as any inspecting general, but with a sweep of the arm worthy of RSM Tucker at Larkhill, he returned the salute. My pipe was firmly clenched between his white teeth.

Ten days later I was saluting again, this time dressed almost as regulation demanded, in khaki-drill service-dress, Sam Browne, shirt, tie and red-and-blue forage-cap. I had been ordered to report to General Quinan at GHQ Baghdad.

An elderly major, introduced to me only as an Arab Liaison Officer, was with the GOC. He paid little attention whilst the General looked over my maps but woke to full alertness when General Quinan asked me about our reception by the Arabs. He seemed to find my report humorous for he grinned inanely and at times appeared to be suppressing giggles.

I saluted again, left the office in company with this silly major, accepted his invitation to the GHQ Mess and, after the third gin, dared to ask him what had been so funny in my precise report of events in Tel Afar.

'That's it,' he replied, 'Tel Afar. Do you know when last there were British troops in Tel Afar?'

I did not. No one had briefed me in history.

'Twenty odd years ago. A company of Manchesters. They were massacred, major, captains, subalterns, troops – every damn one of them.'

With no care at all for the censor I wrote for Jane an account, lavish in detail and lush with atmosphere, of my month-long engagement as T. E. Lawrence then, suddenly frugal of time and creative energy, I copied my posturing masterpiece for my family. Acknowledgement from both sources reached me on the same day, some five or six months later. Jane's was unimpressed, indeed grudging: 'You seem to be enjoying yourself hugely dashing about the desert dressed up as Valentino. You should be made to fight your silly war here, California isn't much livelier than Newcastle. In fact it's about as exciting as Gateshead on a wet Sunday. Me, a sophomore! At least now I know why the word "sophomoric". I'm off to Washington if I can fix it. We're bound to be dragged into this mess and I want to see it where things are real.' Bess was much more enthusiastic. 'Dad, Julie, I, we all read your long letter about your warm welcome at Tel Afar (we can't find it on any map).'

Thirty years later, when Bess died, I found my original letter among her papers, the pencilled writing faded almost beyond legibility but the soggy war-time paper still, I swear, smelling of sweat. With others of my letters it was in a file marked economically but precisely 'Jack – War'.

It was after Tel Afar that I was sent to the Summer Camp of the Royal Military College to give to the cadets a crash-course in the science of gunnery. I doubt that the military sophistication of my students was much advanced by my lucid exposition of angle-of-sight, bracketing, meteorreports, wind-factor and beaten-zone and I hope that I contributed nothing to the success of their only bellicose operation, the assassination seventeen years later, of their young king, but I remember that, so nauseated was I by the fetid condition of the camp latrines, that I ate almost nothing all week. Thinking myself qualified by my experience at Tel Afar and this further exposure to the Arabs, I wrote to the giggling Arab Liaison Officer at GHQ asking for his intervention to have me seconded to Glubb Pasha, the World War II successor to T. E. Lawrence.

I never received an answer. Instead I was ordered back to the Regiment, now under canvas at Khanaquin.

Khanaquin was hotter and dustier than any other place in Iraq and I was in the Oil Company swimming-pool, enjoying a brief respite from the appalling conditions, when the news came that we were to invade Persia.

That night I slept in a hole burrowed into the snow high up in the Paitag Pass. I was in Persia, or was it Iran? No one knew.

The 'scarlet majors at the base' had not moved out of the bar of the Semiramis Hotel in Baghdad for long enough to arrange the issue of winter-kit nor had they troubled to provide Aizleforce with air-cover or anti-aircraft guns and we were miserably aware that, pinned as we were between sheer cliffs, we were easy targets even for Persian bomb-aimers. The Regiment gun-towers had stuttered their way up the steep roads, the tanks of the squadron we were destined to support had failed the ascent, which we thought no great disaster for the armour-plating on their antique Mark VIIs would not have withstood an arrow, and as offensive armament each tank had nothing more devastating than one Vickers machine-gun.

Aizleforce was in fact approximately one armoured brigade *sans* armour, and Intelligence passed down the unconsoling information that the Persians were moving against us an Army corps lavishly equipped with up-to-date tanks and 108s (guns which outranged ours) recently acquired from Czechoslovakia.

The news that an Indian brigade had landed at Abadan added little to our ease-of-mind; Abadan was hundreds of miles from the place where we were huddled. We doubted that we would survive the effects of frost-bite and battle with an Army corps for long enough to permit us to join up with the Russians, though we were encouraged by the rumour that our allies had in the field seven divisions and several bomber- and fighter-squadrons.

At the time we did not know that the Russian army in Persia was largely made up of recent conscripts and that the pilots flying Russian planes were, most of them, unblooded and half-trained. Had we been fully-informed about their state of readiness for battle, it is unlikely that the revelation could have added greatly to our dispirited condition for we had all served long enough to have heard – and generally to accept as valid – the military dictum that for training fighting-men three days in action is worth three months on manoeuvres.

However, the presence of the Russians somewhere, however far off, in our campaign-area did at least reveal to us the reason for the invasion. We accepted the cause for war passed to us from on high, that we were there to give teeth to the ultimatum served on the Shah by the Allies, that he must expel the hundreds of Germans masquerading as technicians all over his country. It could even be valid but we perceived a more potent reason; Aizleforce, the Indians and the Russians were all in Persia to open up a supply-route to the hard-pressed Russian armies facing the Wehrmacht; and this perception was our only consolation. At last we were engaged in activities of major con-sequence in the war-effort.

Next morning we moved up to the plateau of Gilan and morale soared.

The sun, so much more benevolent than anything we had known in Iraq or in the hot weather of India, pasture-land, gently flowing streams, trees, florid flower-beds, even the villagers in their costermonger's caps moving among us selling wine and fruit: all combined to convince us that we were fortunate to be here. This was almost another England. The green, rolling landscape and the pellucid air reminded me of the South Downs, of that other Kipling, the man of Sussex, of Belloc and of my own Blunden. Persia was a country worth a battle or two.

And at Gilan we fought our first and only battle of the Great Persian War.

At some time in the inter-war period, some Staff College pundit must have pronounced that, to compensate for the lack of the Gunner Staff which is always present with Division or Corps, any independent and composite formation must have an artillery officer attached to its headquarters. Accordingly I was sent off to Aizleforce Advanced HQ and so it was that I went into my first action in the Middle East bereft of all familiar companions except my driver and a signaller.

The staff at Advanced HQ made no secret of the fact that they did not know what to do with me and had no intention of finding out, so with my driver and my signaller I walked off a few hundred yards and established my own Observation Post. I discovered later that I had seen more of the Battle of Gilan than anyone else in the Regiment. I watched as the Persian infantry advanced, hordes of them it seemed, moving forward platoon by platoon in line abreast as if to the instructions of some eighteenth century drill-book. They were but a few hundred yards from where I lay when, somewhere to my left, a machine-gun opened fire. The horde became a rabble, men scattered in every direction except forward, most took off smartly towards the sanctuary of the distant hills.

High in the lenses of my binoculars I glimpsed an irrelevance: spurts of dust. I re-focused but took seconds to convince myself that what I saw was not a squadron of tanks but a procession of large saloon-cars, some blue, some red, one dun-coloured, one white, all sleek as if fresh from the motor-show.

The procession halted. I concentrated on the first car. The driver dismounted and, with a gesture that would not have disgraced the Savoy doorman, flung wide the rear door. Legs appeared and I could see the sparkle of highly polished riding-boots followed by sharply-tailored breeches and a tunic buttoned to the neck. All the cars had stopped and all disgorged similar tailor's dummies. They formed a group, the chorus-line from a Lehar operetta.

I estimated the range, reminded myself that I was detached from the Regiment, wondered if even so I should pass through fire-orders and then I heard a drum-beat in the distance. Five seconds, another thud, then another and another. Gun fire! I observed the fall of shells and for a moment I was riled: either the gun-layers in T/R Battery were damnably inefficient or else one of the Forward Observation Officers had chosen to ignore the instruction, which had come to Gilan all the way from Whitehall, that we were not to risk inflicting casualties on the enemy unless 'casualties among our troops are imminent'. All four rounds had landed precisely on target.

It was as if I was looking at stills from a cheap one-reeler: a tangle of metal, all that was left of a blue Buick, the white car in flames, another car reared up like one of the San Marco horses; and then the projector jerked back to life and I began to laugh. This was indeed a one-reeler, a Ruritanian comedy performed by the Keystone Cops. Two of the tailor's dummies were running, as fast as their riding boots and breeches would allow, towards distant Teheran and as I watched the bullets from one of our machine-guns, mischievously accurate, spat dust from the ground immediately behind their heels. The dun-coloured Mercedes skittered through a tight half-circle and sped away, one door still open and flapping like a sail from a shattered mast. A red car bounced drunkenly across the ground, slowed and stopped. Two figures tumbled out and flung themselves onto the running-board of the Mercedes. One lost his grip, fell, picked himself up and ran. The other was still clinging to the Mercedes when it disappeared into the hills.

I did not stop laughing when I heard a rushing sound overhead. I could not stop laughing even when twigs began to fall all around me but I came to my senses when a shell exploded not fifty yards from where I lay.

My signaller grabbed my arm and pointed. Far out to the right there was movement. Smoke and dust obscured my view but I dismissed as inconceivable what I thought I saw. I looked again and it was still inconceivable – but true. No one would believe me but even so it must be reported. Sadly one of our O.P.s had seen it too and so I was denied the distinction of being in all history the last Gunner Officer to give the order 'Target: cavalry'. Four shells bracketed the target neatly and what would have been the last cavalry charge against the British Army never materialized.

The Great Persian War was over and I felt guilty. Not for a moment had I been conscious of any of the feelings that my reading had taught me should have been mine in action, not fear, not exhilaration, not even compassion for those helpless Persian conscripts. But for the intrusion of farce, it was all for me very much as it had been when I went with my father to the panorama at Waterloo.

Even so, I would have my tale prepared for telling and retelling. I sent off my driver and signaller in the truck. I would walk back to the Regiment. I skipped and slithered my way across a little valley and almost I fell over a khaki-clad figure, asleep face downward under a tree. Plush with my recent military prowess I was affronted. He must have skulked away from his unit. Angrily I set my foot against his side and rolled him over. A face glared up at the darkening sky, the red hair topped by a hideous red skull-cap, the shirt, black with congealed blood, shivered with the movement of a horde of bloated insects. For a moment, ludicrously, I thought of Thackeray, of George Osborne dead on the field of Waterloo.

I could not stop myself. I began to sob and then, having first looked round to see if there was anyone watching, I leant against the tree and puked.

Two days later we were at Kermanshah. The Russians, we were told, had halted somewhere equidistant from Teheran. They moved closer to the capital. We moved to Hamadan. The Russians entered Teheran and so did we.

For a few days, until their political commissars took over, we fraternized with our allies and for all the three weeks that we were in Teheran we revelled in the illusion that we were back in Europe, an illusion supported by Riza Shah's follies. There was an opera-house with no company and scant foundations; a magnificent railway station but no trains; our Regimental Mess was in the Persian Army Officers Club, a building so ostentatious that by comparison the Depot Mess at Woolwich was like a NAAFI canteen. The Shah had imported a battalion of Hungarian hostesses to service the night-clubs – and the brothels. There were delicatessens owned by German Jews, the vodka was excellent, cigarettes good and cheap, caviare almost free.

At the European Club we danced each evening with the wives of the resident European community lent to us by their husbands who stayed in the bar buying us drinks as tokens of gratitude for our heroic endeavours in saving their throats from Persian knives.

At the end of the third halcyon week I was handed a signal ordering me to proceed immediately to Eritrea.

8

Chianti in Africa

At the time I did not question why it was me who was sent scurrying over two thousand miles, to take on an assignment which could have been undertaken by almost any one of the many War Substantive captains who were even then rotting in Middle East depots. I was neither elated nor perturbed. I had no wish to get myself killed and I was not displeased to be freed for a spell from that sense of not belonging which oppressed me when I was with the Regiment, but I was conscious of some dismay that yet again I was to be distanced from the business of war for which I had been trained. Even so this was promotion, and a chance to satisfy my curiosity about strange places. The demons who then controlled my fate were at all events unchallengeable. I shrugged and packed.

I travelled by unit truck from Teheran to Baghdad, across the desert by Nairn bus to Haifa, in the car of a senior naval officer to the Canal, on to Cairo again by truck and on by Nile-steamer, train and truck to Keren and so eventually to Asmara, there to luxuriate for three months.

I was in Eritrea and, as we were told time and time again, Eritrea was a province of Abyssinia which we now call Ethiopia. Yet today when it enters into our consciousness almost daily with sad stories of disease, drought, famine and persecution, the word Ethiopia, even the word Abyssinia, springs no reminiscent recognition unless it be of *Prester John* and the headlines blasted by Mussolini's bombers.

In all the time I was in Eritrea I met but one Abyssinian, a tousled youth wearing what I took to be a Guards bandsman's short grey cloak, and from my conversation with Haile Selassie's son I can recall not one word. Abyssinia was for me another country and in Abyssinia another war. News from that front filtered through to us like despatches from the Round Table and even the enemy there seemed bent on removing Abyssinia out of our reality into a vanished century. What consonance could there be between us and an army commanded by a duke? Dukes had been mustered out of all armies after Waterloo. Abyssinia was for us a wild, mystic country where wild, mystic men roamed and roared.

Orde Wingate, their bandit leader, I had met once but I could hardly credit that the scruffy, topeed face I saw occasionally in home-town newspapers, the *Egyptian Gazette* and the *Egyptian Mail* sent to us with crates of cigarettes and bully-beef from Cairo, was the face of the shy, immaculately-tailored Gunner colonel with whom I had talked poetry on a Mess guest-night. Boustead Bey had come down to us from the hills and he became my friend. I had known something of his story even before the War, of how he was the only man alive who had both the King's Pardon and the King's Commission, for his was a name often mentioned in the home of the widow of that other great man of Everest, George Leigh-Mallory, but biographical knowledge was not sufficient to persuade me to associate high adventure with the quiet, affable colonel who, almost nightly, in his Sudan Defence Force Mess, shared with me his whisky-bottle and conversation about cricket and books.

Abyssinia, Ethiopia, call it what one chooses, was to me remote, outside my cognisance, and so it remains to this day. Eritrea was for a while my country and yet the Eritrea of the Eritreans today, so often the subject of press comment, means nothing to me. In all the vivid clips of memory that stay with me from 1941 there is present but one Eritrean, a small goat-boy watching enviously as, with another officer and two pretty nurses, Jean Lindsay and Flora Macdonald (her name was not Flora but Flora inevitably she was), I unpacked a picnic-hamper; all that holds me in community with the Eritrean freedom-fighters is that, even after almost half-a-century, still I refuse to recognize their country as part of the dominion once ruled by the Lion of Judah.

In 1941 Eritrea was a country and that country ours. Ours and the Italians'! The Eritrea I knew had been Italian long before the War, long even before Mussolini's successors gave political authority to social fact. It remained perversely Italian even after we had fought our way up the harsh, rocky slopes at Keren. This was Europe in Africa, Italy under a tropical sky, and for that a blessed relief from the sand, the grubby towns and the stinking bazaars which, those few days in Teheran apart, I had come to accept as my environment. Asmara was in fact by two years the first Italian city I ever saw.

The upper-class was Italian; so were the garage-hands, the shopkeepers and the waiters in the Italian restaurants. There was an Italian brothel offering the services of Italian girls and an Italian cinema showing pre-war Italian films. There was an Italian slum, on the far side of town from the elegant quarter where I had my self-ordained luxurious three-roomed flat in a villa, like all others in that district, set in a scrupulously-tended garden well back from the tree-lined boulevard. Each morning at ten minutes to eight I walked over to my car. My Italian chauffeur held open the door. I said 'Good morning' to the Italian lawyer from the flat below, who was just leaving in his chauffeur-driven Lancia, waved to the Italian doctor in the next villa, and left for the office.

By custom – or it could have been by regulation – those brief greetings and dealings with shopkeepers and waiters were my only social contact with my neighbours or with any civilian Italian.

With those other Italians, the hundreds in the prisoner-of-war camp, our relationship was ambiguous. We did not despise them; 'There but for the grace of Wavell and Slim go I'; but we held over them the gift of patronage. If it served to enhance the ease of our lives, we could arrange for any one of them the illusion of liberty and there was represented in that cage almost every skill that a marvellously versatile nation could offer as support to our comfort: barbers from every city in Italy and from many in the United States, a tailor who boasted that, before the war, he had worked only for Count Ciano, cabinet-makers, mechanics, watchmakers, even two portrait-painters. At the Officers' Club, in what had been the Italian Governor's Palace, we danced to a band led by a violinist from the orchestra-pit at La Scala. My Italian prisoner-of-war batman was a genius with a cocktail-shaker, his cunning he had perfected behind the bar in New York's 400 Club. There were but five of us in what we liked to call the Active Service Mess, five charged with the defence of Eritrea against the slim possibility that the Italians came back at us across fifteen hundred miles of desert. Our meals were prepared for us by a master-chef from an Italian Atlantic liner.

We had our enemies, but they were not our Italian prisoners, not our Italian neighbours and certainly not the Eritreans. All the animosity that was in us we reserved for our compatriots, the civilians-in-uniform of OETA, Occupied Enemy Territory Administration. Many out-ranked us; the Chief Sanitary Inspector was a major, the Superintendent of Posts, a full colonel (or so we told each other); but, with the overt approval of our own commander – Archie Douglas, a Rifle Brigade colonel recovering from wounds suffered in the Desert – we conceded to no one in OETA any of the customary military courtesies. By our accounting, OETA officers spent their days operating the black market, their nights in bed with Italian girls, the wives of our brother-enemies in North Africa.

The responsibilities allotted to me by my status as Operations Staff Officer I carried out dutifully but without energy or enthusiasm. We had available to us as guardians against the unthinkable only one battalion of the Welch Regiment, two companies of half-trained infantry from one of India's princely states, and the reinforcement sent to us out of Rider Haggard, Boustead Bey's Sudan Defence Force. No guns. No armoured cars. No tanks. No air cover. For this meagre force I dreamed up field-exercises, the battle-order handsomely strengthened from my imagination. I reconnoitred the slopes of Keren for it was there, where so nearly the Italians had held us, that in our turn we must stop an Italian invasion. Occasionally I flew in my little reconnaissance plane from the clear, cool air of Asmara down to the Red Sea, into the hell-hole of Massawa, there to drink pink gins with the Naval Staff Officer, who had at his disposal, as I remember it, two small armed-merchantmen and a few motor launches. I consoled myself and my mess-companions for our impoverished condition with a variant of the antique Army jest: 'If Mussolini and Hitler do decide to retake Eritrea we can hurl them back by sheer force of numbers; we can turn out OETA.' But most of my ingenuity I gave to supporting my four colleagues towards their prime objective, to trapping OETA officers into courts-martial.

Deprived though we were of military might, short though we were in the privileges of rank, we had one powerful ally in our skirmishes with OETA, one irresistible support to our arrogance: we had under our command 54th General Hospital and in that hospital an array of handsome nurses. Army nurses are sensitive to the subtleties of military protocol; it took more than a colonel's rank-badges to persuade any of them to dine, dance or dally with an officer from OETA. That they left to the Italian girls.

Only once, on the morning of 8 December 1941, did I wake to any thought that great events far away from the Asmara Officers' Club could have consequence for me. Then, when news came of the Japanese attack on Pearl Harbour, I knew a sense of relief. My other country, the United States, was relieved of the guilt of neutrality. Not long before I had received a letter from John Stewart Bryan: 'If the US doesn't get into this war soon,' he had written, 'Virginia will.' On 8 December I wrote to him congratulating him on his achievement, and to Jane a long letter with the sentimental superscription 'Dearest Ally'.

The end of my placid Eritrean episode came to me with no more logic than had its beginning. A signal from Cairo: my Italian batman packed my bedding-roll, I shook his hand and promised to meet him in Verona, after the War. I collected a travel-warrant, said goodbye to Jean, to my colleagues and my driver and set off to find my new regiment, somewhere west of Alexandria.

I was in the Desert, I was in the War but not for long. I had hardly mastered the names of the Number Ones on my newly-acquired guns before I was trundled back to Egypt in an ambulance.

I had no wish to be buried, for months, years, perhaps for the duration, waiting for my dossier to come to the top of the mountain of files of unattached officers and I was by that time sufficiently versed in the ways of the Adjutant-General's department to know that even in the Army one can at times be master of one's own fate. As soon as I was convalescent I limped into GHQ and asked for a posting.

The Deputy Assistant Military Secretary read my record, raised his eyebrows and informed me that I had twice been recommended for Staff training. The lists were full for the Staff College and the Junior Staff School. I might have to wait for months for a place. I knew that a few British officers had been sent to the United States Staff College and Leavenworth was many thousands of miles closer to Washington D.C. – and Jane – than Haifa or Sarafand. I was, I argued, by my American education peculiarly qualified for liaison work with the American forces. DAMS looked again at my papers, nodded and posted me on temporary attachment to Allied Liaison Staff which had its offices just round the corner from GHQ and which dealt with almost every Allied army except the American.

Many envied me my succession of short-term and generally interesting assignments. I was a captain on Staff pay; Asmara, Cairo, Ismailia, Beyrouth were all places where I could indulge my sybaritic enthusiasms; and the Staff School at Sarafand, more like a university than an Army unit, gave me intellectual exercise such as I had not enjoyed since my senior year in College. Only when I was with Force 292 was there even the slimmest possibility of danger, and because the operation which we plotted so hopefully – landings on the Aegean Islands – was hideously successful in satisfying Whitehall intentions for us, that we relieve pressure on the Allied assault on Sicily by bringing down upon our little force the fury of German bomber-squadrons diverted from Norway, even that danger was short-lived.

Part of me was content to be a perpetual twelfth man, versatile and at short notice reasonably competent in a variety of roles, but I was again plagued by a sense of remoteness. I had seen enough of the harsher realities of war to know that I wanted no more shells, bullets or land-mines and yet I was dissatisfied with my lot. Since I had left Scotland I had travelled widely in countries which in all my life I could never have seen had there been no war; I had proved, at least to my own satisfaction and apparently to the Army's, that I could manage tasks which before the War I and most who knew me would have dismissed as far beyond my competence; but I had not yet convinced myself by continuous performance that I was capable of meeting the demands of real soldiering, that I had yet fulfilled the purposes which had been mine when I volunteered. Had I remained where I had been placed in September 1939, in Information Services, my contribution to winning the War must have been far greater than so far it had been in the Army.

In Scotland I had experienced the comfort of assimilation into a close society, an extension of the sodality which I had enjoyed at C.H. and at William and Mary. From that experience I had learnt that this was a benefit I could draw from life in the Army. But in India, Iraq, Iran and Eritrea, as still in my foot-loose days in the Middle East, the patterns of my existence were anything but communal, always I was conscious of being a spare number. I had many acquaintances but very few intimates. (It is of some significance to the perceptiveness of my assessment of my situation that from my Army associates of that time only two remained as friends after the War: Terence McMeekin, a fiery Manxman, my immediate superior at Force 292 HQ and later a knight, a lieutenant-general and Steward of the Tower of London, and Rajadurai Rogers, in Asmara a corporal-clerk.)

The War was passing me by and so in a sense was the Army.

Cairo, in which I returned again and again in those months, symbolized on a larger scale what was happening to me. When I had seen the city first, on my way from Teheran to Keren, it had been the capital of our known world. Now the role of history-maker had passed to the other end of the Mediterranean and Cairo was left to play out an imitation of its former glory.

Even so, Cairo was no bad place to make the best of a bad job. In Cairo the only danger I found was that I might fall victim to the uninhibited advances of my landlady, a White Russian who spoke no English, whose French was worse than mine and who was old enough to be my mother. Even that risk vanished when 54th General Hospital was moved from Eritrea into Egypt, for thereafter I made no secret of the fact that much of my ample spare time must be dedicated to Jean Lindsay, a Scot from Northampton, quick-witted, intelligent, delectably nubile, with but one disconcerting habit: her manner of meeting my pomposities and arrogancies by putting out her tongue with on its tip her one false tooth.

Convinced as I was in those months that my military career was, to all intents, at an end, I set myself to the vocation which I had boasted as mine since I was seven years old and it was in Cairo that, at last, I became a professional writer.

I suborned Larry Babcock, the war correspondent of *Fortune* whom I had met first on the road to Teheran, to introduce me to the editor of one of Cairo's two English-language newspapers and Larry, who had read not one word written by me, performed his role as intermediary with such enthusiasm that I was commissioned to review for the paper such theatrical performance and concerts as were available to Cairo audiences.

It was a more propitious beginning than I would have dared to assume. Noel Coward, Josephine Baker, Gabrielle Brune, Avril Angers and Alice Delysia came to Cairo during my brief regime: I not only reviewed their performance, I met them all and I have still in my archives a photograph which proves that once I showed the Pyramids to Victoria Hopper. Hugo Rignold conducted regularly at Music for All. There were plays staged with professional competence by Service groups.

Writing brittle notices for the *Egyptian Mail* delighted me but did not satisfy entirely my wish to make myself a man of letters. I resolved to produce an anthology of Middle East Forces writing.

I turned first for advice to two literary Old Blues. Keith Douglas was cool; Keith was always cool, but he promised me a poem and promised also to design the cover. Pip Youngman Carter, now moved to Cairo from Baghdad, looked at me superciliously through his monocle, offered me the backing of *Soldier* magazine and took me to lunch at the Turf Club.

I was advised that the Dean of the American University in Cairo held the keys to all doors that opened upon the esoteric culture of English-speaking military expatriates in Egypt. It was for me the most fortunate advice that ever I received in all the time I was in the Middle East.

Worth Howard and his wife Muriel, a concert pianist, merit a place in the history of the war in the Middle East which has never been granted them. Before the United States entered the War they had already contributed much to the ease of spirit of men and women whose need for entertainment and relaxation could not be satisfied by the wrigglings of the belly-dancers at Dolls' or even by the well-intentioned efforts of ENSA. After Pearl Harbour, Worth devoted much of his time and rare skill as an organiser to fostering Music for All as a civilized refuge from the barbarity of war and of the inhibitions and prohibitions of Service life, as a civilized club where all, irrespective of nation or rank, could enjoy quiet, comfort and the solace of good music. To the privileged many, Worth and Muriel conceded an extension of these benefits. They gave to us something which most of us had not known for years, hours in a home. Every Friday afternoon they held open house at their home in Maadi, one of Cairo's more elegant suburbs. Every Friday afternoon house and garden were filled with guests, British, Americans, New Zealanders, brigadiers and privates, sergeants and colonels.

I cannot tell how many from the Middle East forces owed to the Howards the preservation of their sanity, morale and the consoling sense that there existed in the world still some civilized values. I can only give as statistical evidence to freshly-remembered gratitude that when, several years after the War, the Howards came to London seventy ex-Service men and women came from all over Britain to the party my wife and I gave in their honour; I do not doubt that had they gone to Chicago or Wellington, to Oshkosh or Wagga-Wagga, the response would have been no less eager.

My meeting with the Howards was even more consequential. Their Maadi house became my Cairo home. There I went whenever I felt dispirited and often when I did not. My one Cairo Christmas – a season which makes even the most hard-bitten aware of loneliness – I spent at Maadi and with me Colin Chivers, my school-days' friend. When I had given up my digs with the White Russian terror, always when I returned from an excursion into battle or from some arduous trip into the desert, it was to Maadi that I returned immediately for a hot bath, for the efficient ministrations of the Howards' *saffragi*, Mohammed, for the laundering of my filthy uniform, for a bed with clean sheets, for pancakes and maple syrup at breakfast and for hours of peace playing with their daughter Kathy or listening to Muriel at the piano. The friendship of the Howards gave me consolation for all my discontents and it endured and was extended after the War to take in Muriel's brother, Lloyd Sprague, his wife Iva and their family and thus opened to me as almost a second American home-town, Corning, New York, the hometown also of Steuben Glass and Pyrex.

Worth encouraged my anthology project. Nothing came of it; before I was ready to look for a publisher I was moved yet again, and this time definitively out of the Middle East, and all that I can boast for it even retrospectively is that I had accepted as worthy of publication the early work of authors, then unknown, who later achieved eminence.

It was, however, the preparation of that anthology which prodded me into literary activity more appropriate to what I thought to be my calling than extravagantly sophisticated contributions to the Arts page of the *Egyptian Mail*. I was determined to represent myself in *Middle East Writing* and to that end I wrote a short story, in almost every detail autobiographical.

This I showed to Worth, who praised it without reservation. Forty-two years later his opinion was confirmed by higher authority when, as part of the celebration of the fiftieth anniversary of Penguin Books, John Lehmann and Roy Fuller published a selection from the ten glittering years of *Penguin New Writing* and there was I, flattered and humbled, in the company of Eliot, Pasternak, Lorca, Auden, Graham Greene, Orwell, Capetanakis and many another of the acknowledged grandees.

Immediately, and not with any intention to demonstrate my literary skill but rather as a frugal and uncensorable means of communicating my recent experiences, I copied my story to my sisters and to Jane and filed away the original for use in the Middle East anthology. 'The Pipes' might well have been the last short story that ever I wrote had it not been that, within weeks of its composition, I suffered an experience far more shattering and in its consequence far more enduring than going up on a landmine.

For two, perhaps three, months I had heard nothing from Jane. Though hitherto she had been a dutiful and frequent correspondent, at first I was not greatly concerned; ships carrying mail across the Atlantic and out to the Middle East were only too often torpedoed and we had no faith in Army Postal Services; but eventually I sent off a cable. Next day I received Jane's reply: 'All OK letter follows love Jane.'

No letter followed until the disastrous campaign in the Aegean Islands was over and then it came not from Jane but from her father. It was the letter of a man ashamed of what he must write and deeply conscious of the pain his words must cause. Jane was married and had been married already for six months, long before her reassuring cable and, as I calculated, some weeks before she had written to me her last customarily loving letter.

In my years overseas I had read many dismissal-notices, served upon my friends and my subordinates by welshing girl-friends and wives, but never before had I heard of a 'Dear John' written by the culprit's father.

Even so, at first reading, my reaction to Harold Playter's letter was petulance. In Iran, Iraq, and Egypt I had ordered from local silversmiths several small pieces and had had engraved on them a monogram; J.M. would serve for both Jack and Jane Morpurgo. All had gone to Jane. And she was now Mrs John McCormick.

I put the letter in my pocket, determined not to read it again until I was among friends. An orderly handed me a signal. I was posted out of Middle East Forces to serve on the headquarters' staff of 139 Infantry Brigade in 46

Division at present in Italy. I would not have cared if I had been ordered to join the Chindits fighting behind the Japanese lines in Burma.

In the Howards' garden I read the letter over and over again. Then I stared at trees, grass and flowers and saw nothing. 'After the war', the soldier's one sure hold upon sanity, had been snatched from me. Bereft of that charter for eventual happiness I could, I would, cut short my future. I would see to it that I fulfilled my prophecy, for months forgotten, that I would not live to see the end of the War.

Worth counselled me. 'Write it out of your system', he urged. 'You need something else of your own for your anthology. Here's a theme ready-made. What happened to you has happened to thousands like you. Write for them – and for yourself.'

I lay on my bed and began to fashion a short story. It was not yet truly my own but in it Jane was no longer Zuleika. Now she was Daisy Miller, her artificial world

> redolent of orchids. . . and orchestras which set the rhythm of the year, summing up the sadness and suggestiveness of life in new tunes. . . something within her was crying for a decision. She wanted her life shaped now, immediately, and the decision must be made by some force. . . of love, of money, of unquestionable practicality. . . that was close at hand.

Jane had found her Tom Buchanan, her John McCormick, and I saw him clear, flabbily handsome, with sleek greased hair, and gold tooth, wearing a spider-waisted blue jacket, a bright green tie alive with vicious red snakes, and brown-and-white co-respondent's shoes.

'Letter at Dawn', a melodramatic salve for despair and self-pity, was published a year after 'The Pipes' and I did not see it in print until I was safely back in England. Neither story would have found an accommodating editor had not my sister Julia ignored my instruction that the manuscripts were intended for an audience no larger than the family but, as it was 'The Pipes' which opened the door into the entrance lobby to my career with Penguin, and so eventually to almost all developments in my professional career, and it was the very act of following Worth's advice to 'write out' my anguish which burst the barrier of timidity which had hitherto made me nothing more than a private writer. In the months that followed, even though I was hectically engaged in area reconnaissance, writing operation orders and almost hourly in the battle-zone, I poured out verse, stories, reportage – and almost all found a publisher.

So it is that, if I owe nothing else to Jane, it stands to her credit or discredit that after my false start with the *Egyptian Mail*, I became at last a professional writer.

Jessie Playter foiled my one attempt to take revenge by refusing to pass on 'Letter at Dawn', but, still long after the War, I could not dismiss Jane from memory and at times her shadow dimmed the brightness of my marriage. Whenever I was in the States, I rehearsed the abuse I would hurl at her if we chanced to meet. We never did, but then, thirty years after I had read her father's letter, came the hideous sequel.

A chance remark made in the Senior Common Room of the University of Leeds by a visiting American dignitary gave me the news that Jane's mother was still alive and, eventually, her address. On impulse I wrote and back came a letter, warm and gossipy, but with not a word about Jane. If ever I was near St Augustine I must arrange to call in.

When next we were in America I left my poor wife to suffer the tawdry pleasures of Miami Beach and took a plane for Jacksonville. Jane's sister Patsy met me at the airport and on the forty-mile drive to St Augustine, after several hesitant starts, she told her sad tale.

Some time in 1951 Jane had gone with her husband to a convention in New York and there, in an hotel bedroom, she was discovered by a maid just in time to be revived after taking an overdose of sleeping-pills. Her husband had flown her back to their home in Puerto Rico and then he had returned to New York (what greater wisdom could be expected of a man who wore co-respondent's shoes?). Two days later Jane's nine-year-old daughter found her mother dead. She had shot herself with her husband's revolver.

> How should I your true-love know
> From another one?
> By his cockle-hat and staff,
> And his sandal shoon.

No, not Ophelia 'garlanded with sweet flowers'.

It was not the tragedy of early death which overwhelmed me, but a sense of grievance: for so long I had lived with the certainty that, somewhere, out of my reach but still lovely, Jane existed, that I felt as if I had been robbed of part of my own past. It was not the fact of suicide, unexplained and inexplicable, but its manner which battered me to tears: that glorious voice silenced, all that vitality, all that charm ended, that beauty, shattered, raped by a pistol-bullet.

Patsy's sad tale should have written *Finis* to my account of Jane but soon after my return to Leeds I began to receive letters from Jane's daughter. Patricia had not known of my existence until she heard of me from her grandmother and aunt after our reunion in Florida. Now she begged to meet with me to talk of her mother when a girl.

Twelve months and a half-dozen letters later I flew to San Juan. I waited for an hour or more at the airport. Patricia did not appear. The next three days I spent close to the telephone in my bedroom at a luxury hotel, too proud to pick up the phone but praying for a message. The phone never rang.

It was as if I had been forced to relive the agony of the Maadi gardens and as then so now in a San Juan hotel-room treachery sprang some small coil of inspiration. It was there that I wrote the longest poem that ever I attempted, the only poem of mine (other than a few satirical verses) of which I am proud.

9

Faculty for Storm

I left Cairo and Egypt without regret. In India, as later in Greece, I found consolation for the rigours of Service life in affection for the civilian society which surrounded us but, like most of my contemporaries, I loathed the Egyptians, a feckless, thieving rabble and almost certainly treacherous. I remembered and could not forgive how the back-streets of Cairo and Alexandria had sprouted swastikas when Rommel threatened to break into the Delta, how miraculously those swastikas became Union Jacks after El Alamein. I compared these seedy, scrofulous, resentful imitation-Europeans with the dignified, hospitable Arabs of Tel Afar and knew that I had no wish to meet one of them again in all my life. And now that Egypt was no longer a base for operations,we were returning Egypt to the Egyptians.

Even so it was not so much liberation from Egypt as pride and pleasure in the quality of my posting which made me euphoric as I moved off to join Eighth Army.

Service sentiment is laden with strange anomalies. Brigade is the furthest forward of formations which has at its headquarters Staff-trained officers and appointment to its headquarters staff is consistently coveted by graduates of Staff colleges. At Brigade, I knew, I need no longer accuse myself of being one of those 'lords, trimly dress'd, talking / So like a waiting gentleman / Of guns, and drums, and wounds – God save the mark.' At Brigade I would be a real soldier, at Brigade I would no longer labour under that sense of inconsequentiality, of not belonging, which for the previous eighteen months had overshadowed even my most perilous excursions into the battle-zone.

My term of military frustration was ended. My personal sorrows I could not forget but I was consoled by the thought that as an operations staff-officer on the headquarters of a brigade involved in the Italian campaign I would have little time for moping. My effulgent post-War had been snatched from me but *après la guerre* might never come, and immediately there stretched out before me a future, spiritually, intellectually and physically both exhausting and satisfying.

My optimistic prognosis turned out to be more than justified. So it is that there stands out from all my recollection of war the sensational paradox that I, who shivered whenever a shell landed close by, who enjoyed comfort and preferred luxury, was in all my Army service never so content

as I was with 139 Brigade, though for months on end in the thick of battle
and, for a year or more without respite, suffering the miseries of a campaign which visited upon those who fought it miseries akin to those suffered by our predecessors in Flanders from 1914 to 1918. When it did not
rain it snowed. We were bogged down in mud. We faced trench-systems
and fortifications. Eternally, or so it seemed, there was another river to
cross, another mountain-range to scale. Yet I was happy, fulfilled and, perhaps in consequence, better at my job than I, or anyone else, would have
dreamed possible.

Almost in the moment that I joined the Brigade, and ever after, I discovered another cause for ease which had not entered my premonitory calculations. For the first time since I had volunteered myself out of the
Highland Field Regiment, I was neither an outsider nor a stand-in but, as I
had been at school and at college, a member of a close community and to
that community significant. Long before I left,I knew the name of every
officer in the Brigade and was known to all.

Immediately I was admitted to a special relationship with the Brigade
Intelligence Officer. Not long down from Oxford, Geoff Lindley's military
ferocity and his occasional bursts of frivolousness seemed at times out-of-
kilter with his aspiration to the priesthood, but not then nor ever after
could there be any doubting his sincerity or his care for his friends. Often
we were on duty together through long nights and tense days, and then, as
during infrequent but much welcomed sorties out of the line, I listened as
he raved on about his fiancée, the most beautiful, the most talented, the
most pious girl in all the world. At first I was envious, bruised by these
reminders of my shattered past, these promptings to awareness that my
future was blank, but soon I came to share as if by right of experience in
his devotion to Jeanne and her family. The process of identification was
not difficult. When Geoff spoke of weekends at The Eyrie in Radlett it
stirred me to relive happy times with the Leigh-Mallorys at Godalming, or
with Francis Hirst and his wife when the Editor of the *Economist* had gathered together promising young men and women in their lovely house at
Midhurst, once the home of Richard Cobden.

My sense of identification with Geoff's future family-by-marriage was
made all the more immediate because already reading and even writing had
made me familiar with Jeanne's father, Emile Cammaerts. I knew and
admired his book on English nonsense literature, I had read his life of
Rubens and his biography of King Albert of the Belgians and he had made
an entrance, if admittedly as a supporting character, in a paean mostly dedicated to Conrad, in an essay on writers who perform the miracle of writing
in a language not their own, which I had contributed to the William and
Mary literary magazine. Geoff made others of the family my familiars long
before I met them: Tita Brand, Jeanne's mother, the first Gloria in Shaw's
You Never Can Tell and Desdemona to Frank Benson's Othello, her broth-

er Francis, then somewhere in France as British Liaison Officer with the French Resistance, and her beautiful actress sister with the unlikely name Kippe.

During the last two years of the War I spent much time with Geoff, both in and out of action, but in battle even more with the Brigade Commander. Soldiers, like children and Australians, seldom look for originality when choosing nicknames,and so to most men in the Brigade Allen Block was 'Chippy'; it was by some perverse recognition of unusual intimacy that, except on the most formal occasions, he allowed me to address him by his Christian name.

Measured according to the history-books, the years which I served under Allen, the years of the Italian Campaign and the Greek Civil War, were the harshest of my Army career. I was not often out of range of the enemy's guns. From all that time I can recall very few nights when I slept for more than five hours and many when I slept not at all. In 'sunny Italy' rain was incessant and, as had our fathers in Flanders, we waded through mud. In Greece we were engaged in house-to-house fighting, the most bitter of all military endeavours. Yet paradoxically, I remember those years as among the most contented of my life. As seldom before in my military career, and then only for a few weeks at a time, my capability was recognized, and my capacity for remaining clear-headed for long hours in tense situations. At last I felt fulfilled.

Allen was too sophisticated in handling men to be fooled by my shallow pose of imperturbability. Indeed, years later, in the bar of his London club, he recalled for my benefit two occasions when he had come close to advising me to make my post-War career in the theatre. The first was in a ruined house at Saludeco, under the shadow of San Marino, just before the assault on Rimini and I, by his still flattering account, sat at a dining-table, a glass – 'a fine crystal filled with excellent Valpolicella' – at my side, obstinately setting to paper his operation-orders 'while mortar-bombs exploded all round us'. The second, in the Greek Naval College in the Piraeus, me transmitting his instructions to our battalion commanders and apparently unaware that it was only because the windows were high above our heads that we were safe from ELAS bullets. But I owe it to Allen that, by taking them for granted, he encouraged my performances.

It was Allen also who erased the last, shabby vestiges of my supercilious contempt for Regular officers and replaced it with unbridled admiration and affection for the Army and for all who have made the Service their vocation.

Mere brigadiers are seldom mentioned in war-histories; most military historians regard them as little more than obedient henchmen of the great generals.whose names remain forever resonant in the annals which record a nation's pride. I served on a brigade staff in some of the tensest moments of the War and I know that these are the commanders who bear the full heat of battle, and that often in conditions no more conducive to calm or calculation than those endured by the subaltern in command of the point-platoon, that these are the men who must make the decisions which will decide the course of a battle – or even of a war.

Allen Block's name does not appear even in the most exhaustive history of the Second World War. I accept that the claims that I make for him will be dismissed as products of extravagant pride in the achievements of 139 Brigade, but I will argue against a whole regiment of experts who have never heard a shot fired in anger that it was his skill, his coolness and, above all else, his capacity for winning the devotion entire of his subordinates, which contributed most to the Eighth Army's capture of the Gothic Line; that it was his ability in handling a rag-bag of units which kept ELAS out of Piraeus and, at the last, opened up the road to Athens; and, for good measure, I will add that had it not been for his genius as diplomatist, most of the local population would have turned against us.

Allen seemed never to be dismayed by shells, bombs, bullets or mines – perhaps he too was an actor *manqué* – but, to me even more amazing, he was never put out by the vagueness of instructions from on high(and the orders we received, particularly in Greece, were often not only vague but also contradictory). Grave and unshakeable in adversity, triumph he greeted with a mischievous smile, as of one who says 'I told you so; whatever they predicted I knew we could do it'. He could be hard;but no officer or man in his command ever questioned his humaneness.

As then we calculated age,Chippy was elderly and he looked much older than his years, not so much because his hair was white (at the end of four days without sleep in Piraeus,I myself found several harsh streaks of grey in my otherwise jet-black hair), but because there was in his eyes, undimmed by the habitual twinkle which made him look like Mr Pickwick with red tabs, a gleam of reminiscent sadness. He had served in the First War and, near as I was to him when he was called upon to make some of the most awesome decisions of his career, I came to recognize how permanent was the impact of that vicious experience. Indeed, it was borne in upon me that we of the Second War benefitted hugely from the fact that, like Allen, so many of our commanders had been subalterns in Flanders. Not for him, not for any of them, the gruesome prodigality with lives which had turned 'a country useful to the race' into a British grave-yard. He was determined and efficient, but though he saw it as his prime responsibility to win every action into which he launched his brigade, so also did he think it his duty to avoid needless casualties. Every man in the Brigade was his to cherish,and every man killed or wounded he marked against his record as leader and commander.

I learnt more about soldiering just by being close to Chippy than ever I was taught in all the courses I attended in six-and-a-half years' service and, I like to think, more about what later came to be called man-management (a term which he would have considered condescending to the men he managed). Though I never acquired his insouciance when walking through minefields, I did achieve a parody of his disregard for danger which was at least good enough to convince me that I was not afraid.

There were others at Brigade, at Division and in our supporting units who became much more than amiable colleagues. Of these, my friends, some parade still in well-ordered ranks in Italy and some rest forever in the sad, green loveliness of the war cemetery overlooking Phaleron Bay. A few, Geoff Weymont of the Manchesters and our Senior Padre, Ken Oliver among them, remained my friends even in the less gregarious society of peace-time.

Both Geoff and Ken were good soldiers and Ken, because his soldier's sense made him alert to situations which would call for his pastoral care, the finest Army chaplain that ever I met. I doubt that I ever mentioned Jane to either of them but these two did more than anyone else, more even than Geoff Lindley or Chippy, to pull me out of the mire of self-pity in which I was wallowing. Both shared with me loyalty to Christ's Hospital,and by giving me back an important part of my past all unwittingly they restored to me some hope for my future.

There was in the moves of these four – Ken, Allen, Geoff Weymont and Geoff Lindley, my closest friends – a common factor which I noticed even in Italy. All four were devout Christians and as such it seemed awkward intimates for one who could come no closer to their faith.than adherence to an empty but sternly Protestant agnosticism. It is a paradox that I cannot resolve, even in retrospect, that I found so much comfort in their friendship unless it be that, bedevilled as I was by uncertainty and fear, I found refuge in their certainty.

It is the consolation of comradeship, and not only with these four, and the ease of spirit which comes with unending mental and physical activity, which I remember as I look back to Italy in 1944. Episodes, incidents, some tragic, some frivolous I can recover, and almost all are, as campaign history, inconsequential. There are thrown on to the screen of memory snapshots, stills without prologue or epilogue but to these I cannot give the decency of chronology, not even with assistance from Eric Linklater's brisk little history of our campaign. We of the Eighth Army remember 'with advantages' Salerno, Cassino, Anzio, Faenza and we carry proudly-blazoned as battle-honours other names, the Gothic Line, the Winter Line, unknown to cartographers or the compilers of gazetteers but, though I have returned a dozen times since the War, the scenes that still come insistently to my mind whenever the word Italy is spoken are all cameos: Ken and I standing in a Casualty Clearing Station to which Geoff Weymont had been taken, after a mortar-bomb severed his leg when he was waiting outside Brigade Tactical HQ for me to go with him for a few days leave; black silk sheets neatly folded on the bed in a room in which, though it faced the Germans, I had chosen to billet myself because it was warm and dry; a fifteen-year-old prisoner, one of the Nazi Youth, a cigarette hanging impertinently from his lips; Jean Lindsay in a green dress walking nonchalantly up the shattered main street of a village just out of range of the enemy's guns,where the Brigade was stationed for a few days in reserve. Since the War, I have written often of the Florence of the Medici, of Michelangelo, Giotto, Dante and Petrarch, but though I cannot reconstruct why I was there so far away from the Brigade in the company of a South African major, the Florence that springs immediately to memory is the Florence I looked down upon from the hills, the Florence that I did not visit until fifteen years had passed. Ever since that day in 1944, I have found it difficult to persuade myself that the bridge which I saw blown up by the retreating Germans was not, as then I thought, the Ponte Vecchio, nor can I erase repugnance for a blasphemy that was never committed. After-knowledge allows me to identify the tunnel filled with terrified refugees all as it seemed shrieking at me '*multi bambini, Capitano*' as the railway-tunnel under neutral San Marino, but where was the Triangle? It was in the Triangle that 139 Brigade suffered its heaviest casualties and, as I believe, it was in the Triangle that there occurred the incident which still, after almost half a century recurs in my nightmares: the sight and sound of a boy, a subaltern of the Durham Light Infantry, being blown to eternity because I would not, could not, pay heed to his premonition. But ask me to mark the Triangle on a map and I could do no better than wave my pencil vaguely somewhere close to that straight thick line, Route Nine, which for so long pointed our way northwards towards victory. For the rest I see rain, mud and an endless procession of rivers and blown bridges.

One scene stands out as uniquely identifiable, if not by map-reference then at least by chronology, and the memory arouses in me the same smug satisfaction that was mine when first I looked down at it. As preface to the assault on the Gothic Line, the whole Eighth Army was moved from the western to the eastern flank. 139 Brigade was in the van and I forward with the Brigadier's advance-guard.

Every bridge was blown and it was only by the superhuman efforts of our sappers that we were allowed to make any progress at all. We came finally to the last river before the assembly area allotted to the Brigade, a deep scar in open country, and surprisingly dry. There was, however, an inhibition to advance more sinister than flowing water; we were now within range of German guns and it seemed that all Kesselring's artillery was concentrating its fire-power on the only feasible crossing-place.

I climbed to the top of a small hill and studied the landscape beyond the river. I was satisfied that there was in all the country I could see no suitable vantage-point from which the enemy could observe the fall of shot and that, therefore, he must be using a fire-plan calculated from the map. For an hour or more I watched as shells battered to rubble the ruined bridge. Ten minutes of silence and then, for a minute, a bombardment so intensive that whilst it raged not one vehicle could have survived the crossing. The Boche, ever systematic, was loosing his fury every ten minutes in one-minute bursts.

Allowing at either end a minute for eccentric behaviour by some German gun-crew, we moved the whole brigade across in eight minute dashes. We suffered not a single casualty.

Twenty-four hours later, after a barrage from our own artillery heavier, we were told, than anything since Poperinghe, we attacked the Gothic Line.

We lived with a grievance. Even as we were fighting our way up the length of Italy, Allied forces were bursting across north-western Europe. We did not begrudge them their share of adulation; many in the 21st Army Group had fought alongside us in the Desert: but we resented the fact that whenever we tuned in to the BBC we heard ecstatic accounts of their exploits and nothing whatsoever of our own bitter struggle. *I m Westen nichts neues.*

Resentment lingers on. In 1985, when the newspapers, the radio and television were celebrating the fortieth anniversary of the end of the War, there was scarcely one word about Italy. For all that the bubbling recorders of victory cared,we of the Eighth Army in Italy, like our fellows of the Fourteenth Army in the Far East, might have spent the last year of the War in a Butlin's holiday-camp.

This shrugging-off of our endeavours was, even so, less vicious and less bruising to our pride than the treatment to which 139 Brigade and all engaged were subjected when we were moved to Greece. There is no conflict more tragic than civil war, no military experience more harsh than street-fighting, but when we were in Greece in the last months of 1944 and the first of 1945 we were exposed to attacks more damaging than anything that ELAS could mount, to a barrage of abuse by the British Press and to continuous sniping even from the Palace of Westminster. We heard ourselves reviled as Fascist jackals, as brutish louts who spent their days and nights callously shooting down noble fighters. With but one exception – Richard Capell, music-critic turned war-reporter – even the correspondents nominally attached to our force ('nominally' because we saw none of them except Capell) filed despatches rich with admiration for ELAS heroics. We nominated the BBC and not ELAS as our most-hated adversary!

Something in the blood of the Anglo-Saxon answers eagerly to the needs and the pleasures of Greece. I was not reared a classical scholar. It is Greece and Britain, Britain and Greece that is my delight; for me the call of Greece is most strident when I hear it from the voice of Byron, Trelawny or Rupert Brooke, but most compelling when I remember the amiable tones of Captain Damirallis RHN, my beloved Dami, and of Colonel Prokos, my daily and day-long companions during the Civil War. Through them I have come back to Pericles and Solon, it is they who remind me still that our struggles in the streets of Piraeus and out from Patras towards the vineyards of Achaia Klauss were not unworthy of honour as sequels to Missolonghi and Navarino.

Notice of my second venture into Greece was served upon me by a despatch-rider somewhere near Ancona. I looked longingly at the lovely beaches bordering the Adriatic, handed over to the local Area Commander the sheaf of notes and the sketch-maps I had prepared for a Brigade rest-area, and drove to make rendezvous with Chippy at Rome Airport.

There, after a confused and confusing briefing by some lordling from Supreme Headquarters, we were packed into a Hercules, the Brigadier, his driver, his jeep, two signallers and me, as Tac HQ for 139 Brigade. Part of the Brigade Headquarters Defence Platoon, we were told, would be flying after us next day, the rest of our small staff and two battalions of infantry would be moved by sea.

That night we spent in an hotel on Ommonia Square. Just two months after liberation, Athens was already superficially a city at peace. I had not seen a neon-sign advertisement since September 1939. Trams clanked through the streets. In the hotel bar young women, all beautiful, all elegantly dressed, flirted deliciously with smart young men from the Royal Hellenic Navy and with officers from the Greek Mountain Brigade, the very men who, but a few weeks earlier, I had seen mustering their troops for the hazardous assault across the vast open plain of the Rimini airfield.

Next morning we were served bacon-and-eggs and quantities of delicious coffee by obsequious waiters and even when, with the Defence Platoon, we took up new billets high on the slopes of 'Athens' other hill', Lykabettos, it seemed that this was a rest-area far more luxurious than any that I could have found in Italy.

Chippy accepted an invitation for his three officers to dine with some of our new Greek neighbours. We ate *dolmades, orechtika, moshkari* and sweet *glika*, drank pints of *ouzo* and *retsina*, managed a glass of mavrodaphni, more than one glass of M. Barbaresso's finest Greek brandy, and were in no way embarrassed when we were hugged and kissed by every female in the party, four little girls, their two mothers, three grandmothers and an old lady who bragged delightedly that she had once been invited into bed by Venizelos. Her wicked laugh seemed to imply not only that she had accepted the invitation with alacrity but that, though close to ninety, she would do the same for us if only we could be rid of all these chattering chaperones.

Next morning Chippy and I stood on the terrace of our billet drinking black coffee and eating freshly-baked croissants with butter and jam, all brought to us by the same hospitable neighbours. The view was magnificent, unbroken across to the Acropolis and to the bay. We could even pick out the snipers lying on the flat roofs below.

Chippy was called to the phone – an ordinary civilian phone, even that was for us a novelty. He came back looking puzzled. Some Communist firebrands were threatening the prison; Land Forces Greece wanted us to intervene. 'Stupid clowns' he mumbled, 'what can we do with half of a miserable defence platoon commanded by a boy who hasn't yet browned his knees?' He looked at me. 'You've nothing else to keep you occupied

till the Brigade gets in. Take 'em out and. . . .', he imitated the instructions
he had received, 'see what you can do.'

We commandeered a bus as transport for the platoon. I took the
Brigadier's jeep and driver, armed myself with a street-map and a tommy-
gun, and set off in search of the prison. All the houses were shuttered, the
pavements all empty and there were no trams.

I rounded a corner at the head of my little force and found my way
blocked by a barricade built of dustbins, wardrobes and a battered
Chevrolet. As I moved to inspect the obstacle, a party of men came out
from a nearby house. All were dressed in some sort of uniform. All were
festooned with weapons, sub-machine guns, revolvers, knives.

Their leader, a huge bearded man wearing on his British-issue forage-
cap a red star, saluted me courteously, smiled as if in greeting to an old
friend and said 'No Exit'. This, as it turned out, was the sum of his English
vocabulary; in the next ten minutes he repeated the phrase a dozen times;
but I could not be sure if it was traffic-instruction or threat. I despatched
my driver to conscript an interpreter, a terrified sixteen-year old girl, and
through her as best I could I explained that I had my orders to relieve the
prison-guards, his countrymen, and to replace them with British soldiers,
his allies. He would not wish to bring down upon himself the wrath of his
country's liberator, the great English general, Scobie. My interlocutor
grinned, saluted, shook his head and repeated 'No Exit', but he offered no
protest or opposition when we cleared away the barricade.

As we passed through he saluted yet again, but as I drove on at the head
of my formidable convoy I flexed every nerve that I had and entered upon
the unenviable heritage of the British Army: I was attempting to hold apart
two adversaries. Greek met Greek; I was in the no man's land between
them and denied the right to fire upon either.

There was no shooting. We relieved the guards. On my way back to
Lykabettos we passed the place where I had encountered my first ELAS
fighters. Some small urchins were playing at soldiers in the detritus of the
barricade. One pointed a stick at me, his finger close to an imaginary trigger, then he threw down the weapon, raised two fingers to a V-sign and
shouted '*Zhito* Winston Churchill'.

That afternoon I drove to Phaleron to reconnoitre billets for the
Brigade. The road took me close to the Acropolis and I thought, not of
Iktinos, but of the greatest visitor who ever came this way, and of the
stinging rebuke that he delivered to the Athenians as he stood 'in the midst
of Mars' Hill': '. . .And the time of this ignorance God winked at; but now
commanded all men everywhere to repent.'

In the next months I was given cause to think often of St Paul. Many
times I was in the home of dedicated members of EAM and once, for
twenty-four hours, a hostage in the headquarters of ELAS. Always there
were smiles, ouzo and baklava,but I was never allowed to depart from
among them until I had 'debated at length' with certain philosophers the

'rights and wrongs of Marxism' and always when I had my say, 'some mocked, and others said, we will hear more of this matter'.

In Phaleron I commandeered several luxury hotels along the shore-road and here, yet again, it seemed that we were destined for an idyllic respite from war.

Early in the morning of 3 December, I drove with Chippy up the long straight road that leads past the Acropolis and the Fix Brewery from Phaleron into the centre of Athens. On the way we passed processions of men and women carrying banners. We were called for conference with General Scobie, General Officer Commanding all Allied forces in Greece.

Many of the wilder parts of the country were still in ELAS hands; the King was delaying his return from exile until he knew the result of a plebiscite, those who were now governing in his name had made appointments offensive even to moderates, there was tension everywhere and some rioting.

The room was warm, my Grande Bretagne armchair comfortable, Scobie made his report casually, in a quiet voice, and the sound of a car backfiring in the street below heightened the impression that he was telling to a small group of club-cronies stories about the eccentric behaviour of a much-loved maiden-aunt.

Another back-fire, yet another, and then the illusion of tranquillity exploded to the unmistakable sound of rifle and sub-machine-gun fire.

Since 1944 I have read a dozen accounts of the events in Constitution Square but, as each is weighted with the political prejudices of the chronicler, I do not know if the police were provoked or if their action was premeditated.

As we left the Grande Bretagne, I made an appreciation of the situation which faced Chippy and me. Had there ever been presented to an eager enemy two positions so ideally located for control of an open road as Mars Hill and the Fix Brewery?

ELAS tacticians were not näive; they had riflemen in both positions before we drove past and already they were sniping at opponents invisible to us. Apparently they considered us unworthy targets but I could not help reflecting that a stray bullet is no less lethal than a round inscribed with the name of its victim.

That afternoon EAM called a general strike, that night we took up positions defending the port of Piraeus to secure landing-facilities for reinforcements from Italy.

Next morning ELAS cut the road to Athens and we held perhaps four hundred yards, from docks to ELAS outposts.

We set up our headquarters in the Greek Naval College, an easy target for ELAS snipers, and from there Chippy directed operations with an emasculated Brigade Staff strengthened by three Greeks – Colonel Prokos of the Mountain Brigade, Admiral Vulgaris's Flag Captain, Captain Damirallis RHN and his Flag Lieutenant, an exquisite out of Corfu by way of Spetsi, 'the Greek Eton', whose English would have honoured Eton-on-Thames – and an elderly Canadian major who until a few days previously,had thought himself in Greece to bring rehabilitation to a devastated country and relief to its people.

It was Dami who confirmed my burgeoning philhellenism. Gentle in friendship, ferocious in battle, he was never still save in moments of crisis, always argumentative unless the circumstances of action demanded immediate acquiescence, and always good-humoured. In this, like Colonel Prokos, he paid me the rich compliment of accepting my authority without demur for I was the Brigadier's ventriloquist's dummy.

Under command we had two of our battle-hardened battalions, a handful of Greek Marines, a few companies of recently-levied and terrified National Guardsmen, a ragbag of men from the Service Corps, and the Sappers who had been sent out from England to man the ports. We had our own field ambulance but no other hospital facilities: our artillery we had left in Italy, our only armour was the infantry's vulnerable carriers and, until the last days of the fighting when the gods in Whitehall permitted a sortie against the otherwise unassailable refrigerator-plant on the far side of the estuary, no air-cover. Daily, hourly I looked covetously out into the bay where lay a flotilla of destroyers, frigates, armed merchantmen, Greek, British and Canadian, their guns muzzled by order of Westminster.

> And ships, by thousands, lay below
> And men in nations; – all were his
> He counted them at break of day –
> And when the sun set where were they?

This was Blockforce and in the next weeks, fighting its way house by house, street by street through Piraeus and out towards General Scobie's troops battling to meet us, Blockforce wrote its record on the shifting tablets of Greek history, freshly remembered while a king sat on the Greek throne but, like Blockstreet (named for Chippy at the end of the fighting by grateful Piraeans), expunged from legend when the Socialists came to power.

My name, too, was entered, briefly, in Greek chronicles. We knew that our every movement was swiftly reported to ELAS by its many sympathizers in Piraeus. Chippy decided to take advantage of this leaking sieve. We would lead ELAS command to believe that we were mounting a sea-borne attack against the coast behind his lines. Morpurforce was formed. To give the impression of substance, six of our carriers laden with petrified National Guardsmen drove round and round in the dark streets, as close as I could bring them to ELAS without drawing his fire, then on to a jetty where we loaded all on to LCTs and put out to sea. For two hours I drank sweet tea and Navy rum with the Lieutenant RNVR commanding the ships of Morpurforce. For two hours almost to a man the National

Guardsmen were sea-sick. Then we retired to port, landing, close to the Naval College, out of hearing of ELAS and of any informer.

The fighting in Piraeus was fierce and nasty, fiercer and much nastier than any I had experienced. The enemy was well-armed, well-led and determined. We had around us a civilian population, justifiably nervous and in part disaffected. It was our job to defend them but it was no less our task to reassure them, to feed them and to root out the ELAS spies. All this Chippy managed,even whilst he was directing hideously complex operations. His manner, pitched nicely somewhere between stern schoolmaster and kindly uncle, his diplomatic skill and his obvious fairness won for him, and for us, the affection of most Piraeans.

Though at times we woke to the fact that we were defending the wrong against the wrong, our determination was spurred by the news that several hundred RAF ground-staff had been captured by ELAS on isolated landing-strips and taken off in a march as horrific as any inflicted by the Japanese. It was made almost hysterical by the knowledge that every success of ours ELAS answered by taking hostages, by tortures and executions.

When I was not manning Headquarters or commanding Morpurforce, Chippy set me to calling upon some of those who, left behind our slowly advancing forward positions, were thought to be obvious leaders and perhaps ELAS sympathisers. It was in the performance of this duty that I discovered for myself the best billet I ever enjoyed, in the home of M. Barbaresso, the brandy-king. No fellow-traveller he, I had won his gratitude already by ordering a guard upon his brandy-store immediately upon its liberation – not to prevent its recapture by ELAS but to protect its desirable contents against our ever-thirsty Geordies. As reward he gave me his guest-bedroom, bathroom *en suite*. Be it two o'clock in the morning or four in the afternoon: whenever I returned from the Naval College there was waiting for me a uniformed maid carrying a silver tray bearing a silver coffee-pot and a bottle of Director's Bin Barbaresso Brandy, at whatsoever time I woke there she stood again, as if she had been watching over me for the first sign of waking, that same silver tray in her hand, and on it a fresh white linen cloth for my bedside-table, coffee, more brandy and a platter of sweet cakes.

Early in Christmas week we were told by GHQ that, at last, and much too late, we were allowed to call for fire from the Navy. At daybreak one morning a cutter came to take the Brigadier and me out to the Canadian armed-merchantman flying the Commodore's pennant. Festooned with map-cases and equipment, I did my best to clamber up a swaying rope-ladder as if it was the Duke of York's Steps. I floundered onto the deck as the honour-guard saluted Chippy. The grinning Number One swept me up. 'Your boss is breakfasting with mine before we talk. What can we do for you?' In all the war-years I knew no comfort more luxurious than a hot bath and so, despite the Barbaresso *en suite* bathroom, it was for a bath that I asked. I was soaking happily in three feet of steaming water when there was a sharp rap on the door. In came a huge Marine who set a plank across the bath and on it knives, forks, spoons, a cup and saucer, a glass – and a white napkin. He went out and came back immediately with a plate of ham-and-eggs and another with on it a stack of pancakes, then out and back again with salt, pepper, mustard, jam, honey, marmalade and a pitcher of water all of which he dressed in a disciplined rank on the floor beside the bath. This regimental ordering completed he straightened, thrust his thumbs to the seam of his trousers, bellowed 'Number One's compliments, sir. Eat hearty', right-about-faced, and marched out of the bathroom.

I blessed the North American habit of serving iced-water with all meals, groped for the pitcher, filled the glass, and gulped. Pink gin! And at six in the morning!

In the Commodore's cabin, over maps and Canadian rye, we prepared our plans, the Gunnery Officer and I, for those moments in a supercilious professional alliance against our naïve seniors. I negotiated the rope-ladder down into the picket-boat with supreme confidence.

Dami greeted us at the landing-stage, his face gloomy. The order freeing naval guns had been rescinded.

A few days before Christmas we linked up with General Scobie's men. On Christmas Day, Churchill and Eden arrived and, though there was still fighting in the back-streets, we smuggled them up to Athens in an armoured command-vehicle. Archbishop Damaskinos, much-respected by all Greeks, became Regent and the liberal General Plastiras, Prime Minister.

By New Year's Eve we had most of Piraeus under control and our patrols were moving out into the country. It was then that we heard for the first time tales of how three months earlier, many a starving Greek village had handed over to the men of 3 Corps Australian, New Zealand and British survivors of the 1941 campaign who, for three and a half years, they had refused to betray to the Germans and whom the villagers had never allowed to go hungry.

An armistice was signed on 11 January at Varkiza. Immediately we planned a celebratory party for the next night. I begged of M. Barbaresso that we be allowed the use of his handsome drawing-room and he begged of me that he be permitted to present to us several cases of wine, a case of brandy and, so that the rejoicing might be truly Anglo-Hellenic, a bottle or two of *ouzo* and a bottle from his pre-War hoard of Johnny Walker. Stephanie Damirellis was summoned from Athens to join our planning-committee.

Early in the afternoon of 12 January two hitherto unknown Greek ladies arrived with armfuls of greenery and flowers and set to decorating the Barbaresso drawing-room.

Even without these floral arrangements and even without M. Barbaresso liquid benefactions that party would have been memorable for we were in party-mood, euphoric not only because our hideous business in Piraeus was successfully concluded, but also because we sensed that before 1945 was out we would be back in our own homes. It was, however, Stephanie Damirallis who made the occasion superlative. She conscripted her sister Alex and a dozen friends, all young, all pretty and all, we were told, married – though only Stephanie and Mme Prokos, whose husbands we considered to be unquestionably members of our Mess, brought their menfolk with them. And all were dressed as if they had just stepped out of the salon of Molyneux or Dior. How, after four years of occupation, they managed such elegance was, and remains, a mystery but I contend that there are in all the world few who can match for *chic* Athenian young women from the prosperous classes.

The next weeks were festival. We were dined handsomely by the Prokos, by Admiral Vulgaris (soon to be Prime Minister). by Athenians whose names were unknown to us until we read their invitations. Most nights I slept in Dami's flat off Station Street, most days I toured Athens with Dami, Stephanie, Alex or Alex's husband as guide.

Late in January, Geoff and I went to the re-opening of the Opera. I refuse to myself the research which might disabuse me of a myth long-cherished: that on that occasion I heard the young Maria Callas singing the title-role in Massenet's *Manon*.

Also in January I wrote the most difficult operation-orders that ever I was called upon to devise. There was to be in the Kifissia quarter of Piraeus a great celebration of the Second Liberation, the naming of a street for Chippy (ever after, from our meagre understanding of the Cyrillic alphabet and our deliberate confusion with the name of a brandy less glorious than our own Barbaresso, we called it Metaxa Mplock Street), a service in the Cathedral, and a march-past of all the forces that had been ours during the Civil War.

It was the march-past which caused me to spend hours wrestling with a slide-rule. The National Guard had never before performed any ceremonial duties; I suspected them of shambling; the Service Corps and the Sappers are admirable but not noted for their drill; I had little idea what to expect from the Greek Navy; our own sailors and even our own Leicesters had not performed in this fashion for years; and the Durhams, being Light Infantry, marched at a faster pace than all the rest.

I stood on the saluting base behind Chippy, General Plastiras, the Mayor and the Bishop (he taller and even more dignified than Plastiras, who must have been all of six foot three). The parade was worthy of the Household Brigade on Horse Guards Parade; the Durhams did not tramp into the ground the contingent of Piraeus Boy Scouts.

In the Cathedral, all officers of Blockforce HQ were placed next to the Bishop, standing, and facing a vast and standing congregation. The Bishop's address was long and all Greek to me but I noticed that every few minutes he, and with him all the congregation, bowed to us and always on the same words. I strained at my limited Greek vocabulary and then I had it: 'Sons of Byron'.

News from Italy and from north-west Europe convinced us that for 139 Brigade the War was over and then, suddenly, carnival ended. I was called to HQ. Again I was set to establish Brigade Tactical HQ, this time in Patras.

Aboard a destroyer bouncing across rough waters, Chippy explained the situation while I struggled to avoid the disgrace of returning to the sea the evidence of Royal Navy hospitality. Patras had been placid throughout the Civil War; it was said that ELAS had defeated our liberators – at football; but the Communist commander had refused to accept the terms of the armistice. In the last days there had been some sporadic shooting in the country around the town and the tension in Patras threatened an eruption of violence. Once more we were to go in 'to see what could be done'.

Patras is the unloveliest of Greek cities. Denied in war-time even the cheerful bustle of a ferry-terminal, its few 'ancient' monuments – a Roman Odeon, a Byzantine church, a basilica (built in 1836) and, on the hill above the town, a ruined Frankish castle – all seem apologetic, as if Patras is guiltily aware that it can never match Athens, Salonika or even Corinth. Long ago Patras led the Achaean League, long ago Patras welcomed Cleopatra, and not so very long ago, in 1821, it was here that Archbishop Germanos raised the city's patronal flag as signal for the re-birth of Greece, but the only whisper of ancient glories that ever I heard from men of Patras was that it was here that St Andrew was crucified.

We of 139 Brigade added little to Patras legend, and I nothing whatsoever. I wasted much breath on squabbles with my opposite number on the staff of 11 Indian lnfantry Brigade about the comparative seniority of our two brigadiers. I quoted the *Army List*, which I had never seen, and the unquestionable authority of General Scobie's written orders, which I waved brazenly in his face. His man, John Hunt (later the conqueror of Everest),was more gracious than his mouthpiece but, either because he felt that 139 had seen enough of civil war or because he recognized John Hunt's superior knowledge of the local situation, Chippy gave to the lndians most of the prime tasks in the limited engagements which were necessary to clear up Patras and its environs and, diplomatic as ever, couched all his orders as requests. So it was that I was with the Gurkhas when they liberated the winery at Achaia Clauss a few miles out of Patras. ELAS offered only token resistance; the spirit of Marxism was cooled by the sight of the Gurkha *kukris*.

I could not foresee that Achaia Clauss, like my initiation by fire at Gilan an affair too comic to be memorialized as a skirmish, would be my last battle-honour.

Dutifully I placed sentries on the winery. Hopefully I drove straight into town to report my concern for his wines to the proprietor. Infected perhaps by his Bavarian antecedents, he received me coolly and offered as return not even a glass of *retsina*.

10

This Way to the Aviary

On VE Day I fretted in a Naples transit-camp. With hundreds like me who had been posted home after serving overseas for more than four years, I was confined to camp by some upstart Area Commander who feared that if we were let loose into the streets we would celebrate the most momentous victory in all history by tossing a few Italians into the Bay. On that evening I and Hector McQuade, Senior Grecian in my final year at C.H. and for the last years Medical Officer to a Field Regiment, could not go to the opera as we had every evening in the previous week, so we sat morosely sipping the extra tot graciously allowed to each officer by the High Command and listing mournfully the names of our friends who had died to purchase for us this double whisky-ration.

The Brigade had returned to Italy early in April. Chippy, exhausted by his efforts in Greece, was promptly hospitalized but before he left he persuaded his successor that, because I was so near to 'Python', I must be left at Base when the Brigade went back into the line. Somewhat to my own surprise I found myself protesting that I must finish my task with 139 Brigade and, when all my arguments failed to move first Chippy and then Brigadier Finlayson, I went off to Base, rebellious, glum and bereft even of the services of my driver, Gunner Thompson, and my batman Gunner Cottage. (Thompson was a Leicester and Cottage a Forester but I could never grow accustomed to the title Private. Gunners they were to me and Gunners they had become to all at Brigade.) I had been for so long part of a community that I could no longer find myself in isolation.

Two days after VE Day we were loaded on to a troopship, American and so, by the severe custom of the US Navy, dry. For twelve weary days we plodded homewards, the men close to mutiny and I, by accident of seniority, O.C. Royal Artillery, and Hector, Senior Medical Officer, tempted to lead an assault on the bridge.

After dark on a rainy evening we docked at Liverpool. The men crowded the rail, their equipment buckled, their kit-bags by their side. Hector and I waited for orders in the ship's austere lounge. At long last, a Movements Officer came aboard – another of those 'scarlet majors'. There would be no troop-train for London until next morning; no one was allowed ashore

We let him go back to his luxury billet, then Hector and I left the ship.

Close to the dock-gates we found a Liverpool policeman and to him we poured out our sad story of two officers and fifty men, all veterans of some of the War's fiercest battles, all victims of American puritanism and British bureaucracy. He took us to a public-house and hammered on the back-door as if he meant to waken all the Scouse dead. The publican poked his head out of an upstairs window and, seeing below two Army officers and a policeman, hurried to unlock his door without so much as putting on a coat or a dressing-gown. The policeman's version of our story was even more dramatic and even more tragic than ours. I left Hector in the bar, went back to the ship, found a sergeant who marshalled our men – Gunners and RAMC only. I issued instructions – one pint, no more – and we marched through the docks, as smart as any Royal guard. The men behaved impeccably: one pint each and many courtesies to the publican's wife.

They marched off at the sergeant's orders and I asked for the bill. The publican and his wife whispered together, then he turned to me. 'For you gentlemen there is no bill.'

I had not warned my family of my return home. I rang the bell. Bess opened the door, looked at me and, without greeting, turned back into the house and yelled up the stairs. 'It's Jack, he's a nigger.'

Within days I was bored. I loved my sisters and my father but since I was eleven years old I had always been a visitor in my own home. All that had happened to me in the last few years was to my sisters incomprehensible and to my father explicable only after tiresome scene-setting. They talked of the Blitz and of friends unknown to me and always there was the question to which I had no answer: 'What do you do now?' The War in the Far East was not yet over and it had been rumoured throughout the Army that staff-trained officers would be required for the invasion of Japan. Against the terrifying implications of that rumour stood calculations inspired by Army Command Instructions: I was due to be demobilized in June. But what then?

At David Roberts's suggestion I went to Oxford. There, after an interview no more searching than that which six years earlier had sent me to Larkhill, I was told that, if indeed I was demobilized in June, there would be a place for me in the Extra-Mural Department. I was not enthralled by the prospect but it was something.

Back home I found new orders, as ever from the Army generously littered with initials and parentheses. I was to report forthwith to the War Office to serve as GSO II (PR) in PR2 (lb).

I found myself a second-floor flat in a Notting Hill Gate cul-de-sac, self-contained but with bath and cooker in one small room outside my front door, and from there, each morning at 8.20, I walked to the corner and caught a Number 88 bus to Whitehall. But for my medal-ribbons and my rank-badges I might have been a bank-clerk.

Although at first I resented the postponement of my recovery of the delightfully unglamorous title of Mister as an unwarranted imposition by an ungrateful Sovereign upon the free-will of a subject who had served him for long periods in hard stations, and although my sense of grievance was heightened by the paucity of work, there were some compensations. Once a month I drew my whisky and cigarette rations from (of all places) the Tower of London. Eminent authors and journalists – R.C. Hutchinson, Christopher Buckley, Eric Linklater – came to my room as suppliant writers to a publisher whose desk-drawer was full of blank contracts.

With Eric I became immediately intimate and our friendship continued until his death. I regret that in all our cheerful meetings in London and Edinburgh, though we talked of many things, most of all of the comparative qualities of various malt-whiskies, seldom after our first meeting did we exchange reminiscences of war, and never did we speak of our mutually-held knowledge of the life of a British student in an American university.

I had admired Eric's work since first I read *Juan in America*, and I had bought *Poet's Pub* on August Bank Holiday 1935, the day which heralded the seismic revolution which turned me, and thousands like me, from humble book-borrowers into proud book-collectors but I cannot boast that it was I who trapped him into the net of PR2 (lb); early in the War he had written for the War Office the story of the Highland Division; but it was I who summoned him to Whitehall to discuss a history of the Italian Campaign.

He came unheralded. The door opened a few inches and through the gap appeared a bald head disfigured by a hideous scar. The eyes of the disembodied head scanned the room; I had been at the War Office only a few weeks and it was obvious that I was not the man he expected to see at the desk.

That meeting, as so many of my meetings with Eric, continued in a pub and he made me do most of the talking. He was ridiculously humble in the presence of someone whose battle-experience was so much more recent than his own.

In 1945, the Public Relations Directorate was a wonderfully convenient base from which to reconnoitre my future. First General Sir John Beith – Ian Hay, author of *The First Hundred Thousand* and *The Middle Watch* – and then his successor, the newspaper-proprietor Lord Burnham, had filled PR with khaki singing-birds, with authors and journalists in uniform. All but I had well-established contacts with the Press, with publishing and with the BBC, and these contacts all were eager to share with me. I was duty-bound to sustain and improve relations with the media. This duty I performed assiduously, lunching almost every day with some victim whom I had persuaded to be lavish with his expense-account by hinting that I had at my disposal, through channels not entirely proper, an overflowing reservoir of enthralling war-stories.

Such time as I spent at my desk I gave to drafting poems, articles, stories and letters of application for civilian jobs for my ATS secretary to type. I never rose to the pinnacle of immaculate impudence climbed by my predecessor, Denzil Batchelor, who dictated his weekly sports' columns for *The Leader* and *Picture Post* over the War Office telephone, but I worked hard and more successfully than I had dared hope.

I liked to think of myself as a nineteenth-century Radical but my literary aspirations were more potent than my political prejudices, and I was in no way affronted when I was taken up by the group of intellectuals and *soi-disant* aesthetes gathered around George Orwell and his left-wing *Tribune*. They thought of me as a poet but, once I had escaped the threatened sanctification of a libel-action instituted by Auden, I abandoned all pretension to be myself part of the answer to the vilification of my war-generation – that we had produced no poetry – which had aroused my ire against my most distinguished senior and, contentedly, allowed myself to be cast as one of *Tribune*'s regular reviewers of history, literary history and biography. Blunden passed me on the *Times Literary Supplement*; I found my own way to the *Birmingham Post*. My ego was dented by the enforced anonymity of the *TLS* but I was delighted that I had climbed so soon on to the slopes of the book-reviewers' Parnassus, and the *Post* gave me for review all that I requested. With these two journals, but not with *Tribune*, my association continued placidly for several decades.

I had phoned Lehmann immediately upon my return home to thank him for his patronage of an unknown soldier-writer. On the telephone he was generous about my work and he professed eagerness to meet me. A day or so later he called me. Could I come to a cocktail-party that very night?

There was gathered in Lehmann's flat the cream of the literary establishment. Some I recognized: Cyril Connolly, looking like an exquisite prize-pig, Rosamund Lehmann, beautiful and elegant; some were identified for me by Daniel George, after Lehmann had greeted me, the only person who spoke a word to me all evening.

Even so, as obstinately I drank beer, a drink I abominate, in a dim corner of the room, I was elated and when I left, despite Lehmann's perfunctory farewell, I knew that I had arrived.

But never after did Lehmann agree to publish anything written by me until in 1985, amazingly, he selected 'The Pipes' for the *New Writing Anthology*.

Although, this one unexpected and inexplicable set-back apart, I had reason to be delighted by my progress, I was not content. Wisdom demanded that I find for myself a job in civvy-street. Free-lance literary journalism would never pay the bills on Clanricarde Gardens, nor keep me in the style to which the Army had accustomed me. I toyed with the notion of completing my doctorate but I had lost such little affection as once had been mine for the dusty loneliness of research and I knew myself to be too old for the uncommitted habits of my student-days. My assault on the literary world was sensationally successful but, as a serving-officer still, I was prohibited from broadcasting. Even so, the BBC accepted, for reading by others, all three pieces I submitted. Only Lehmann resisted my advances. It was Lehmann, however, who had previously given me most encouragement and I knew already that recognition by *Penguin New Writing* was tantamount to membership in the literary MCC.

I was sixty years older than I had been six years earlier and much older than I am today – and I had no wish to end a pedagogue. Yet what other fate is presaged by a Ph.D? I had been hardened by fear, by boredom, by excitement, by responsibility, yet paradoxically, my capacity for self-discipline and pious application had been eroded by being forever a pawn in someone else's chess-game and by the reassuring knowledge that there were always others around me sharing both my terrors and my boisterous relaxations. It followed that, for reasons other than financial and yet made insistent by finance, I must settle myself into some organisation.

Even more compelling upon my ambitions: I had long-since discovered that I had no liking for ivory-towers. In the Army I had found also a liking for administration and, as was confirmed by my superiors, some capacity for giving orders. In that strange hiatus between the familiar realities of war-time soldiering and the terrifying uncertainties of a civilian existence in an England at peace, the fulfilment of my literary ambitions became a probability but none wished to know that I needed also a job, with authority, in some organisation appropriate to the skills I believed I possessed. Hundreds, like me well-versed in the manipulation of range-tables and the drafting of operation-orders, were coincidentally searching for civilian employment. Such few replies as I received to my numerous applications were courteous but non-committal. I was interviewed twice, by the BBC and by the British Council; both interviews ended in much the same way as the letters: 'Try again when the date of your demobilization is certain.'

Looking back, I see that my career was shaped in those months in 1945 and 1946. Had it not been that I was obdurate in my determination to live a double-life, as writer and as administrator, I might have accepted my immediate literary success as preface to uninterrupted dedication to a career as man-of-letters and so might have made for myself a reputation more substantial than ever it has been. I doubt that I would have found the contentment that has been mine as Sunday-writer, seizing respite at my desk from the complexities, perplexities and pleasures of administration, enjoying the privilege of privacy and strenuous effort just because it was a change from busy-ness.

In 1945 I was bitter, my disappointment made rancorous by stories told in all the pubs around Whitehall, by officers in like circumstances to mine, of how one had faced a panel chaired by a man several years his junior but never in the Services, another – a veteran of Dunkirk and Alamein with an MC and Bar – rejected because he had no experience, and yet another – but recently the youngest battalion-commander in the Eighth Army – turned away because he was said to be too old to set foot on the bottom rung of the commercial ladder. All the best jobs, and even many that promised less, had been taken years back by men who had kept their heads down throughout the War.

I had cause for misery more immediate and more profound than career-frustrations. I was lonely.

Fires are frozen for those who sit alone.
Here, where so often you two watched with me,
The wanton ashes wilt, the warmth has flown,
Iced by my solitude.

I found one old school-friend but already I sensed in Bernard Taylor that desolation of a spirit – once so ebullient but now desecrated by years of lonely responsibility in command of an ML and by his failure to find civilian employment worthy of his many talents – that bruising of the heart and mind which would bring him at last to his death in a mental hospital, a war-casualty no less than Peter, Basil and John. Ross Hook and Colin Chivers were still somewhere overseas, Geoff and all my friends at Brigade HQ were in Austria.

My cousin Betty had married an American bomber-pilot. I spent one week-end with them, happily recidivist as I demonstrated Guards' drill to Swede's Mess-companions, and before she left for America Betty did her best to fill the void in my social life by supplying me with a raft of telephone numbers. One after another I took her ballet-dancer friends to tea at the Savoy or dinner at Quaglino's. All were handsome, all amiable but with them, as with my family, there was always that impediment to mutual comprehension created by the unshared years.

When the news reached me that both John and Basil were dead I had thought briefly that Basil's sister might take his place in my life. That notion I had dismissed as fatuous but now, when the full burden of my desolation was upon me, I was not so sure for at very least Moyra would be a link with a cherished past.

I sought her out, our two families watched and whispered, but even at first glance I knew that Moyra was not built to be a D'Artagnan and knew too that the ploys for her immediate future which formed immediately in my mind were not of a kind likely to fulfil the unabashed hopes of the senior Morpurgos and the senior Hewitts that our reunion would write the first paragraphs for a neat, happy and romantic concluding chapter to a story hitherto overladen with tragedy.

I knew that Moyra was now 19 years old and knew therefore that she would be no longer a pretty but pestilential infant but I was not prepared for the metamorphosis. This was a handsome and delectably nubile young woman. The pertness was still perceptible – not then nor for many years thereafter could I persuade myself that the primitive advice which so often John and I had offered to Basil had been made by the years inapposite – but pertness was now something dangerously akin to coquetry and the impudent grin now a provocative smile.

Dutifully I told myself that either I misread the signals or else that they were unintended. How could it be otherwise from a girl as devout as Moyra and in most things so conventional? How could it be otherwise from one, as she, reared to a stern Ulster Protestant morality? But I cared little for devoutness and for six years I had lived in a society which cared even less for all those conventions which were not its own, a society which, because it had no future, cared not at all for morality. I came close to shattering a friendship which in the event has lasted to this day only because on the brink I rediscovered scruples which I thought I had mislaid for ever.

Moyra was Basil's sister. Their parents had always treated me as an almost-son. Basil was dead, I the only son left to Marshall and Evadne Hewitt. *Ergo*, I was Moyra's brother. Moyra was now obviously and abundantly adult but the age-gap between us had been widened by my experience of war and she seemed by aeons younger than the Service girls with whom I had roistered on the *Ormonde*, in India, the Middle East. *Ergo*, alas and on all counts, it was my bounden duty to defend her against all assaults by brutal and licentious soldiers and at that moment, though I was not tempted to brutality, I knew of no soldier more eager for licentiousness than me.

For months whenever we were together my conscience battled with my *libido* – and for many years thereafter, even when we were both happily married, she to a man I liked and respected, there was no armistice. Even so, in those months which followed VE Day I was never more content than I was when in Moyra's company and she, being ignorant of the turmoil she occasioned, I do believe not unhappy in mine.

But one topic was by tacit agreement taboo and that the topic uppermost in our minds. We never mentioned Basil.

In those months I had good reason for depression but there was worse to come and the worse devastating.

A few weeks before the bomb on Hiroshima blasted the last remnants of purpose out of my military existence I met a girl who, immediately, almost drove Jane from my mind, the girl I was determined must marry me – and she was already married.

In the first days of my disembarkation leave before ever I was called to the War Office, dutifully I invited Geoff's fiancée to dine with me at Prunier's. The food was superb and, in an England still severely rationed, remarkably lavish. Through the first course we talked about Geoff, through the second and through the third. Over the coffee Jeanne asked me to tea at the family home.

I went to Radlett expecting no more than the hospitable reception due to Geoff's closest friend. I came away convinced that the Fates were bent on punishing me for the miracle of survival.

Jeanne met me at Radlett Station. We entered the Eyrie through the kitchen door having somehow shrugged-off in the garden an assault by a regiment of small children. I was introduced to Jeanne's mother (and that the only introduction of the day), a fine-looking elderly woman with a sparse matting of silver-white hair, wearing a loose-fitting dress of an antique pattern which, as later I was to discover, she never varied except by colour. I was immediately affected by her voice, deep and resonant; I heard only a couple of sentences and I knew how it was that Tita Brand had enthralled Shaw, Benson, audiences at Stratford, the Royal Court and in theatres all over Europe and America, but then I suspected, what later I found to be slanderous, that the warmth she showed to me was no more than a fine example of theatrical virtuosity.

I remember being amazed that a big woman with a big, almost masculine voice, knocked so timidly on her husband's study-door and that the words 'Kim, Jack's here' were spoken in a whisper, as if she was talking to pew-neighbour in the middle of a sermon.

Emile Cammaerts – a tall man but bent, as if apologizing for his height, his grey, soft and ragged beard flecked with red hairs and tobacco-stains, in his mouth a pipe exuding foul-smelling smoke – put his hands on my shoulders and said, 'So this is Jack who takes up so much space in Geoffrey's letters.' There was just a touch of something exotic in his accent.

One arm in mine, the other in Jeanne's he led us into a large sitting-room. There we were joined by Mme Cammaerts and, almost immediately, by several young women and most of the children I had seen in the garden. As so often happens when a welcome stranger is thrust into a long-established community the conversation was awkward. The women gossiped across me – not with any intention of excluding me but as if I had always been a familiar – about matters to them everyday. Michael had managed a complete sentence; the grocer in the High Street had kept for them some under-the-counter eggs; Helen had grazed her knee; a new curate was to preach his first sermon at the parish church. Only Emile paid particular attention to me and at that first meeting he won from me admiration and affection which never after faltered. He talked, not of trivia, not of the weather, not even of Geoff, but of poetry and war and, most flattering of all, about my literary ambitions.

The door opened and a girl came in carrying a laden tea-tray. It was unmistakably an entrance; all conversation was silenced, Martha had upstaged a whole cast of Marys; but this Martha had all the advantages. She stood for a moment posed in the doorway, smiled across at me as if we were old friends, then walked the width of the room, set down the tray on a table in the window-alcove and began to fill the tea-cups. Jeanne said something to me but I had no thought for her words. All my attention was centred on that tall slim figure, its every movement a delicious conspiracy between art and nature.

She came to sit on the sofa beside me; once she asked after Geoff, once she offered me more cake and once she answered a question from one of the children. Though I willed her to speak again so that I could listen to that skilfully modulated, soft but clear voice, she uttered not another word and I, for the first time in many years bashful when close to a woman, could think of nothing to say.

Jeanne walked with me down the hill to the station. 'I like your family', I said vacuously, and then, again a boy who cannot keep from talking about the topic which is uppermost in his mind, his latest love, 'Nan's a beauty, isn't she?'

Jeanne was casual – 'Nan, a beauty? She's a good-looker, true, but I'd hardly call her a beauty' – and I indignant, 'She's the best-looking girl I've seen in years. I'd put it higher than that if she wasn't married to your brother.'

Jeanne changed the subject but on the platform she spoke the words I had been longing to hear, 'Why don't you come down for a weekend?' Then she ruined the invitation, 'Can you manage Saturday week? Nan and Marie won't be here so we'll have plenty of room.' I nodded, my dismay outfacing courtesy, and Jeanne chatted on. My train was already signalled when something she was saying recaptured my attention, '. . . just like my mother, Kippe gave up the stage when her first child was born.'

My mind raced back over all that had happened that afternoon and found sense but no more comfort. There was no good reason why I had assumed that the lovely girl was Jeanne's sister-in-law and surely there had been only two actresses in the sitting-room, Mme Cammaerts and my sofa-companion.

'Kippe?' I asked lamely and Jeanne replied, 'You should know, you sat gawping at her most of the afternoon.' Then, assuming that I was doubting the name, she went on, 'Yes, Kippe it is; not a nickname; Catherine Noel Kippe in fact; Kippe without an R. My father was so excited by the advance in 1918 that he forgot his English and insisted on naming his new-born for the first village re-captured by the Belgian Army. The parson almost dropped the baby into the font when he heard he must christen her Kippe.'

'She's married?' I asked, inanely forgetting that I had been told she had two children. Jeanne bridled. 'Of course she is. Her husband's with the Pioneer Corps somewhere in the Middle East. The two little boys are hers, Pieter and Michael.' Then she softened and a touch of sadness came into her voice. 'Pieter, the Belgian way, with an I, after our younger brother who was killed with the RAF.'

In the train to St Pancras and for weeks thereafter I consoled myself with Army snobbery, petty, rancid and, I knew, ludicrous but still comforting. A girl as precious as Kippe had no need to waste her loveliness on the Pioneer Corps. 'As a golden jewel in a pig's snout. . .'.

I had seen so often the consequences of Dear Johns and myself had suffered bitterly from betrayal. I had no wish to inflict pain on Kippe's husband but, as with each return visit to Radlett, interest became more and more obsessive, so did I more vehemently justify myself to myself with this unworthy rationalization: for two years the Middle East had not been a theatre-of-war and service in the Pioneer Corps was not and never had been real soldiering.

Soon I had better cause for the assault upon which I was determined and cause also for hope that it would be successful. Kippe had married young, early in the War, to one who had been a fellow-student at RADA and, if somewhat obliquely, she confided to me that she had come to doubt the wisdom of a decision taken at a time when the impulses of the moment were undeniably persuasive.

I convinced myself that I was embarking on a noble cause: I would make her truly happy – and, as an afterthought, her children also. We no longer troubled to hide the fact that at Radlett I was now Kippe's guest but Tita, to my eyes amazingly innocent for one who had passed her younger days in a profession not notable for fidelity, seemed unaware of what was happening and Emile watched us, thoughtful, compassionate but, because he was so utterly convinced of the irrefragable condition of matrimony, still without fear that anything disastrous would come from our affection.

Kippe and I were like children playing 'Let's pretend'. We were simulating a courtship, but we were not children, we were in love and we knew that our love had no future. 'Would she could make of me a saint, Or I of her a sinner.' Cravenly I decided upon retreat. I would stay away from Radlett and I would stay away from Kippe.

The excuse for honourable disengagement came with a letter from Austria and for a week or so as I considered its contents I thought that the gods had at last relented, for here was a way both to escape my personal predicament and to secure my professional future. Brigadier Finlayson wanted me back with the Brigade, he had discussed the practicalities with the Divisional Commander and General Weir with the Military Secretary. If I would postpone for a year my right to demobilisation I would go to his headquarters as Brigade Major and – an even more intriguing possibility – if I would apply for a Regular commission I would have his support, Chippy's and the GOC's and there would soon be available to me a plum appointment at Division.

I did not see this invitation as in any way a threat to my literary ambitions; Bernard Fergusson and other acquaintances had demonstrated to me that it is possible to follow the professions of soldiering and writing in tandem; and almost I plunged. Had I done so I might be writing now as a

Major-General (Retd.) or as the central character of a notorious court-martial – and almost certainly as a bachelor – but inevitably, if illogically, I took the letter to Kippe.

I did not wait for her reactions. As soon as I was with her, I knew that I could not tolerate an overseas posting.

Still, our plans might have remained what they had been from the start, no more than idle dreams, had it not been for the bombing of Hiroshima and Nagasaki. Atom bombs blasted all purpose out of my military life but, much more significantly, they made me uncomfortable in the Cammaerts home.

There was at The Eyrie no evidence of antagonism to me. Indeed my affection and respect for Emile deepened with every meeting. I listened with delight when he spoke of his friendships with Chesterton, Elgar and Maeterlinck and I was no less enthralled on those rarer occasions when Tita told of her life with her mother, the *diva* Marie Brema who had sung for Wagner and created for Elgar the Angel in *The Dream of Gerontius*, and of her own career at Stratford and the Royal Court. Even though I was tempted to question how Emile could reconcile his Leftist dogma with his fervent Royalism and to comment that some of the younger members of the family were closer to Stalin than to Clement Attlee, I managed to meet with a polite smile the communal enthusiasm for Socialism. I could ignore the seemingly incongruous dedication to High Anglicanism. 'Your family', I told Kippe, 'is so High that you look down on the Pope, mine so Low that we look up to the Methodists.' Compline, Mass, Eucharist, Confession: all these I could slough off but not their unanimous condemnation of the action which forced the monstrous Japanese to surrender, which to my War Office informed estimate saved the Allies millions of casualties and which allowed to Geoff, to Francis and to me the prospect of living on into old age.

As is my wont when faced with people or theses which I cannot abide, I took refuge in surly silence; my sulks hurt Kippe; that I could not endure and so I stayed away from Radlett and we began to meet in town.

In my flat over lunch – assuredly a chaste meal – and under a portrait-photograph of Jane, which for all my scrupulous preparations I had somehow forgotten to remove, for the first time I insisted on discussing divorce at length.

The canon of her faith, the convictions of her family, her profound sense of duty and concern for the future of her children: all served to persuade Kippe that divorce was unthinkable but I noticed, with mounting hope, that even so she was ready, almost eager, to consider it, if only as an abstract concept, as something that happened not to her but to other people – and even they reprehensible.

Conscious that I, who shared none of her inhibitions, could not advance my cause by denying her principles, I turned to practicalities. I began to set up an Aunt Sally, thinking that before I had finished erecting it I would find some way to knock it down. I did not mention what was truly in my mind, that her marriage was a mistake, its future unpropitious, that I needed her and was confident that together we could make a good life for the boys. Instead, as if it was the only obstacle before us, I complained that I had no career, no money and no possibility that I could afford to keep a family.

I did not then appreciate how cunning was my shift of ground. In all my life I have never met anyone so utterly unconcerned with security as is Kippe. Before I had completed my account of my pitiable and helpless condition she interrupted and, as if already all countervailing arguments were thereby dismissed, proceeded to explain how we could manage well enough until such time as my career blossomed.

For several months thereafter there were hesitations, even *voltes-face*; but never after that luncheon in Clanricarde Gardens was I without optimism.

My gods must have laughed when they appointed Allen Lane, himself a shifty lover, to knock my Aunt Sally out of sight. The jest has kept them laughing for more than forty years for our lives became intertwined with Allen's.

Somehow I managed to keep separated from the perturbations of my private life my busy-ness as a writer. When I read the notes from Lehmann, polite but firmly dismissive, I knew how Adam must have felt when he was expelled from the Garden of Eden but I found solace for my failure in my immediate conquest of another Penguin journal. *Transatlantic* was a wartime venture designed to capture and enlarge the interest in things American forced upon the British by the new Grand Alliance and by the presence in their midst of tens of thousands of young Americans. It had never come my way during my years of real soldiering; I doubt that many copies reached the British Army overseas, which was perhaps just as well for Anglo-American concord because to us, the serving soldiers, the Alliance was a cross we knew we must carry but preferred to ignore, associating it as we did with sinister rescue-operations in the Kassarien Gap, with Mark Clark's flamboyant and unnecessary march on Rome, with crates of coca-cola landing on some tenuously-held beach, with the mischief wrought by American diplomats and politicians as we fought our way through the bloody murkiness of the Greek Civil War, with too much pay, short overseas tours, a riot of medal-ribbons and, most deleterious of all to affection, with readily-verifiable rumours of conquests by British-based Americans of the wives and girl-friends of absent British servicemen.

Back home, and a copy of *Transatlantic* in my hand, I saw that for me this was an obvious market. An Englishman who had been an undergraduate in an American university was in those days a rarity. In that select club of missionaries who had survived the cannibals' stew-pot I was the only member who had qualified for Penguin publication by reason also of membership into the aristocracy of *New Writing*. The editor of the sister-magazine could but share my view that I must write for him.

It was that editor, Tom Fairley, who persuaded Allen Lane to summon me to his London office.

There was nothing sensational in the manner or peculiar in the circumstances of our first meeting that could have persuaded even the most percipient soothsayer to predict that this was to be for me a seismic rendezvous, that in time I would be twice Allen's heir, his biographer and the grandfather of his grandchildren. For the moment I was just another volunteer for service in a revolution, marching forward to be inspected by the revolution's instigator and leader.

We met in a tiny and untidy room, Allen gave me a glass of white wine and glared suspiciously at my rank-badges, my burnished Sam Browne and my campaign-ribbons. I saw a brisk, handsome man in his early forties, looking like a yeoman-farmer who had submitted himself to the scrupulous attentions of the best barber and the most exclusive tailor in London.

He spoke first, his tones, sharp and chilly, denying any eagerness that I might read into his words. 'Tom suggested we should meet, you've written sometimes for him and for Lehmann.' It was a statement not a question. I nodded and for the next twenty minutes, until I exhausted my capacity for making autobiography at once decently modest and sufficiently self-important to persuade him that I merited a job with Penguins, he stared absent-mindedly out of the window. I tried to explain my predicament, suspended ambiguously and indefinitely between military and civilian existence. Allen grunted. My attempts to make relevant to a career as publisher my time as shivering mouse among academicians sounded vacuous even to me. Wisdom, inspired by his occasional but, it seemed to me, consistently deprecating glances at the formalized evidence of my military pretensions, prevented me from saying too much about the last six years. And what, after all, had they contributed to my potential in a publishing-house? An itinerant's knowledge of twenty-six countries, some experience of gun-positions, tactical headquarters, and night-clubs in Bombay, Cairo, Teheran, Athens and Rome.

Allen signalled the end of the interview by offering to refill my glass. I refused. Without a smile he shook my hand and thanked me for coming. Then, when I had hailed a taxi, he changed his mind. 'Going to the War Office? Drop me off at Whitehall Court.'

In the taxi he spoke but once. 'Gunner, eh? Used to be a Gunner myself. T.A. Nonsense, but we had horses on the Government.'

He stood on the pavement while I paid off the cab. He put out his hand again and for the first time I saw what I was to see so many times in the coming years, a mischievous smile, the grin of a boy who knows that he has done wrong and does not regret it. 'Public Relations, eh? Could be useful. I'll think about it.' He vanished into Whitehall Court and I walked glumly the few yards to the War Office.

When I arrived next morning at my office there was a message on my desk. 'Ring Allen Lane at Harmondsworth.' On the phone he was laconic.

'Come to lunch; I want to talk to you. Silverbeck, Stanwell Moor. 12.30.'

'Today?'

'Why not?'

I had no answer. I commandeered a staff-car and a busty ATS driver and arrived at Silverbeck, Allen's elegant William the Fourth house close to what is now the end of the main runway of London Airport, just in time for the first of five gins.

So did eight other guests. I was entertained exclusively by Allen's wife, Lettice, a pretty, intelligent woman who appeared to have no interest in publishing and no knowledge of why it was that I had been invited. Allen ignored my presence; throughout lunch he addressed to me not one word; but over coffee he demanded that I go with him on a tour of his gardens.

I have no interest in horticulture, Allen was an enthusiastic expert and in all that long hour my torpor was broken and my impatience relieved only for a few moments, when he interrupted his interminable lecture to talk to two nude little girls paddling in a pool.

At last we arrived back at my car. The driver scrambled out of the back seat, wrenched her tunic across her bulging chest, crammed her cap over her straggling hair, held open the door and managed something she took to be a salute.

I summoned courage. 'You wanted to talk to me!' It was inane; he had been doing nothing else for sixty minutes, but he smiled, again that naughty-boy smile. 'Ah yes, that's it. Knew I had some reason for getting you down. At Penguins we don't buy advertising space. I'm setting up a Public Relations Department. You're in PR. The job's yours if you want it. Can't pay more than about five hundred a year. When can you start?'

Only twice in almost thirty years did I get the better of Allen Lane. This was the first time and I contrived my victory by judicious silence. I did not tell him that my skills in the technique of public relations were about as significant as the small typewritten label on my office-door, PR2 (lb).

I stopped the car by the first call-box on the Bath Road. In those days before vandalizing became a popular sport call-boxes were even so always occupied in moments of high excitement or emergency. This one was filled – literally so – with a huge corporal and his tiny girl-friend. The phone was off the hook but talking was not their employment. I rapped on the glass and, perhaps impressed by my rank, they came out looking sheepish.

'Sorry', I said. 'Urgent.'

I phoned Kippe. 'It's on. Penguins have offered me a job. Now we can plan that divorce. And I've just seen the girls our boys must marry.' She was as excited as I, her questions urgent and curious but she said nothing about divorce or about my premature proprietorial claim upon Pieter and Michael before those infuriating pips which invariably interrupt the most important telephone conversations. I fumbled for small change and found none. My driver had come away without her purse.

When next we met, Kippe put up a fine performance of shared pleasure in my good fortune but I saw it as an act; something had happened which made delight impossible. I pressed her and it came out. She had heard from her husband; he would be home in a month, a couple at the most.

'We must tell him.'

'Of course I must tell him.'

'And then what?'

She answered only by repeating my question, 'And then what?'

A week later Geoff arrived from Austria and I had to go back to Radlett to join in the planning for his wedding. He, Jeanne and all her family received me as warmly as ever but I was over-sensitised and I imagined that there was resentment, even anger, underlying their easy acceptance of the man who for so long they had known would stand as Geoff's best-man.

Late in September, on the night before the wedding, I stayed at The Eyrie but for most of the evening after dinner I kept out of the family circle, excusing myself on the grounds that I considered it part of a best man's duty that he polish the groom's belt, shoes and buttons. In recent weeks the pressures upon Kippe had become more vocal and intense. 'As a faithful daughter of the Church it is your bounden duty to abandon this attachment before foolishness traps you into sin beyond redemption': in my imagination I could hear the unctuous counsel and so angered was I by my certainty that Kippe's family and friends would use her churchmanship as prime agent for engineering our separation that, for the first time in my life, my agnosticism was soured by hatred. If *caritas* could be driven out by obsequious attention to the dogma of the Church then, thank God for my disbelief. I was tempted to face my persecutors in open debate and might have done so had it not been that still (as indeed for ever after) I could not bring myself to attack Kippe's faith and had it not been that, as each day in my bath and each night in my bed, I rehearsed the dialectics which I would use to destroy the opposition, an impish familiar whispered words into my ear which turned fury into self-mockery. 'Though I speak with the tongues of men and of angels, and have not charity, I am become as sounding brass, or a tinkling cymbal': I prepared myself to enlist St Paul as my junior and I glimpsed triumph in debate when I recalled that the 1881 New Testament uses invariably the word 'love', so convenient for my didactic purpose, in preference to the 1611 word 'charity'.

Seeing Geoff and Jeanne on their wedding-day so earnest and so content as we listened to Cranmer's wondrous orotundities, my black mood was temporarily dissipated but, traitor to my own convictions, I did not deny to myself the masochistic ecstasy that came from fancying that these glorious words were being spoken for Kippe and me. Only when the parson came close to the injunction 'Those whom God hath joined together let no man put asunder' did the sceptic in me stop the ears of the romantic.

I was burdened by other substantial perplexities. Each time I asked for confirmation of my Penguin appointment, Allen Lane answered with an evasion: we must wait until I knew when I was to be demobilized; my status must be precisely established; there was as yet no office for me at Harmondsworth. His trimming I kept from Kippe, for fear that it would deprive me of the most practical item in my catalogue of persuasion.

It was not until I was well-entrenched at Harmondsworth that I discovered that for two years before he met me Allen had been promising the post of PRO at Penguins to the very man who had arranged that first meeting, to his close friend Tom Fairley, but I soon learnt that disloyalty in this kind, like the evasiveness with which he served me, was endemic to Allen's nature.

For months Allen denied me certainty. Many times in the years that followed I, and many others, suffered in similar fashion. The simple, the direct, was to Allen anathema. A man of unquestionable genius and the only truly original publisher I met in a career that brought me into close contact with most leaders of the book-trade in all the continents, nevertheless he was incapable of standing by his own decisions. He was besotted by the process of negotiation; so much so that he shirked its conclusion. In his dealings with his fellow-publishers, but even more patently in personal relations, today's clear affirmative became for him tomorrow's perhaps. It was as if he studied Machiavelli whilst suffering from a hangover, as if he was a skilful but eccentric chess-player who, having planned and executed moves intricate beyond necessity, over-turned the board just before the game was won. Even the most trivial issue he felt compelled to complicate. Always he cavorted, always he blurred the edges of decision so that those with whom he was dealing could not know where they stood, so that all definition must remain susceptible to his whim, so that for him there would always be an escape-clause.

Made impatient by Allen's havering, early in the autumn of 1945 I put Penguins out-of-mind and set off again in a grim search for some other key to the door to life as a civilian. Carefully drafted letters, phone-calls, interviews, lunches at West End clubs brought nothing but a sequence of hedged promises. Then, suddenly, one of my earliest applications re-surfaced. I was summoned to Broadcasting House and, after ten minutes of idle talk, I was offered appointment as Talks Producer, North American Service, at a salary of £440 a year, my duties to begin as soon as I wished after demobilization.

I called Allen Lane and, when I announced to him that Penguins must prosper or founder without my assistance, to my surprise gently he set out to dissuade me. I would be lost in the morass at Broadcasting House – 'Might as well become a Civil Servant' – there were no limits to my future at Penguins. He had given much thought, he said, to planning for my indoctrination into the ethos of Penguins. As it would still be several months before I was out of the Army and as I had told him (I had not) that my duties at the War Office were by no means onerous, would it not be sensible for me to pass some of my spare time in the Penguin atmosphere? I could go to editorial meetings. 'Just a second, let me look at my diary', and then, his voice over-loaded with histrionic amazement, 'I see that we have an editorial panel fixed for tomorrow morning'.

I was tempted and I fell, but I did not then realize that by chance I had put my finger on the trigger of the only weapon which could force Allen to stand and deliver. Tell him that some prize that he coveted was about to fall into the hands of someone else and he would sell his daughters, his wife and his mistress to seize it for himself. This, his collector's mania, made him often and with good reason unpopular, but it was a powerful factor in his success and in the success of Penguins, for it was this that impelled him to colonize for Penguin dominion over all the continents of the world and of the mind, this that persuaded him to enrich the Penguin list with all manner of titles foreign to the original concept, this that brought him to create that marvellous variety of series – Specials, Pelicans, Puffins, Pocket Scores, Classics, the History of Art – and against all precepts commonly acknowledged by book-publishers, encouraged him to establish a wide range of periodicals. 'Let's have a go'; I was to hear him speak those words a hundred times; they were the key to his philosophy of publishing and from them stemmed the achievement. He and his creation must be every-where and in everything and so it was that Penguins became universal and of all publishers the most polymathic.

Next morning I went to the Bureau of Current Affairs, 117 Piccadilly, to the office of William Emrys Williams, Chief Editor of Penguins, Allen's closest adviser and friend (later the Secretary-General of the Arts Council) where all major Penguin meetings were held. In the boardroom there were also gathered Williams, Allen and a larger, less mercurial version of Allen, his brother Richard (with Allen and another brother, John, who had been killed in the War, the founders of Penguins). Allen's secretary, Tatyana Kent and a fair-haired, bird-like woman, Eunice Frost (a superb manager of authors and almost obsessively dedicated to Allen and to Penguins) fol-lowed me into the room. Next came another, like me in uniform, Peter Messer, a major in the United States Army, who it seemed was to work with me in Public Relations, though which of us was to be the senior none vouchsafed for many months, and, finally, two men of much the same build but in manner, tone and appearance as unlike as any two can be.

One was Edmond Segrave, neatly. conventionally dressed, his balding head and his nose ostentatiously ruddy as if he had spent months sun-bathing with all other parts of his physiognomy protected. The other had a face scarred by excised tattoo-marks. He wore a suit of massive tweed, a red shirt, a shocking-pink tie and on one hand a grey suede glove. He car-ried a large gladstone-bag and, before ever the meeting had started, he tipped its contents carelessly on to the polished table. Books, books and ever more books. This was Alan Glover, the unacknowledged genius of

Penguins and the best-informed man I have ever met, as knowledgeable about Russian literature, psychoanalysis and the more obscure religions – to most of which he had been converted at some time in his life – as he was about cricket scores or bus time-tables, and the only man I have ever known who could correct galley-proofs whilst strap-hanging in a rush-hour tube-train.

Glover took me at once into his care. It was he who identified for me each of those present. Segrave, he whispered, was the Editor of *The Bookseller*. At the time the information meant nothing to me, but within weeks I was to discover significance that would stay with me for the rest of my career. *The Bookseller* is the most influential of all book-trade journals, the Epistle to the Corinthians sent out weekly for the enlightenment of publishers and booksellers.

There was about my first Penguin editorial board, as about most of the Penguin meetings I attended over the next twenty years, an air of inconsequence and something which, long after, Eunice Frost described to me as 'glorious amateurishness', that, had I not been so overawed by my good fortune at being present among the arbiters of enlightenment, as a collaborator in the making of reputations and the breaking of authors' hearts, I might have taken for carelessness. Much of the conversation was casual, gossipy and to me incomprehensible, but we went through the pile of books at great speed as if by the prompting of some corporate chemistry. Most of the titles were offerings from those same, hard-faced, hard-back publishers who, only a decade earlier, had refused to co-operate in Allen Lane's lunatic experiment and who had at that time delightedly forecast his impending bankruptcy.

Segrave fidgeted but said nothing. Glover snapped out summaries of readers' reports and his own monosyllabic verdicts, 'Yes', 'No', 'Could be', and Tatyana Kent sorted the books into three neat piles. Richard Lane smoked his pipe, muttered calculations and occasionally scribbled figures in a small note-book. Allen was palpably the central figure, the chairman, but he directed nothing. Sometimes he pursed his lips, from time to time he smiled, grunted, scowled or nodded but it was not until his brother announced that some book which was about to be moved to the Yes file was bound to prove uncommercial that Allen intervened to any effect.

'Should we do it?' he asked Glover.

'It's an important book, the best of its kind for years.'

Allen looked enquiringly at Williams. Williams nodded.

'We'll do it. Why not?' said Allen, 'Swings and roundabouts, roundabouts and swings.' This was another of his favourite texts and another with which I was to become delightedly familiar.

Williams's interpolations were of a different order and many of them far from the proclaimed purpose of the meeting. Frequently he launched into lengthy and scabrous accounts of the private lives of the authors whose works we had accepted or rejected. Once, when we had been in session for almost two hours, he left the table, scrabbled at a desk in the window, returned to his seat clasping a magazine and began to read aloud from the work of a young poet. Williams's own Welshness became more obvious as he read and his slight speech-impediment exaggerated the bitter humour of the verse.

This was my introduction to Dylan Thomas. Williams's irrelevant entracte may have been no more than an expression of boredom with our routine proceedings, but I like to think that it was a deliberate statement of standards, a reminder that there existed, somewhere in the world outside that pompous board-room, genius shrieking for attention, literary authority that reduced to the puny status of efficient hackdom most of the books on the table before us.

Williams finished his reading. There was no comment but the interruption seemed to serve as a cue for Eunice Frost. Hitherto she had been no more than Allen's shadow. When he nodded she nodded and when he glared she scowled but now, responding to some hint that I could not catch, she launched herself into an elegant exposition of matters that were in no way connected with the books that had been carried to the meeting in Glover's gladstone-bag. All in the room were alert and even I, in my ignorance, was caught up in the fervour. This was the real business, the breath that kept alive the unique flame of Penguins, we were discussing plans for 'originals', for Pelicans, for Penguin Modern Painters and for Penguin Specials.

Allen rattled out dates and print-runs, Richard costings, Williams and Glover added an occasional gloss to Eunice Frost's summaries of the qualifications of some chosen author or a note to confirm her view that Penguins should turn its attention to some new subject.

Eunice Frost's passion seemed exorbitant, for there was no argument; again that strange corporate chemistry was at work and all present seemed to be unerringly aware of what was right for Penguins.

Eunice ended her oration. Allen pulled a sheaf of envelopes from his pocket, sorted them on the table and found what he required. 'I met an old boy at a party last night. He has an idea for a book. . .'

I could not then know that, for the third time in twenty-four hours, I was hearing a phrase that, echoing and re-echoing through the years of my Penguin experience, was to stay with me for the rest of my days as the epitome of Allen's especial genius.

Segrave's fidgets were by now offerings to St Vitus and ever more often and ever more ostentatiously he looked at his watch. Richard Lane took pity on him. 'Edmond has a lunch-date. Shouldn't we deal with his business and let him go?'

Segrave, it appeared, had already written and published in *The Bookseller* a series of articles on the short but brilliant history of Penguins. The firm planned to gather them together as *Ten Years of Penguins* and to give the pamphlet world-wide and free distribution.

For the first time that morning Allen noticed my presence. 'We keep in touch with our readers by sending them lists, a publicity magazine, *Penguin Progress* and such items as this *Ten Years of Penguins*. It'll be your business to see to it if you come to PR.'

The instruction was too vague for my staff-trained mind and I refused to notice the conditional but Allen had already forgotten me, swept up in the excitements of an anniversary celebration. Nothing delighted him more than this, the serenading of a Penguin birthday, the brutal and public dig in the ribs of those who had prophesied that Penguins would not last so much as one year.

Should *Ten Years of Penguins* be enlivened by illustrations? By drawings, perhaps, commissioned from some suitable cartoonist? The names that flickered around the table – Arno, Bateman, Fougasse, Thurber, all in the first division of British and American cartoonists – bolstered my awareness that I was close to the higher slopes of Parnassus. There was no suspicion of ludicrous ambition; it was implicit that any of these great men would be glad to drop whatever he was doing to accept a commission from Penguins. But when the moment of consensus arrived and all, with the possible exception of Allen himself, settled on Osbert Lancaster, I knew for the first time that I had not only arrived but arrived as an equal. I spoke. I had knowledge denied to the others; Lancaster was at the Embassy in Athens and still enmeshed in the affairs of a nation that had come but recently out of one brutal civil war and was threatened with another.

Allen stared out of the window. The others listened with due politeness as I explained why I doubted that Lancaster would be available. Allen dragged his attention back into the room and, as if I had never spoken, continued the earlier discussion. Not Lancaster, not Thurber, not even Peter Arno (who had helped to make the Lanes' first fortune), not any of these already bloated masters. It was Penguin's business to find and foster new talent. We needed for *Ten Years of Penguins* some promising new artist.

At once elated by my privileged status as the source of information not available to these sophisticates and deflated by Allen's disdain, I blurted out 'What about Jon?'

There was a long, embarrassed and embarrassing silence then Glover asked 'John who?'

Almost I was angry. As well ask of any man who had been through the Western Desert, Italy and Greece 'Who was Montgomery and who was Alexander?' I tried to explain that Jon's 'Two Types' cartoon in *The Crusader* and the *Eighth Army News* had held our morale as surely as leave-passes, cigarette-rations or ENSA concert-parties but I was flogging the air. Only Richard Lane showed any sympathetic interest. Allen stared once more at my uniform, my rank-badges and my medal-ribbons. 'No illustrations, I think. Just good, clean design.'

I took it as a snub but it was in truth another revelation and this time a symptom not of genius but of weakness. Just too young for the First War and, because of his professional achievements, by the outbreak of the Second far too important to the national effort to be allowed to take up again the commission he had held in the peace-time Territorial Army, Allen was wrong-footed in the presence of soldiers and resentful of old soldiers' tales. This strange and unnecessary sense of guilt would cost him dear in the next few years, when the first genuine competitors to Penguins entered the market and built their reputations and financial stability almost entirely on the war-books which Penguin rejected as ephemera.

All unconsciously Segrave hauled me back into the magic circle from which I had been so summarily dismissed. 'If no illustrations' he said, 'perhaps a trifle or two of light verse. As you all know, I have a certain facility in the writing of humorous poems. My friends Chesterton and Belloc frequently said to me. . .'

Richard Lane filled his pipe. Glover dug me in the ribs and Allen actually winked at me as if he thought I must see the joke.

'Not this time, Edmond. Just good design and your fine prose.'

There were still three books on the table. Two were turned down without debate, the third was about to be accepted but Allen's wink had given me courage. This was a book I had destroyed only weeks earlier in a *Tribune* review. I damned it for the Penguin editors in a voice as powerful as any that I had ever used on a gun-position and with a fluency of which I had never thought myself capable.

Without spoken orders or protest from the others Tatyana moved the book to the 'No' pile.

This was power!

Segrave, Richard Lane, Eunice Frost and Bill Williams left. Allen moved towards the door, then turned and put his hand on my shoulder. Once more he looked disparagingly at my military trappings. 'Do you have a degree as well?'

'A B.A. and half a Ph.D.'

'Good Lord!' – But now he was smiling. 'Glover' he called across my shoulder, 'fill him in will you.' Then to me: 'Can't give you lunch today but we'll see you again at Silverbeck soon.'

He bustled out of the room then poked his head round the door, his eyes bright with mischief. '£440 a year, wasn't it?'

He was gone before I had time to acknowledge that I had been admitted to the Penguin aviary and confirmed in my vocation. I was half-way down Piccadilly, hopping over the cracks in the pavement in a manner entirely unbecoming to a staff officer and almost a publishing gentleman before I realized that Allen had slipped his hand into my pocket and filched a handful of five-pound notes.

In the next weeks I went often to 117 Piccadilly, and on occasion to Harmondsworth. There, sitting in some office temporarily vacant, I dictated replies to letters by the hundred from admirers all over the world. Many correspondents enclosed money and asked that we send to them as they were published all thrillers, all poetry, all history or all books on current affairs and I suggested to Allen that we make active the hint by establishing within the Public Relations Department a direct sales system. Either because he did not know or, more likely, because he did not care, Allen did not tell me that his 'Let's have a go' set Penguins in contravention of an edict of the Publishers Association.

Nor did he ever suggest that I be paid for my moonlighting.

The expected blow fell: Kippe's husband was back in England. I took her to within a hundred yards of a Knightsbridge hotel and, after a melo-dramatic outburst shamefully inconsistent with my well-bred intention to show myself gracious in defeat, I watched as she walked back into matri-mony. Her customary grace had vanished; she shambled like one who drags a great weight.

A week later Kippe announced to her parents, to her husband and, after much cross-examination about my willingness to accept a ready-made family, to me that she intended to make her future with me.

Kippe's husband accepted the verdict gracefully, if not with equanimity; her brother Francis, just back home with as evidence to his formidable rep-utation as a Resistance leader a DSO., an MC and a Croix de Guerre *avec palmes,* acting according to principles which in his case did not include High Anglican dogma, remained neutral; the rest launched against Kippe a united, fierce and unrelenting assault.

It was a tactical error, for there is in Kippe as in so many gentle and hes-itant people a sturdy streak of obstinacy. She can be cajoled but vehemence only strengthens her determination to do as she thinks fit.

The decision to despatch Emile to open up a front was much more shrewd, for there was affection between us and in debate we spoke the same language.

In the years that followed, I lunched with Emile once a month at his club and the ritual never varied. A man almost untouched by vanity, he was even so inordinately proud of the fact that he had been elected to the Athenaeum, at the same meeting which picked Montgomery, under some rule which allows to the Committee the right to bring in to that consor-tium of eminence men even more distinguished than those who ordinarily put themselves forward for membership. Being a Belgian and therefore by definition a gourmet, his pride in the Club did not extend to its cuisine. Throughout each meal he groused about the quality of Athenaeum cook-ing and, the meal ended and his bill paid, he led me into the hall, crammed on his head his filthy hat, asked me where I had left mine (though I had told him a dozen times that, except perforce in the Army, I had not worn a hat since I was eleven years old) marched me to the door, and there announced to me and to the many who could hear 'Now we will go to your club where the coffee is at least drinkable.'

At our first Athenaeum encounter, however, there was none of this. At lunch we might have been two strangers meeting for the first time. He searched frantically for some comfortably impersonal topic, the paintings of Rubens, the harsh injustice meted out by Allied propaganda to King Leopold of the Belgians, the amiability and genius of his friend Chesterton. Lunch over, he took me up to a little room at the top of the building (which ever after when I was a member I avoided), sat me down and gathered himself for an assault. We were both embarrassed, I because I knew that he had written a book attacking divorce and so was fearful that a divorce in his own family might be used against him by his enemies, and he, as generously he admitted, because his own history opened up a gap in his defences. In Belgium, before ever he met Tita, he had himself been involved in a much-publicized relationship to which he and his *inamorata* had allowed the name of marriage.

I was in no mood to use the weapon of *tu quoque* but I saw no reason to hold back knowledge that long since he had pronounced Kippe's first marriage a mistake. This was my only thrust; for the best part of two hours we fenced.

From me: the Church condemned divorce; so be it, let the Church also live by its own vaunted doctrine of forgiveness. From Emile: Kippe would be denied the solace of Holy Communion. From me: not necessarily, there were bishops and priests sufficiently gifted with charity to allow a divorced woman to take wine and bread. From him: our actions must hurt Tita and disrupt a contented and united family. From me: none need be dismayed by Kippe's happiness. Uncharacteristically he fumbled for the precise English words when he spoke of Kippe's husband, and the suggestion that after all he had been through in recent years he deserved better than rejection was withdrawn almost before it was offered: 'No, that's not a good argument; I know you haven't been idling at the Ritz'. And then, as if a momentary lapse in scrupulous advocacy forced from him a compensatory concession, Emile allowed freely that he did not deny my love for the children. 'It is just. . .', he paused, laughed and quoted:

> Where be his quiddities now, his
> quiddities, his cases, his
> tenures, and his tricks?

I repeat myself and I see that repetition cannot shift you.' He elbowed himself out of the depths of his chair, stood rarely erect, put a hand on my shoulder and said 'All my principles forbid me to give you my blessing; my love you will always have, you, Kippe and the boys.'

We found allies and in unexpected quarters. In its own austere, Evangelical fashion, my family was as fervent against divorce as the Cammaerts but my father fell in love with Kippe at their first meeting and, as we stood on his door-step saying good-bye, he turned to me. 'She's my daughter,' he said, 'get her for me. It's your best chance, perhaps your only chance.'

My sister Bess came to be introduced to Kippe and the boys. Her verdict, delivered in her habitual headmistressy tones, was no less enthusiastic if a deal more ambiguous. 'I'm sorry for her. She's right for you but I'm not so certain you're right for her. I doubt if the two of you will last together but you'd better try it. Poor girl.' Then she softened, 'She's all you've said she is. Don't hurt her and for God's sake don't do anything to hurt those adorable boys.'

We began the seedy process of divorce.

Despite his words to Glover Allen had launched a new series of evasions. When I broke to him the news that had filtered down to me on the War Office grapevine that my demobilization had been set for April 1946, he answered that there would be no office free for me at Harmondsworth until July at the earliest.

I was not amused. I now had responsibilities for the lives of three others and I had no intention of wasting my hard-earned gratuity on giving amusement to Allen. I appealed to Bill Williams and Bill understood more than any other of Allen's collaborators, both the tortuous mentality of his friend and the severity of the practical problems which that tortuousness imposed on his victims. He produced a compromise. When I left the Army I could work as a salaried editor at the Bureau of Current Affairs until Harmondsworth was ready to receive me.

The Bureau was Williams's eventually unsuccessful effort to continue in peace-time his highly successful war-time venture in adult education, the Army Bureau of Current Affairs. In the war years I had paid little heed to ABCA and, indeed, I had kept as far away from all Army educational activities as my ingenuity would permit, for I was sensitive to the threat to interesting service, promotion and spare time implicit in my degree and research fellowship and I had no wish to have foisted on me the unenviable and unhonoured role of Unit Education Officer. Nevertheless I was dimly aware that ABCA had been wondrously effective in informing the Services about the larger issues of the War and it was exhilarating to find myself tied to the two institutions, ABCA (if only in its post-bellum state) and Penguin Books, which had magicked the successors to Wellington's despised soldiery into well-informed civilians in uniform.

However no sooner did Allen hear that I was digging in at 117 Piccadilly than he found me an office at Harmondsworth.

In that same week I was demobilized, an event honoured by a grateful country by the presentation to me of a shapeless suit, a trilby, a letter signed in facsimile on behalf of His Majesty by the Permanent Secretary of the War Office, Eric Speed (yet another Old Blue) and a gratuity of £400.

So ended my long career as soldier, almost seven years that had seen me in many countries, in circumstances often harsh and often strangely luxurious, often terrified, sometimes discontented and yet, in sum, perversely happy. I had learnt affection and respect for men who in peace-time would never have crossed my path. I had discovered a self I had never known

before, a more resilient and yet less self-satisfied me. And so began my new
life. I was a publisher, I was a writer, I had an almost-wife and two very
real and very rumbustious children. I was ready for anything and eager for
everything.

11

Peripatetic Penguin

When, at Blunden's suggestion, John Hayward invited me to edit Leigh Hunt's *Autobiography* for his Cresset Library, I felt much as Scott Fitzgerald when Scribner's accepted *This Side of Paradise*. I wanted to tell every passing stranger that I had been summoned to join a literary company which included Gide, Eliot and Veronica Wedgwood. That it was Hunt I was called to edit gave me especial delight, for since my school days I had felt a peculiar empathy for this, the least of my three greatest schoolfellows, and my sense of community with him had been enhanced by the coincidence of transatlantic background. I did not presume any equivalence between my activities or aspirations and the achievements of the mighty Coleridge or the inimitable Elia, but I could pretend to myself that there was some affinity with Hunt, like me at once author and editor and, sitting now at my Penguin desk, I had some little authority for my dream that the day would come when I would discover for my generation its Keats or its Shelley.

Throughout my career, deaf to my own opinion that the roles of publisher and author are antipathetic, sometimes hectically but always to some degree, I have been involved in these two closely-related but mutually contradictory careers. Both have given me much satisfaction and from the emotional and mental strain imposed by attempting to run the two in tandem, I have learned at least discipline and a measure of cunning in dealing, as author with my fellow-publishers, as publisher with my fellow-authors.

When Hayward also encouraged me to write my first full-length book, excitement became ecstasy but the burden forced upon me by the call to continue at one and the same time my Penguin responsibilities, the scrupulous scholarship demanded by the Cresset Library, and the creative necessities of *American Excursion* persuaded me to construct for myself a severe regimen. This regimen, though it is utterly distasteful to my indolent nature, I have maintained ever since with but minor amendment.

In those neophyte years the long hours at Penguin, the time taken in travelling to and from Harmondsworth and the need to be with my newly-acquired children, made it inevitable that writing began at nine in the evening and continued far into the night. So it was that almost every evening after dinner, Kippe and I carried the boys from the Clanricarde sitting-room where they had their beds into our tiny bedroom and set to work. Together we broke up the immaculately-completed jigsaw Hunt's 1851 *Autobiography* and traced the pieces to their original setting in his misbegotten *Lord Byron and Some of His Contemporaries* and in his voluminous journalistic output. Together we compiled the comprehensive Index. (The only index in all my books which is my own.) The first rough drafts of my Introduction to the Cresset Library edition and of *American Excursion* I dictated for Kippe to take down in long-hand. Her exotic spelling and her dashing calligraphy made the product a secret document incomprehensible to all but Kippe, me and an expert cryptographer, but this nightly routine had consequence far more significant than immediate practicality. We were collaborators, wondrously together both in effort and enthusiasm. This was for us a potent ritual, the true solemnization of matrimony. Together we shared the tensions, common to all authors, of those hideous months between completion of typescript and production. Together we revelled in that thrill which comes with opening the parcel of advance copies. Together we suffered that other awful pause between publication and reviews. And together we basked in the sunlight of approval.

I had not expected that Hunt's *Autobiography* would arouse much interest outside the academic journals, but many reviewers must have felt, as I, that here was an unjustifiably-ignored book by a fellow-professional. Even the popular press noticed it and all the reviews were warm. In a fashion that, since, I have myself followed on many occasions and which is close to being *de rigueur* for eminent literary critics, Harold Nicolson used the opportunity presented by the publication of the *Autobiography* to write an elegant essay revaluing Leigh Hunt's place in the Romantic Movement. He paid no heed to my sturdy defence of Hunt against Dickens' flagrant libels but he did deign one gratifying prophecy: my edition, he forecast, would remain as standard for all the twentieth century and probably for all time. We could not hope for praise in this generous kind for *American Excursion:* indeed I was already sufficiently hardened by Penguin experience to the harsh statistics of reviewing that I expected no notice at all for my simple account of student-days in America. We were, therefore, surprised when reviews began to appear in all the obvious journals – and even in the *Daily Express* – and not a little elated by their unanimous approval. Pleasure turned to dread, however, when Graham Hutton breached the anonymity which at that time masked all *Times Literary Supplement* reviewers, announced that he had *American Excursion* from the *TLS* and whispered in my ear dire predictions of the savaging he intended for my precious book.

Graham's review was close to being effusive; this was better than a reprieve from damnation for here was praise, proclaimed in the most august and most influential of all reviewing journals, from the author of *Midwest at Noon*, a book which then, as still today, I rank among the most percipient of all the many British books on America.

For my edition of the *Autobiography* I was paid £75 outright. *American Excursion* sold just enough copies to cover the £100 advance, but my Leigh Hunt is in all reputable libraries and is forever being cited by literary historians; and the *succès d'estime* of *American Excursion* led almost immediately to my being granted a place of honour among British authorities on all things American. I received bids for articles from *The Times, Men Only, Lilliput, Windmill* even from the *New York Times*, and it was *American Excursion* which enshrined me as a frequent and regular contributor to the BBC and led, not long after, to my selection as Denis Brogan's partner in the ludicrously popular 'Transatlantic Quiz'.

At Penguins, Allen allowed no severe job-demarcation to his still tiny staff. I remained PRO but it was not long before Public Relations became a small part of my duties and editing my principal responsibility.

It was not easy to manage all that was required of me at Harmondsworth and the sudden rush of commissions from other publishers, from editors and from the BBC. Something had to go. I abandoned versifying and story-telling.

Although at times I have mourned the death of my creative self and though on occasion I have attempted to resurrect him – with occasional light-verse and, until all markets vanished, with short stories – the crude measure of the bank-balance allows me no regrets. I cannot remember a day when there was before me no commission waiting to be fulfilled. I do not pretend that I could have been a rival to Graham Greene. I know that I lacked the inspiration and the skill which would have won me a place in the anthologies of later twentieth century poetry. I am content – almost – that I have been for forty years a competent, unapplauded lock-forward in the literary Second Fifteen.

In that first decade after the War there were often strident siren-calls which came close to luring me away from the profession I had chosen. Almost I entered that *galère* which is peculiar to our times: almost, I became a radio personality. Through no effort of my own, but I suppose from heredity, I was blessed with a voice which can caress a microphone and given also a convenient if dangerous ease with words. Once I was released from the Army's prohibition against public performance immediately I became a favourite with some BBC producers and, because the Corporation is devastatingly inbred, my original mentors soon passed me on to their colleagues so that there was scarcely a week when my name did not appear in the *Radio Times*. I wrote plays and documentaries both for adults and for the Schools Programme. I gave pontifical talks on the emergent Third Programme and spoke often, if less pompously, on the Home Service, but most often I appeared in what have since come to be called 'chat-shows' and, in company with the most popular broadcasters of the day, Gilbert Harding, Lionel Hale, Robert McDermott and his wife, Diana Morgan, in those silly and ludicrously remunerative party-games which then, as still today, filled so many programme-hours.

It credits me not a whit that for much of what I was then doing my contempt was profound; I accepted with howls of delight the cheques that came regularly from Broadcasting House; and even now I must temper my supercilious disdain for this part of my career by confessing to persistent pride in an achievement which I believe to be unique among broadcasters: by the miracle of recording I appeared simultaneously on the Light Programme – in 'Twenty Questions' – and on the Third – as contributor to a prestigious series (so prestigious that it was later translated into book-form by a distinguished American publishing house) to which the other contributors were Bertrand Russell, Perry Miller, Martin Cooper and John Lehmann. I am well-nigh certain that no other broadcaster has ever received from the BBC two invitations as disparate as those which came to me by one post, one to discuss over the air with Boris Pasternak the philosophy of literature and his reactions to winning the Nobel Prize, the other to compère 'Housewives Choice'.

For several years I chaired the Midland Region's weekly 'Behind the News' and somehow held to order – and to the topic in hand – my superlatively articulate colleagues, Noel Annan and Jacob Bronowski. I was a regular in 'Town Forum', precursor to the ever-popular 'Any Questions', and from platforms all over the Midlands I handed down opinions which, until the moment the question was asked I had not known I held, on subjects as varied as euthanasia and professionalism in sport. Twice I persuaded the BBC to despatch me on long missions to North America, once on a journey so miraculously contrived by me that it included visits to ghost-towns in the Rockies, to ranches in Texas, to sleepy villages in New England and, of course, to Williamsburg.

And there was 'Transatlantic-Quiz'. Even now, more than thirty years later, sometimes when I am introduced to an elderly stranger I see in his eyes a spark of recognition and hope that he will exclaim 'Nye and Morpurgo', '*Barnes Wallis*', '*Allen Lane: King Penguin*' or even 'The National Book League', but invariably I am given the accolade 'Transatlantic Quiz'.

Even at the time the Quiz did not satisfy me as did the rest of the galli-maufry which paid for the early education of my children; I thought of it as little more than an exhibition of intellectual acrobatics, but it did give me, in every week for more than a year, before we recorded an hour on the air with New York, with Christopher Morley, John Mason Brown and Alistair Cooke, and several hours each week with Denis Brogan. Those prefatory conversations were generally more stimulating than the broadcasts – and by courtesy of the BBC I was able to order for Kippe luxuries denied to her in still-rationed Britain, nylon stockings and nylon under-clothes.

Once we were, all of us but Hale, together in New York, Lionel chairing Denis and me from Langham Place. The BBC, puritanical as ever, refused to publicize this superb example of the competence of its engineers for fear that the British public might attack the Corporation for prodigally paying the airfares for Denis and for me. (We were, in fact, both in the States on quite other business.) Once during the long run of 'Transatlantic Quiz' I suffered hideously from the light-headedness of a colleague who in all other respects was possessed of a head as quick as a computer. In those more generous days, the BBC was in the habit of placing a bottle of whisky on the studio table. I relished the Corporation's alcoholic charity as much as any man but never before a broadcast. We were twenty minutes into our two-hour recording when suddenly I noticed that the bottle was almost empty and, at just that moment, I caught sight of Thomas Radley, the producer, gesticulating frantically from behind his glass screen. Then Lionel pushed a note across the table, and on it: DOESN'T MATTER WHAT YOU SAY, KEEP TALKING. At that moment Denis Brogan's head came to rest on my shoulder. I doubted that even my powerful voice could drown the sound of his snores.

It was Denis who taught me the art of the quiz-programme. At the end of our first recording-session I asked timidly if I had performed adequately. 'So-so', he replied, 'but you're thinking. Never think, just say what comes first into your mind; it's almost certainly right.'

I first came to suspect as fragile the overt security of my success as broadcaster when I heard gossip about the callous treatment meted out to Robert McDermott by the Corporation. Bobby had behind him no supporting career; all that he earned came from his free-lance broadcasting; but from those activities he prospered hugely. Then, suddenly, one of those mysterious potentates of the Corporation whose names are unknown to the listening and viewing public, whose faces are seldom seen even by regular broadcasters, circulated a memorandum to his subordinates, something to the effect 'We are using McDermott too often'. Every producer took that warning as addressed to himself; for a year and more Bobby earned not one penny from the BBC.

I noticed but did not heed the danger-signal, and even when Gilbert Harding took it upon himself to articulate a warning that the BBC is the most fickle of patrons, I remained unconcerned.

For all that I did not share his well-known proclivities, Gilbert had accepted me as friend and pupil from the day when first we met, in a studio in the Langham, and soon after he had extended his amity to Kippe whom, ever after, he treated with generosity and infallible courtesy – this despite his reputation for rudeness. He was probably the most tragic exemplar of the evanescence of notability based entirely upon broadcasting; I doubt that any under forty would now know his name; but in his heyday his fame was greater than Danny Kaye's and more resplendent than T. S. Eliot's. A man possessed of a phenomenal intellect but utterly without creative power, he forced himself upon the world's attention by blatant aggressiveness, by surliness in the studio and braggart behaviour in public places. Not once in all his stellar career did he appear in a programme which exercised his mental capacity. By making himself the most loathed man in Britain he made himself Britain's best-loved broadcaster and is now forgotten – but not by me. For me it is his unflagging charity, his generous enthusiasms for the more serious activities of one in years as in reputation so much his junior, that sustains him in my affection. I remember in detail none of the many broadcasts in which we were teamed, but I recall vividly his warmth and his frequent kindnesses.

Once – it must have been in 1952 – when Kippe and I took him to dinner, at a restaurant we could not afford, he indulged in his customary practice of abusing the waiter. Not I but Kippe had the courage to rebuke him. 'Gilbert,' she said, 'Stop behaving like an ill-mannered school-boy.' He subsided, smiled, kissed her hand and for the rest of the meal behaved immaculately. Back in his flat in Weymouth Street he grew diffident. Palpably there was something on his mind and I demanded that he bring it out. Still he hesitated. 'You're writing a lot these days?' I nodded. 'All else goes well?' I nodded again, though at that time it was not quite true. At last it came, not as a question, nor as advice directed at me but as a state-ment of self-evident generalization. 'Radio and television deal only in ephemera. No man who has anything else to give should waste his life producing artefacts for immediate hurling into the trash-can.' Then he turned to me. 'Take care, dear boy, no less than their products so also are those who oversee their production will-o'-the-wisps. All-powerful today, tomorrow they have vanished into Surbiton. Put not your trust in BBC producers. Set not the care of your lovely wife and your delightful children in Langham Place. Unless, as do I, you are ready to spend most of your days at the bar of the Bolivar, unless, as am I, you are prepared to appear in any programme however fatuous to which you are summoned, there can be for you no certain career as broadcaster, no security, and, I do believe, no satisfaction.'

I noted but ignored his words. Not until I joined Nuffield and of my own volition began to refuse, as beneath the dignity of the Foundation's Assistant Director, broadcasting assignments, did I accept the force of his advice. Almost imperceptibly the number of engagements declined – and then there were none.

By the time, five or six years later, when I was again eager for BBC contracts, many of my sturdiest supporters had retired or had been elevated beyond influence and the producers who had used me only to favour their friends were determined to punish me for spurning their graciousness. With time and a new generation of hierarchs, I came back not infrequently to both radio and television but now generally as a suppliant, as spokesman for a cause or when, by reason of some other activity in which I was engaged, I was the obvious candidate. Never again did I hear on my tele-phone that flattering summons, 'Jack, can you fit in an hour at the studio. . .' and certainly I am no longer. as in my broadcasting heyday, one of the gilded few whose voices create flutters of recognition in the hearts of switch-board operators, whose faces set travellers in tube-trains to nudging and to whispering recognition, but regrets are few for my vanished notability and I am content that I did not put my faith in the feckless and arrogant princes of a careless monopoly.

There was little or no casual relationship between my glory-days as a broadcaster and the Golden Age of Penguin, but the two were coincidental and I revelled in both.

Harmondsworth was at that time a pirate-ship, better, a privateer dashing but honourable, its objectives such treasures as could be found anywhere on oceans charted and uncharted, its ultimate intention the conquest of empire, imperial dominion over all the continents be they continents known to geography or the continents of imagination and scholarship. To those years, the last of war and the first of peace, belong most of the developments which have made Penguins unique in the history of publishing; the Classics, the first Penguin Million (Bernard Shaw), Penguin Modern Painters, the Archaeologies, the Histories. To those years belongs the maturity of the Pelican series, the stabilization of Puffins as first, finest and greatest of paperbacks for children.

We were as yet virtually without competitors in Britain, though in the United States several emulators had appeared, all but one of them (Bob de Graff's pioneering Pocket Books) set up by refugees from Penguin. In Britain, only Pan Books could come close to us for turnover or the number of titles and Pan piped an editorial tune so unlike ours as to set it in another world. Sensing Allen's aspiration to universal dominion and because as an ex-soldier I was in a sense flattered by the public enthusiasm for books about the War, I tried to persuade him to take such books as *The Dam Busters* and *The Wooden Horse*; both went to Pan, and sold in millions. I argued for Fred Majdalany's *The Monastery* (still, by my reckoning, next only to Linklater's esoteric *Private Angel* as novel about the Italian campaign), and for Douglas Grant's *The Fuel of the Fire* (the *Undertones* of my war and still the most unjustly forgotten book of the Second War). Glover, Williams, Eunice Frost, none of them with any Service experience, paid no heed. Only Dick Lane, a war-time naval officer, showed any interest and it was well-known at Harmondsworth that, though Dick's capacity with figures was admirable, he was not to be regarded as literate. Allen remained stony and, by icy disinterest, denied to Penguin not only some fabulous best-sellers but also titles which, by all other accounting, belonged assuredly within our list.

Other than war-books nothing was to us off-limits. 'Let's have a go' and 'Swings and roundabouts, roundabouts and swings': these, Allen's bromides, were the epigraphs to the richest chapter in Penguin history.

I doubt that in 1947 Penguin employed one-twentieth of the number which today serves the firm at Harmondsworth, in Kensington and at Ringwood, near Melbourne, and the hierarchy was undefined. Beyond all question Allen was Captain, navigator and most of the other officers. Dick was Paymaster, forever immersed, as first I had seen him, with notebooks full of calculations but already, unjustifiably but by Allen's malevolence, Dick had become to most of us a joke. ('Pay no attention to Dick', Allen said to me once when, by chance and for a week, I was but for Dick left in total charge. 'He doesn't know anything about anything.') Glover was First Mate, the paradox of exotic omniscience and meticulous organisation so useful to the firm that I name him as, with Allen, the true founder. Eunice Frost, and, after he had been brought from Switzerland to Harmondsworth by an impulse of Allen's and at immense expense, Jan Tschichold, were senior deck-officers. Eunice was superbly energetic, and useful for her vast acquaintance among authors and artists, for her capacity to lure them into the Penguin net and for her skill in handling them once caught, and 'Little Tschich', the acknowledged apostle of the lower case, for his magnificent contribution to Penguin design, yet another of those qualities which had made – and held – Penguin unique among paperback houses. For Bill Williams's position the naval metaphor fails. On his weekly visits to Harmondsworth he was honoured as a visiting admiral – and he was proclaimed as Chief Editor though that role was truly Glover's – but I came to suspect that Allen kept him as prompter and, as often was needed, as hatchet-man and because the society was forever changing, he needed an immutable. Harry Paroissien, the new Sales Manager, and I were not quite made easy as members of the ward-room. Commissioned Gunners, perhaps? We were included in all the meetings of senior staff and more significant to our status, we went almost daily after work with Allen to the bar of the Peggy Bedford, where most of Penguin's more devious plots were laid and we were frequent visitors to Silverbeck. Even then, as I substantiated when much later I came to write Allen's biography, I sensed that there was an inner cabinet – Allen, Dick, Bill, sometimes Glover, but never Tschichold – which considered matters never disclosed to us, and, for our part, Harry and I, always with Glover, kept our own Mess in the Blue Diamond, the greasy-spoon next to the Penguin building, and there, over a noxious lunch, we hatched out our plans for the future of Penguin.

It was Penguin policy to enlist to serve as General Editors for all series men of indubitable distinction in their particular disciplines and it was, therefore, a break with precedent when Allen turned to me, a full-time employee, to edit the Second Series of *Penguin Parade*, the eclectic companion to the élitist *New Writing*. His brief was curt: 'Here's a set of the First Series; you can do as well, even better; have a go.'

I settled my target in the centre of the Penguin and Pelican range, I would aim not only for short stories and verse but also for authoritative and popular articles on the arts, on politics and on social policies.

I looked for contributors for the most part among the rising generation but with a leavening of the established and eminent. I turned first to my friends. After much cossetting and not a little bullying Sydney Carter produced for me an article, elegant and sensitive, on a topic which was then, just after the publication of the Fleming Report, as it is still today, cause for vehement debate: the Public Schools. John Trewin, the Elia of my generation, wrote on the theatre. Presuming on a brief acquaintanceship acquired at one meeting when, monocle firm in his eye and newly-famous as one of Wingate's column commanders beyond the Chindwin, he had lectured at the Staff School, I approached Bernard Fergusson and he offered an amusing little short-story set against the tumult of pre-War Palestine. Douglas Grant I encouraged to versify, and whenever after I looked at the files of *Penguin Parade* my pride and pleasure was touched by regret that Douglas abandoned poetry for scholarship. Blunden gave me a sheaf of poems, none of them among his best but even so finer than most I might have acquired, and all unknowingly added to my prized possessions examples of his exquisite calligraphy. Emile Cammaerts wrote for me an essay on William Dobson, a seventeenth-century painter hitherto unjustly relegated to near-oblivion.

From without my own circle I commissioned Maurice Collis to predict for *Penguin Parade* the artist who, twenty years on, would be held in greatest favour. He settled on Louis Le Brocquy, his article was supported with good colour-plates – and, for eight pounds, I bought for myself Le Brocquy's *Tinker Girl*.

I planned a sequence of 'Chapters of Autobiography' to include Harold Abrahams, thirty or more years before *Chariots of Fire*, Learie Constantine and, the first to be published, G. Murray Levick, doctor to Scott's last and fateful expedition.

Periodical publishing requires skills and support-systems quite other than those which bolstered Penguin's phenomenal success in the book-market. In war-time, when the public was eager for print, Allen had managed well enough on both fronts but, the War over, he soon realized that he must concentrate where his strength lay. He killed off *Parade* after only four issues and without recrimination ('No go; we'll try something else'). Soon after he put an end to all our other journals even the jewel in his crown, *Penguin New Writing*.

'Something else' he was always ready to try.

We were gathered in his office for a meeting of senior staff. Allen paid little attention as Dick recited stock-figures and the record of sales; all his interest was concentrated on the runway at Heathrow. Suddenly he turned from the window and, as if he was announcing bankruptcy or the death of a treasured friend, he proclaimed 'We're getting into a rut.'

Dick abandoned his recital in mid-sentence and, incapable of sensible response, we all gaped. Allen repeated himself, 'We're in a rut', and then, and I was sure his eye fixed upon me, he went on. 'A rut, I say, someone have a new idea.' My Penguin career had thus far lasted but six months and in that moment I was convinced that six months and one day was all that I could expect. Allen's eye still upon me, I reached towards Heaven and grasped the offering of the gods. 'We've done books, let's do music.'

The words out and I, as I thought all others in the room, was shocked by their extravagant vacuity. 'We've done books. . . as if even Penguin could ever exhaust the possibilities of the printed word. 'Let's do music. . .' I did not even know what I meant to suggest. But Allen merely turned back to contemplating a taxi-ing plane and Dick returned to the statistics of our stewardship.

Back in my office in the Nissen hut behind the main one-storey brick building I was busy dictating letters when Allen's head appeared round the door. 'Music? What's all this about music?'

Somehow I had to give flesh and bones to my spectral notion and again the gods took pity. 'Pocket scores', I replied, and Allen's head vanished.

I went off to lunch at the Blue Diamond. Allen was waiting for me on my return, as was his habit, sitting on my desk and, as was also his habit, reading my correspondence. 'Pocket scores. Get it moving.'

I knew no more of music than Lang had taught me and nothing whatsoever about music publishing. For once Glover could not help; musical he was, but Wormwood Scrubbs, as a conscientious objector during the First War, and proof-reading on the *Daily Herald* and the *Reader's Digest* had taught him nothing about the techniques of music-publishing. I phoned Kippe and sent her scurrying round London buying up all the pocket scores she could find.

I wrote to Lang; Lang gave me an introduction to the conductor Robin Jacques. Jacques proposed as General Editor for the new Penguin Pocket Scores the composer Gordon Jacob. Jacob came to tea in our flat in Philbeach Gardens, next to the Earl's Court Stadium. At that time I knew none of his works, but I found him immediately sympathetic and immediately sensitive to the imperative that, if we were to launch a new Penguin series, we must prepare as rousing opening ten titles and all of them popular.

Severally Kippe, Jacob and I wrote down our favoured ten. When we compared our lists eight titles appeared on all three; Beethoven's Fifth, Mozart's number Forty, a Bach Brandenburg. . .

Thus was born the Penguin Pocket Score series. For Kippe and for me, and I have little doubt for Gordon Jacob no less, the triumphant clash of cymbals was heard on the first occasion when, at a concert, we saw members of the audience dutifully following the orchestra from a Penguin Score.

The first and most intimately-engaged of my several Penguin episodes came to an end as surprisingly and as abruptly as it had begun. I was alone with Bill Williams in his office at 117 Piccadilly, clearing up my papers after an editorial meeting and Bill reading his mail. Abruptly Bill walked across the room, closed the door, offered me a gin and poured one for himself, stammered a conventional toast and then blurted out 'A.L. thinks you should get some experience outside Penguins.'

I knew already that Allen, for all his bravura, was never his own executioner, but I was so amazed by Bill's statement that I could find no words in reply. I had become, more and ever more obviously, one of the small and privileged group which guided Penguin through the difficult post-War seas. I had launched the Pocket Scores. Much of the editorial preparation and all the promotions for the first Penguin Million had been left to me; Shaw had not complained, indeed he had himself written to thank me for my part in what he measured as an unsurprisingly sensational success. I had set up for Allen, against all the edicts of the Publishers' Association, an efficient and profitable direct-mail service. And all this I had managed whilst editing *Penguin's Progress* and *Penguin Parade*, whilst answering all letters from our readers, and whilst organizing all our publicity. I had good reason to believe that Allen looked upon me as a friend; I was frequently at Silverbeck and there much cossetted both by Allen and by Lettice Lane. Not once in all my time at Harmondsworth had Allen found cause to damn my efforts or to rebuke me.

Even now, with behind me much knowledge of Allen's erratic nature acquired by personal contact, by research and by conversation with others his disciples and victims, I find it difficult to read back cogency into my first experience of his ruthlessness. Perhaps he was eager to be off with the old before he was on with the new, but no successor took my place for several months. Perhaps he was just bored with me or else feared that by some otherwise unstoppable mechanism I might become too powerful. Even, it could be – for such long-sighted machiavellian elaboration was not beyond Allen – that he had it in mind that by enlarging my experience I might eventually be all the more useful to Penguin.

At the time I could only go to Kippe to tell her that I would soon be unemployed and the four of us all dependent on free-lance earnings. Our situation was made all the more hideous because I had received an invitation to lecture in the United States. This I had discussed with Allen and it was only after he had expressed confidence in the possibilities – for the firm – inherent in such a tour that I had accepted.

Throughout a long night we gnawed at our predicament. Should we cancel the tour? It was unthinkable that another and similar opportunity would come my way for many years; even this chance was miraculous for I was not yet blessed with a reputation that inspires a summons to the lecture-circuit. I had written to Dr Swem telling him that we would bring with us the Dunmore Papers. I had written to Tim, though I was not certain that he had survived the War. Bob de Graff of Pocket Books, met first with Allen, had offered us the use of his apartment for the New York leg of my tour. Eventually, rationalizing the defence of my prize by adding together the fees that I would earn from my lectures, we decided to damn caution. We would go to the States and leave the search for another job for our return.

I decided upon a posture of indignant righteousness and next morning I stormed into Allen's office. It was empty. Deflated, I collected my mail and trudged to the Nissen hut. Allen was perched on my desk and before I could speak, he grinned his naughty-boy grin and said: 'You've been bullying me for months about a History series. Get it for me, a history of England, six, seven, eight volumes. Get me a history of the world, and, while you're about it, see what you can do about biographies.'

He left hurriedly and without so much as mentioning, or giving me time to mention, my conversation with Bill Williams, but in seconds his head appeared again at my door. 'You've been doing some work for old Bertie Christian; I'll have a word with him.' Then: 'With that rogue Peter Baker, too, if you like. Can't stand the man, but he might make a publisher, if you can keep him honest.' Allen's head vanished.

Only a trifle reassured, even so we argued ourselves into making the American tour. All else apart, this was to be our honeymoon. Having come at last, and almost unsullied, through all the squalor of divorce proceedings, we were married in a Kensington registry-office that could have doubled as funeral-parlour by a registrar who must have been in his spare time an undertaker. The wedding-party, the Roberts, the Glovers, Sydney and my sister Bess, represented the whole of my British life to that date except my Army service but there was no plenipotentiary on the bride's side. I bankrupted myself to meet the costs of the wedding breakfast, David announced that in the Registry Office for the first time ever he had caught me suffering from stage-fright, my words inaudible, and as we took them in a taxi to meet his sternly teetotal father, Lord Clwyd, we fed peppermints to him and to Peg.

Our first voyage was made magical for me, more wondrous than any, even my first by the *Ausonia* to Montreal, because Kippe was to be with me, but I was obsessed by doubts. We were leaving a Britain still battened down to rationing, disfigured with scars inflicted by the Luftwaffe, a country more dispirited in victory than ever it had been in the harsh years of danger. Many Americans had fought nobly in distant places, many had died and many had mourned, but for the majority in the United States the War had not been immediate. There had been no bombing and no threat of invasion, the United States had not suffered that hideous consequence of war, the elimination of international potency and shattering of economic health which blasted Britain. I feared that I was about to introduce Kippe to a history which ignored the preceding eight years of my life.

The first dramatic symbol of adventure into another existence was blatant before ever the ship ceased to be hawser-bound to the familiar. We arrived in Southampton early in the morning, went immediately to the ship's dining-saloon and there on the tables were plates of white rolls and dishes full of butter. As we ate our gluttonous and unaccustomed way through grape-fruit, cornflakes and two or three lavishly embellished rolls, we watched guiltily as dock-workers finished their pre-sailing tasks before going home to their meagre, rationed breakfasts. I demanded kippers as aperitif for bacon, sausages and eggs; I had not yet recovered from the dreams, insistent throughout my war service, dreams of fair women but often of fair women carrying salvers of kippers, thick, juicy and delectably browned.

Six days at sea, luxurious even in the Tourist Class then, at dawn, we entered New York Harbour. I insisted that Kippe must join me on deck and she, who ordinarily does not recognize that 5 a.m. is on her watch, this once accepted that my bullying was justified. The New York sky-line seen at dawn from the Harbour, the light going out in the office-buildings in consonance with the vanishing stars, the dark blue sky turning to grey and then to white behind the skyscrapers: this is a sight as amazing – and as beautiful – as the Taj Mahal under a full moon.

Ashore we found a message from Swem. 'Welcome home but do tell your dear wife that New York City is not in the United States; it is the capital of Hell.' There was nothing from Tim.

We went off to Connecticut, Massachusetts and Vermont. New England in the fall is more beautiful than anywhere else in the world, the colours of autumn there more varied and richer than elsewhere, the weather at once balmy and bracing. Daily Kippe was growing ever more susceptible to its seductive charms and I was resentful, impatient to show her my own Virginia. Though I was remarkably ill-equipped to serve, as I was supposed to serve, to introduce Americans to the development of English letters during the War years and though I was dismayed by the variousness of the audiences I faced – on one night four hundred undergraduates, most of them ignorant freshmen, and the next twenty or so members of the faculty of some college, among them several whose names I had known from the title-pages of books set for courses at William and Mary – once I was on my feet I found lecturing easy and a pretence of authority by no means difficult. I can boast – for they have told me so – that it was from me on that first of several lecture-tours that many Americans first heard the names of Joyce Cary, Sidney Keyes and Keith Douglas.

Back at the Institute in New York, I was told that every day since we had left for New England there had been a phone-call from Washington D.C.: No name, no telephone number but always the same raucous voice and, if with abundant adjectival variation, always the same message, 'Tell that Limey bastard to get off his butt and come on down here.'

My cousin Betty had adapted quickly to American mores. Her accent was overlaid with American inflections, her vocabulary with Americanisms and, though our relationship remained as ever close and she as affectionate and as polymathic, it was when observing her that I began to appreciate how dubious was my conceit of dual nationality. I would never be an alien in the States, but the War, and perhaps marriage, had strengthened my Britishness and I knew that however plush the temptation, I could never apostasize.

After a few days in Alabama, I was even doubting the validity of my affection for the South. This was not the Dixie I had promised to share with Kippe. This was Faulkner's 'accurst' country, a land trapped in its own seedy myth, its obsolescent grandeurs flaking, its air soured by the scents of rotting magnolia blossom. My shame and Kippe's disgust for the blatant racism of the middle-aged Scarlett O'Haras, the jumped-up Mrs Snopes and over-blown Mrs Compsons who, whilst a terrified black maid waited upon them at the University Club, shrieked to each other their disdain for 'nigger-servants' persuaded us to abandon our plan for a three-day break in Mobile.

It was close to midnight when, with assistance from Directory Information, I got through to Tim. His response was immediate and typical. What were we doing 'faffing about' down there? Tuscaloosa, Alabama? 'Jesus Christ.' We were to fly to Washington next day – 'If there's a plane from that one-eyed, one-horsed fundamental orifice.'

I asked for the address. He gave it, grudgingly, as if anyone in America's capital would know the way to the residence of Arthur B. Hanson. An hour later Tim called. He and Jane – this the first that I knew of his marriage – must keep a dinner-engagement. He would leave a key at the reception-desk.

We flew to Washington through a storm appropriate to my reunion with Tim, took a taxi downtown and carried our shabby pre-War suitcases across a thickly-carpeted lobby. The receptionist, platinum all over, did not look up from manicuring her nails. I asked for Mr Hanson. 'Out.' 'Is Mrs Hanson in?' 'No.' I asked if there was any message for me. 'No message.'

We turned away. I counting out in my mind our statutorily-limited supply of travellers' cheques. The receptionist called after us, her voice proclaiming pride in a miracle of comprehension, 'You're Jack.' I nodded and took the key she offered. Her eyes were brisk with suspicion. She looked from me to our cases and back again as if to indicate that it was none of her responsibility if the Hansons were fool enough to allow into their apartment, unchaperoned, bums still reeking of the box-cars.

For half an hour we sat, uneasy, on the edge of our chairs. Then, to Kippe's dismay, I searched for whisky. 'You can't, you don't know Jane.' Another half-hour and I announced that I would take a shower. 'Don't leave me; they might come back.' It was well after midnight when we heard a roaring in the corridor and a pounding at the door sufficiently violent to wake the President in his bed at the White House. I opened the door and a fury hurled past me shrieking as it went a torrent of scabrous abuse. Tim leapt up the six inches he needed to get his arms round Kippe's shoulders and clung there, his hat still on the back of his head, as he kissed her. From somewhere out in the corridor. a gentle voice welcomed us home.

At last I was back in my America and Kippe with me, for herself and for me accepted.

Tim's eyes had hardened, there were lines etched into his face but in manner and in character this was still the Tim of our student-days, his generosity, his energy, his enthusiasm, his unmatchable loyalty masked, but masked only to those who accept his poses, by cynicism and by sophomoric abusiveness. And so he has remained for forty years, unchanged even by success and prosperity, as warm and as active in the service of his friends now that he is one of Washington's most influential lawyers, a Major-General (Retired) in the United States Marine Corps Reserve, a business tycoon on two continents and America's leading authority on the law of libel.

As for Jane Hanson: she stands, unique among women and rivalled by very few men, as a match for Tim, her gentleness a foil for his barbarisms, her occasional asperities check-mate to his roarings and her loyalties, as his, beyond shifting.

William and Mary set out for me the welcome reserved for a favoured son and, for my sake and her own, immediately made Kippe an honoured if honorary alumna. More obviously than most small towns in America or in Britain, Williamsburg has a sizable and identifiable *haut monde*, the hierarchy of the Restoration, the more eminent members of the Faculty, the President of the bank and some from that substantial group of senior officers of the United States Armed Services who have retired to Tidewater. In 1947, as patently and generously on all our many subsequent returns to Williamsburg, this group opened its doors to us and by its warmth made evident that we must think of ourselves not as visitors and most certainly not as tourists but as Williamsburgers who just happened to spend most of their lives away from home across the Atlantic and, perhaps for that very reason, more to be cherished than any stay-at-home.

If there is such a thing as a typical American small town, it is most certainly not Williamsburg and, though the Main Street of Corning, N.Y. is virtually a replica of a thousand other Main Streets, a town which boasts more Ph.D.s to the square yard than any other in the United States cannot be regarded as typical of anything. It was not in search of Middle America that we went first to Corning, nor yet to associate with some of America's most subtle technologists and it was not even to view one of the world's finest collections of glass that over the years we returned again and again. We were there to be with Muriel Howard's brother Lloyd, his wife Iva and their family.

Even so, it would not be difficult to caricature Iva Sprague as one of those infuriatingly pleasant and devastatingly smug American middle-class women who delight each other by talking about the good they do to lesser and less fortunate beings. It would be easy but it would be wrong. Iva was forever on the move; there was scarcely an underdeveloped country she did not know and her motives for travel were always more philanthropic than touristic but she made sure that she understood the civilizations she was visiting and wherever she went she left behind her some genuine benefit. If there was in her benevolent spirit any trace of the Helen Hokisson lady it was her conviction, by no means rare among Americans, that the richest benefaction she could confer, be it on Chad or Upper Volta, India or Greece, was access to the American Way of Life.

Abroad or at home, Iva was never happier than when she was organizing, something or someone. She organized me, in 1947 and on every one of my subsequent visits, and among the richest benefactions that she conferred on me was that she organized me into friendship with George Kahrl and his family.

My first acquaintance with George, in Elmira, close to Corning and hitherto known to me only as one of the homes of Olivia Langdon's 'Boy', Mark Twain, opened my eyes to the depth and spread of American scholarship and, by extension, led me to appreciate the realities of British academe.

I had been reared in a society which accepted almost without question the high opinion that Oxford and Cambridge have of themselves and, if with chauvinistic reservations, of each other and, until I went to William and Mary, I was as convinced as any Oxbridge don that just as there are in Britain no universities worthy of mention in the same breath as Oxford and Cambridge so also are there on the other side of the Atlantic only a handful – Harvard, Yale, Princeton and, by strenuous exercise of magnanimity, perhaps a State university or two, Chicago, say, California or Michigan – which merit the next breath. William and Mary I thought of as an aberration, like C.H. *sui generis*, an institution out of time and out of the context of American educational institutions, but I had never shaken off a sense of guilt, a feeling that by rejecting Oxbridge I had somehow betrayed my heritage. I met George at little Elmira College, a scholar as profound as any in either Cambridge or All Souls and, I can add from subsequent experience, a teacher as dedicated and as effective as any who hands out sherry in the elegant surroundings of Merton or the House.

I have watched over George through the long years he has given to the study of David Garrick, many times I have dined with him and Faith Kahrl at his beloved Garrick Club (where else?), and I have even allowed him to take me walking with him in the woods of Upper New York State or along the shores of Maine. Our two families have grown together. For all this I am grateful to him but for nothing more than for that first revelation, that William and Mary was not unique, that there are even in smaller, less renowned American colleges, academics of high quality, that the Oxbridge-Ivy League pretensions are suspect.

Since that first meeting I have met many others like him: Dan Young the biographer of his great predecessor at Vanderbilt, John Crowe Ransome; at the tiny and isolated College of Idaho, the distinguished folklorist, Louis Attebery and a dozen more; and in many unexpected places I have found institutions as true to my idea of a university – or John Newman's – as the grand academy's on the Cam, the Cherwell or the Charles. My respect for British redbrick and for many a humble American college is profound and, if not without reservation then sufficiently persuasive to make my advocacy strident – and often provoking even to my indulgent but Oxbridge colleagues on the Christ's Hospital Council. But, when first it was aroused by George Kahrl and Elmira College, I did not expect that it would be confirmed only a few days later at an institution but recently a State agricultural college.

Nor were our first experiences at Michigan State College encouraging to admiration. We were met off the train by the Dean, an 'Indiana Englishman', one of those Americans who knew little of England but worship everything they do not know, a middle-aged man wearing country tweeds and carrying an umbrella. He showed us round the sprouting campus reciting for each embryo building its cost in millions of dollars, dropped off Kippe to lunch with the Faculty Wives Club and took me to speak to the Lansing Rotary.

Arrived back in our hotel-room I found Kippe close to tears. 'Do you have to lecture this evening?' she asked. 'Your talk may not be all that erudite but it's far above the heads of anyone here.'

At dinner before my lecture I was seated next to my chairman for the evening. The name Smith reveals little but I soon discovered that he was a Canadian and a poet. I had fled from UNB innocent of all knowledge about Canadian literature except that forced on me by New Brunswick's pressing and unmerited pride in its three poet-sons, Charles and Theodore Roberts and Bliss Carman, and so at that Lansing dinner-table I was settled in a predicament which I have suffered many times since. I must attempt intelligent literary conversation with a writer whose name meant nothing to me, whose works I had not read. My embarrassment was eased by Art Smith's quick and incisive wit and by the fact that he had spent part of his childhood in London, a mile or so away from my own Canonbury, in the very same street where my cousin Betty had lived.

Kippe, the only female in the party, was placed next to the Dean. Suddenly, even over Art's reverberating voice, I heard him ask 'The grouse-shooting season, when does it begin?' I leapt to Kippe's assistance, 'August the twelfth'. 'And when does it end?' I left Kippe to her own inadequate devices.

The lecture might have been for me a happier experience had it not been that an audience of some three hundred was almost unnoticeable in a hall built for two thousand.

We went back to the Dean's house for drinks – one weak Martini for each guest and two for me, the distinguished visitor – and to listen to a programme of English records; songs from the music-hall of the first years of the century, then the Massed Band of the Brigade of Guards. I knew what was coming and it came, the Guards playing 'God Save the King'. The whole company rose, Kippe and I and my new Canadian friend looking awkwardly at our shoes. I did not foresee what would come next from the Dean. In tones redolent with delight in the unique possibility, and no less patently indicative of the end of the celebrations, he announced:

'Ladies and Gentlemen, the King.'

Art volunteered to drive us home and no sooner were we in his car than he exploded. We must not leave thinking that all in East Lansing were like the Dean, next day we must lunch with him and his wife Jeanie. Art brushed aside my excuses. He would see to it that we caught the 2.30 train to Chicago.

At noon next day Art swept us up. At one o'clock we were on our third gin. At 1.30 his six-year-old son came home with a young friend; both carrying air-rifles. Art broke off in mid-word a scabrous account of his first meeting with Geoffrey Grigson, grabbed the gun from his son's hand and, all the time lecturing his son on the dangers of fire-arms, he waved the offending weapon, 'You never can be sure; it might be loaded.' A crack, to me in that confined space reminiscent of the deafening noise of a twenty-five pounder heard from the firing-seat, and a salvo of pellets scattered into the freshly-painted ceiling. Frenetically Art hurled his son's gun into an armchair, grabbed the gun from his companion, sprang to the telephone and dialled, all the while waving the weapon in one hand like a drunken cowboy celebrating in a saloon, and poured into the phone a torrent of abuse. 'Pete says he got the gun from your brat. No sane mother ... There was I calmly rebuking the boys for carrying dangerous weapons-of-war, coolly warning them of the unpredictability of fire-arms. . .' He waved the gun. Another crack and another barrage of pellets.

At half-past two we sat down to lunch but only three of us; Art we left behind in the sitting-room making phone-calls. By five o'clock there were gathered in the Smith house more than forty guests. At two o'clock next morning we were put into a car to be driven to Jackson, thirty miles away, to catch the night-train. As we opened our eyes to the slum-approach into Chicago, Kippe informed me that she thought, she could not be sure but she thought, she had heard me promise to return next year to teach at Michigan State. I shrugged. They were a good lot, I said, and bright but by the end of the evening they were all drunk. Even if the promise had been given, which I doubted, by now it would be lost in the anguish of hang-overs.

We had been back in England for only a week when I received from Lansing a letter formally acknowledging my gratifying acceptance of a nomination to serve for one semester as Distinguished Visiting Professor in the Department of English at Michigan State College.

That nomination I accepted as blithely as if I had been invited to a cocktail-party, then lost it in the litter of unpaid bills and moved to the more fascinating business of turning my singed Penguin into a phoenix.

12

Poets and Philanthropoids

At the very moment when it became evident that henceforth I must support a family of five on an income even less certain than that paid to me, grudgingly, by Allen Lane, we elevated ourselves to squirearchy. Hypnotised by the house, the village and the Essex marshes, we bought New Hall in Bradwell-juxta-Mare close to the Blackwater Estuary.

Seen through eyes made cautious by experience,this extravagance was folly on a lunatic scale but I assured myself,and Kippe, that my career was blossoming; in addition to my work for both Christian and Peter Baker, my editorship of the Penguin Histories, 'Transatlantic Quiz' and two other radio-series all my own, I was reviewing regularly for the *TLS*, the *Birmingham Post*, and *Books of the Month*. Given the seclusion of a country residence I could add to my free-lance earnings sufficient to meet a huge mortgage (at 3³/₄%!).

In the Essex volume of his *Buildings of England*, after several ecstatic paragraphs about Bradwell Lodge across the road, Pevsner dismisses New Hall in six words, 'an attractive little Queen Anne house', a phrase which shrieks proof that his researchers did no more than glance over our front gate. There is a six-inch gap between the original Tudor building and the elegant brick facade, with window-tax windows, added by some early eighteenth-century owner to give to his farmhouse the dignity of a gentleman's residence. By the standards of Blenheim, Chatsworth or Bradwell Lodge, New Hall is not big, but I question that even the Duke of Marlborough or the Duke of Devonshire would describe as small a house with thirteen rooms set in three acres of lawn, orchard, rose-gardens, with a mulberry-tree, two fig-trees and grape-vines under glass.

The owner of Bradwell Lodge did so describe it. Tom Driberg, our Labour MP, formerly William Hickey and later Lord Bradwell, invariably referred to New Hall as 'the pretty little house across the way', and invariably I riposted that ours was the former manor-house, his no more than a converted rectory, that there had been a house called New Hall where ours now stood three hundred years before Henry VIII built what is now a wing of the Lodge for Anne of Cleves, that New Hall (all but the Queen Anne mask) was more than two hundred years older than the wing added to the Lodge by John Churchill of Chelmsford, with embellishments by Robert Adam and Angelica Kauffmann and a belvedere later used by

Gainsborough.

Despite his disdain for our house and despite his unsavoury reputation, Tom was warm-hearted and the rays from his *Roi Soleil* reached out often to touch us, his humble neighbours, and some from his resplendent court, John Freeman and John Betjeman among them, became also habitués of New Hall. Tom's marriage to a sensible, middle-aged Lancastrian gave to Winston Churchill the opportunity for one of his most scabrous witticisms, 'buggers can't be choosers', and the arrival of Ena as chatelaine at the Lodge encouraged Tom to enrich the splendour of his seigneurial parties. We seldom refused a summons but often, sipping exquisite sherry from a superb Beilby glass, I came close to choking on the wine as I observed the ineffable Socialist compromise: a white-jacketed, white-gloved butler bowing to Mrs Driberg and announcing, in tones that would have honoured Jeeves, 'Ena, luncheon is served'.

We were at Bradwell for only six years and yet for all of us to this day, even for Kay, our only daughter, who was born in the house on a day ominously stormy, New Hall remains the family home; so settled in our loyalties that I have never dared to return, not even when I am on my way to Margery Allingham's house across the water in Tolleshunt D'Arcy (as Pip had it, "forty miles to drive but a mile to spit'), not even to enquire if New Hall still stands as host to the seventh member of our family, the member who refused to move on with us and so brought all of us, even the adults, close to tears, New Hall's amiable and caring ghost. Years later, when I returned at last to the craft of the short-story, I made him the hero of a fiction that has in it almost nothing that is not fact except the names of people and places and so he walks still in the pages of *Blackwood's*.

There is logic in our fidelity to New Hall, for it was our shared experience at Bradwell which set us beyond the range of schism. By blood and the letter of the law ours were two families but ever after in all that matters we were one.

Although for a dedicated townsman it was out of character, my eager acceptance of a rural retreat worked as I had forecast. Commissions poured in. Charles Ede invited me to edit for the Folio Society the writings of that lovable old liar, Edward Trelawny; the BBC to compile and present on radio a history of America illustrated by ballad and folk song; Glover to join him in the planning of the Penguin Poets (a series launched with a flourish in 1950 and by some unfathomable Penguin sleight-of-hand reissued in 1985 as a 'great new series') to which I myself contributed the *Selected Keats*; Dennis Cohen enlisted me as a scout for the Cresset Press. Then there was a roar from Olympus; *The Times* ordered me to write the text for a book the paper planned to send to the States, one copy to every family which had lost in the War a son, a husband or a father who had gone into battle from a British base.

That for this prestigious volume the nabobs of Printing House Square approached me, the humblest *naik* in their service, was flattering and I did not resent the fact that for 20,000 words I was paid only five pounds more than I received for a leader in the *Literary Supplement* but such was the dedication of *The Times* to its policy of anonymity that I was sworn never to reveal my authorship (a vow which I have kept until this moment).

Even in the catalogue of the British Library my book is ascribed to the only name which appears on the title-page, the author of the 500-word Preface, Winston Churchill, and it was only after months of pleading and conniving with a *Times* editor that I was allowed one copy of my own book for my own bookshelves.

Through all this time I was travelling regularly to London, to Broadcasting House, to Berners Street to Bertram Christian's Christophers, and to Crown Passage off Pall Mall to help Peter Baker establish an educational list, and through all this time I was preparing the Penguin Histories.

From the moment when he hurled me naked into the world, Allen acted as if he was innocent of all offence. Indeed, whereas in my years at Harmondsworth he had been unfailingly amiable, now he treated me as an intimate and treasured counsellor. More often than in the past we were bidden to Silverbeck parties, three or four times in every week he phoned to seek my opinion on some Penguin venture, to pass on malicious gossip about Dick or a rival publisher, even to retell for my delight a story about the wondrous doings of his small daughters but, perhaps because he was convinced that my time in the office had taught me far more about the Penguin ethos than was known to other and in this sense uninitiated series-editors, he gave me no brief whatsoever for the Penguin Histories. 'Get me a history of England, a history of the world...'!, that was all.

Enthused by this trust, and certain that I could complete his limited brief ('Get me historians who will be the leaders of their craft in twenty years time'), I set about reconnoitring the field.

The leading historians of the age, Trevelyan, Ensor, Stenton, were none of them too haughty to shun an emissary of Penguin. I saw them all and, almost without exception, each one hinted his own candidacy for the authorship of a volume in the Penguin *History of England*. I became marvellously dexterous at turning away scholars whose works had been my icons since my days in David Roberts's study and, somehow, from almost every one of them I dragged the counsel I needed. In Cambridge, Trevelyan led me to a young Fellow of Christ's, Jack Plumb, for my eighteenth century volume; Frank Stenton set me in pursuit of Dorothy Whitelock for *The Beginnings of English Society* and, unashamedly but, as I later discovered, with percipience entire, assured me that there was in all the world but one young historian as well-qualified as he to write our book on the early Middle Ages: his wife and former pupil, Doris Stenton. Ian Richmond for *Roman Britain*, I discovered through an old acquaintance at King's, Newcastle. With Myers of Liverpool for the later Middle Ages, and a fellow-member of the Reform, Maurice Ashley, for the seventeenth century I had my *History of England* complete, except for the volume which some publishing second-sense persuaded me was likely to be the most immediately popular with the general public and which, therefore, must appear in our first batch. I wrote for an interview to Sir John Neale, the most eminent of all Tudor historians.

Neale I had met before the War, when he came to talk at one of those weekend house-parties given, for his selection of promising young men, by Francis Hirst, but I had not expected from Neale the warmth that he showed when I called at his rooms in University College, London. He spoke of Hirst, he spoke about the great benefits conferred upon popular education by Penguins and Pelican and then, his ebony-black teeth flashing and more bluntly than any of his distinguished predecessor-advisers, he offered himself as author of the Penguin *Tudor England*.

Dare I reject the author of *Queen Elizabeth,* a scholar who more patently than any other except perhaps Trevelyan had bridged the chasm between academic and popular history? How could I so contrive dismissal without giving offence?

Neale grinned, and those black teeth shone again. 'You don't want an old hack who's written it all a dozen times? I don't blame you.' He then began to dictate a list of possibles, all as later I discovered, his former pupils.

I was scribbling furiously when there was a knock at the door. Neale looked up, clasped his hand to his head and said '*Ecce homo*'.

Bindoff and I crossed the road to a Gower Street pub and passed a glorious evening talking about cricket. I did not so much as mention Penguin until after I had heard his third story about Wally Hammond and even then all the glories of Tudor England could not prevent me from telling the tale of how once at the Horsham ground I had seen Duleep literally pocketing a slip-catch whilst all others, batsmen, fielders and spectators, looked for the ball by the boundary ropes.

Then, at last but for the next half-hour, I preached my Gospel to the Penguin historians.

A few weeks after that evening, I had the synopsis and a couple of sparkling chapters of *Tudor England*. A week later Bindoff had his contract and – the shame of the memory overwhelms me every time I pontificate on publishing techniques to audiences of young aspirants – only then did I go to the London Library to find Bindoff's previous books.

There was only his doctoral thesis and, as is not uncommon to its kind, that almost unbelievably ponderous. For the best part of a year I looked apprehensively in every post for the typescript that must herald the end of my second Penguin career.

It came. I read it through once and was enthralled, a second time, and I knew that I was midwife to a classic. Almost forty years and millions of copies later Bindoff's *Tudor England* is still in print. Bindoff went to two Chairs in the University of London. He never wrote another full-length book but generations of students, teachers, scholars and general readers – and his royalty-statements – have confirmed the faith that was mine at the end of that second reading.

With the History of England planned and in preparation I began to move, slowly and now more cautiously, to a history of the world. Over the months I found authors for China, Japan, France, Spain and Portugal, New Zealand and India. Australia I commissioned; the typescript has not yet been delivered; but all my endeavours failed to unearth a suitable author for Canada and, though I did not articulate my thoughts, there was one subject I held back. I wanted the United States for myself.

It was an impertinent notion. My knowledge of the Colonial, Revolutionary and Federal periods was not insignificant, Dick Morton had given me a solid if somewhat biased over-view of the War between the States, and much reviewing of Americana had filled in some gaps in my knowledge but I was far from confident that I could find in myself the dexterity to handle the woof and the warp, the complexity of themes that must be brought together – and in one flowing narrative – by any historian who attempts a one-volume history of a nation.

I tried my hand at a chapter. Several times I drew up synopses. The task began to terrify. Palpably the United States must have not one but two volumes; the very enormity of producing a thousand or so pages of manuscript was daunting.

I thought of looking for a collaborator but decided, with consummate arrogance, that there was in all Britain none except perhaps Brogan who could match my purpose to produce a history of America as it were from mid-Atlantic. Brogan was in the Trevelyan-Stenton-Neale class and so by distinction disqualified from the Penguin race. The Penguin *History of the United States* must wait.

I set off for Michigan State College, leaving Kippe to care for a new-born baby and the two older boys both suffering from mastoid. Within days of my arrival in East Lansing, I sensed that I would have little difficulty with the professorial role. That same blessed adjutant, the actor in my make-up, came to my aid whenever I was faced by an audience.

As a temporary bachelor I was less successful. C.H. had taught me to make a bed more meticulously than any hospital-nurse, but I possessed no other domestic skills whatsoever, except some limited capacity as a curry-cook which I could exercise only if I had the assistance of three or four kitchen maids, and I would have starved had it not been for the abundant hospitality of my temporary colleagues and their wives. I missed Kippe and the family and would have pined like some Victorian miss had it not been for the readiness with which I was accepted as an addition to the social and intellectual life of the community.

Michigan State had almost shed the chrysalis of State agricultural college and its English Department was bursting with lively academics, most of them young, most of them ambitious and all of them as energetic in party-going and party-giving as they were in writing books.

East Lansing prompts response again to the Elian cue, 'Bring back to memory': Elwood Lawrence, Adrian Jaffe, Wallace Moffett (who was always about to produce a definitive study of Harold Frederic and did produce the noblest roses in Michigan), Arnold Williams, who seemed so earnest until one noticed the twinkle that never left his eyes even when he was talking about the Wakefield Mystery Plays (and whose wife, Sally, from North Carolina, cooked baked beans more succulent than any that ever I ate in Boston, 'the home of the beans and the cod':), John Abbott Clark (who wrote elegant little essays for the *Saturday Review of Literature* and established around him a little coterie of colleagues and students all ready and able to talk on any literary topic, ancient or modern), and Bill McCann, in a sense an outsider, because he was not an academic but a local businessman, and yet as erudite as any in that circle, a man almost as polymathic as Alan Glover – and the editor who introduced me, and thousands of others, to Ambrose Bierce.

Over the years I have returned often to Michigan State and over the years our various homes became virtually English suburbs of East Lansing, but two names stand out from those months as Distinguished Visiting Professor as from the years of association which followed, the names of Russ Nye and Art Smith.

When first I visited East Lansing, Russ had been off in Cleveland working on his biography of George Bancroft, the American statesman and historian, for which he later won a Pulitzer Prize. There was no braying of trumpets, no sounding of propitious tocsins when, on my return, he met me at Lansing railroad-station; I thought of it as no more than a gentle courtesy from the Chairman of the Department to which I was to be attached; and I do not remember that in all the four months of my stay I so much as mentioned to Russ the Penguin Histories. The contracts for the *History of the United States* were not exchanged until another two years had passed and it was not until 1955, five years on, that the two volumes appeared, but I do recall that within weeks of my arrival I suspected that, if only I could bully him into collaboration, I had found my partner.

We had much in common and our differences, though always vigorously expressed, never spurred us to antagonism. As did I, so did Russ refuse to recognize the boundaries drawn across the intellectual map for their own convenience by academic historians.

As was I, so was he as interested in the literature of the United States as in its political or economic development. As did I, so did he take pleasure in folk-song, ballad, myth, in all those evidences of a nation's character which later he was to pioneer as an academic discipline, Popular Culture. We were both of us fascinated by the records of ancient military campaigns. Most significant of all as portent, we were neither of us shackled by concern for the petty opinions of academic historians; scholarship mattered to both of us but not footnotes and we both considered history an art to be shared with an audience as wide and as varied as we and our publisher could reach.

I was, perhaps, better informed than Russ about early American history, the Colonial, the Revolutionary and the Federalist periods, he much more expert on the nineteenth and twentieth centuries, though Dick Morton's tuition had given me a sufficiency of knowledge so that I could at least keep up with him on the War between the States. My Johnny Reb prejudices made a useful foil for his damn-yankee sentiments, just as my Britishness was so useful counter to his devout Americanism.

Together – if we could come together to produce the first history of the United States written by an American and an Englishman in collaboration – we might be able to create not so much a chronicle as a biography of the nation.

When at last we settled to our task we were five thousand miles apart. We wrote, each of us, the sections most appropriate to his expertise, exchanged our efforts and re-wrote. Soon neither of us could tell with any certainty which of us had written the original version.

We did not foresee the phenomenal sales of Nye and Morpurgo, neither of us dreamed that the two volumes would stay in print for more than twenty-five years, would be reissued in 1990 or that, in the interim, they would be translated into six languages. In 1955 we would have dismissed derisively the suggestion that for the rest of our days our two names would be linked together as surely as are the names of Crosse and Blackwell, Abercrombie and Fitch, Fortnum and Mason – or Laurel and Hardy.

Collaboration is a process inimical to amity. Gilbert hated Sullivan, Sullivan despised Gilbert, fifteen years after the publication of Nye and Morpurgo the affection between me and two of my most cherished American friends, Mel Jones and Ed Riley, almost foundered in the planning of the history of William and Mary. When I wrote for Thames and Hudson the text to support a collection of pictures of Venice by a distinguished German photographer, a resident of Switzerland, the consequence was a public quarrel on the only occasion we met, and a vitriolic three-column attack on me written as a leader for the *Neue Zurcher Zeitung* by my collaborator (the vitriol inflamed not by what I had written of Venice but by six paragraphs in an earlier book, *The Road to Athens*, in which I had enjoyed myself proclaiming my distaste for all things Swiss), probably the best publicity that ever I received for any of my books. In our collaboration, friendship with Russ Nye and his wife Kay was strengthened.

Art – on the title-pages of his many books always grandiloquently A. J. M. Smith – had transformed my first visit to Michigan State from drab, dutiful performance to hilarious farce. My second, as all *reprises* whether acted out in East Lansing or in the Eastern Townships of Quebec, he made into an experience profound and seminal. Yet, with Art at centre-stage, as generally he was whether out in society or in his own home, there was always comedy and with Art, as with all great jesters, scarce hidden under frivolity, anguish. His wit was quick and sharp, but in verse he exercised it most effectively and most often when he wrote of those overtly serious subjects which occupied his mind: God, death and poetry itself. His verse was painfully personal, but he was of all men I have met the most gregarious. There is in his poetry a quality of quiescence, but he was never still; even when listening to music he marched around the room at the pace of a light infantryman, booming impromptu and wicked rhymes about pompous colleagues or ignorant critics. His intellect was most comfortable when it was centred on the seventeenth century but nothing pleased him more than driving fast cars and fast boats faster than their designers had ever intended – a process made terrifying for his passengers by his habit of punctuating endless monologue with elaborate gestures, with the infallible courtesy which persuaded him to look directly at his audience, even if it was in the back seat of his car.

Art was a compendium of paradoxes. It was the contradictions in his history, his spirit and his manner which made him a fascinating companion but it was also the contradictions which spurred his anguish.

Since his undergraduate days at McGill, he had been both a leader among Canadian poets and the most active and most articulate advocate for Canadian literary independence but his own work was profoundly influenced by Cisatlantic masters, by Rilke, Yeats, Donne and Vaughan. By the time he won the Governor-General's Medal in 1943 he had made himself a foreigner to Canada by taking on American citizenship. (The cock crowed thrice and for him its mocking tones were made all the more strident because to the end of her days his wife remained defiantly and proudly a Canadian.)

Even his superlative service as propagandist for Canadian letters created for him a kind of critical schizophrenia. Striving to arouse Canada to accept its literature as an important element in its heritage, he was himself trapped into the very pretension which he himself castigated so vigorously, to make of 'every Saul of Tarsus . . . a Paul.' A critic who, because he was himself a poet, understood better and wrote more perspicaciously than most about his great and much-loved predecessors, Donne, Vaughan, Herbert, he was forced by the demands of advocacy to slip into hyperbole about Canadian poetasters such as Charles Mair or William Henry Drummond.

He attacked the provincialism of Canadian literature yet almost throughout his career he was himself a victim of Canadian incest, his poetry admired almost exclusively by other Canadian poets; if there was any bitterness in Art Smith, it was for the ignorance of his work outside Canada. He, who as a young man had been launched, with a fanfare, in England as one of Geoffrey Grigson's New Voices, was ever after shunned by London and New York, the capitals of English-speaking literature.

That very energy which he dedicated to the Canadian cause of itself contributed to frustration. He produced the two best anthologies of

Canadian literature (his *Oxford Book of Canadian Poetry*, a unique effort to reconcile the two almost irreconcilable traditions of Canada, the English and the French), several other anthologies and a plethora of essays on Canadian themes, but all these endeavours left him with little time for his own poetry.

It is the slimness of his output which I regret. I regret nothing else about my long friendship with A. J. M. Smith. He honoured me by allowing me to see the pain that was sometimes upon him but not once did he let pain disturb his generosity and not often did he let it dim his ebullience.

I returned home from Michigan just in time for Christmas, elated by my first experience as professor, enriched by many new friendships and with a few dollars in my pocket, to find waiting for me a letter from Bertram Christian. He had sold Christophers; one of the small rocks on which I had been given cause to believe that I could build family security had gone to Chatto and Windus.

From our first Christmas together, Kippe and I had thrown ourselves wholeheartedly into Christmas celebrations. We had added to the conventional rituals some customs of our own devising (which continue in our family 'even unto the third generation'). Pieter and Michael were now old enough to enjoy the festival with us but also old enough to sense despondency and that year, for the first time, we had in our family an *au pair* girl, Hildegarde from Holland, precursor of a long line which has given to our children 'sisters' and to us 'daughters' and 'grandchildren' in many countries; and also two young Americans, Nan Jones and Marianna Brose, both recent graduates of William and Mary, for whom we were determined to stage a Christmas worthy of Dingley Dell. We resolved to forget Christian's letter for a week.

St Stephen and St Nicholas rewarded us. On New Year's Eve Peter Baker phoned from his home in his Norfolk constituency and begged that I take over as Managing Editor of the Falcon Group.

In the years immediately after the War, the opportunities for a new publishing-house were generous. Even in 1950 the public had not yet satiated the hunger for print endemic in the entertainment-starved war years, a new generation of authors had grown to maturity which had no established publishing loyalties and there were ripe fruits for plucking, several even of the most distinguished American writers who during the War had been cast off by their London publishers. Falcon had almost everything which was required to allow us to seize the chances; a young, enthusiastic and well-informed staff, contacts in many fields and, we thought, money. Almost we made it, almost we settled the Falcon Group as a leader in the post-War book-world, and the omens were bright which forecast for the firm prominence and prosperity in the 1960s and 1970s. All that we lacked was integrity at the top and it was on the naïve dishonesty of Peter Baker that all our hopes foundered.

Our headquarters – a few shabby rooms, above a greengrocers and a greasy spoon café, in two houses, adjacent but without access from one to the other except by way of the street – was an unlikely place from which to launch an assault on the omnipotence of such as Macmillan, Hodder and Methuen, but we had crammed into those slum quarters a galaxy of rising stars – Paul Scott, Roland Gant, Sean Jennett, John Frost, John Trevor Brown – every one of whom was destined to shine somewhere in the book-world firmament. On the rare occasions when he put his mind to it, for all his faults – and they were many and obvious to me as soon as I began to work intimately with him – Peter Baker was no mean judge of a book. By way of his father, Reginald Baker, partner to Michael Balcon at Ealing Studios, he gave us access to the film and theatrical world; by way of the Members' Bar at the House of Commons, to the world of politics. Our only geriatric, and he at the time perhaps fifty years old, Charles Wrey Gardiner, was himself an indifferent poet but his dedication to poetry was intense and shrewd, his acquaintance among poets and critics wide and catholic, so that we were set fair to challenge Faber's hegemony among publishers of verse, and with his Grey Walls Classics series (to which I contributed a selection from Lewis Carroll) we established ourselves as competitor to the Penguin Poets.

As Managing Editor, I enlarged Falcon Educational, the bread for the butter and jam of our general list. I commissioned Gordon van Praagh to write the first science text-book founded on the heuristic method (and his *Chemistry by Discovery* held pre-eminence in that genre for many years after Falcon had collapsed). I launched a series of drama texts, the titles all selected from the lists of books set for School Certificate but the Introductions and explanatory material written not by the schoolmaster-hacks who generally edit school-books but by distinguished critics, by such as J. C. Trewin and Muriel St Clare Byrne. With *Life Under the Tudors* and *Life Under the Stuart*s I opened a series of background histories which, because each contributor wrote only one chapter, allowed us to slip the bonds of extant publishing affiliations and which, because many of the authors were eminent and none of them pedants, soon proved as popular with general readers as with schools.

As for our core trade-list, we bought Scott Fitzgerald and Erskine Caldwell from America (our revival of Caldwell's *Tobacco Road* sold two substantial printings before publication), commissioned autobiographies from Ivor Novello and John Gielgud, reprinted Radclyffe Hall's *Well of Loneliness* and, with *Scott of the Antarctic* and *The Blue Lamp*, pioneered that easiest and, I do believe, shoddiest route to comfortable sales-figures, the book-of-the-film. I made a deal with James Laughlin of New Directions for first refusals on the British rights for all the titles in his avant-garde list. Our catholicity allowed me to follow Allen Lane's dictum 'have a go'; if one experiment failed there were always others to essay; and Falcon prospered. Or so it seemed, but there was a flaw in our success, the slippery behaviour of our Managing Director. I spent more time chasing after Peter

Baker, to the Palace of Westminster or the Junior Carlton Club, in the hope of persuading him to sign cheques for printers, for author's royalties or even for the fee owed to some wrapper-designer who depended on our ten guineas for food for his family, than ever I gave to managing or editing. Often he bought me drinks, sometimes he gave me lunch – usually at Prunier's – but always there was some reason why payment must be deferred.

Baker's reluctance to meet our financial obligations he extended to my own salary. At the end of my first month as Managing Editor the cheque paid to me was drawn for £40 short of the sum I had been promised and, despite my protests and Baker's insistence that I had suffered no more than a clerical error which would be immediately corrected, so it continued for six months.

Then I was summoned to meet the Chairman, Peter's father. Mildly, as if talking to a refractory child, he rebuked me for my discontent, then, just as mildly, he asked my age. I could not perceive relevance in the question but I told him that I was thirty-three. He grinned disbelief as if at some tale of Munchausen or Brigadier Gerard. 'Oh no you're not, you're really only in your mid-twenties. You can't expect me to count as publishing experience your years in the Army, and I'm damned if I'm going to pay all that money to a boy of twenty-six. But I'll be magnanimous; I'll pay you at the rate proper to a twenty-eight year old.'

For the first of only two occasions in my life, fury outweighed my customary prudery. I exploded an obscenity, slammed out of Baker's office, collected my private possessions and never went back to Falcon.

But a week later at the Carlton Club, Harry Legge-Bourke, Baker's fellow Tory MP and a sleeping-partner in Falcon, read me a Household Cavalryman's homily on loyalty.

The Falcon Group stumbled into bankruptcy and Peter Baker into gaol for forging Sir Bernard Docker's signature on a guarantee.

Yet again there had been snatched from us that element of security which made feasible a career largely free-lance and now crisis was imminent because the time had come to settle Pieter's schooling and so, by reason of our determination to treat all four children in like fashion, to project the proportion of our income which, for at least the next eighteen years, we must dedicate to education.

These were matters about which Kippe and I had argued violently almost from the day we first talked together. Then she had been inclined to favour the State system, but she had come to accept as persuasive my refusal to condone an education for our children potentially and almost certainly less rich than that with which I had been blessed and, though there lingered on some vestiges of her prejudice against public schools and a considerable bias against boarding education, practicalities won her round. My more fragile arguments had little effect. She could find no fallacy in my assertion that evidence from our own youth-time made my advocacy unanswerable, that she had been continuously miserable at a day-school and I consistently content as a boarder, but it did not convince and nor did my *tu quoque* that whereas her day-school was guilty of all those follies which are customarily associated with 'academies for the daughters of gentlemen' it was undoubtedly a public school; my superb C.H. was a public school only by the most finicky interpretation, but the fact that the nearest day grammar school to Bradwell was fourteen miles off and inac-cessible by bus convinced her.

It would have delighted both of us, Kippe almost as much as me, had we been able to accept the logic of my reasoning but when we approached the Clerk he informed us, firmly if courteously, that our prosperity set us outwith the income-limit prescribed for admission to Christ's Hospital – a verdict which stupefied us and which would have amazed our bank man-ager. I was tempted to make some cunning adjustments to my programme, a process not too difficult for a free-lance, but I was strangely reluctant to play tricks with C.H. and, if I did persuade some of those who hired me to postpone payment until the next financial year, it was unlikely that we would have sufficient funds for immediate needs. Instead we wrote four cheques, each for ten guineas, to four great schools and hurled ourselves into the mysterious and debilitating task of inspecting appropriate prepara-tory schools.

Then, for the first and only time in my life, I began to study the Appointments Vacant column in *The Times*.

The interview granted me by the Trustees of the Nuffield Foundation was even more awesome than that which had opened for me the gate to Christ's Hospital and far more searching than that which had sent me on my way to a commission. I sat for an hour or more at one end of the long, polished table in the elegant dining-room of the Foundation's Decimus Burton house at the corner of Regent's Park, with facing me a panel of ten inquisitors, Vice-Chancellors, Heads of Oxbridge colleges, Fellows of the Royal Society, and as the hour droned on so did I grow ever more con-vinced that I had been insane to submit myself to such torture. There were moments of respite, as when the Principal of Glasgow University com-mented that I was fortunate to have as referee the former Principal of Aberdeen, Willy Fyfe, and when the Principal of Somerville, a lady with a face like an eagle but a kindly smile, revealed the surprising information that the Foundation had made enquiries about me from Penguin and the even more surprising news that Allen Lane had responded ecstatically, but nemesis arrived when one of the Trustees, as terrifying for his great height as for his steely eyes, growled 'You have behind you some interesting experience but you know nothing of the sciences'.

It was strangely reminiscent of Teddy Edwards's comment at my C.H. interview, but I was sick of being badgered and my reply was of the same order of defeatist impertinence as the response I had given when asked by the Officers Selection Board why I wanted to be a Gunner. I glared at

Alex Todd, Professor of Chemistry at Cambridge, already a Nobel Prize-winner and later Lord Todd, Master of Christ's College, and snapped, 'I may not know much about the sciences but I do know that most scientists can't write English'.

Three days later a letter from the Director, Leslie Farrer-Brown, invited me to accept, from the beginning of the next month, the post of Assistant Director of the Nuffield Foundation and Assistant Secretary of the Nuffield Provincial Hospitals Trust, at a stipend which made us wonder if we should add Eton to the list of schools for Pieter and Michael.

There were at the time few jobs more gilded than those of senior employees at Nuffield Lodge. My office, furnished as a sitting-room with antiques, looked out over large gardens to the Canal and Regent's Park. The dining-room, in which I had faced the Trustees, was the setting for many more comfortable occasions, for lunches and dinners blessed by good food, fine wines, fat cigars and fascinating company. Wherever I went I was welcomed unctuously as the man from Nuffield, his pockets filled with gold.

Farrer-Brown was an indulgent boss who interfered not at all in the work of his senior colleagues and if in the years when I was with him in company with my intimates, sometimes I smirked at his obsession with the Honours List, subsequently, and particularly after I had myself experienced the miscarriage of several hints and promises, I came to sympathise with the frustration that he suffered at a time when service with Nuffield was a moving-staircase into the House of Lords but he, the Director, garlanded with no more than a CBE.

My other colleagues were all polymaths, most of them amiable and two, Kit Huxley and Gordon McLachlan, became almost immediately much more than just colleagues.

Kit, the Foundation's Fellowship Officer, cousin to Aldous and Julian, brother to Michael and Gervase and brother-in-law to Elspeth, mocked himself as 'the stupid Huxley' but his impeccable tailoring, clipped moustache and picket-straight posture proclaimed him for what he had been, a brigadier, and denied all identity with that shaggy if brilliant clan which I had encountered briefly years before at the Leigh-Mallorys. Yet he was a connoisseur of paintings and procelain, a sophisticated critic of books and music and always a stimulating, amusing companion.

Gordon, the Foundation's Accountant, was then, as he remains to this day, without any of those pernickety and desiccated traits which are too often manifest in those who follow the profession. Even his appearance damned caricature: stocky, ruddy complexioned, with a nose that must have been broken even more often than mine, he looked what in fact he had been, a first-class Rugby-footballer. His enthusiasms were all of a kind which made friendship between us easy; Rugby football, of course, Scotch whisky, of course, books, the theatre and above all the ballet, on which he wrote with authority and charm for *Twentieth Century*. Mary, his wife, I met first in somewhat unpropitious circumstances when, it must have been well past midnight, after a Trustees meeting and a lavish Trustees dinner, Gordon and I routed her out of bed to join us in one last drink. She forgave me then – and Gordon too, I suppose – and, in a fashion which is not always possible in relationships that have their origins in day-time and professional contact between husbands, our friendship was immediately extended to include our wives. And so, happily, it has continued for many decades after Gordon and I ceased working together.

Settled in such luxurious circumstances, surrounded by likeable colleagues and by a host of lively and eager contacts and blessed with a brief which conferred upon me the duty to act as patron for many fascinating projects, I was left with little cause for complaint.

I soon discovered that, though superficially the two jobs were unlike, in essentials my role at Nuffield was much as had been that which I had exercised at a Penguin editorial desk. As at Penguin I had given part of my time to the consideration of unsolicited manuscripts, so at Nuffield I was dealing daily with appeals for grants. Just as for Penguin the most intriguing of my responsibilities had been to predict the topics which would arouse public interest a year, two years, even ten years ahead, and to find authors capable of satisfying that interest, so now I was ordained to act both as prophet and recruiting officer.

Thus it was that, when television was still in its infancy, the Foundation had already decided to investigate the effects of the medium on young viewers. To direct our researches I found Hilde Himmelweit, a scholar with a stiletto-sharp intellect and, to me almost as persuasive, of physical attributes and charm of a kind that never before and never since have I seen in a sociologist.

We came, also long before it had become a hobby-horse of the quality-press and politicians, to considering Britain's generally contemptuous attitude to industry, to applied science and to technology, and the potentially disastrous consequence for the national economy of the inferior status of the sciences in our schools. Though myself a shameful and shamed product of these prejudices and qualified to talk of the sciences only by one year of Density in the Third Form at C.H. and one term of Geology at UNB, I was active in establishing with the British Association for the Advancement of Science the Science and Industry Committee and its research programmes. By involvement I learnt at least some sophistication about the problems handled by the Committee and its research team but, though I could not fail to notice their seminal influence, I cannot pretend that I ever understood two other offspring of this activity at whose birth I served as one of the attendant midwives. I am still mystified by Nuffield Science and Nuffield Mathematics.

Not all my activities were as portentous as these. Some indeed were, by Nuffield's grandiose standards, picayune, as when I went as the Hospital Trust's plenipotentiary to establish on the island of Alderney a twelve-bedded hospital.

When, years later, Gordon McLachlan informed me that the Alderney project should have been ruled *ultra vires* before ever it was launched, he added to my pride in being the effective Founder of the smallest hospital in the British Isles retrospective gratification in my success as an illicit philanthropist. Even so, I hold my many visits to Alderney in delightful recollection most of all because it was then that I was introduced into the company of the author of *Mistress Masham's Repose* and *The Sword in the Stone*.

Tim White was the most hospitable of men; for him an empty glass – his own or his guest's – was a blasphemy and even when he was sunk deep in depression (a not infrequent occurrence),he saw to it that neither he nor his guest could blaspheme even for a moment. Sober or, as more often happened, some distance on the wrong side of sobriety, his mind remained sharp. He was witty, at times even comic, shrewd in his judgements of men and books and with each glass of whisky his opinions of his fellow-authors and the literary establishment became ever more deliciously slanderous.

I found no comparable pleasures, no pleasures of any kind, when I went as emissary from Croesus into institutions dedicated to the care of the mentally disabled. I was too squeamish to support with ease a place in the audience set to watch psychopaths acting out their fantasies. Though I did take some consolation in silent laughter when, at the end of the performance, the pioneer of that mode of psychotherapy took me aside to give me a long, detailed and lurid account of his own sexual adventures and misadventures. On those many other occasions when I was locked in an office with the Medical Superintendent of an asylum – announcing that I carried with me riches almost infinite – I could summon neither comfort nor laughter. On the face of each and every Medical Superintendent I saw the same look, patient and tolerant. He had heard it all before; give me but a few minutes of prefatory extravaganza and then I would reveal myself as Napoleon or Jesus Christ.

One of my Nuffield projects stemmed directly from my publishing experience and allowed to me use of techniques learnt at Penguin, Christophers and Falcon. I urged upon the Trustees interest in the state of the learned journals.

The world of scholarship is dutifully concerned to publish the results of research but its audience, though word-wise, is generally tiny and so uneconomic, its financial resources slim, and those responsible for editing, production, promotion and distribution generally amateur and not infrequently inept.

I turned to Bob Lusty, then at the height of his career with the lively publisher Michael Joseph, to make a report and, on the strength of his conclusions and my recommendations, the Trustees decided to offer advisory services to the two austere bodies nominally responsible for British Scholar-ship, the Royal Society for the Sciences, the British Academy for the Humanities and the Social Sciences.

The Royal allowed to me the full dignity of membership in its Learned Journals Committee and for several years after I had left Nuffield I continued to serve, the only participant in its affairs who did not write after his name the homage-inspiring initials FRS.

Mortimer Wheeler, Secretary of the British Academy, would have nothing of the kind; he would take Nuffield money but he could do without Nuffield advice and he had no wish to install a rival who might challenge, in however trivial a fashion, his status as patron-in-chief; but Rik Wheeler paid to me personally a compliment far richer than professional acceptance. He gave me his companionship.

Mortimer Wheeler was at that time as well-known to television audiences as Gilbert Harding. Tall, craggy, flamboyant, an amateur soldier who had risen to the rank of brigadier, Rik was an unchallenged and unchallengeable leader among British archaeologists and the most skilful publicist of their craft. His talk, delivered in a key more than a trifle higher than one expected from a man of his build, was a treasure-house of anecdotes – about digging in India, about soldiering in the Western Desert, about the foibles and fallibilities of his eminent colleagues – and his wine-cellar was as rich as his conversation.

There were, throughout my time at Nuffield, reservations and perturbations which not infrequently disrupted my contentment. Although I was still writing – indeed most of the first draft of the *History of the United States* was completed in week-ends away from Nuffield Lodge – and was not greatly dismayed either by my abdication from broadcasting or by the BBC's abandonment of me, my conscience was bruised by my impotence to use my position as an agent for patronage on behalf of those modes of activity, literature, music and the other arts, which had always meant so much to me. I was disturbed, too, by an inhibition which I discovered to be common to all the great foundations: the prejudice which made it far easier to secure huge funds for grandiose projects proposed by a great institution than ever it was to find a few hundred pounds for the support of an undeniably worthy but humble scheme put before us by an unknown, if verifiably competent, applicant. Most of all I was made uneasy by my own divided condition. There was I, by day a patron, intimately involved in making decisions which conceded tens of thousands of pounds to supplicants and living in the style of a latter-day Medici,but both as benefactor and beneficiary all that I did was financed out of the admittedly ample pocket of a man I met only twice. And there was I of an evening still worrying about the state of our overdraft, mortgage repayments, school-fees and, sometimes, butcher's bills.

Even so I might have continued, perhaps for the rest of my working-life, as a generally contented distributor of Lord Nuffield's fortune had not some mischievous djinn brought to my attention a terse advertisement in *The Times*; 'Director required for national cultural institution'. At the time,

I was not even greatly concerned that no reply came to my letter, addressed to a box-number, asking for enlargement of that unrevealing announcement.

I owe much to Robert Lusty. I know little of his achievements as Deputy Chairman of the BBC but I claim to be qualified to judge as superlative his work as a publisher at Michael Joseph and at Hutchinson and I hold that his combination of commercial acumen with editorial perceptiveness and integrity made him rare in his kind. For forty years and more he has been my friend, often my patron, and I am not insensible to the debt I owe him for persuading me to write the biography of Allen Lane. But I cannot be certain that I should honour him for retrieving my letter from the waste-paper basket to which, with dozens of other similar exploratory letters, it had been consigned, and thus setting himself up as the *deus ex machina* who brought me to the National Book League.

Six weeks after I wrote that letter, I was bidden to 7 Albemarle Street to meet the hierarchs of the National Book League. Any casual observer must assume that 7 Albemarle Street is one of the finest town-houses in London's West End and so it is for two floors. Built by that Marquess of Granby who, for losing his wig at the Battle of Minden has since been made eponymous for more public-houses than the Duke of Wellington or Lord Nelson, its ground floor boasts one huge and elegant salon used by the NBL as an exhibition-gallery, its second floor several handsomely-proportioned rooms, one of them named for Fanny Burney whose ghost is said to haunt the place. In thirteen years she never vouchsafed herself to me (to the best of my knowledge when alive she visited the house only once, and then briefly). But the pride of 7 Albemarle Street is the magnificent cantilevered staircase sweeping up from the oval central hall to the first floor.

On the day of my interview I was not taken up the ceremonial staircase, nor was I ushered into any of the dignified rooms. Instead I was placed in a lift which must have been installed by the Marquis of Granby himself and decanted into an upper-floor slum.

I was settled at a trestle-table covered with what I took to be an Army Surplus blanket, before me three men; Joseph Compton, the League's retiring Chairman, Kenneth Potter, Chairman of Longmans and the Chairman-elect, and a grey-faced Scotsman, the Treasurer, William Balleny. Compton I knew already. An eager hanger-on to the hems of the literary establishment, he was as famous for his exquisite calligraphy as he was for his execrable poetasting. It was not easy to warm to Balleny, the caricature of a Scottish accountant, crabbed and dour. For Potter my liking was immediate. It was Potter who did most of the talking, his talk punctuated by huge and friendly chuckles, and it was obvious to me that, though there were three men behind that Army blanket, there was but one vote.

In appearance florid and in manner, despite those chuckles, austere, Potter chose to present himself as a hard-nosed businessman who despised the arty pretensions of the trade ('the only books I ever read are my company's account-books') but from that very first meeting I sensed that I could work with him and my confidence was never confounded. Then, and in several meetings thereafter before I took up my post as its Director, he stressed his conviction that the League could serve best the cause of books -even the cause of the book-trade – by holding itself patently independent of the publishers, printers and booksellers who, just because they contributed substantially to its funds, thought themselves entitled to direct its policies. Later I discovered that 'substantially' was accurate only by comparison with funds brought in from other sources, that the trade subscribed meanly, grudgingly and only after much coercion, that the League teetered perennially on the brink of insolvency and that much of my time and energy must be wasted on the nauseous business of raising funds. But at that first meeting as Potter spoke so did I become ever more convinced that the mantle he had already cut for me would fit. As ever the League was in crisis, but the opportunities before it were immense – if only it could find a leader, energetic, courageous and able. I would have unqualified responsibility for the public relations of the whole book-world, my brief I could interpret almost as I wished and I would have his unreserved support.

I fell for Potter's blandishments with only one reservation, that I be permitted to appoint my own subordinates.

All seemed set for a future more glorious because more useful, more influential if less gilded, than anything I could achieve at Nuffield. I closed my mind to the gibes against my predecessors that were rehearsed gratuitously for my indoctrination by acquaintances in the trade. Under their direction – so ran the complaint – the League had frittered its resources on preaching to the converted. I vowed that in part at least so it would continue with me as its head, for that very metaphor refuted the condemnation it was intended to carry. Had not the Church suffered the degradation of empty pews just because all passion had vanished from its preaching to the faithful? We must fashion a new congregation but we could not afford to lose the confirmed.

Leslie Farrer-Brown and the Nuffield Trustees had been unfailingly kind to me and I could do none other than agree to their request that I remain in post until my successor had been found; the delay also suited my purposes, for I wanted time to plan my strategy. For two months the stairs to my Nuffield office were the steps to Canossa, with almost every day some member of the NBL staff as it was then constituted crawling up on his knees to entreat me to retain his services. I was more ruthless than I would have believed possible; I had my eye on several adjutants more suited than these to the battles ahead.

At the end of two months, Farrer-Brown gave a valedictory dinner for Kippe and for me and we were presented with a noble set of ales to add to our growing collection of eighteenth-century glass. (Another year would pass before Gordon told me that outside an antique shop he and Kit had come close to street-brawling over the selection of those glasses.) Gordon took over my responsibilities for the Hospitals Trust and, after he had divorced it from the Foundation, directed its activities for the next thirty years and made himself Britain's leading independent authority on the Health Service and an expert on the administration of medicine, honoured all over the world.

I had no difficulty in persuading Potter of the validity of my appreciation of the situation at the NBL nor did he question the plan of attack which I outlined in several meetings with him during that two-month interval between gazetting and taking up command; for the most part, I was merely articulating conclusions already in his mind. (Military metaphors were as acceptable to him as to me.)

It was my opinion that hitherto the League had frittered away its resources by attempting to attack on too broad a front. I planned to select, and to reconnoitre before attacking, limited but significant objectives. My time at Nuffield had taught me that prefatory research is the civilian equivalent of military reconnaissance.

My first objective, I told Potter, was also in all probability the richest prize of all. We would go for Britain's schools. If we could enhance the use of books in schools we would be serving education, adding to the prosperity of publishers, both educational and general, but, most important of all, we would be ensuring the future of books by creating for use in later years a reservoir of readers. If by sound research, we could establish standards for Local Education Authority expenditure on class-room books and school libraries which we could use to shame laggard administrators and miserly politicians, by supporting propaganda about money with information, with scrupulously selected book-lists and exhibitions, we would persuade even those we lambasted to accept our services.

Even before the two months were out, I approached the Association of Education Committees. Its Director, Bill Alexander, did not trouble to disguise his suspicion. He knew, he said, all that there was to know about the NBL: it was nothing but the publishers' poodle and at that no Crufts prize-winner. I was indignant; I insisted that I would not discuss the past and then, illogically, proceeded to argue that all was now changed, that I had been assured by Kenneth Potter, and he the most powerful of all educational publishers, that henceforth it would be accepted by all his colleagues as a tenet of faith that the NBL could only serve books well, and therefore the trade, if its independence from trade control was respected. Alexander continued to look sceptical but somehow my conviction that I was speaking nothing but the truth, that the League under Potter's chairmanship and my direction would be left unfettered to carry out unbiased investigation and to provide unprejudiced advice and services, won him over. Once won, he was immediately the most fervent of allies. Provided, of course, that the NBL did most of the work, he would so arrange matters that our report on school book-expenditure would be given the *imprimatur* of the Association and as such recommended to Directors of Education, to head-teachers and, this he added with a grin as if showing me a long spoon use-ful for supping with the Devil, to the Department of Education and Science. We must make our report annually and to this end we would set up a joint steering-committee with him and me as alternative chairmen. Even, and with another grin, this time almost sadistic, he agreed to my more contentious suggestion that we publish each year an LEA book-expenditure league-table, and so bring down upon those who did not live according to our standards the condemnation of the public.

And so it continued for all my thirteen years at the NBL.

Kippe accepted with no obvious show of reluctance my announcement that, now that I was to be responsible for the salvation of a struggling organisation, I must reduce even more my literary and journalistic com-mitments. This decision would deny to us the second-night tickets for concerts, theatres and the opera which I had been receiving as a junior Mollie Panter-Downes, writing a monthly letter for a Canadian magazine (*Mayfair* was not grand enough to be invited to first nights). But that, said Kippe, would spare her my favourite outburst of hate for Sylvia Fisher, the current *diva* at Covent Garden and the only person in the world who could make me dislike *Fidelio*. And, Kippe added in her most audible stage whisper, 'Give it six months, at most twelve, and you'll be back to scrib-bling.'

She was less complacent when I urged that we leave Bradwell. In the time when I was at Nuffield we had tried a variety of domiciliary patterns, for me Bradwell and back every day, for me a flat in London and Bradwell at the weekend, for the whole family a cottage in Highgate and Bradwell only at weekends. With this last arrangement we persisted for almost two years after I moved to the NBL, but at last we agreed that we must move.

There would never be for any of us a worthy substitute for New Hall but we were fortunate when we found Oxhey Hall, another Tudor farm-house, an anomaly of dignity set in a field but a few hundred yards from a council-estate somewhere between the bric-a-brac of Watford and the stiff-backed, mock-Tudor pretensions of Moor Park.

Travelling up from the Dengie Hundred to Liverpool Street, I had remained always anonymous to my bowler-hatted stockbroker train-com-panions because we did not own a yacht. From Moor Park to Baker Street on the 8.23 I was similarly spectral; I played neither bridge nor golf.

But on the last train back to Moor Park, as often as not, Kippe was with me. The NBL had bought two slaves for the price of one. For thirteen years, Kippe served as hostess and supernumerary exhibitions-officer. Not once in all that time, nor ever after, was her contribution acknowledged.

13

Spokesman for Barabbas

I entered upon service with the NBL confident that, by purge and replacement, I had equipped myself with a compact group of efficient colleagues.
That my complacency was in all but one instance justified was demonstrated in the succeeding years, and it was not until a decade had passed that I
woke to the realization that, by retaining and advancing to responsibility a
man already on the staff, I had established in high office a Benedict Arnold
in a shiny bowler hat, pin-stripe trousers and a black jacket. For the rest,
my appointments were shrewd and the first three blessed with consequences as happy for our family as they were beneficial to the League and
the book-world.

It is symptomatic of the grudging attitude of those we served that not
one of the many chronicles of the NBL so much as mentions by name any
one of these three, Monica Anderson, Joy Heiseler and Barbara Kyle, who
in those hectic and often troubled years gave unstintingly time, skill and
loyalty, and that only three Chairmen – Potter, Michael Hornby and
Stewart Mackintosh – paid public tribute to them or to any other member
of the staff.

A senior executive is only as good as his secretary and, as I prepared to
go to the League, I gave much time to the selection of my Personal
Assistant. I did not doubt that I would be mobbed by applicants; publishing
exercises attraction for young men and young women far more powerful
than its meagre rewards merit; nor was I surprised when most of the girls I
interviewed seemed to be better qualified for the chorus-line at the
Windmill or the pages of *Tatler* than for a seat behind a typewriter and a
telephone, but I was disconcerted when two candidates added to their
recital of qualifications blatant offers to accept the *double-entendre* implicit in
the title.

I resisted these seductive and flattering propositions and took instead
Monica Anderson, a recent History graduate of the University of London,
a lively, intelligent young woman whose integrity was evident even at our
first meeting and whose fidelity has warmed me ever since.

I had first met Joy Heiseler when she was a guest at a luncheon party
given in honour of the Editorial Committee of *The Christ's Hospital Book*
before we lurched into St Paul's Cathedral to celebrate the C.H.
Quatercentenary. The Inland Water Authority seemed a long way from

the NBL but I needed an administrator, thorough and experienced, and I was not mistaken in Joy. She delighted in a party, and there were many parties at the League, but her zest for partying she never allowed to interfere with her work. In the next thirteen years, with care, skill and enthusiasm, she filled every senior post up to and including Deputy Director, yet she never turned away from the humblest jobs. I have seen her often – as I have seen also many of her senior colleagues – just before an exhibition, shifting heavy glass cases, carting piles of books and then, a half-hour or so later, there she was by my side, immaculate, ready to greet some eminent guest. Thirteen summers in a row I worked with her as in her elegant calligraphy she prepared place-cards and seating-plans for the Cricket Match lunch. Always it seemed that the umpires would be out before the task was finished, always, before the first visitor arrived at Vincent Square, there she was stretched out in a deck-chair, dressed as if for the Royal Enclosure at Ascot. But of all that I, the League and the book-world owe to Joy, our greatest debt is for her sensitive care for an underpaid and overworked staff.

I brought in Barbara Kyle to be my closest and most senior colleague by subterfuge. Some months before I had piloted past the Nuffield Trustees a grant which would allow her to quit her post as Librarian at the Royal Institute of International Affairs and to undertake recondite research preparatory to devising a new library classification-system. She needed a base for this work; I offered her a room close to mine in 7 Albemarle Street.

At almost no cost to ourselves we would have immediate access to advice from one of Britain's outstanding authorities on libraries, but I had motives more consequential and Barbara knew them for what they were. Potter had met Barbara and his spies confirmed his opinion and mine that she was ideally suited to be my deputy. As ever he was delighted by what he took to be a machiavellian scheme but he uttered a warning, the first audible rumble of a storm that would threaten me throughout my years at the NBL.

I wanted Barbara, he wanted Barbara, she wanted to come but were I to appoint her as Deputy Director our captious supporters would murmur that I did so only to exalt my own status and all would complain that the League could not possibly afford the profligate salary demanded by one as distinguished as Barbara Kyle. He advised me to give her an office, to tell no one and to bide my time.

Barbara was then in her mid-forties. A big, handsome woman, there was in her character and characteristics nothing whatever that matched her to the conventional if calumnious portrait of a librarian: unworldly, parchment-faced and timid except when some inconsiderate reader threatened to disarrange her neatly drilled book-stacks. She looked, acted and spoke more like the jolly headmistress of a progressive but well-disciplined girls boarding-school. She was shrewd, whole-hearted in her zeal for the causes we served and never subservient – not even to me. She neither needed nor troubled to hide her confidence in her own intellect, fools she suffered sadly and bullies not at all, but she was clubbable and devoid of all pretentiousness.

In the first ten years, my conviction seldom flagged that at last I had found my vocation. By the efforts and activities of these, my no less dedicated colleagues, I would contribute hugely to dismissing as false prophets those Jeremiahs who for all my life had been predicting the imminent death of the book. First it had been the silent film which had been cast for the role of murderer, then wireless and after that successively the talking-picture and television. I would prove to them that the book was still very much alive, the printed word still the most adaptable, the most convenient and the most effective way of communicating enlightenment and entertainment. Despite Potter's warning, it took me some time to discover that, though the hitherto unconverted were not unwilling to listen to our carefully-articulated sermons, though Ministers, the heads of national and international institutions, Ambassadors and High Commissioners were not only ready to become allies but also, not infrequently, to call upon the League to service their own projects, it was often in the trade, among those very people who, in financial terms, would be most obviously beneficiaries of our success, that we found critics, sceptics and obstructionists. Potter had suggested that the League was condemned to walk an endless tight-rope between service and subservience to the trade. I was soon persuaded that the League's Director must perform that balancing-act whilst standing on his head. For thirteen years I managed that feat well enough – and then I fell off.

Although during my term in office I and my colleagues brought in from other sources considerable sums of money and though we had the unflagging support of our private members – and they essential to us also as the outward and visible sign that we were not as Bill Alexander had averred, 'the poodle of the publishers' – we could not survive without subscriptions from the trade. They came in, but never in sufficiency to relieve me of the task of begging outwith the book-world, and usually only after much cajoling, hectoring and, when we could so indulge, bullying.

Retrospective assessments in this kind are, of course, heinous generalizations. There were many noble exceptions, two of the trade Chairmen, pre-eminently, Potter and Michael Hornby (and these two, as I thought significantly, heads of two of the most successful empires in the book-world, Longmans and W. H. Smith), who never spared themselves or the firm's funds and there were several others (most of them, as I thought no less significantly, among the shrewdest publishers in the land). Bob Lusty, for example; our closest neighbour across Albemarle Street at Number 50; Jock, the sixth (or is he the seventh?) John Murray; Desmond Flower of Cassell, a connoisseur of books, wine and French literature, who was the only man I ever met who could speak either English or French impeccably with a cigar in his mouth; and that exquisitely eighteenth-century publisher of notably twentieth-century books, Fred Warburg; Ian Parsons of Chatto and Windus – himself editor of the best of all anthologies of First War poems – who supported the League whole-heartedly, worked on its committees and who, when they saw cause for criticism, paid me the compliment of voicing it to me rather than whisper it to cronies in the bar of the Garrick Club.

Others more remote were even so invariably amiable to the League. Despite his suspicion of my name, T. S. Eliot did not remove his name from the list of Vice Presidents, almost a membership list of the Order of Merit, on our notepaper and on the rare occasions when I asked for his assistance he was quick to respond, but I did not flatter myself or the League nor yet credit Sir Geoffrey Faber or Peter du Sautoy for the ease of our dealings with Faber and Faber. That, I suspected, we owed to another Faber director, Richard, the son of the poet Walter de la Mare and to my wife. Dick's father had been a close friend of my father-in-law and as children Dick and Kippe had played together in the family gardens at Richmond and Radlett.

It was not likely that I would ever persuade Allen Lane into ardent membership of the NBL, for his aversion to co-operative effort was notorious. Indeed, when tentatively I asked him to join the League's committee, he replied only with scabrous comments on the ability, integrity and parentage of almost every one of his fellow-publishers active in the League's councils, but almost as soon as I was installed he took to accepting invitations to our various functions and, rarely for him, on occasion actually came, though I could never foretell whether he would bring with him his wife or his current *inamorata*. He also adopted the habit of dropping in, sometimes twice in a week early in the evening, to drink my white wine, to hear from me the latest trade gossip and, more and more often, to try out on me his latest ploy. Once, when he had outlined to me some scheme even for him more than ordinarily byzantine, he articulated my use to him and to Penguin at that period in our erratic relationship. I was, he said, his human thermometer. If, as at that moment, I loathed what he proposed, I looked glumly at the ceiling. If I thought his notion potentially sound, I grunted, raised my eyebrows and proceeded to cross-examine him like a lawyer trying to trap a criminal into admitting perjury. But when I approved of something he suggested, I interrupted before he had finished his exposition and talked for half-an-hour until he was convinced that it was I who had thought of it first.

Penguins co-operated readily in all our projects – and already by 1956 we could not have staged without them an authoritative current book-list nor could we have published a worthwhile subject book-list – but even in the years when I was regularly Allen's thermometer I could not extort from Allen a subscription that was much more than a token. Sir Stanley

Unwin on the other hand, a man every whit as notorious as Allen for tight-fistedness, was invariably generous with money, time and, most of all, with counsel.

In the 1920s, Unwin had been one of the founders of our parent-body, the National Book Council, and it could have been his conviction that he was always right that made him so steadfast in his loyalty to the institution he had helped to create. Certainly Unwin was not reticent about his infal-libility. The story is told that when his nephew Philip, having read the typescript of Unwin's autobiography, *The Truth about a Publisher*, advanced the gentle criticism that the book might be improved if, just occasionally, the author admitted to an error of judgement, Uncle Stan replied without pause 'But I'm not writing fiction'.

I can vouch for his parsimony, and for his generosity. When. my appointment as Director was announced, he invited me to lunch at the Reform Club ('1.15 in the Coffee Room' – and so too late for pre-lunch drinks). We sat, studied the menu, then he pushed across the table one of those pads which members use for their lunch-orders. 'I see you're also a member here.' But at the end of lunch, whilst I was paying for my own meal, he wrote a handsome cheque in favour of the NBL.

It was not easy to hold the League from becoming, what too often it was accused of being, a mammoth literary society, its motivation uplift, its achievement booksiness, but we strove hard, and on the whole successful-ly, to demonstrate that, like Elia, in book-matters the League had 'no repugnances', that we were as much concerned with *A First Course in Homological Algebra* as with the works of Dickens or a slim volume of verse from an obscure publishing-house in Pontefract, as much with *The Care of Reptilian Pets* as with *A la recherche du temps perdu*.

To this end, as also to fulfil the comparable catholicity of a brief which imposed upon us the duty to act at one and the same time as informed props and allies to habitual book-users of all kinds, and as missionaries to those still unconverted to the benefits of print, we were called upon to employ a plethora of techniques. Much of our work in this kind – statisti-cal research, the preparation of travelling exhibitions and book-lists and the activities of our unique Book Information Bureau, presided over – before, throughout and long after my regime by the self-effacing but omniscient Jane With – was continuous and undramatic; so undramatic that it passed almost unremarked by the media and by most of our critics and so patently continuous that, though these were labours central to our utility and the heaviest burden upon staff time and upon the League's meagre budget, when I look back on the years when I directed the NBL even I see all as hourly, daily, yearly chores unrelieved by sensational episode or exorbitant triumph – unless it be triumph that over those years, the skills and hard work of those who had immediate responsibility for these activities brought in from all over the country, and indeed increasingly from any part of the world, ever more and more demands for their services.

We produced reports on library supply in schools, in medical and nursing education, in industry and in the developing countries. We published book-lists on an almost infinite number of topics, the Book Information Bureau answered hundreds of queries every week, we staged exhibitions not only in schools and libraries but also in cinema-foyers, at trade-shows, at Congress House, at meetings of Women's Institutes, in churches and at wine-tastings (the second of these almost fatal to Antony Kamm who, because he was the only male at that time available to serve as guardian and guide to our display and therefore uniquely qualified to circumvent the embargo imposed by Guy Prince, the head of the shippers Lebegue, against perfume at a tasting, spent the whole of his first week with the League drinking the best clarets and burgundies). All this was routine and at the time it was the grand occasions which won us most attention just as it is those more glamorous events which come most readily to recall. The Antiquarian Book Fairs, for example, which, with the Antiquarian Booksellers Association (incidentally the most amenable of all the many trade associations with whom I dealt), we launched in 1957 and held annually thereafter, when our gallery was filled with the stands of sellers of rare books and our bar with bibliomaniacs from all over the world. Or the Beatrix Potter Exhibition which gave me for the second time in my life the extraordinary sight of a queue in the street waiting for admission to a book-event (the first, outside W. H. Smith in Baker Street when, to honour Bernard Shaw's ninetieth birthday, Penguin published its first Million, ten volumes of G.B.S. each in an edition of one hundred thousand.

My pleasure in the success of the Beatrix Potter Exhibition was not a little reduced by the shame that was mine for being, in all those thousands who flocked in – among them Sir Barnes and Lady Wallis who demanded from me a private showing – almost certainly the only one who had never read a book by Beatrix Potter.

I was more at ease with the British Army exhibition which we staged first in our gallery and then in the grandeur of Edinburgh Castle, yet it was that exhibition which caused me an embarrassment which remains with me even as I write.

I had begged from Sir John Murray the loan of the manuscript of Byron's *Childe Harold* so that we could have it on display, opened at the Eve of Waterloo passage. Sir John had agreed but with certain conditions: I must myself bring it across the width of Albemarle Street under police escort, no one but I and a named member of our staff must be allowed to handle it, and it must be kept by day in a locked and humidified show-case and at night in a safe. All these conditions we fulfilled and then the Duke of Gloucester announced his intention to visit the exhibition. His expertise and enthusiasm in all things military were matters of public knowledge and, because for a few days in Asmara I had served as one of his aides, I knew that he had other enthusiasms. I filled my whisky-decanter and my cigarette-box and thought myself well-prepared for a Royal visit. I was not ready for the first remark made by the Duke when he entered the gallery. He had heard of our prize exhibit and now he could fulfil the ambition of a life-time, he could inspect the manuscript of *Childe Harold*. 'Seraphs might despair.' With Sir John's eyes on me I opened the show-case, took out *Childe Harold* and, palpably denying to royalty all but a distant view of 'revelry by night', I set my shoulder to block the outstretched ducal hands, and turned the pages. Every photographer in the room exploded his flash-bulb to record my republican impertinence.

For another of these grandiose and prestigious exhibitions I asked Allen Lane to lend us his own copy of Penguin Number One, *Ariel,* inscribed by André Maurois to Allen Lane, an exhibit less sensational than *Childe Harold* and, by the measure of the sale-room, far less valuable than many we were accustomed to display, but in its own way as precious and more seminal than any.

I did not intend to sleep in the gallery alongside a security man as I did when we had the Queen's Gutenberg Bible in the building, and we were not called upon to employ the services of the Metropolitan Police to escort it from Harmondsworth, but I was dismayed when Allen brought it in himself, dragged it, unwrapped, from his overcoat pocket and promptly used it as a coaster for his wine-glass.

I was well-advanced in recounting the latest rumour about Robert Maxwell when, seemingly apropos of nothing, Allen remarked casually 'Jack, you've been here long enough. You're coming back to Penguins.'

It was an order not a request, but I protested that I had been with the League for less than two years and that at all events I had never left Penguin, I was still General Editor of the Histories.

Allen smiled, held out his glass for a refill, asked me if I could spare time in the next week to attend a Penguin sales conference and changed the subject back to Maxwell. But when he was ready to leave, with his hand on the door-knob, he grinned his naughty-boy grin and said 'I know, you know that I must have a second-in-command I can trust, just in case. . .'

The selection of heirs-apparent was for Allen a hobby only a little less pleasing than dismissing his anointed successors. I had no wish to end in the moat of Caenarfon Castle; in the next few months I went several times to Penguin gatherings and there was tacitly accepted as Prince of Wales but, though still he came regularly to my office, I could never persuade him to discuss terms. Within six months – and for another three years – my translation to Harmondsworth was forgotten.

The advertisement which had summoned me to the League 'Director required for major national cultural institution' – was a job-specification far less than adequate. I was called upon to be administrator, fund-raiser, choreographer and producer to a dance-troupe composed almost entirely of *primas*, ambassador for British books abroad, committee-man, con-man, father confessor, public relations officer for the trade, impresario, secretary of a social club, if at one remove, manager of a restaurant and bar (the actual manager one of the League's characters, Lou Fisher, a large, cheerful lady who would do almost anything for the NBL provided I introduced her to those of my guests she thought worthy of her attention, Michael Wilding, Allen Lane or Prince Philip), broadcaster, editor, travelling sales-man, cricket-selector – and always politician.

As public demonstration of the League's unique status, balanced between the trade and the users of books, the authors of our constitution had legislated that the chairmanship of the Executive Committee be held, two years about, by a prominent representative of the commerce of books and an *Éminence* from some other walk of life.

While Kenneth Potter was Chairman, I could leave to him much of the politicking, the endless in-fighting, necessary to keep the League indepen-dent and solvent; those he could not persuade, he bullied into acquies-cence. My second trade Chairman was no less effective, for though Michael Hornby's methods were never, as Potter's, uproariously ruthless there was no weakness in his gentleness – and who in the Trade would dare risk the displeasure of the Vice-Chairman of W. H. Smith. An upright man in both the metaphorical and the physical meaning of the adjective, he carried with him still the resonances of the Guardee he had once been, his superbly cut dark suit, pearl tie-pin offering no hint of his association with a chain of High Street stores but for all that he was unfailingly courte-ous, even to the humblest member of our staff, and to me invariably both friendly and supportive, and though the Edwardian *persona* was genuine, Michael was a modern businessman, tough, efficient and dedicated to effi-ciency, and shrewd. Himself a noted collector of rare books (and son of one of the most famous of all collectors) he was of all my Chairmen the one best qualified to understand the duality in the League's purposes.

Even so, when once in every year he played in the NBL Cricket Match, Michael was all Edwardian, his back as straight as his bat in the block-hole, his moustache as trim as his wide flannels and, perched on his carefully brushed grey hair, a small colour-ringed cap.

'Oh my Hornby and my Barlow long ago.'

The eminence and the strength of Hornby's predecessor in the Chair were alike faded. In the 1920s and 1930s Wyn Griffith had written one admirable book on his Great War experiences and some undistinguished verse; when I was at Penguin we had published his sensitive study of his countrymen, the Welsh; but he had become, like Joseph Compton, one of those minor scribblers who are useful to make up numbers on committees. It was, I suppose, no fault of his that he was an Income Tax inspector; though his profession did not help me to love him, it was because he was a trimmer, a man who went always with the majority, that I found him of little value as ally. The other two non-trade Chairmen under whom I served, David Eccles and Stewart Mackintosh, were both of them indu-bitably eminent and both men of mettle.

When first I encountered David Eccles I came, as poacher to his gamekeeper, to the Secretary of State for Education as advocate for increased school book-expenditure. He was courteous and attentive but no Minister of the Crown gives way easily to a plea for more spending of public money and he made me work hard through several meetings before he allowed me to see that if ever I was engaged in preaching to the converted it was with David Eccles; that, as no Minister of Education with whom I had dealings – not even Edward Boyle, who was later our Deputy Chairman and later still himself a publisher – he was dedicated to the cause of books. Although the League was small beer for the man who had stage-managed the Coronation, for a Privy Councillor who had served in several Cabinets, I was not surprised when after Harold Macmillan's Night of the Long Knives, David agreed to become the League's Chairman. I knew all the gibes hurled at him by the Press and I despised his politics just as, had he known them, he would have despised mine, but he believed in the NBL and he gave to it as much care as he would have given to any affair of State. Sometimes I was disconcerted by his habit of nodding-off in the middle of some portentous discussion, but I never knew him to miss the thrust of the argument and I never knew him to fluff a brief.

There is within every adult male a schoolboy struggling to be let loose. Once a year my imprisoned twelve-year-old was allowed an hour or so of glamorous liberty as I strode round Lords with Douglas Jardine, selecting the team he was to captain in the NBL Cricket Match, a task to which he gave as much care as he had applied to winning the Ashes – and a great deal more charm. So it was that the child that once I had been was on the road north before me when I heard that Dr Stewart Mackintosh, Glasgow's Director of Education, with whom I had arranged a meeting, was H. S. Mackintosh of West of Scotland and Scotland who, on 5 October 1929, just a few days after my conversion to the true faith, had played for Scotland and Ireland against England and Wales in the Rowland Hill Memorial Match.

At our very first meeting, Stewart confirmed his place in my pantheon of heroes by admitting without provocation that Scotland's need for the kind of services the League provided was greater even than England's; England, he said, was the land of books, Scotland the land of the One Good Book; and ever after he was one of our most ardent supporters. He joined our Scottish Committee as soon as it was formed. He sat with me and William Beattie, Chairman of that committee, the National Librarian and unequivocally acceptable to Scotland because he was the foremost authority on Robert Burns, when we selected Mary Baxter to be the League's first Scottish Officer, and it was his swiftness of foot and his charity which allowed to Mary and her small staff suitable and suitably inexpensive premises. It was also Stewart who conspired with me to so arrange the calendar for the NBL Scottish Office that all of the Winter meetings of its Committee were held on the day before an International at Murrayfield, a ploy which I had learnt at Nuffield, and it was he who supplied me with tickets for seats above the half-way line.

Later, as Chairman of the League, as always in Glasgow, Stewart was a formidable leader of the pack. A grin on his face, his red hair bristling, his head down, he brushed aside all opposition as if it was no sturdier than the netball-team of a girls' preparatory school. But if there was glory to be won he passed the ball to me. It is my good fortune that I have always been on the same side as H. S. Mackintosh.

Potter, Hornby, Eccles and Mackintosh understood that, if the League was to fulfil its role as spokesman, lobbyist and missionary, it must first establish and then hold its authority as unimpeachable, dispassionate advocate for books and, by extension, also the authority of its principal spokesmen. In this task we were almost immediately successful and thereafter few days passed when we were not asked for our views, advice or assistance by the media, by Government or by national and international organisations. Perhaps a hundred times in every year either I or one of my colleagues appeared on radio or television.

My first chance to demonstrate the League's effectiveness as lobbyist came when the Post Office, indulging in one of those spasms of philistinism not infrequently suffered by Government departments, announced the abolition of the privileged book-post rate. I gathered a deputation which included the Archbishop of Canterbury, Harold Nicolson, the Poet Laureate and Field Marshal Sir Gerald Templar. In the gentleman's toilet of the Post Office Building in Newgate Street I made rendezvous with the Secretary of the Publishers' Association, who had just left the Postmaster-General's office with his own deputation of *commerçants*, heard what arguments had been advanced to justify vandalism, briefed my eminent colleagues and went in to beard Charles Hill.

It was fortunate that Potter was still Chairman when I was asked to join a British delegation led by Quintin Hogg, then Secretary of State for Education, bound for Virginia to join in the celebrations of the 350th anniversary of the first permanent British settlement in America, for I doubt that his successor would have had the perspicacity to comprehend or the courage to condone the acceptance of an invitation to participate in a ten-day-long *tamasha* which seemed to have no bearing on books. I argued, and Potter needed no persuasion, that we could not afford to turn our backs on this propitious signal that authority was prepared to accept the League as truly 'a major national cultural institution' and its Director as fit companion for representatives of those other and well-established institutions who were included in Lord Hailsham's party; the Church, the Universities, the City of London, the BBC, the Royal Academy, the Royal Colleges of Music, the four constituent parts of the United Kingdom, and the City Livery Companies which, in the first decade of the seventeenth century, had stood as godfathers to the infant Virginia Colony. I reasoned also that ten days in such influential company would furnish me with contacts of inestimable value to the League.

In the previous year, under the leadership of the Governor, a group of prominent Virginians had come to London to prepare the way for British participation in the Jamestown celebrations. I had been present at several of their functions but in my personal capacity as the only British graduate of William and Mary. Now I was invited to represent British books and literature.

Even so the sociable experience of 1956 was an advantage in 1957 – and ever after, for it was then that Kippe and I struck up friendships with Parke Rouse, the Director of the Jamestown Foundation and his wife Betsy, and with Edward Riley, the Director of Research at Colonial Williamsburg, and his wife Annette.

Our association with the Rileys began, indeed was created, by the oratorical ineptitude of distinguished political figures, one British, one American. Kippe and I stood at the back of the room listening to the mumblings and grumblings of the Leader of the London County Council, to the fractured grammar and hesitant speech of the Governor of Virginia and we were torn between shame and laughter. Close to us were two Virginians of about our own age, a handsome pair and she exquisitely dressed. It soon became apparent that they too were suffering from the same cause. We escaped the shame of public disgrace by establishing a quartet and whispering to each other our despair for the quality of our leaders. Ever since when we meet with Annette or Ed Riley we recall County Hall – and always we giggle.

When we left London none in the delegation knew that I was on my way to a homecoming, that I knew Williamsburg, where we were to be housed, as well as most Williamsburgers, or that the riverside close by the little church at Jamestown had been the setting for some of the best alfresco parties of my college-days. On the plane my pride burgeoned when I saw John Keith, Master of the Skinners Company, preparing himself for immersion in American history by reading Nye and Morpurgo, but once in Williamsburg my unique status as a returning wanderer was made obvious by the familiar greetings of many of our hosts, and I became the recognized source for all those items of information – where to get a hair-cut? should one tip the eighteenth-century-garbed guides? where's the Post Office? – which are not customarily revealed to distinguished visitors.

Once the formal celebrations were over, the British party was packed into a Greyhound bus to be rocketed round Virginia. The livelier members of the delegation, prominent among them the Keiths, Brian Faulkner, then Chief Whip and later Premier of Northern Ireland, and Raleigh Trevelyan (in the delegation for the part that his ancestor had played in a fated settlement prior to Jamestown), settled themselves in the back seats of the bus – 'the Steerage' – with me as licensed Punchinello and, for all the distinction of its individual members, as a group behaved as rowdily as a football-team returning from an away-game.

Every evening we were lodged in some luxury hotel, every evening there was a banquet in our honour and every evening, just as I was collecting my winnings for the wagers exchanged on the length of speeches made without invitation by 'Denis the Menace'! (Sir Denis Lowson, but recently Lord Mayor of London), some local dignitary, a class-mate at William and Mary, sidled up to me, bade me to his home 'for a real party' for which he would round up other alumni and to which I must bring such other of my British friends as I chose to invite.

At the end of the last banquet, in Roanoke, the Minister's Private Secretary, speaking in his master's voice, rebuked me for my behaviour. I was neither surprised nor shamed, but I was taken aback when the Private Secretary went on to explain the cause of my disgrace: I never invited the Minister to join these revels. So it came about that the Secretary of State for Education made his last journey in a Greyhound bus wearing a Confederate hat.

There was in those ten days of delicious recidivism much that was warming and much that was hilarious, but one hour that was uniquely moving. The President of the Honourable Society of the Cymrrodorion, the representative of Wales, who had served in the Great War as a sergeant in the Royal Welsh Fusiliers, had asked to be allowed to lay a wreath at Fusilier Redoubt where his regimental comrades had died in the last gallant but futile stand of the British Army in the Battle of Yorktown. The guardians of the battlefield were hesitant about the propriety of thus honouring the enemy but, at my request and prompted by my judicious hint that the Fusiliers had been originally a Maine regiment and so remotely affiliated with the United States Marine Corps, Tim pulled rank, out-flanked the National Park Service and at the appointed time three of us, all glittering and clanking with medals, marched through a guard-of-honour of Marines, at the salute John Cecil-Williams laid his wreath. A Marine bugler played 'Land of My Fathers', and John spoke a few words in Welsh which, for all that anyone in the audience knew could have been a plea to the Devil to hold Washington and Rochanbea to all eternity stoking hell-fires.

With as much military dignity as we could recover from our past, we had managed a ceremony, noble, generous and to the best of my knowledge unique in the long and glorious annals of the British Army. I doubt that ever before or ever since has a sergeant been honoured with an escort composed entirely of field rank.

My second venture abroad as Director of the NBL was much more obviously relevant to books. For the first time since the War, the Government wanted a British presence at the Leipzig Book Fair but, for reasons never explained to me and probably explicable only to the byzantine minds of Foreign Office potentates, did not want to give the delegation official status. All was ordered in the name of the NBL: even the money which paid for the trip was so laundered before it reached me that not even the most alert East German agent could have established its provenance.

Seven of us flew directly from Heathrow into East Berlin, with me two publishers, two booksellers, the Editor of *Penrose Annual* and my PA, Monica, now Monica Mosam. We spent one night in an hotel looking out on dark streets and over the ruins of Unter den Linden to the neon signs of West Berlin. The next day was hot and the road to Leipzig empty, dusty and boring. Arrived in Leipzig, we were allowed ten minutes to wash before we were taken to the huge conference hall where the opening cere-mony was already in progress with many and long German speeches. Someone was well-launched when we were marched down the long cen-tre-aisle and deposited in the front row. I gathered that he was introducing the Minister of Culture.

The Minister droned on and my head drooped. It could well have been a half-an-hour later when my neighbour nudged me. 'What's he saying?' he whispered. I summoned my School Certificate German and remem-bered Norman Birkett telling me of the apology offered by the interpreter to the English-speaking judges at Nuremberg when there was a break in the otherwise simultaneous translation of Goering's evidence, 'Sorry, gen-tlemen, I'm waiting for the verb', but I did not need to wait, the Minister's menacing gestures in our direction made his animosity evident and then, just as I caught sight of the Union Flag among all the Eastern bloc flags on the wall behind him, I caught the meaning of two words the Minister was spitting towards us. He was reviling us as 'Western pornographers'.

National dignity demanded that I rise haughtily and stalk from the hall with my six colleagues in my train but indignation without transport was futile. We were in Colditz without an escape-committee. The proceedings came at last to an end and I was contemplating some theatrical protest when the Minister leapt down from the platform, advanced menacingly towards me, placed his hands on my shoulders and, as if we were both Frenchmen, kissed me on both cheeks and said in too-perfect English, 'It is indeed a great honour and a great pleasure to welcome bookmen from the land of Shakespeare to this, the oldest and greatest of the world's great gathering of men of the book.' Then, chuckling, he added, 'Pay no heed to that,' he nodded at the rostrum, as if it had been that inanimate object which had vilified me and my professional colleagues, 'that's for the televi-sion audience. Come, let us seal the amity between us with a flagon of our fine DDR sparkling-wine.'

The brief which I had been given on appointment was bland: to do all that was within the power of the League to promote the use of books. Because at that time no one dreamed it possible that the League would ever acquire an international reputation sufficiently sturdy to incite demands for its services outwith the United Kingdom, not I, not Potter, nor anyone else had thought to define the geographical boundaries of our domain and at first the invitations which sent me to Jamestown and Leipzig were regarded as exceptional, but as time passed so did the number increase of obligations to activity abroad. We were asked to stage a British

Book Week in Geneva, a Children's Book Show in Moscow and Leningrad, to attend conferences in Munich, Amsterdam, Zurich, Vienna. . . , to nominate a member of the League's staff to serve on the jury of international book-prizes.

It was by no means always essential that I go myself as response to these requests. I sent Antony Kamm and Jessica Jenkins to Russia and Antony also to South East Asia. I interfered only once in the Russian venture. 'Impossible,' I said to Kamm when in high excitement he phoned from Moscow to order for immediate despatch by diplomatic pouch, as gift for the most important of visitors to our exhibition, a Shetland wool sweater, 'even Mrs Krushchev cannot have bust measurements as extravagant as that.' And I was wrong.

However, when for example the United States and Canada severally asked for an exposition of the workings of the League, which both countries were thinking of imitating, it was considered imperative that our representative be the Director, and not infrequently I was bidden by name. Once routines were established, a staff competent to carry them out and Barbara Kyle as my most effective deputy, not I nor any member of the League's Executive Committee had qualms about my generally brief absences from London.

For me, an obsessive wanderer, all this traipsing round the world should have been a delight and so for the most part it was, though I seldom saw more of foreign countries than is visible from hotel bedrooms and committee-rooms. I seized upon any and every opportunity to go to Holland, next only to Greece my favourite country in Europe, and I learnt a great deal, though much of it but sad scepticism from all my ventures onto the international scene. Strident internationalism, I soon discovered, is too often no more than a front for virulent nationalism; shrieking good-will between all nations from the roof-top only a noisy farce designed to divert attention from the clamour of conflicting chauvinisms in the conference-room below; and from my experiences on international juries, I gleaned more wisdom about the realities of power-politics than ever I had from history-books or newspapers. ('You vote for my candidate this year; next year yours will have my vote'; the Scandinavians, the Dutch and the Greeks invariably with the British in an alliance whose principal motive it was to thwart that other unchanged, unchangeable and far more aggressive union, the German-speaking bloc; the French invariably for the French.) But my overseas commitments were not, as some of my critics hinted, neither exercises in self-aggrandisement nor paid vacations and, in one sense at least, in total they deprived me of part of my experience for which no itinerant pleasure could compensate, the companionship of my family.

Ostensibly for the convenience of participants, most meetings of international juries and international committees are scheduled to span weekends and, perhaps by malodorous coincidence, many of my more extended commitments coincided with school holidays. In the thirteen years when I was so often away, Pieter and Michael progressed from preparatory school to matrimony and parenthood, Mark from kindergarten to reading Law at the University of London, and Kay from her cradle to boarding-school.

Neither at the time, nor in hindsight when the scale of my deprivation became obvious to me, could I indulge in self-pity. Christmas was always sacrosanct, in every year we managed a family holiday (but, though by contract I was entitled to forty days leave, only once and then when we drove to Greece in preparation for my book, *The Road to Athens*, for longer than two weeks). Almost by chance, I was on hand for most of the children's more spectacular triumphs. I was in the school hall when Pieter played Lady Macbeth, premonitory whisper to his career as one of the BBC's most skilled television producers. It was I who drove Michael to Aldershot to collected the tropical uniform especially designed for him when he was selected to be the Army cadet ordered to accompany the Queen on a Royal visit to India. I stood on the touchline when he captained the Hertfordshire Schools Fifteen, combating with my smug boast that he owed that honour to my early coaching in the art of catching a rugger-ball Kippe's even more patently smug conceit that he was there because as a child he had profited from her brutal training in tackling. I was there, my hand in Kippe's, when, in court-dress and scarlet gown, as Head of School he gave the valedictory speech for Fred Shirley, the rogue-genius Headmaster of the King's School, Canterbury. (Nothing of omen in all of this for Michael's subsequent achievements as one of Britain's most successful and popular authors of children's books.) I was at Hurlingham to watch Mark in the Junior Wimbledon and I was in the audience when Kay's school performed a play of her own devising about Mary, Queen of Scots – with Kay, of course, as Mary. Whenever I could I read to the younger children after they had gone to bed or, with the whole family and every one of us demanding 'to play the lion too', read plays together. In the years before Michael made apparent his despising of my skill by dismissing ball after ball into the neighbouring farm-yard, for hours on end, I bowled at the nets set up in the Oxhey Hall garden. But in those years so seminal for the family, I was away too often and when I was in London too often kept at 7 Albemarle Street or in some professional sociability until late at night, so often that I am given cause to wonder how it came about that we remained and remain in all but one heart-breaking circumstance a close and devoted family.

Had I been possessed of the wisdom which comes only with afterthought, I could have spared myself many of the journeys I made to the Continent to attend meetings of the International Board of Books for Young People. Even at the time, I went principally because I was determined that Britain must raise a powerful voice in its affairs to counter the overweening and *schmalzisch* influence of the representatives of the German-speaking nations and to dispute the omnipotence of their leader, the founder of the organisation as of the International Children's Library in

Munich, the admirable but, as I thought, almost always wrong-headed Jella Lepman.

My ignorance of the Beatrix Potter gallimaufry is symptomatic of a flaw in my vaunted literary catholicity which, long before I moved to the League, I had elevated to the status of symbol of faith. As a child, though I rollicked through Henty and Harrison Ainsworth, I read them because they were 'history'. I revelled in Kipling, Stevenson, Fenimore Cooper and Mark Twain but I was never exposed to those cat-sat-on-the-mat picture books which are said to delight infants. At the Christ's Hospital oral examination I claimed in all honesty as my favourite novel *Vanity Fair* – a verdict unchanged even after sixty years as book-addict, and when in time I came to bed-time reading for my own children I discovered that, providing my performance was suitably dramatic, they were as readily contented and I not bored by *Treasure Island*, the *Ingoldsby Legends*, 'John Gilpin' or 'The Incident at the French Camp' – anything with narrative or rhythm – as ever they were with even the best of self-proclaimed children's books.

To justify my illiteracy in children's literature, I developed a thesis which, when driven out of patience by their shrill advocacy, I developed for the most discomfiture of the middle-aged Vestal Virgins who are everywhere the devout guardians of children's books. There is, I argued, no such thing as children's literature, only books that are comprehensible and pleasing to children. Almost all of the acknowledged children's classics – *Huckleberry Finn*, the two *Alices*, *The Last of the Mohicans*, *Kim*, Lear's *Nonsense Rhymes*, *Treasure Island*, *The Lord of the Flies*, even *Jane Eyre* and *Christmas Carol* – are as popular with adults as they are with children and of these, with the possible exception of Carroll's two masterpieces – and even those two as exception dubious – not one had been designed by its author exclusively for children and, because more personal a more satisfying thrust, not one, not even the *Alices*, had been commissioned by a children's book editor.

It was a thesis not without force but riddled with flaws and it could not serve me well when I was abroad as the lonely ambassador for all British children's books, even for the books of Enid Blyton. I went well-briefed by the experts on the League's staff and at all events, when engaged in international debate, though sometimes it was my task to advance the cause of some particular author or one title, most often it was my task to run interference, to ensure that no principles were established which would operate against the interests of Britain, to speak up for the whole canon of British children's books.

UNESCO committed to the International Board of Books for Young People the responsibility for compiling a list of characters from the past appropriate as subjects for biographies intended for young readers and hinted that funds would be made available to support their publication. The Swiss representatives, urgently supported by the Austrian and the German, stated, not as a proposition but as a *sine qua non* of the Board's selection, that we include no fighting-men. We must not encourage children to glory in war. A provisional list was prepared by the Swiss. It so happened that at the meeting when it came before the Board for finalization before being forwarded to Paris, I was representing not only Britain but also Canada and the United States. I asked: 'Why not Montcalm and Wolfe? Why Booker T. Washington but not George? Did they not know that Harriet Beecher Stowe was 'the little woman who started a great war'? And if Mrs Stowe why not the noblest hero of that war, Robert E. Lee? Edward Jenner, Florence Nightingale and Elizabeth Fry were all in the list. I wanted Cromwell, Wellington and (these with pointed acerbity) Wavell and Montgomery, and I announced that I would use my veto (I was not sure that veto was within my power) if a selection was proposed to UNESCO which tended to deny to British children all knowledge of Horatio Nelson.

The Dutch, the Scandinavians and the Greeks applauded and for once I had the support of the French. Napoleon Bonaparte was not in the Swiss list.

The German-speaking nations had been accustomed to dominating the affairs of the International Board, the International Library, most of the international book-prizes, and consequently to exorbitant influence over such funds as were available from international organisations for the encouragement of children's books, so they resented the growing strength of a disloyal opposition. In an attempt to limit our potency, the Austrian delegate proposed that as we were engaged in the business of words, in future votes must be cast according to the number of languages for which each national representative was plenipotentiary.

The effrontery of this suggestion – four votes to Switzerland! – sharpened my wits. I seconded the proposition, adding modestly that henceforth I would have nine votes, one each for English, Gaelic, Erse, Manx, Cornish, Welsh, Lallans and Norman French.

Herr Doktor from Vienna protested, his pedantry outstripping his indignation that I had offered only eight qualifications.

As sweetly as I could, I apologized for forgetting to mention that in book-matters Eire was conjoined to the United Kingdom. Surely I was entitled to a separate vote as representative of the independent Republic.

My Dutch colleague joined in. In fluent German, a language which ordinarily he refused to utter in public, and then in fluent English, he demanded for himself an extra vote for Frisian and then went on to argue casuistically that he did not intend to concede omnipotence to his dear friend from Britain who, if this amendment to the constitution was carried, because so often he was deputed to represent also countries too distant to attend meetings, would have not only his British votes but also the vote of the United States, the two votes of Canada and the forty – or was it four hundred? – votes of India.

No more was heard of the Austrian proposition.

The cast-list for these meetings seldom changed and I, on children's books the least informed of all present, depended hugely on the sophistication common to all in the bevy of handsome Nordic ladies who, generously and to the evident annoyance of our opponents, called themselves collectively 'Mr Morpurgo's Vikings'. For them my affection was real but for most of those who faced us, when I was not watching anxiously lest their machinations produced consequence inimical to British books, I knew only contempt – and, I fear, showed it. For most, but not for Jella Lepman. She was my Rommel, we fought but I admired her.

There was about Jella a mystery which I never dared ask her to solve; quizzing Jella was as unthinkable as interrogating Queen Elizabeth the First, Hecate or the Fairy Godmother, each of whom she resembled when the appropriate mood was upon her or the character convenient to her purpose. Did she take up her mission because she was by background, temperament and even feature type-cast to be the titular head of the Commonwealth of Children's Literature, or did she conjure up a new *persona* to suit the role? Which came first, the pumpkin or the six white horses?

In 1945, after the surrender of Germany, Jella took it upon herself to declare war on both conquerors and conquered to build what she herself called 'a bridge of children's books' between victors and vanquished. She badgered the mightiest men of all the great powers, crowding them into alliance, forcing them to become collaborators in turning her ideas into realities: the International Board, the International Library, the Hans Andersen Medal. Herself a United Nations in one person, born to German Jewish parents in Latvia, she held a British passport, had served in the American Army, was a resident of Switzerland and had children living in Canada and Italy. She carried with her through life a rag-bag of qualities and qualifications which she used as ruthlessly as a saint. She could be as tough as any of the hierarchs – American generals, British statesmen, German industrialists – she bullied into supporting her projects, or she could play for their persuasion the part of frail and helpless woman pleading for the assistance of a strong man. I heard her one minute oozing treacle over some mawkish children's book and the next, a gin-glass in one hand and a cigarette in the other, unravelling with wit and pungency the complexities of *geo-politik*.

Jella's fervour was undeniable and almost irresistible. I might have become her acolyte had it not been for her sentimentality, and the nauseous earnestness of those she chose to be her house-carls. As it was, in all the meetings when I sat under her chairmanship we were only once allied: when one of the Swiss delegates, and she among Jella's devotees, proposed a ban on smoking in the committee-room.

Fencing with Jella Lepman was no easy sport; it was easier to score points against the other leaden-footed Teutons who set themselves up as the champions of children's literature and not all that difficult to lunge for a kill, but I was never quite comfortable as plenipotentiary for British children's books. I was much more at ease and, at least in the short run, much more effective when I took on the role, made available to me at the request of UNESCO, which allowed me to serve as emissary for British books in general among the nations of the Third World, and which brought me in time to being proclaimed somewhat extravagantly by the Indian book-trade journal as 'the *guru* of the Asian book-world'.

In places where book-professionals met there was at that time much wailing for the loss of our traditional hegemony as book-suppliers to the Third World, much gnashing of teeth for Government's refusal to support with funds and sponsored activity our efforts to combat the invasion of our long-established markets by the Americans and the Russians, both with ample and freely-given resources of their governments.

I wailed as vociferously, gnashed my teeth as ferociously as any. I mouthed the clichés (clichés only because they were statements of the obvious) as if I had invented them: political influence is heir to the book; trade follows the book; train an Indian engineer or farmer on British text-books and when he comes to authority he will buy British machinery. And now, at UNESCO's expense and with the advantage of my unimpeach-able, detached status as Director of the League, I had before me a unique opportunity to do something about it. Better still, and undeniably appeal-ing to the romantic in me, whilst helping Britain I could help the Asians to help themselves, I could advance literacy in countries where illiteracy is as endemic as poverty, as devastating as famine.

UNESCO asked me to devise and direct a seminar, to be staged in Rangoon, on the provision of reading materials. I was to go first to Burma to make the local arrangements, then to tour the Sub-Continent (and, for reasons never vouchsafed to me, also Iran) to select participants and, when the three-week seminar was over, to go again to Ceylon, India, Pakistan and Iran for detailed discussions with governments and professional bodies preparatory to writing for UNESCO a detailed report on the organisation-al and training needs of the region.

The challenge excited me, though acceptance would take me away from the family for at least five months, and I was only a little deflated when the Executive Committee of the League passed unanimously a reso-lution supporting acceptance, principally because one of its most vocal members pointed out that, if I did not go, UNESCO would almost cer-tainly invite an American – or even, perhaps, a Russian.

Rangoon in the early 1960s epitomised the dark ages which followed the fall of empire. Never since the end of the Alompra dynasty much more than an important provincial city, even so it must have been in its day one of the most attractive towns in Asia, set as it is around lakes and along the Rangoon river, with wide streets lined by the elegant houses built by teak-wallahs and Colonial officials, with the substantial, if generally pompous, Government offices built by the British when Rangoon was made the cap-ital of a Burma separated from India, and dominated by the glittering Shive

Dagon Pagoda. Now the surface of the principal shopping street menaced the springs of cars and was, like all the other streets, marred by piles of uncollected refuse; most of the houses had not been painted since the beginning of the Japanese occupation, and even the gold leaf on the Pagoda was visibly flaking. Rangoon, and indeed all of Burma not in the hands of dacoits, for a century the charge of efficient if foreign administration, was now controlled by Burmese administrators, all of them inexperienced, many of them indolent and not a few corrupt.

It could be because the Burmese were convinced that in 1942 we had deserted them that there was in Burma little evidence of that lingering respect for British institutions, that persisting ease with visitors from Britain, which I found so often in India, Pakistan and Ceylon. Only once in all my time in Rangoon did I hear any overt reference to Burma's British heritage, and that a back-handed tribute.

If a mania for gambling is an Irish characteristic, then the Burmans have right to their boast that they are the Irish of Asia. Of all the facilities originally established by the British only the race-course was by our successors regularly and meticulously groomed. I was invited to a meeting as guest of the Stewards, because almost all the stewards were either Cabinet Ministers or high officers-of-state, an honour tantamount to being a guest of the Government. My principal host, the elderly Chief Justice, who entertained me with reminiscences of Cambridge in the 1890s, marked my card and thereby presented to me an opportunity unique in all my life to make money by betting on horses. In the Stewards' box, after an elaborate lunch, he fell asleep. At the end of the third race he woke and asked me if I knew what was wrong with Burma. Correctly, I took it to be a rhetorical question and, first looking round the box to make certain that all his powerful companions were listening, in a voice that could indeed have been heard in Mandalay, he said, 'My dear chap, the trouble with this country is that most of our Cabinet were educated at the London School of Economics.'

The economic philosophy of the Government of Burma may have owed much to distant recollection of Harold Laski, but the social and political mores of the upper echelons with which inevitably I became involved revealed a running battle between reactionaries, who sought to restore to Burma the grandeurs and hierarchical structure of the Alompra regime, and closet Communists, eager to impose upon their countrymen uniformity, equality but not liberty. The leaders of the contending groups seldom argued their cases in public for on one thing all those leaders were agreed: that the business of running Burma must be kept in the hands of a tiny élite; and all were gifted with a remarkable capacity for chicanery and procrastination. And, if I was to make any progress, first I had to square both the Guelphs and the Ghibelines.

I was billeted in the Government Guest House on the fringe of the city, my only companions an Indian Christian servant and my elderly deputy, also an Indian but a Muslim, who in all his life had never ventured further from his home in Delhi than Agra. Each night I lay in my bed listening to the lullaby of rifle-fire and I did not get up to enquire whether these were fired by adherents of one or the other of the parties then contending for dominance or by the dacoit. Each morning I sat on my balcony sunning myself whilst Henry served breakfast – orange-juice, porridge, bacon-and-eggs, toast and coffee – then dressed and went down to be driven to the office in a rickety Government Buick.

Hamid Ali Khan, my deputy, soon found cause to complain about my casual habits. The dignity due to my office did not allow, Hamid explained patiently through his grey beard, that I flounce down the stairs carrying my briefcase. Instead, he advised, I should sit with him in the large ground-floor lounge until my car arrived then ask him to ring the bell for Henry, order our bearer to fetch all that I needed, and go out to enter the car whilst the chauffeur held open the door and Henry packed my impedimenta – on to the front passenger seat.

We were allotted two adjoining offices on the third floor of the Burma Translation Society and Hamid also objected, most courteously, to my calling to him through the paper-thin walls between our offices. If I required his services or his advice I must ring for the *peon*, bring him up three flights of stairs, by his hand pass the Director's compliments to the Deputy Director and request the Deputy Director's company in my *dufta*.

To all intents the Burma Translation Society was a publishing- house, but financed by the Ford Foundation and for the most part staffed by American experts. Because it was maintained by Ford and used by Americans, the Burma Translation Building was in good repair but, perhaps because most of the American staff spent little of the day in their offices, Ford had not troubled to instal air-conditioning. So it is that most of the papers that remain in my possession from that time are liberally spattered with evidence of sweat. The only air-conditioned rooms in Rangoon, other than those in the homes of my American colleagues, were the dining-room of the Prime Minister's Residence, and the Stewards' box at the race-course.

Twice I was bidden to dinner by U Nu, then Premier of Burma. He advised me to avoid travelling on the State air-line ('all our planes are held together by string') and he watched maliciously as I pretended to enjoy the betel-nut which he had forced on me, but I could never penetrate his inscrutability and learnt from him nothing whatsoever about the present state of Burma or about his plans for the national future. He did, however, provide a platoon of infantry to escort my car when I went to view the Pegu temples. I was much more terrified by the casual manner in which his conscripts handled their fire-arms than ever I could have been by the *budmarh* who, according to U Nu's cheery gossip, regularly attacked travellers on that road.

Some of the seminarians who eventually assembled in Rangoon were there only because they were related to a Minister or a senior civil servant, some were already qualified editors, printers or booksellers, a few – notably Qumral Hassan, a young painter and book-designer from East Pakistan, who might have attained a world-wide reputation had he not been murdered a few years later in the Dacca riots – were rarely talented, but all were enthusiastic and all convinced that, by establishing efficient machinery for preparing and distributing reading-materials, benefits would accrue beyond the immediate advancement of literacy, that an improvement in the machinery of publishing was an essential first step towards progress in agriculture, health and industry.

Despite the soggy Rangoon weather, the participants worked diligently under the tutelage of a small staff, mostly Americans seconded from the Ford Foundation's local staff. They studied design, editing, printing, contract, stock-control, sales, and promotion. We even managed a practical exercise, seeing a small book through from writing to a run of one hundred copies.

I was a kind of headmaster. In addition to my pedagogic duties I was called upon to hob-nob with dignitaries – Ambassadors and Ministers – to make innumerable after-dinner speeches and to preach whenever I could find a pulpit, usually on the text 'British books are best'. As missionary I was for those three weeks better-placed than my American colleagues, who were forced to take words like Baskerville, Times New Roman, 'blurb' or 'sale-and-return' as clues for a paean to the virtues of books from the United States. I was also as headmaster responsible for the pastoral care of the students, most of who, like my Deputy, had never before been away from home and, as is I believe not uncommon for headmasters of co-educational establishments, in the middle of one night I was hauled out to rush to hospital a very pregnant young woman, a book-designer from Ceylon.

By strenuous argument and by reiteration my American friends and I converted most of the participants to our belief in the need to hold both the commerce of books and all ancillary non-commercial organisations free from control by Government. When I returned to Teheran, Karachi, New Delhi and Colombo, it was immediately obvious to me that many of the Ministers and senior Civil Servants with whom I spoke favoured governmental control over publishing even closer than was already imposed, and that some were intent on creating a governmental monopoly in book-supply. All promised energetic support for the new training-schemes and promotional organisations I proposed to recommend for UNESCO sponsorship. Each and every one had visions of thousands of dollars from Paris to enrich his department and more power in his own hands.

I determined to make independence the central theme of my visit to UNESCO.

The journey back to Paris took twenty-three hours, six of them spent counting the gekkos climbing the walls of the waiting-room of the airport to which the plane had been diverted and betting myself that the temperature would top 100 degrees. There was only one other passenger in the

First Class of the Air France plane and four stewardesses, each of them armed with a bottle of champagne. I heard but did not register the information passed to us by the captain that all France was blanketed in snow.

Kippe had flown to Paris, carrying with her my winter clothes. She had spent the night in the arctic airport lobby, dressed in an outfit newly acquired to honour our reunion, and warmed only by an occasional cup of tepid coffee. When, eight hours late, my plane landed, I marched down the steps in my tropical suit, dismissed with my diplomatic passport the attentions of Immigration and Customs, and strode past my shivering and furious wife.

For all the next three days I coughed and puked in a Paris hotel bedroom.

I submitted my report. The response was immediate and gratifying: I was given leave to select four of the seminarians for further training in England.

Thereafter there was silence broken only by letters from me demanding the refund of the fifty dollars I had spent on taxis in Calcutta, Bombay, and Lahore, and letters from UNESCO rejecting my expense-account on the grounds that I should have used public transport. To my comment that I doubted if any of UNESCO's finance officers had ever ridden a bus or a train in Calcutta, there was no reply, and it was not until I threatened to tear up the unused voucher for twenty times as much supplied to me by UNESCO to meet charges for excess baggage that I received a cheque for fifty dollars.

Almost a year later I went, again as UNESCO Consultant, but this time only for a month, to Madras to direct an almost identical seminar. I wrote another report. When, yet another year on, a different UNESCO department wrote asking me to nominate an expert capable of advising on the organisation of book-supply for the new readers of Asia, I suggested that they search through their filing-cabinets – and sent Antony Kamm to Asia.

Fifteen years later, and I no longer the almost-accredited emissary for the British book, I was again in Karachi and New Delhi. My Pakistani and Indian friends, formerly students at Rangoon or Madras, arranged reunions. They greeted me warmly but there was grievance in their eyes and indignation on their lips. Why, they asked, had UNESCO done so little to encourage the book-programmes of Asia? Why had UNESCO failed to use its abundant influence to prevent the institutions fathered by my reports becoming virtually Government departments? Why had I deserted my faithful acolytes?

Thus, though the fault was not mine, it was I who at the last bore all the opprobrium of denying to my Asian friends the fulfilment of those aspirations which I myself had taught them to cherish. Even at the time when I was still working for the advancement of Asian publishing, and still hoping that, somehow, I could circumvent UNESCO inefficiency, dilitoriness, callousness and downright chicanery, and so justify the confidence placed in me which had won for me the title '*guru* of the Asian book world', my mind was so filled with these activities and frustrations that I dismissed as trivial a coup in a quite different kind which now, with the benefit of hindsight, I hold in pride as among the greatest and certainly as the noblest of all my NBL achievements and, for all my life, as the only extended exercise in deceit which has left no scar on my conscience: the invention of the NBL Prize and its award to John Masefield.

Like many of my generation I had taught myself to slough off as mere childishness the enthusiasm with which once I had read 'Reynard the Fox', *Sard Harker* and *Odtaa*, but my indignation was aroused when Masefield's daughter came to me with the sad tale that her aged father was suffering penury. Indignation excited me into action. I drove to Masefield's home near Oxford.

The Poet Laureate's welcome was warm but the house was cheerless, cold and damp. In the hope that I might find among them some that would fetch a handsome price in the sale-room, I asked Masefield to show me his treasures. There were manuscripts by the dozen and holograph letters from almost every notable writer of his generation, from Yeats and Eliot, from Kipling and Bennett, and all had served to make perpetual feast for the mice who shared the house with Masefield and his daughter.

I came away depressed. It was I and my countrymen, I and my generation, who by our callousness had engineered this brutish treatment of a noble artist. Something must be done, but what I could not at first envisage for I was inhibited by concern that I do nothing to bruise further the Poet Laureate's pride. I decided to write to Thomas Lamont, son of that Thomas Lamont who had been Pierpoint Morgan's partner and himself for many years a friend of the Masefields.

A few weeks later I faced Lamont in the penthouse of the Morgan Guaranty Trust Building on Wall Street and found him more than willing to help but no less than I sensitive to Masefield's feelings. For more than an hour we exchanged ideas as to how we could ensure for Masefield an adequate income for the rest of his life without giving offence. At the last I ventured a proposition which pleased Lamont. With his money the NBL would establish a prize to be given, not as are most literary prizes to a young hopeful, but to an elder statesman of literature who had, in the opinion of a named and suitably distinguished jury, in his life-time contributed largely to the general good of English letters. For this Prize we would have but one candidate, John Masefield, but that would be a condition known only to the jurymen.

This condition I have honoured until this moment but the story of the NBL Prize is a worthy chapter in the history of English literature in the twentieth century and I am convinced that my fellow-conspirators – Thomas Lamont, his brother Corliss and my fellow-jurymen, Rupert Hart-Davis and the Editor of the *Times Literary Supplement,* Arthur Crook – will excuse this belated revelation all the more readily when I reveal also that for some years I have been convinced that we did not deceive Masefield and that he was grateful to us for leaving him with his dignity unsullied.

In his Will he left me twenty pounds as token of gratitude for my 'friendship and kindness to an aged poet'.

The happy outcome of our ploy was marred by one inconvenient post-script. For the rest of my time at the NBL I was forever fending-off recommendations for the NBL Prize proffered by ardent advocates of elderly writers, even T. S. Eliot, and some of them as prosperous as Mark Twain.

14

Other Men's Lives

My secondments to UNESCO brought benefit more attractive to some of my employees than delight in any good that I might do to Asia's new readers and more immediate than enhancement of British exports. For the period of my absences, the League was relieved of my salary and the League was always so penurious that even this picayune economy was significant in the unending struggle to avoid bankruptcy. However, the number of UNESCO consultancies available to me was limited, it was evident to me that I could undertake no more if I was to remain both the League's Director and truly a husband and father; the death of Barbara Kyle left me for the moment without a suitable deputy and, as Kippe had foreseen, I was not content as an author who, though still pouring into print thousands of words, wrote almost always with only one purpose in view, the enlargement of the book habit.

Allen Lane's intervention opened to the League an opportunity to improve its finances and to me both variety and yet again the enthralling prospect of myself as his successor.

When, casually during one of his evening visits to my office, Allen had first mentioned his intention to establish a school-book list, I had argued against it with all the cogency I could muster. The text-book, I insisted, was outmoded, made obsolescent in part by his own success, by the utility of Penguin and particularly Pelicans as supports to class-room instruction; the addition of an educational list would force the firm to adopt publishing techniques in which it was not skilled; would create confusion in an Accounts Department unaccustomed to the discounts customarily given on school-books; and could not be successful unless Allen took on a number of additional and expensive representatives sophisticated in the business of travelling educational institutions. But, when it became obvious that, whatever countervailing advice was offered by me or anyone else, Allen's compulsion to be everywhere and in everything made Penguin Educational Books inevitable and, when he offered to me the task of adding flesh to his skeletal ambition as preface to returning full-time to Harmondsworth as his deputy, I succumbed.

As ever, once he had made an idea into a reality, Allen did not interfere in the processes of implementation. He left to me the appointment of editors and, after some obligatory haggling, he agreed to rent from the League as offices for his new subsidiary the slum adjacent to the elegance of 7 Albemarle Street,which had its own entrance, and therefore its own address, on a side-street and, convenient to my purposes, access by way of a back-door from my office.

There I installed the editors. With them I devised a list and within a year Penguin Educational showed promise of becoming a viable addition to Allen's empire. We had even established a foot-hold in a new form of educational publishing, which in the years soon to come was to grow into a gigantic rival to conventional commercial publishing: the production of books designed to support television series.

By that time there had been added to the chain which held Allen and me together a link more sturdy and potentially more enduring than any urged by common experience, by shared commercial interest and tempered by sociability. My son Michael had married Allen's daughter Clare.

This circumstance, so propitious for the future happiness of our family owed nothing to any skill of mine as match-maker or organizer of dynastic marriages, and nothing to my percipience as gazer into crystal-balls but just a little to my impatience to return to writing.

Over eighteen years Kippe and I had seen much of Clare, one of the two little girls I had met first when they were paddling naked in the Silverbeck pool, but the Lane children and the Morpurgo children had never been brought together. Then, at Allen's suggestion, Clare came to the NBL to consult me before hitch-hiking through Greece with her sister.

Several times in the preceding years I had subverted the implication of Horace's affirmation that 'it takes money to holiday in Corinth'. My first return to Greece I contrived by emulating G. K. Chesterton *en route* to Paradise by way of Kensal Green; I so ordered my UNESCO itinerary that it was essential to stop over in Athens. My second came to me through no exercise of cunning: as consequence of an invitation to join, as lecturer on Byron and his fellow-philhellenes and on the Greek campaigns of the Second World War, one of those superbly organised and superlatively expensive Hellenic cruises. My third was when, with all the family except Pieter, already working as Stage Manager to the Scottish Opera, I made my preliminary reconnaissance for *The Road to Athens* .

The first return had been brief, just two days in Athens spent for the most part with the Damirallis; the third, staged at a time when I could not get away for more than fifteen days, allowed little time in Greece because we travelled by train to Brindisi and thence by ferry to Patras. But, though I was seldom free to roam as I would have wished, the episode with Swan's Hellenic Cruises gave me a rare opportunity to fill the gap in my own ardent philhellenism created by my move at the age of thirteen from the Classical to the Modern Side. I was free to attend all the ship-board lectures by my expert colleagues, some of them the world's leading authorities on the civilization of Ancient Greece and Greek archaeology, and because I was committed to only one shore-based lecture (at Missolonghi,a drab little town and utterly without Byronic resonance), I had ample energy left for all the scrupulously-guided site-visits.

Yet it was not so much the improvement of my Classical knowledge which made that cruise for me memorable: not the experience of declaiming Homer from the walls of Troy (of course in Rieu's Penguin translation), not even the licence to rehearse to an attentive audience my own trivial Aeneid in Cos, Samos and Leros and in the bullet-spattered streets of Piraeus. It is true that my vainglory was much enlarged because there was in the front row of that audience for all my lectures a pudacious blonde, one of the very few young women on the ship and certainly the prettiest, who sat, her large blue eyes fixed on me as if I was Michael Wilding's identical twin. It was not until a chance remark revealed to me that her determination to miss not a word I uttered was not a tribute to my charms, nor yet to my erudition, but symptomatic of her amazement that there was aboard that ship and actually talking at her a man who had seen battle only a few miles from where she sat; for Vanessa aged nineteen the Aegean Campaign and the Greek Civil War were, as Marathon or Salamis, ancient history. It was the unique opportunity for demographic observation which on that cruise delighted me most. Already when we gathered at Victoria Station for the train to the cross-Channel ferry I counted in my putative audience one hundred identical shoulder-bags, three monocles, four Old Etonian and five Vincents ties (but not one Hawks which must tell something about the differences between Oxford and Cambridge), and later I discovered that we had with us two duchesses, four peers of the realm, seven knights, a Queen's Counsel and five other lawyers, twelve doctors, an American millionaire and six relatives of my fellow-lecturer Lord David Cecil.

When Clare came to collect from me tips on travel in Greece, I had far-advanced preparations for my definitive *Road to Athens* tour, by car through Holland, Germany, Switzerland, Liechtenstein, Austria, down the length of Italy to Brindisi, by ship to Corfu and on to Igourneritsa and thence to Athens and down into the Peloponnese. At the end of a long and cheerful evening, it occurred to me that Clare would be in Greece at the same time as us and I gave her a copy of our itinerary.

A few weeks later we arrived in Corfu. We had booked rooms in a ship-scrubbed flat on the third floor of a house in the poorest part of town, accommodation found for me at short notice the previous year by a sergeant in the excellent Tourist Police. Our host and hostess had between them not one word of English, and, twenty years after the Treaty of Varkiza, I had mislaid both *demotic* and *katharavous* but, as soon as they had finished hugging and kissing us as if we had returned from long exile, somehow they managed to explain that an English lady had that very day been asking for us. I mistook their meaning and assumed that the unnamed visitor was middle-aged, what the Victorians called a decayed gentlewoman, and in all probability the local representative of some British charity dedicated to the preservation of Corfu's itinerant cat-population or the revival of the *tsintsiberra* industry. Nevertheless we were curious and, once Mark and Kay were in bed, Kippe, Michael and I walked across the hill to a house marked for us as the English lady's residence by our host on a grubby street-map.

Even as I knocked, Medusa flung open the door and stood there, her arms akimbo, glaring menacingly from me to Michael, from Michael to me: no men must ever pass her portal. I tried my little Greek. She replied in shamingly fluent English, 'the hour is late, my ladies are all comfortably in their beds'. I pointed to my watch as if to suggest that 9.30 was in Corfu no inappropriate hour for making calls but when, to her demand that I name the lady and explain my relationship to her, I responded with some inarticulate mumblings, her suspicion was intensified and she was only a little mollified by Kippe's saccharine intervention. She had but two English ladies in her house; she would see what could be done; she promised nothing. She slammed the door in my face.

We waited in the street for five minutes, dousing the mounting fires of impatience with hyperbole on the beauty of the blue-velvet night-sky. A first-floor window opened and, Juliet in a diaphanous nightgown, Clare stepped out onto the moonlit balcony.

The legend as Michael and Clare tell it is that three days later they were engaged to be married, and we were no sooner back in England than they announced their intention to us and to Allen and Lettice Lane. As at that time the Army regarded matrimony as an inhibition to the professional zeal of young officers, and did everything it could by way of discouragement, Michael insisted on quitting Sandhurst.

The Lanes were happy with the match and we could have asked for nothing better than the addition of Clare to our family but we were greatly troubled by the thought of Michael entering upon married life before he was twenty, and without a profession. None the less I was not prepared for the flurry of excitement in the uppermost echelon of the Army. On three successive days I was taken to lunch by generals, captains when I was a captain or field-officers when I was a field-officer, who urged me to persuade the boy to postpone marriage at least until he was commissioned.

Michael and Clare were married, Michael left Sandhurst and in due course I became grandfather to Allen's grandson, Sebastian.

It was no surprise to me when, as an aside to some insignificant conversation, Allen remarked that it might be a good idea if Michael spent some time working for Penguin – 'just to get to know about publishing' – and I did not doubt the veracity of the rumour which came to me that he was hinting that Michael change his name to Lane. A caring if erratically energetic father, because he could not credit any woman with the capacity to rule a great empire, his dynastic ambitions were thwarted by the fact that he had no sons. I knew that, when young, not only he but also his parents and his brothers had changed their family name from Williams to Lane to make certain Allen's succession to his second cousin, 'Uncle' John, founder and proprietor of the distinguished publishing-house, John Lane, The Bodley Head.

Penguin Educational did not die, it slipped out of existence, its small list absorbed into the great maw of Harmondsworth, but for a while my relations with Allen continued as before and still from time to time he spoke as if some means must be found to bring me back to Penguin.

A second grandson, Horatio, was born and then, by adoption, a grand-daughter – 'no jewel is like my Rosalind'. We went often as weekend guests to Allen's farm near Reading and there played endless games of Murder; often he arrived unheralded at my office-door, and so it was that when Harry Paroissien, by then Deputy Managing Director, invited me to lunch, I accepted without premonition. Even when I found Bill Williams with Harry at the table, still I believed that we met for informal discussion about some new Penguin projects.

And so at first it was as I studied the menu and sipped whisky, all talk casual, amiable and cheerful. Suddenly Williams took from his pocket and placed on the table before me a sheet covered with neatly-typed figures. 'Your NBL salary', he stammered, 'is a matter of public knowledge; most of your free-lance income comes as royalties from Penguin but we have allowed another £300 for earnings not known to us. Allen calculates that you can afford to give the children an annual allowance of two thousand. Agree to that and he will match it. They should be able to survive.'

For a moment I was silenced by this impertinent prying into my finances, by this arrogance and by this inequitable proposition made on his behalf by a millionaire to a man who had to borrow to pay school-fees. Then I gulped my whisky – 'purge me with hyssop and I shall be clean' – slammed down the glass and, in a voice that must have been heard by Charles Forte in his office at the top of the building, I roared out 'To Hell with you both and to the lowest circle in Hell with Allen Lane' and stormed out of the restaurant.

In all the few years that were left to him I never again communicated with Allen, not even through an intermediary. My indignation was righteous, he had blasphemed against friendship, yet there remains with me still a sense of shame for my refusal to recognize that what I had experienced was no more than particularly blatant evidence of traits in Allen with which I had long been familiar; his zest for labyrinthine machination and the cowardice which made him prefer the use of hired assassins to face-to-face confrontation. I am ashamed, too, that I did not recover sufficient charity to attempt reconciliation. Allen held the pack, it was he who dealt patronage or dismissal, but the joker was in my hand. I was surrounded by a loving family and warm-hearted friends and, in his last years when he was a sick man, lonely and even – if admittedly through his own folly – for all practical purposes deprived even of his Penguin throne, I should have striven to revive a friendship which, just because it was at once consistent with professional interest and not marred by power, dependence or subservience, gave to him more pleasure than most of his acquaintanceships.

In the two years when I was working both for the NBL and for Penguin, the League was brought as close to financial stability as it ever had been or ever would be. A headquarters in the West End of London, so essential to maintaining both our prestige and our respectability as a national organisation dedicated to books but not the hireling of the trade, was always a burden on our resources but in those years that burden was considerably reduced by the rent from Penguin and with it at least part of the responsibility for my salary and, an ever greater contribution to solvency, we had attracted support for our various projects from industry and from foundations. The Penguin assignment brought me a variety of contacts useful for the fulfilment of the League's polymathic responsibilities.

The League's prestige seemed assured. The demand was ceaseless for our routine services and there was scarcely any development involving books, major or minor, in which we were not represented. As instances, but only as instances, when the Foreign Office established the GB–USSR Association to oversee cultural relations with the Soviet Union, I was invited to serve on its Executive Committee; when the Arts Council set up an unRoyal Commission to consider the reform of the obscenity laws not only I ,but also Clifford Simmons, by then my Deputy, were included in its membership. I was unique on the GB–USSR Executive for I had never been to the Soviet Union and I contributed nothing to it, except perhaps by nagging the Executive to include books in programmes, by the instincts of other committee-men generally centred on the theatre, music, the cinema and ballet; but I contributed perhaps just a little to the Arts Council's report on the obscenity laws.

I had been present in court throughout almost every session of the trial of *Lady Chatterley's Lover*. D. H. Lawrence as poet I had always admired but his reputation as novelist I considered over-blown and, though I had been one of many who advised Allen Lane that he could not exclude it from the ten titles making up the Lawrence Million, I had never found *Lady Chatterley's Lover* anything but pretentious and boring. Even so my detestation of censorship was devout and it heartened me greatly to see such as Basil Blackwell and Stanley Unwin on their feet in the Central Criminal Court giving evidence for Penguin and T. S. Eliot walking its dreary corridors waiting, more or less patiently, to add his eloquence (an opportunity he was not granted). I was tempted to applaud when my brother-in-law, Francis Cammaerts, dismissed the Crown Counsel's innuendo that surely this was not a book he would allow to his fourteen-year old daughter with the crushing comment that it was from her that he had borrowed the copy he read, and when Griffith-Jones Q.C. asked of another witness the even more fatuous question about the suitability of *Lady Chatterley* for 'your housemaid', I turned to Hans Schmoller of Penguin in triumph. 'Now', I said, 'we have the jury on our side.'

Despite the monstrously prejudiced summing-up by the judge, I was proved right but even so, I was not convinced that the verdict had proved anything, except the worth of the jury-system, or persuaded of the adequacy of the 1959 Obscene Publications Act. As I think every other member of the Arts Council's Working Party, I entered upon our deliberations certain that we would come to recommend a new Act and perversely conscious that the revised legislation must include some means whereby the public could be guarded against pornography.

For six months we debated and examined witnesses. Not even the lawyers among us could arrive at a satisfactory definition of obscenity. We found only one witness, David Sheppard, Bishop of Liverpool, who confessed that he had been 'corrupted or depraved' by reading a book, and we came unanimously to the opinion that, if that elegant batsman and severe churchman was an example of depravity, we should recommend that the Government subsidize the publication of obscene literature.

The Working Party reported, unanimously and at length, but said little. We could not define obscenity but that which we could not identify we knew to be loathsome. Pornography we found obnoxious and a menace to society, but no more inimical to the public good than censorship. The 1959 Obscene Publications Act was vague, its implications elusive, but we could think of no way to improve it. In essence: best not tamper with the not-so-good lest the product be something devastatingly worse.

The League's prestige and its advance close to the borders of solvency owed all to the efforts of its small but enthusiastic and energetic staff. Most of our senior employees were young women, many of them married, there was seldom a time when there was not at least one of them evidently pregnant and since those days I have often wondered how long the League – or for that matter any other organisation with minimal resources and exorbitant responsibilities – could have lasted had we been forced to accept all those obligations to female staff which have since become either statutory or by public sentiment made well-nigh inescapable. We had neither the money nor the space for a crèche. We could not have afforded maternity-leave and, as would have been even more intractable, the activities of many of our departments were so esoteric that it took months for those responsible to make themselves expert.

My wife and my daughters-in-law will deride my boast that I am no male chauvinist, though even they will admit that I have been always a strenuous advocate for equal pay. I abhor some of the sillier and shriller protestations of the women's liberation movement. I disdain the assault on the Authorised Version and Cranmer's Prayer Book which would make all references to the Almighty read like some official form, alternatively He or She (strike out whichever does not suit your prejudices). I mistrust academic or critical attention to what has come to be called 'feminist literature'. For me Emily Dickinson is a major poet, Jane Austen perhaps the greatest of novelists, literature is indivisible and I see no reason to flatter with attention Wilhelmina Stitch or Barbara Cartland just because they are women. I resent for my wife the contemptuous look and the supercilious question 'But what do you really do?' which so often comes to her when she cites housewife as her profession. (This to a woman who, voluntarily but reluctantly, gave up the stage and has since cared for large houses and gardens, reared four children, collaborated whole heartedly in her husband's career and even so has found time and energy sufficient to run as a so-nearly successful Liberal candidate for a seat on the County Council held without contest by the Conservatives for forty years.) I am convinced that the more virulent feminists by their virulence harm their own cause. But, sadly, experience at the League gave me reason to question the practicality of many of the moves towards equality between the sexes which sentiments and reason persuade me to espouse.

I lost to matrimony and parenthood several of the key members of my staff, among them my two closest and most diligent aides, Monica Anderson and Jane Buxton. Not all the satisfaction of working in an organisation seminal to so many elements in national and international life could compensate for the derisory salaries I could offer, and many of those who presented themselves as potential replacements were attracted to the League not because they were interested in furthering the cause of books, but because they assumed that all of 7 Albemarle Street was as elegant as its first two floors or because they found enticing the prospect of lunch-hours in Mayfair. Often there was a long and debilitating interregnum between the departure of a vital and experienced staff-member and the appointment of her well-qualified but inexperienced replacement.

At the last, but only after several futile experiments, I found a worthy successor to Barbara Kyle. No one could match Barbara's intellectual agility or her uninhibited forthrightness but as was Barbara so was Clifford Simmons dedicated, prepared to work often long into the evening, and he had what Barbara lacked, long experience in the trade.

Fortunately for me, for the League and, I truly believe, for the whole book-world, there was no hiatus between the departure of Jane Buxton and the arrival of her successor. Nansi Pugh, though in all probability old enough to be Jane's mother and, measured in terms of professional experience, by far her senior, was already working part-time in my outer office as Jane's assistant.

In all superficials, but not in diligence or efficiency, the contrast between the two was to me at first startling. Jane, a comparatively recent graduate of the House of Citizenship – the forcing-house for well-trained, upper-crust secretaries founded and managed, a whip in one hand and a book of etiquette in the other, by that sister to Simon Legree, Dorothy Neville-Rolfe – was young and exquisite, her capacity for management, as was appropriate for one reared by Miss Neville-Rolfe, veiled by charm and sociability. Nansi looked and behaved like everybody's maiden-aunt or, perhaps more accurately, like a maiden-aunt who has spent many years in far-off countries – as indeed she had, as senior secretary at Shell in Shanghai.

There have been in my life, as in the lives of all men and women, individuals who are unforgettable and unforgotten though my time with them has been brief, our association often casual and even though they have exercised little or no influence on my career or character. I have been but thrice to Australia and when I was there, Henry Lathwell, his wife Peggy, Robin Paul and Rozanne Turner were none of them significant to the purposes of my visit, yet whenever I think of Australia it is these four, my former student, Wayne McKenna, and Ian Shaw, my first Christ's Hospital presentee, who come immediately to my mind. Williamsburg has been home to many who have fashioned my course but for me Williamsburg means not only Tim Hanson, Swem, Miller, Jones and Bryan but also George Sands – a NASA chemist and next to Alan Glover the best-informed man I have ever met – and his wife Peggy, with whom I have spent a dozen evenings. Not infrequently, when I was what is ludicrously called a radio-personality, I was asked to name those individuals who had etched themselves into my memory. If that same question was put to me now I would have to offer for the last thirty years two seemingly disparate answers: Jim Dodd – the very Irish porter at the University of Leeds, a one-time 'tail-end Charley', a polymath, the best-read man in the School of English and still my prime source for campus gossip – and (I intend neither pretension nor impertinence) the Duke of Edinburgh, President of the NBL in my last years as Director General.

There have been through all my years others who have slipped into my life as it were side-long, without obvious cause or portent, who have nevertheless stayed by me as friends ever since. Eric Pearce, for example, I met first on a liner when we were both on our way to be students in the United States. A few years later, as a pilot in the Fleet Air Arm, miraculously he survived a horrendous crash, but it is not my admiration for his courage in rebuilding his life which enters his name in my chronicle, rather gratitude for his unthrusting loyalty.

For me, as I suppose for most men, there have been some, like Eric, the back-stage hands – and at times the claque – to my drama. Nansi Pugh was not one of these but I cannot be sure whether I should number her – with my father, David Roberts, Swem, Tim Hanson, Allen Block and, above all others, Kippe – among those who have fashioned my performance, or whether she should be listed with the supporting cast, like all these others cherished in recall but nevertheless a bit-player.

Nansi was my Personal Assistant, my professional *alter ego,* through a period of my life most fraught with frustration and despair. That role she performed with matchless efficiency but Nansi the executive's secretary is only the frame; it is for the picture itself that I hold her in affectionate and grateful recollection.

Confident in her ability as a highly competent secretary, as author of several successful children's books and as regular contributor to leading periodicals, Nansi blasted with sarcasm any colleague, however senior, who did not meet her severe professional standards; because dishonesty and disloyalty were beyond her comprehension and so outwith the beaten-zone of her sharp wit, those who committed these heinous offences she dismissed with awesome silence and a look of disgust. She was free of that urge to flaunt unique possession of knowledge which compels so many even of the best men and women to pass on confidences and so, at a time when I was busy with extravagant plans and my spirit bruised by the cowardice or malice of those who thwarted me, I talked freely with her as with none other. Her advice was always sound, and she punctured my excessive optimism just as she made my anger bearable by shrewd comment, often expressed in ribaldry which would have amazed many who were not aware, as was I, of her skill as an author of satirical verse and her habit of writing pungent letters to the press.

Next only to lack of integrity, Nansi detested pomposity or rudeness and, if the offender was, by reason of his status, placed beyond the reach of her rebuke she used her talent as mimic to release pent-up abhorrence – if only for my benefit. One of the trade's grandest grandees, a regular visitor to my office, was in the habit of handing her his coat and umbrella without so much as a 'please', 'good day' or a glance in her direction. At the end of his visit, when, with exorbitant courtesy, she had shown him to the front door, she would return to my office and pose in front of my desk. There she stood, for a blissful moment self-magicked into a Victorian hat-rack.

Nansi had her favourites among my visitors, Desmond Flower among them (though invariably she came back from escorting him out of the building puffing at a pencil), and there was only one who roused in her distrust too powerful to be assuaged by mimicking.

Mark Longman, Potter's successor as head of his family firm, at the time when Nansi was with me, Deputy Chairman of the League and so destined to be its next Trade Chairman, was never guilty of discourtesy or pomposity and it puzzled me that Nansi chose him as her *bête noire*. I put the question to her. She replied with a diatribe more splenetic than any I had ever heard from her, and with a warning which I dismissed as product of a flexible imagination. Longman, she insisted (she never conceded to him the courtesy of title or Christian name), was my evil genius – and the League's. He rides with the hounds, always in the middle of the pack and never daring to jump fences but at the kill he will be there, gloating. 'He's no gentleman,' she added, 'too many of his forebears were gentlemen.'

Nansi was essentially a private person but a private person thrust by circumstance into public affairs. Close though I was, it took me time to piece together her history – her childhood in China, her flapper-days in Shanghai and Sydney – and even longer to discover her inner self, her affection for her native Wales and her profound if undemonstrative faith.

For most of the time I knew her she was a sick woman and often in great pain. Soon after I left the League she was taken into St Thomas's Hospital. Two weeks before she died she wrote me a letter of such warmth and wit as seemed to deny the imminent end, and with it she sent a book, her collected poems:

> What matters whether it be East or West
> Prodigal blossom or a bud alone,
> If I still know, however harsh the death,
> That one green bud can roll away the stone?

Most of the many projects which we developed in those years were enlargements or variations of the activities which we had made routine. The most ambitious, however, had its origins in my missions to Asia and in the requests for assistance or advice which came to us from all over the world. I was convinced that the time had come to draw the League's hitherto uncharted frontiers so that they include all the English-speaking countries except the United States and, if reluctantly, Canada.

The organisation I planned in detail. For the benefit of our British constituency I argued that, if we were forced to offer actively those services which already we provided when the unprompted demands came to us, by so doing we would increase hugely our membership and so reduce the item-cost of each and every activity, we would expand British book exports and, coincidentally, we would provide for many countries a seminal central book-organisation which few of them had either the will or the funds to set up for themselves.

My paper on the Commonwealth Book League (a hesitant title, which I knew must be amended to meet the susceptibilities of Eire, South Africa and Pakistan, though all three were by sleight-of-hand still within the aegis of British publishing) was received by the officers of the League with limited enthusiasm and considerable scepticism. My plan, they said, was excellent, my reasoning faultless, but where would we find the money to launch the scheme and how would the trade react?

I approached the Commonwealth Secretariat, the Foreign and Commonwealth Office, two foundations and a millionaire who had previously helped the League. The response was much as I had expected, not damning but hardly exhilarating. All but the Commonwealth Office said much the same thing: that, once the Commonwealth Book League was established, almost certainly they could find money for its sustenance – providing the others came in. Whitehall offered me encouragement, even its blessing, but no funds.

I sent my paper for comment to Ron Barker, Secretary of the Publishers' Association. He invited me to lunch and, three hours, a steak (two for Ron) and a bottle of whisky later, he advised me to forget that I had ever dreamed up such a sure way to professional suicide. My case was sound, he did not doubt it, and it just might work but the NBL had always been suspected by some elements in the trade and recently there had been much murmuring about its growing influence and many hints that something should be done to cut it to size. 'Just think what this could do', he slapped his hand on my paper. 'You're suggesting an organisation which, if ever it got going, would be more powerful than the Publishers' Association, the Booksellers' Association, the Federation of Master Printers and the Library Association rolled into one,' and he asked if it were true that some well-meaning idiot had put my name forward for the Honours List.

I ignored this question, which I thought irrelevant even when he added that Balleny had been trying for a gong for at least a dozen years, but I argued as vigorously as I dared against his central thesis and at last, after three more whiskies, he agreed to test my paper on his President, a publisher *sans rapproche*.

A week later Ron phoned. 'Thumbs most definitely down. He says he'll see you in Hell before he allows you to build an empire within his frontiers.'

He had fired a shot across my bows which I was too angry to notice but I was in no mood for a fight. I was facing a disaster much more devastating than the death of a pet project.

For years I had been troubled by failing eyesight. It was now obvious that my most recent operation had been bungled. A brutish ophthalmologist informed me that there was a slim chance that another bout of surgery might save me from total darkness.

A few weeks before I went into hospital I sat for hours on end in front of my icon, Rembrandt's *Night Watch*, committing to memory every detail, the drummer, the little girl in her golden dress, the flags. . . After the operation, head down and pinned to a pillowless bed and eyes bandaged, I fought to listen to Kippe's voice, but the question was always there, blocking out the beauty and the sense of the poems which, for hour upon hour she read to me: would it be like this for the rest of my days, blackness without glimpse of wife, children or friends, without paintings or scenery, without cricket or Rugby football, without books? No books! Reading was my livelihood and my life.

I was fortunate. The light did not fail. Twenty years and two operations later I can still read though not, as once I could, a paragraph at a glance but now like a child spelling out words to a moving finger. I have never been reconciled to my incompetence nor have I lost a sense of shame for my dependence on Kippe's patience and the care of others, but I no longer mock myself as Blind Pugh or old blind Dandolo. Though not even the most wistful fancy can set me where once Milton trod making the soil glister beneath each hesitant footstep, still I write. The all-knowing Creator, an all-foreseeing Master of Physics, so arranged matters that the point of a pen is so finite that it can be seen and controlled even by a man with only one eye and that eye damnably dimmed.

Before I submitted myself to the attentions of the eye-surgeons and even before I set to paper my scheme for a Commonwealth Book League, my conscience was troubled because I was no longer truly involved in authorship. True, I still committed to paper thousands of words but the effort was akin to the writing of appreciations of the situation and operation orders which had exercised my ingenuity twenty years earlier, and to me no more satisfying. For my own comfort, I excused my literary sluggishness on the grounds that the hours I worked and my journeying in Britain and abroad made impossible obedience to the routine which I have always found essential for literary exercise, but I knew that I was falling victim to the temptation which silences so many would-be writers who practise also a quasi-literary profession, that I was giving so much to the propagation of other men's books that I had neither time nor intellectual energy left to create for myself. Deliberately I set myself to contemplating another book.

There were genuine and practical problems; I could not take on the kind of research that had produced Nye and Morpurgo and my experience as publisher warned me against attempting the kind of book which most I favoured and which would have been simplest to fit into my erratic existence: a volume of occasional essays. Bacon, Hazlitt, Lamb and Chesterton had always tempted me to emulation but their day was past.

I had enjoyed writing *The Road to Athens* and its reception had outstripped my hopes and the expectations of my publisher. The reviewers greeted it warmly, one, Richard Church (and he the one whose opinion I valued most) forecast that it would come to be regarded as a classic among travel-books, but it was more than a *succès d'estime*, in all that Eyre and Spottiswoode series it was the only title which went into a second edition.

There is affinity between the occasional essay and the travel-book. Both are personal, both in form and subject dictated only by the author's whim. Neither is constrained by chronology nor yet, in any obvious sense, by the discipline of logic and, when contemplating the possibility of producing another travel-book, there was evident to me another advantage. Writing as a traveller and freed from all constraints save the generous boundaries imposed by geography, I could even so use such skills as I had acquired – as historian, literary critic, even as soldier and I could make manifest many of my enthusiasms – for painting, music, wine, food – without being forced to pretend to expertise which was not mine.

I thought first of a book on India and Pakistan, but that would necessitate another long journey and I could afford neither the time nor the expense. The Netherlands was my obvious choice. My father had endowed me with a working knowledge of Dutch history; Piet Heyn, van Tromp and de Ruyter were my childhood heroes no less than Drake or Nelson; Rembrandt, Pieter de Hooch and Frans Hals among my favoured painters and, though many of my rivals enjoyed *uitsmeiter, rijstaffes* and *gen-*

ever, oude or *nieuwe*, I was prepared to wager that there was no other English writer who in youth had listened fascinated to readings, in Dutch but translated immediately into Cockney English, from Joost van den Vondel's *Lucifer*. A refresher course in Holland could be managed in week-ends or two-week summer vacations and I would have the delightful and, I was sure, the delighted assistance of my three Dutch 'daughters', Hildegarde, Mieke and Agnes.

Nothing came of my projected book on the Netherlands. My eyesight murdered it before I could produce so much as a synopsis.

In the weeks which followed immediately after the operation I was by no means confident that I would recover even some limited visual facility and the thought that I had suffered so much spiritual anguish and not a lit-tle physical pain and all, perhaps, to no good effect was almost beyond bearing. Resilience is a noble word and I do not flatter myself that it was anything noble in my character but rather pig-headedness which allowed me to pull through. There was, however, something not my own which stayed me against depression.

It is for me, a confirmed sceptic, shaming to be forced to confess that I was held from despair by faith not my own but even at the time, as in all the crises of the last forty years, I recognized how much I owed to Kippe's certainty. Had she been pious, overtly devout, I would have mocked and in derisiveness must have lost the benefit granted to me by her indomitable and unwavering Christianity. As it was, as it has always been I, an unbe-liever, was guarded by her belief.

I was still recovering from the operation when I was offered a sensa-tional opening for professional endeavour of a kind that had never before been presented to me. I was asked to write the biography of Barnes Wallis.

I had known Wallis since my earliest school-days, since the moment when I, a polite little school-boy, carried his suit-case up the Centre Path when he came to Christ's Hospital to talk to us about his airship *R100*. After the War, and particularly after I had fought off Flecker's heinous assault on the revolutionary essay on the future of the Foundation written by Wallis at my invitation for *The Christ's Hospital Book*, we had become close friends and, when the novelist Neville Shute (who had been Wallis's calculator on *R100*) died, Wallis took to using me as his literary and public relations adviser. He was in truth more adept in the art of PR than many who earned from it a rich living, but he was forever complaining about the waste of his creativity involved in satisfying the impertinent curiosity of the public. Never with any serious intent but only to silence his martyr's moans, I took to answering that this persecution would not end until I wrote his biography.

Early in 1967 BBC Television screened an hour-long programme on Wallis, 'Why Not? Why Not?', using the story of his many frustrations to shame the British for failing to profit from the genius of their inventors. Britain's conscience was untouched but the public was intrigued and publishers were quick to see the possibilities.

A week after the broadcast Wallis came to my office and dumped on my desk a bulging file. 'Tell me, dear heart, what do we do about that?'

I could read the letters only with difficulty but I knew what was in them: bids for the rights to his autobiography and requests that he grant permission to have his life-story written. Without thinking, I gave back my cliché, now made particular, 'Now I'll have to write your biography.'

Wallis slapped his hand on the file. 'Done.'

For a week I hovered between ecstasy and despondency. I knew that I was in the happiest of all situations for a writer, I could force the publishers to an auction, but Wallis was in himself almost a history of British aviation and I knew less about aeronautical engineering than I knew about the quantum theory. I had never attempted a full-length biography and here I was, thinking of taking on the life of a centemporary and a contemporary still very much alive. My historical knowledge was for the most part confined to the times of Cromwell, Queen Anne and George Washington; for a biography of Barnes Wallis I must draw the background of this century. The most debilitating doubt came to me last: how could I manage the essential research with eyes that were not yet capable of seeing the food on my plate?

In that very week when I was hesitating, we drove to Oxford to see *At the Drop of Another Hat* and, backstage in the dressing-room of our old friend Michael Flanders, I was almost shamed out of my own physical excuse for refusing this, the best and richest challenge that ever I had faced. If Michael, hideously handicapped and tied to a wheel-chair, could even so commit himself, cheerfully and whole-heartedly, to the cause of laughter then surely, somehow, I must make myself manage, for Barnes, for history and for the enlivenment and enlightenment of readers.

Even so I went to see Barnes in his research-establishment, the club-house of the old Brooklands, determined to cry off.

We were no sooner finished with conventional greetings than Barnes denied to me one of the most cogent passages in the speech of regret which I had rehearsed. Our conversation in my office, he said, had been much in his mind and he had come to suspect that I doubted my competence to present, in comprehensible terms to a generally inexpert readership, an account of his career. (He called it '*R100*, geodetic construction, the big bombs, swing-wing and all that.') I had no cause for concern; given a fourteen-year-old lad who was both numerate and literate, he, Wallis, could teach him in six months enough about aeronautical engineering to allow him to design a plane that would fly. With me, a quick-witted adult, undoubtedly literate and a mathematician, he could do it in six weeks.

I asked what made him assume I was numerate. He brushed my question aside – You were an artilleryman, weren't you? – and while I was wondering whether I should confess to my struggles with trigonometry at Larkhill, he went on to dismiss an objection which, though I would not have dared to raise it, had in the last days occurred to me again and again. He was prepared, even eager, to have his life-story written and he had turned to me because I was a friend. I could have all his papers, private and professional, and he would do all he could to help me but I need not fear that I would have him forever peering over my shoulder, directing what I wrote, censoring what he did not want told.

Barnes pushed his glasses up on to his forehead and said, 'If someone commissioned me to design an aerostat I'd kick him to Kingdom Come if he tried to tell me how to do it.'

I was left with but one valid reason to escape from a commitment which in truth I wanted to accept. I rumbled something about my impaired vision. Barnes looked thoughtful and for moments it seemed that this was indeed cause for him to seek some other biographer. Then he grinned, the confident grin of a man who is faced with an interesting problem which he knows he can solve, and said: 'I'm sure I can dream up some way to deal with that.'

He rang for Pat Lucas, his efficient and devoted secretary, fixed dates for me to return to Brooklands and to his home at Effingham, ordered a British Aircraft Corporation car to take me to the station; took me to the door and said first 'It'll be great fun' and then, 'Paint in the warts as big and black as you see them.'

I sold the book, without benefit of auction, to Longmans but before I signed the agreement, to my publisher's chagrin, I disposed of the serialization-rights to the *Sunday Times*.

A month after the decisive meeting at Brooklands, Barnes's chauffeur delivered to Oxhey Hall a huge wooden box fitted out with lights and magnifying-glasses, devised and built by Britain's greatest aircraft-designer. With the box there was a note in Barnes's bold cursive hand: 'For seeking out all that can be said and much that none other dare say about that wicked old man, his biographer's friend, Barnes Neville Wallis.'

Einstein said that no man shows more courage than he who allows his life-story to be told in his life-time. Barnes did all that could be expected of him and much more to make it possible for me to tell a full and frank story. He gave me uninhibited access to his vast archive of technical and personal papers – even his mother's diary, which he had never dared to read. At his suggestion Molly Wallis passed to me the bundle of letters – courtship in the guise of a correspondence-course in Mathematics – which he had written when schoolmastering in Switzerland and she a medical student preparing to take her First M.B. He gave me another collection of letters from a much later period, carefully presented but for some reason never sent – amorousness strangely but typically interspersed with reports on the progress of his swing-wing experiments. He submitted patiently to hour-long inquisitions in his Brooklands office and his Effingham study. Throughout his life a non-smoker (or so he claimed), whenever I went to Brooklands he saw to it that his cigarette-box was filled, not, he would say as he urged me to fill my cigarette-case, because he wanted to encourage me in a filthy habit but because those cigarettes came at the expense of Sir George Edwards, the head of BAC and Barnes's favourite enemy.

All this Barnes did for me and, as he had promised, he coached me in the principles of aeronautical engineering. He was a superb tutor and, though I never quite succeeded in persuading him that, for me as for those who came eventually to read my book, words must take the place of the mathematical symbols and diagrams he thought to be all the explanation required, almost I came to believe him when he said, 'I told you so, dear heart. Yesterday there was but one man in England capable of designing an airship. Today there are two, you and me.'

But in all the years I was working on the biography only once, and then at my request, did he read or ask to read, so much as one paragraph of my text.

It was not, however, Barnes's magic-box which made feasible the arduous but fascinating search through thousands of the documents. For that, and so for the success of the book, I owe much to my spare-eyes, my long-time friend and part-time research assistant, Elaine Barr, whose mastery of research techniques – learnt in a very different discipline, in the study of antique silver – she applied with meticulous skill to biography and aeronautical engineering, and who won for herself the trust and affection of Barnes and Molly Wallis.

Biography is a complex craft. He who practises it must be narrator, simultaneously defence counsel, prosecutor and judge, and master of two seemingly contradictory disciplines, the historian's and the novelist's. The facts of his character's life – parentage, education, career, dates of birth, marriage and death – are as readily accessible to him, as clear and as precise as an entry in *Who's Who*, but he must use his creative imagination to discover and make visible the inward spirit and the influences which have fashioned his subject's development.

The biographer of a contemporary is faced also with a problem of conscience that does not trouble those who write the lives of men or women whose lives ended long ago. Biography no less than any other historical mode is a quest for truth, the biographer must tell nothing but the truth, but is it essential that he tell the whole truth if by so doing he trespasses on privacy, hurts or damages some who cannot defend themselves?

Qualms of this order were less taxing when I wrote the life of Wallis than they were a few years later when I took on the biography of Allen Lane but there was evident to me a difficulty that did not burden my second excursion into contemporary biography. Wallis was still alive.

Barnes's integrity was beyond doubt, yet in the course of research it was made obvious to me that, even from a man as palpably honest as was he, first person evidence is suspect. He had told so often stories about himself, and particularly about the disdain with which his most original ideas had been received by his fellow-professionals and by Government, that he was convinced that he was telling the truth. Of perhaps a dozen instances, the most flagrant was his oft-repeated tale that for almost two years no one in authority would pay attention to his 'bouncing bomb' theory. I was able to demonstrate, from undeniable written evidence, that he was indulging in fiction.

There was, however, as I waited for his reactions to my book, reason for trepidation more compelling than my fear that he would resent the revelation that remembered and genuine frustration had at times trapped him into dramatizing the truth. A man of paradox, a devout Christian concerned with the welfare of his fellow-men, Barnes had given most of his life, of his remarkable intellectual athleticism, to creating the machinery of destruction. His rare, inventive imagination he used to project Britain, first among the nations, into the twenty-first century, but his moral and social precepts were essentially Victorian. In the last years of his life he devoted himself, his abundant energy and even his money, to the care of the children of others less fortunate than he and for all that he did was revered by all of Christ's Hospital; with his own children he was severe, unapproachable and, it must be admitted, by them feared, even unloved. I had written my book with affection tinged with indignation for the scant respect shown to his genius by his country and for the tardiness of the honour its Government granted, but I had taken him at his word, the warts were there, it could not be otherwise if my portrait was to be faithful, and some were very big and very black.

Barnes Wallis: A Biography came from the printers in mid-December 1971 and a copy was sent immediately to Barnes. That year for the first time we had accepted the inevitable but pleasing fate of grandparents, the status of Christmas guests of our children. Kippe and I were staying with Michael and Clare at their home near Canterbury. On Christmas Eve morning I was in the bath when Clare called through the bathroom door that Sir Barnes Wallis was on the phone. I did not pause to wonder how he had tracked me down but, wet, shivering and offering up a prayer to Sir Thomas More, whose severed head had been taken to that very house by his daughter Margaret, I went to the telephone.

There was no preface, just 'Jack, dear heart, how did you find out so much about me?' and then the greeting, 'Happy Christmas, dear boy and God bless you.'

The book went through three hard-back editions in Britain, was published as a paperback by Penguin and appeared also in America. Barnes and I stayed close but he continued to repeat as history in private, in the press, on radio and on television the self-pitying stories which I had proved to be myths.

Barnes Wallis died in 1979, when he was thirty-four days past his ninety-second birthday. Some twenty years earlier, when in hospital for a prostatectomy, he had forecast on the basis of elaborate and abstruse genealogical investigation that he would die when he was eighty-two years old but after the operation he had amended his prognosis when the satisfied urologist announced cheerfully, 'That will add ten years to your life'.

I knew Barnes well and I swear that all that kept him from troubling St Peter at least thirty five days sooner was his determination to prove to the world the accuracy of his actuarial calculations.

After his death, the two communities he had loved and served so well, Christ's Hospital and 617 Squadron, RAF – 'the Dam-busters', 'Barnes Wallis's Own' – joined together to plan a National Service of Thanksgiving for his life and work. Angus Ross, Treasurer of C.H., chairman of the joint organizing committee and hitherto my friend, dragooned me into giving the Address.

Brisk but clear, as was his fashion, Angus outlined to me the arrangements: the setting, as Barnes would have wished, St Paul's Cathedral; Christ's Hospital boy and girl organists; music by the combined orchestras and choirs of our two schools, by the Boys' School band and the trumpeters of the Royal Air Force; prayer led by a chaplain of the war-time 617 Squadron and by our Old Blue bishop, Ross Hook of Bradford; a colour-party of young men from 617 Squadron laying the Squadron's colours on the altar; a lesson read by the Treasurer of C.H. and my Address. 'Eight minutes precisely. The Prince of Wales has asked to be present, the Lord Mayor will be there, several ambassadors and the High Commissioners; Cabinet Ministers; probably the whole of the Air Staff; God knows how many dug-out Air Chief Marshals, and the Australian, New Zealand and Canadian governments are flying over 617 Squadron veterans. We must get the whole thing through in an hour, not sixty-one minutes or fifty-nine, but sixty. So remember: eight minutes.'

In the weeks that followed I wrote and I honed. I read the results on to tape. Kippe listened, watch in hand, and at last we had eight minutes, 'not one second more, not one second less'.

St Paul's served me well as master-metaphor for the life and spirit of Barnes Wallis. Created by another such as he, a poet of technology, by the man whom he admired above all his predecessors in the Royal Society, St Paul's is the noblest of post-reformation cathedrals, the image of England's faith; throughout his life Barnes had been motivated beyond all else by his religion and his fidelity to the Established Church was immutable. St Paul's has been for centuries the temporal focal-point for England's emotions, the stage on which in times of trial, triumph, mourning and jubilation the English have ritualized their sense of community; Barnes shrugged at both fashion and the capriciousness to which he was subjected and remained defiantly a patriot. St Paul's is the cathedral-church of the City of London; dismissing what others saw as the logic of history, for sixty years and more Barnes worked to sustain, against all aspiring usurpers, London's status as capital of the world. Throughout the years of the Second World War, at just that time when, as never before and never after, his persistence outmatched the obstructiveness of his disbelieving critics, St Paul's stood, ringed by the fires of hate, for Britain, for the Commonwealth, for free men everywhere and for men longing to be set free, the symbol of survival, of endurance and of hope. An auspicious coincidence made my metaphor entire. Scarcely an airship's length from St Paul's there stood until 1902 the gates through which Barnes entered upon his Christ's Hospital heritage.

I had my address ready and then, ten days before the ceremony, Angus demanded four more minutes. ('Shove in a few more paragraphs.') I protested, but he was adamant so I went through the process – writing, reading, cutting, enlarging – all over again and, just in time, arrived at twelve minutes, 'not one second more, not one second less'.

Through every day of every week St Paul's is filled with tourists or worshippers so stage-rehearsal was impossible but I was determined to find my way unaided from my appointed seat and up the winding stairs to the pulpit and the evening before my ordeal I reconnoitred and committed to memory the route.

Next morning, before the arrival of the congregation, I robed and even in those minutes of tension I was conscious that I was about to make history; to the best of my knowledge never before had a William and Mary hood been flaunted in the pulpit which three centuries back had been occupied frequently by the College's first Chancellor (and, I added to myself, discarding historical precision in favour of self-flattering sentiment, also by John Donne). I set my script on the pulpit-ledge and, beside it, the neck-microphone and returned to my seat next to Kippe.

I remember little of the first part of the service though since I have listened often to the magnificent music held for posterity on tape and disc. The Anthem began. I counted my way up the pulpit steps and stood, head erect, my hand feeling for the microphone. It was not there, some moron had moved it.

Below me, in the front row, Kippe watched in horror as my groping hand crept along the pulpit-ledge. She was certain that I was about to tip my text into the lap of the Prince of Wales.

I found the script. The Anthem ended and twelve minutes later, 'not one second more, not one second less', I was ready to count my way back down the pulpit-steps.

15
Lungs of Bronze

In those months when I was coming to terms with diminished visual capacity, I had other and no less cogent reasons for echoing Claudius's moan, sorrows came upon me, 'not as single spies, but in battalions'. Damnation from Bedford Square wakened me from the cosy dream that I could make the League international and, in so doing, at a time when heightened prestige was bringing to us more and ever more demands for our service but little more money, also wrote *finis* to what I thought to be the surest safeguard against bankruptcy. The demise of Penguin Educational deprived the League of rent and set again upon the League's sagging back what could well be the proverbial straw, the whole weight of my derisory salary. My break with Allen Lane slammed the door on my way back to Penguin, shattered beyond possibility of repair my hope, seldom given form even in my own mind and never articulated even to Kippe, that some day I would return to Harmondsworth possessed of sufficient authority to restore to the firm that spirit of adventure which had made the 1940s and 1950s its golden age. Worse still, estrangement from my fellow-grandfather menaced the precious unity of our family.

I need not have worried about Michael and Clare, their affection resisted the strains of divided loyalty, and for the rest I was saved by the surest of all prophylactics, frenzied activity, from falling victim to self-pity.

Such little time as I could spare I gave to the absorbing task of preparing the Barnes Wallis biography. At the League I, with my senior colleagues, strove to enrol more private members and I to hold, and if possible to enlarge, the scale of financial support from the trade. In both efforts our success was limited and, as I reported ruefully to one of the more sympathetic publishers, the need to be forever busy wrestling for funds with those most advantaged by our activities brought back to my mind a complaint I had more than once moaned to an Inspector of Taxes: 'If I give all the time you demand to my Schedule D returns I will have none left to earn a free-lance income on which to pay tax.'

All this busy-ness, the extension of routine activities and the supervision of an appeal to bolster our finances, denied to me all thought of further licensed moonlighting.

Then came the offer of the Chair of American Literature at the University of Geneva. The Officers of the League encouraged me to accept. More, I suspect, from gratitude for a reprieve than out of any wish to compliment me or to salute the honour conferred, if at second-hand, upon the League, the Executive Committee passed unanimously a resolution of congratulations.

My elevation to the professoriate set me to exertions that were more physical than intellectual. My students were polite and earnest, so assiduous in their note-taking that. when once I vented my exasperation with their docility by reciting as preamble to a lecture the opening stanza of 'Jabberwocky', the only response was a frenzy of pencil over paper as every boy and girl in the lecture-hall attempted the impossible task of transposing into Pitman "Twas brillig and the slithy toves. . .', but every Tuesday in term-time I went from Albemarle Street to Heathrow, took plane to Switzerland and, if Geneva Airport was free of fog, arrived at the University just in time to begin a two-hour teaching-session. Every Wednesday I lectured almost without break until it was time to return to the airport for the last plane back to London.

Continental universities are so organized as to deny all possibility of conviviality between teacher and taught. I never came to know as individuals any of my students and I managed little more with my colleagues; indeed, most I never met though once, for reasons by me unfathomable, I was invited to a party given in honour of the most eminent of them all, the Professor of Child Psychology and the History of Scientific Thought, Jean Piaget. At that party my conversation with the great educational theorist was limited to a precise exchange of greetings, '*Monsieur le Professeur*' for '*Monsieur le Professeur*''

It is a perversity of the French – and the Genevois are more French than the Parisians – that, though they use the word *professeur* prodigally their respect is reserved for the incumbents of University Chairs. There we sat far above mere university lecturers, our dignity unassailable, our persons far out-of-range of those humbler, un-Chaired *confrères*. There was in the University of Geneva no equivalent to a British university's Senior Common Room and, as most of the other professors in Geneva's Modern Languages Department spent no more time on campus than their teaching-programmes demanded, even had I extended my weekly visits I doubt that I would have enlarged my acquaintance with my colleagues beyond the conventional salutes we gave to each other as we passed in the corridors.

Such hurried attention as I paid to the city of Geneva reinforced my prejudice against all things Swiss. I was paid handsomely, that I had to admit, but the thousands of international civil servants in this, the cathedral city of goodwill between the nations, were paid even better and their fat, tax-free stipends made exorbitant the cost of the few pleasures available in a city still made gloomy by the omnipresent shadow of John Calvin. (After a few evenings in Geneva I accepted as apposite the antique quip that the statue of Calvin's only peer among the Genevois, Jean Jacques Rousseau, has its back turned upon the city of his birth.) It is true that I ate well, sometimes superlatively, but only by taking a taxi across the frontier into France, and even Geneva's much-lauded free attraction, the view across the lake to Mont Blanc, was consistently denied to me. In two years, every time I looked the mountain was hidden by mist.

I was bored by Geneva and the Genevois, by Switzerland and the Swiss, by most of my colleagues, by all those earnest young people scratching at their notebooks, by hours waiting in airport-lounges and by a procession of Swissair meals. Other than a plentiful supply of Swiss francs I gained from my time in Geneva only regular and duty-free replenishment of my stocks of whisky and cigarettes, the detail useful when later I came to write a book about the Arnold-André Conspiracy, that John André, the handsome dilettante, Elia's 'amiable spy' and pathetic victim of Washington's obduracy, was in part educated at the University of Geneva. But I did not expect that my generally unsatisfactory and unsatisfying experience in Geneva, through no fault of the Genevois or the University, would make possible a débâcle.

Lulled into complacency by the approval of the League's Officers and Committee and made insensitive to danger by the knowledge that, having passed to the *République et Canton de Genève* responsibility for half my salary and all my pension arrangements as recompense for sacrificing my services for one-and-a-half days in a sixty-hour week for only thirty weeks in the year, I mislaid my political antennae. It took me time to wake to the fact that my absences were convenient for those who wished to organize at 7 Albemarle Street a palace revolution.

Even when loyal colleagues reported to me that, always on days when I was in Geneva, Balleny came often to the top floor, I dismissed their fears. It was, I said, no more than proper that at a time when the League was in financial difficulty its Treasurer wished to consult with the Accountant.

I read the omens, accurately but belatedly, when I was told that on his last two visits the Treasurer had been accompanied by the Chairman, Mark Longman. In the week when I received this menacing intelligence the directors of Longmans must have been in continuous session, for every time I rang Grosvenor Street I was told that Mr Longman was in a board-meeting.

A note from Longman informed me, without explanation or apology, that he had called a special meeting of the Executive Committee and that my attendance was not required. I wrote letters to all those I considered to be my stalwarts, warning them that some perfidy was in preparation and begging them to be present at the meeting. (Most, as later I discovered, found excuses to absent themselves.)

Throughout the two hours of the meeting I sat alone in one of the backstairs-offices recently occupied by the staff of Penguin Educational and I was praying to all the gods whose names I could remember but not for reprieve; for that I had little hope, and I was by no means sure that I cared;

but, just as sometimes under bombardment during the War I had found myself praying that none would see me cowering in a ditch, so now I prayed that I would be able to meet *congé* with dignity.

I was summoned to my own office and there, sitting in my own chair behind my own desk, Longman told me that my contract would not be renewed. He offered not one word of regret, not one expression of gratitude for the thirteen years of my life given to the National Book League.

The brutishness to which I was subjected did not end there. The Chairman vetoed a plan to organize a testimonial valedictory gift and had it not been for the vigorous, professionally expert and wondrously histrionic intervention of my friend, Reggie Barr, I doubt that the 'handshake' which eventually came my way would have been as 'golden' as gold paint made it.

Immediately it was revealed to me that there had been opposition to what was in effect my dismissal, most vigorously expressed, as I would have expected, by Stewart Mackintosh and Josephine Kamm, author and mother of my one-time colleague, Antony Kamm, and, to me surprising, by the representatives of the librarians and the printers. Later Longman himself told me that the League's Royal President had expressed his doubts about the propriety of the Executive Committee's action, and Prince Philip wrote me a generous and encouraging letter.

Twenty years on, one of those who had been, at least tacitly, on the side of the vipers admitted to me that I had been treated shamefully but already before I left office the cabal which had plotted my downfall stood on its corporate head. I had been for many years a member of the book-world élite dining-club, the Society of Bookmen. Now I was elected as Honorary member for life and, it could have been to ensure that a closet scandal gave me no grounds to organize a public outcry, I was invited to become Deputy Chairman of the very committee which had got rid of me. A year or so later my name was added to the glittering list of the League's Vice-Presidents and there it shone, if dimly, alongside such resplendencies as T. S. Eliot, Sybil Thorndike, Arthur Bliss and Veronica Wedgwood, until at last the NBL became, what some had always wanted it to be, what I had fought hard to prevent, a trade tool without the cutting-edge of independence.

The wounds from treachery, disloyalty, ruthlessness and ingratitude have never been healed and I mourn still for thirteen wasted years but, though at first my dismay was profound, I was buoyed against despair by indignation and soon found some consolation in the knowledge that, at least in mundane terms, my condition was far from parlous. I was confident that, when it was finished and published, my *Barnes Wallis* would win an audience with a public which had already established Barnes as a cult-figure and, though momentarily I cursed myself for having but recently rejected out of hand a suggestion that I allow myself to be considered for a senior post at the British Museum, there was still open to me a slim chance that I could make active a hint that my name might be added to a very short list of candidates for the editorial directorship of a major publishing group. My Geneva Chair was secure but the grace to occupy it part-time had only one more year to run. Even so, if all else failed, Kippe and I could survive as John Calvin's neighbours.

More than once I have argued in print that in their eagerness to tease consequences out of cause, historians are too often blind to the significance of coincidence and never was my case so amply justified as by the events which, in 1969. changed the whole course of my life.

It so happened that, before ever I was alerted to the imminence of disaster, we had arranged to meet in London friends from Leeds, the University's Professor of English Literature, Derry Jeffares and his wife Jeanne, like Kippe half-Belgian and, by some abstruse genealogical calculation of her own, my wife's distant cousin. The evening chosen for our reunion chanced to be the evening of the afternoon on which Longman had chosen to play Nemesis in hob-nailed boots.

Derry is a man of many parts. The biographer of W. B. Yeats , he had become the acknowledged managing director of the Yeats industry and it was he beyond all others who, as Chairman, had so organized the Leeds School of English as to endow it with prestige greater than that of most Departments of English in British universities and inferior to none. An energetic and skilful manipulator of men and institutions,it is one of Derry's most lovable characteristics that his interest in the affairs of others is never passive, his sympathy for their tribulations always demonstrated by action. He saw a way to lighten my despondency by using to my advantage a tragic circumstance.

A few weeks earlier Douglas Grant, Leeds' and Britain's first Professor of American Literature, Derry's friend and mine, had dropped dead in a Singapore street. Derry asked me to take over his teaching duties for the rest of the academic year and so, for months on end, I spent even more time than previously in planes and airport lounges.

The continental academic year begins and ends later than the British and it was one evening when I was not called upon to extend to Leeds my return flight from Geneva that I came back to Oxhey Hall to find Kippe tremendously excited. Derry had phoned with the news that the University of Leeds intended to offer me the succession to the Chair. Inwardly thrilled, even so to save both of us from disappointment I put on a fine show of sophisticated scepticism: great institutions, I insisted, do not act in such impulsive fashion; I had made no application; there would be before an election all manner of committees; and I added, gratuitously but not without support from precedent, she must have misunderstood Derry's message.

Kippe defended herself vigorously, added, not unreasonably, that Derry already had on his files the curriculum vitae and bibliography I had sent to make feasible my temporary appointment, and challenged me to call him back.

It was by then close to midnight but I rang Derry's Leeds home, was told that both Professor and Mrs Jeffares were away, he on his way to Nigeria (this no surprise; Derry was forever on his way to distant places). I tried the Athenaeum. Yes, Professor Jeffares was staying in the Club but he was not in his room. I left a message and at one o'clock Derry rang back. Kippe's account of their conversation was so close to being accurate and yet so devastatingly wrong that I kept her awake for the rest of the night trying to persuade her, and myself, out of optimism. I was indeed the favoured candidate; the Registrar would be writing to me soon to arrange for a meeting with the Chair Committee.

By the first post that morning I received a letter from the Vice-Chancellor, asking me if I could make myself free to meet him at his office at 11 am five days later.

I could, I did and before we went to lunch with the Chair Committee I was for all practical purposes Professor-elect of American Literature in the University of Leeds. Sir Roger Stevens accepted without demur my condition that for one more year I must continue my weekly visits to Geneva, and he understood my reasons for postponing formal acceptance until I had consulted Douglas Grant's widow.

That afternoon Kippe and I drove out to see Joan. I had stayed frequently in the lovely Georgian house with the lovely name, Manna Ash, but we had not seen Joan since Douglas's death and we were both nervous about her reactions to a friend who, after such a brief interval, impertinently threatened to take on the role her husband had filled with such distinction.

Joan greeted us with her customary grace and a bottle of malt whisky. She was delighted, she said, and it would have given Douglas much pleasure could he have known that it was a cherished friend who was to succeed him.

For all my years at Leeds my pride in my professorship was much enhanced by the knowledge that I was perpetuating the pioneering work of a distinguished scholar, a writer of consequence, a man who, had he not given so much to academe, must have fulfilled his early promise as a poet, but for the first eighteen months whenever I went to my university rooms I pretended not to notice that the door still bore the label 'Professor W. D. B. Grant'.

I faced my future as pedagogue with few but potent qualms. I had had more than my fill of administration and politics and I resolved, so far as was within my power, not to participate in any committees save those I wanted to join. I was accustomed to speaking in public but I could not regard as preparation for the task of teaching third year and graduate students at Leeds my brief and eccentric episodes at King's, Newcastle, Michigan State, the Free University in Berlin and Geneva. For almost a quarter-of-a-century I had been a published author but only once, when I edited Leigh Hunt, had I indulged in the sternly footnoted scholarship generally thought proper for a don. For almost as long, I had written on American literature and history for important periodicals; the syllabus which I had inherited – an inevitable progression from Ann Bradstreet and Cotton Mather to Robert Frost and William Faulkner by way of Cooper, Emerson, Hawthorne, Melville, Mark Twain, James and Emily Dickinson – did not dismay me; every one of them had been at some time subject for extended and often pontifical comment from me sufficiently persuasive to satisfy authoritative editors, but I cared not a comma or an exclamation-mark for the scalpel-criticism favoured by academic critics and always I had held myself haughtily apart from the blood-feuds over dogma between donnish factions. Innocent of all taint from F. R. Leavis, I. A. Richards or Freud, my own literary criticism was unashamedly subjective. A simpleton, no doubt, I knew what I liked – and I knew that I detested Emerson.

I had my articles of faith and these I intended to propagate at Leeds, not as restrictive doctrines but to enable students to move freely across the frontiers imposed upon the study of literature by the conventions of universities.

Already at Geneva it had been brought home to me that Continental students are shamefully ignorant of the history of the American people. In my first week as Professor,I set my class a simple quiz; not one in a group of twenty could differentiate between the Revolution and the War between the States,even when I offered as alternative titles the War of Independence and the Civil War. I hoped for something much better from my Leeds students. (I was disappointed; to the same question the success-rate was four out of sixteen, only two knew that the Pilgrim Fathers were not the first British settlers and only one genius had heard of Jamestown.) I had available to me the statistics of enrolment into the third year course in American Literature. Year after year in my predecessor's time (as ever after in mine), it had been by far the most popular of all the options offered by the School of English as support for the main-stream courses in the literature of England, I suspected, as indeed proved to be the case, that the eagerness of students was aroused by their misbegotten conviction that the United States is the land of shiny modernity, that they would be presented with a reading-list of novels published a year or so earlier by obscure San Francisco publishers and little collections of avant-garde verse, set in deliberately eccentric typography and distributed at their own expense by poets whose names did not and never would appear in any reference-books, and I surmised, as again proved true, that they would be disconcerted when they discovered themselves called upon to look first at Ann Bradstreet, a poet whose life-span coincided with Milton's.

If I was to make the development of American literature comprehensible, if I was to persuade those I taught that the United States, a nation devout in worship of a constitution devised two hundred years ago and in all the world the second oldest, is in many respects more traditionalist even than Britain, I must give time to American history.

I was determined to offer to my students free passage across the severe thematic frontiers policed by those who design the structure of university departments of English, the frontiers which allow only to poetry, drama and the novel the privilege of full-blown citizenship, to literary criticism ambiguous status as some sort of resident alien, but which dismiss philosophy, theology, political writing, history and biography beyond the pale, there to be cared for by other departments. If I followed procedure, I would deny to myself and to my students notice of some of America's greatest literary achievements. We would even be barred from a view of one of the finest prose-poems in the English language, the Declaration of Independence.

I resolved to include in the syllabus Jefferson, Jonathan Edwards, William Byrd of Westover, John Woolman and William James. Perhaps less deliberately, but to my mind with consequence no less disastrous, the custom of literary pedagogy established also demarcation lines demurely obedient to geography. Too often American literature was studied in isolation, as if it is something separate and independent of all association with British literature. I determined that, whenever practicable, I would emphasize those influences, literary or biographical, which supported my thesis of interdependence and I took as title for my Inaugural Lecture 'From that damnable place: the Englishness of American Literature' –

> Can we never be thought
> To have learning or grace
> Unless it be brought
> From that damnable place?

– thereby deliberately provoking many British expositors of American literature and their chauvinistic American masters.

Though I was never able to fulfil all my ambitions, for fourteen years I held to my *credo*. Judgement on my success I leave to those who sat at my feet.

When Kippe and I first discussed the practicalities of our move to Leeds, we comforted ourselves for exile from the metropolis with talk of the excellence of the train-service from Leeds to London. Once settled in Yorkshire, whenever I went to London my first action on arriving at Kings Cross was to confirm the times of trains northwards.

A Londoner by birth and pride, I have said frequently that were I to find myself the sole survivor of some catastrophe that wiped London from the map I would seek consolation by migrating to Paris or New York, to my mind London's only near rivals among the cities of the world. My Paris is the place des Vosges not the faubourg St. Honoré, my New York Washington Square not Park Avenue or Broadway, and my London not Piccadilly Circus or Oxford Street but the squares, streets and alleys round Canonbury Towers. So it had been in Newcastle; I went often to Grey

Street but the Newcastle of my heart was along the Elswick Road and up by Jesmond Dene; and so it came to be that in Leeds I was contentedly a villager in a big city.

Leeds for me is two almost contiguous villages: the University, a mish-mash of Victorian streets, 1920s pomposities and the glass-and-concrete aberrations of post-World War II architects, and, a few hundred yards away across Woodhouse Moor, the inner-city village on the slopes above Hyde Park Corner.

There we made our home for thirteen years, in an early nineteenth century farm-house set incongruously in a street of houses, most of them jerry-built a hundred years after Cliff Cottage. We walked the mysterious ginnels between high walls and lavishly-treed gardens. Our market-place, accessible it seemed by day and by night and always lively, was the Indian general store at the bottom of Cliff Road kept by the Upals. The main roads which made boundary to our village seldom lured us into the city centre just a mile away or out to pretentious Headingley. We had little need of the Yorkshire moors and dales; from our rear-windows, the slums of Meanwood conveniently hidden from us in a dip, we had an unbroken view of an almost rural landscape.

In Leeds a villager, whenever I returned to my own 'the Southron folk' I became vehemently and vociferously Leodensian, flaring my proud *ripostes* to the customary and patronizing comment 'Leeds! There is lovely country that is easily accessible to you.' (Something in like pitying vein I had heard often when back in London during my year as a Geordie: 'Newcastle! It's beautiful along the Roman Wall and you are lucky to be so near to the sea.') Indeed, I would snap, we have Ilkley Moor and Swaledale not far off. Indeed, we had Haworth, Castle Howard, Fountains Abbey and York, places we visited only when we entertained guests from abroad. But we had within the city limits almost everything that civilized man could desire, stores as good as Harrods, restaurants, theatres, opera, concerts. We had our own medieval abbey at Kirkstall and our own stately home at Temple Newsam. And Leeds had what London had not – for who notices London's choked spluttering of colleges? – at its very heart a university, proclaiming by its centrality and visibility that it is truly a civic university.

When we announced our impending move to Leeds, our metropolitan friends and even our children looked at us pityingly, as if we had been condemned to life-long exile in some uncharted, inaccessible arctic waste up near John o'Groats, but once we were settled I allowed none to use unanswered of Leeds the deliberately double-edged description 'a provin-cial city'. I spat back angrily whenever, by blatant emphasis, my Oxbridge associates made pejorative the term 'provincial university'.

It was in truth the cosmopolitanism of the University which made easy my translation from administrator to pedagogue in my earlier years at Leeds. The student-body was drawn from every corner of the British Isles and from all over the world; it was said that Leeds had more overseas students than any other university in the Kingdom. Scholars came to us from all the Continents, some for brief visits, many to teach with us or to undertake long-term research. Leeds professors and lecturers were constantly on the move, teaching, examining or consulting in distant places.

Largely because of the example and leadership of Derry Jeffares, the School of English contributes more than any other department to the congenial bustle which is to a university essential if it is to guard itself against inwardness, intellectual incest and social sterility. and I followed eagerly where Derry led.

In the years when I was at Leeds I went, as invited lecturer or scholar, twice to Australasia, once to Latin America, once to India and Pakistan, several times into Europe and annually to North America. Our home was to all intents an hotel for visitors from other British and overseas universities and, because our previous experience had been more generous than is usual among academics, we added to its register also an international assortment of publishers, poets, novelists, actors, diplomats and soldiers.

Robert Lowell came first, and after him no guest seemed difficult to handle.

Worth Howard had introduced me to Lowell's poetry when, I suspect with intent, he had left on my bedside-table in Maadi a periodical containing some of his earliest published poems,and since the War I had read everything he wrote. I was one of the many who perceived in his work qualities rarely propitious for the future of American poetry but I knew, too, that because he accepted readily and exercised brilliantly the duty of a poet that he shrive his readers of complacency, Lowell made Americans uneasy. For me he stood tall among contemporaries, American and British, for his genius in reconciling the private demands of poetry with public responsibility to comment on the spiritual and political problems of our times. I respected above all his capacity to speak at one and the same time as clarion-voiced advocate for the continuance of the New England tradition and as the harshest and shrewdest critic of the hypocrisies of his countrymen – and of all mankind. But I knew also that the man himself was anything but the quiet rebel as revealed by his poetry, that in social circumstances he could be boorish, that he was apt to be unprincipled in his dealings with women, that he was often in melancholy and even more often drink-sodden. All this was common gossip but that it was true had been confirmed for me by his closest and oldest friend, the anthropologist, Robert Gardner.

Bob is himself a Boston Brahmin, a member of one of those families which, like the Lowells, 'speak only to God'. His forebears had added museums to 'the home of the beans and the cod', his grandmother was that famed Isabella Gardner who sought expiation for her great riches by scrubbing the doorstep of neighbours far less fortunate while dressed in mink coat and pearls. His sister, also Isabella, was successor to Harriet Monroe and Ezra Pound (he for a brief spell) as editor of Chicago's prestigious *Poetry: A Magazine of Verse*. I had met Lowell first in Bob's home in Cambridge, Massachusetts and then, as on the few occasions thereafter when we had been together, he had behaved impeccably but Bob had spoken often about Lowell and so it was with some trepidation that, in my first months as Professor, I advanced his name to the University as a candidate for an honorary degree.

Perhaps because I was new and had not yet had time to make enemies, my recommendation was accepted and I wrote to Lowell.

His reply was friendly – he addressed me by my first name and signed himself Cal – and almost boyish. No other university, not even those with which his association was intimate, Harvard, Kenyon and Vanderbilt, had honoured him with a doctorate. (In the event Columbia beat Leeds by a short head.)

Cal came to Leeds. At the end of the luncheon given at one of the women's halls of residence by the University, in order to get him to the degree ceremony Kippe had to root him out from the bushes into which he had disappeared with a red-headed student-waitress. After he had become Dr Robert Lowell (Leeds) grudgingly, and ineffectively, he recorded for our departmental library a few of his poems and that evening, during a party at our house, he complained whenever his glass was momentarily empty and insulted each of our guests in turn, but when, at about one in the morning, we were left alone he asked shyly if we would care to listen to him reading from the page-proofs of his latest collection of poems. This performance, for us a privilege somewhat diminished by exhaustion, lasted for two hours and continued over breakfast to the moment when the taxi-driver who was to take him to the station was banging impatiently on our front-door.

He hugged me, kissed Kippe and the last that we ever saw of Cal Lowell was his head out of the taxi-window and his hand waving as he was driven down the road. When Kippe went to tidy the guest-room, she found on the bed a package wrapped in newspaper. Inside were four volumes of his poems all signed in a hand which, when deciphered, seemed to give the inscription 'To Catherine and Jack in gratitude and affection from their friend Cal Lowell'.

Leeds, and most obviously the School of English, suffered not at all from the disease of unsociability which infected the University of Geneva and in four years, whenever both Derry and I were in town, scarce a week went by when Kippe and I were not at a party in the Jeffares' home, an ungainly, five-storeyed, late Victorian house overlooking Roundhay golf-course, with a bathroom embellished by Quentin Bell murals.

Jeanne Jeffares pitied me for my lack of faith in her white magic but she was unfailingly benevolent to my whims and, as Derry, lavishly attentive to the care of all her guests.

At the Jeffares' parties academics from Leeds and from universities all

over the world, poets, painters, musicians and prosperous Leeds businessmen talked for hours on end about the arts, about the miserliness of the
University Grants Committee, the dissolute behaviour of some of our colleagues and the indolence of others. We stood on the stairs and in the corridors or we sat, long after the meal was finished. our pleasure in discussion
almost obliterating from notice the discomfiting hardness of the benches.

In those years of delighted debate, Derry and I developed to perfection
a new course for the School of English. We were both of us dismayed by
the miserably restricted literacy of most of our students, even of those who
would soon graduate, ostensibly as experts in literature. We could but
accept that it was no fault of theirs that they had read so little that was not
included in the syllabus of school or university, we blamed it on the continuous and sadistic examination process to which the young are subjected,
but we thought to lift their horizons by instituting a course with a reading-
list of books which all students should have read but most had not, my
Uncle Tom's Cabin for Derry's *Harry Lorrequer*, his *Moonfleet* for my *Prisoner
of Zenda*. There were represented in our list many authors – Chesterton,
Tom Moore, Stevenson among them – who came close to meriting inclu-
sion in a conventional university course but, disparagingly but by no means
dismissively, we labelled all as 'seminal trash'.

We had no hope that we would see our course in the University
Calendar but construction eased a little our consciences, allowed us to for-
get, sometimes for hours, that we were ourselves duty-bound to be
Torquemadas of the examination-rooms.

For several years after my move to Leeds, I was so enthralled by my
new activities that as best I could I shut my eyes to the blemishes in the
society of a big university.

Accustomed as I was to working long hours for fifty weeks in every
year, then and ever after I was irritated by the wailing about overwork set
up by junior colleagues who, for only a little over half the year, were
committed to no more than ten of what university administrators call
inelegantly 'contact hours'. Irritation turned to indignation when I discovered that, though all claimed to be active in research and writing, the
profound works of original scholarship of which they were forever boast-
ing too often materialized as pedantic little articles or nit-picking reviews
in obscure learned journals.

At first I was disappointed, even disillusioned, because so many even of
my senior colleagues were both uninformed and uninterested in anything
that was not immediately relevant to their own expertise. In time I found
some whom I could not diagnose as sufferers from intellectual myopia but
I was never given cause to doubt that there is another and related disease,
paranoid concern to keep petty private empires inviolate against rivals and
potential supplanters, which is endemic among academics. Of this I saw
many examples in my fourteen years at Leeds, to me the most brazen
because it affected me personally, the petty affair of the pioneering course

on publishing established by the School of English.

I was the only member of the University staff who had practical experience of publishing, students from all over the University came to seek my advice about careers in the trade but when, on the only occasion that I was ever asked to comment on the proposed course, I voiced the view that study of publishing was futile if it paid no heed to the practicalities, to contracts, promotion, costings and sales, profit-and-loss accounts, my mild criticism was met with silence and fixed stares such as might be accorded to one who has uttered a Manichean oath at the altar-rail. For all that the course was given in the room next to mine, not once in five or six years was I invited to contribute.

There is a price to be paid for the manifold advantages of belonging to a university which has not been banished into green fields. When lectures finish,students scurry to the pubs, to distant halls-of-residences or to the sordid lodgings which so many prefer to the palaces provided by the University; professors and lecturers, like any office- or factory-worker, take car or train out into the suburbs or to the villages beyond the city boundaries. Neither students nor teachers have much chance of acquiring corporate feeling, the pride of membership in a close-knit community of scholars.

Because our home was closer to the campus than the homes of most of the staff, it was not difficult for us to overcome my initial disappointment that there was at Leeds so little opportunity for contact with students outside tutorial-rooms and lecture-halls. At first, students came to Cliff Cottage only by invitation and even then with some show of reluctance, as if they suspected us of trying for some unjustified advantage, but soon Cliff Cottage became an acceptable rendezvous. Students came to us for advice about their academic progress, about their future careers, about their love-life. Because they found it easy to unburden themselves of the burden of intimate problems to a middle-aged married couple they thought more worldly than is common in academe, we were made father- and mother-confessor to tales of abortions and pregnancies. But mostly they came just to use Cliff Cottage as a cross between a club and a home away from home, to drink our whisky and our wine or to use our bathroom when the plumbing failed in their own sordid lodgings.

There was no similar practical and simple release for the frustration I felt for the almost total absence of social and intellectual contact between academics in different disciplines. I came to know the Medical Faculty, particularly the ophthalmologists, only too well, principally in their non-academic professional capacity, others became to me familiar for their generally inapposite and often lengthy interventions in committees or Senate. But I doubt that I would ever have established intimacy with any outwith the School of English had it not been for my Army background and Jeffares' hospitality.

By the time I joined the University such old soldiers as once there had been in the professoriate had, most of them, either died or faded away into retirement. The Bursar, himself a veteran of the Western Desert, bullied me into accepting, as substitute for my Royal Marine Commando predecessor, Douglas Grant, election to the committee which served as link between the University and the Forces and which supervised, if remotely, the Officers Training Corps and the Air Squadron.

The OTC when first I knew it was much reviled by politically active students and academics, and even by those more charitable but no less ignorant considered to be obsessed by hierarchy. I found still lively in the OTC, as nowhere else in the University, that sensitive care for subordinates, that affectionate respect for superiors which had won my admiration when I was a serving-soldier,and the OTC still preserved that remarkable military capacity to shift in a moment from the unquestioning order of parade-ground or training-area to the easy egalitarianism of the Mess.

I gained much from sitting on the MAFEC (the Services have not abandoned their addiction to acronyms). I went once to Rhine Army and there sat as guest-of-honour at a Mess Night of my old regiment with, spread out on the table before me, all the silver which I had last seen thirty years earlier when I helped to pack it for storage before we left Rawalpindi. I was invited to a Master Gunners' dinner at Woolwich, where I was re-united with my immediate superior on 3 Corps HQ, by 1976 Lieutenant-General Sir Terence McMeekin. I participated in the deliberations of the Regular Army Officers Selection Board, the most scrupulous selection-process that ever I have witnessed. The most useful benefit was access to the OTC Mess, the best and the cheapest club in town, where I talked on equal terms with undergraduates from all the Faculties – the girls the most attractive of all our students – and not only with colleagues from other disciplines but also with men and women who, other than interest in the OTC, had no connection with the University. But the most enduring of the gifts granted me by this association with things military was friendship with Alan Roberts.

Alan, perhaps twenty years my junior, is the most frenetically energetic and the most versatile of all my friends. By profession an internationally renowned medical engineer, he is also an enthusiastic Territorial, a silver-smith, a Justice of the Peace and, though never on the staff at Leeds, an enthusiastic participant in the governance of the University. When first I met him he was Second-in-Command of the OTC. Later he was promoted to command and later still made a red-banded full colonel and an ADC to the Queen, both honours rarely given to an amateur soldier. He has recently achieved the distinction, rare and in all probability unique for a university Pro-Chancellor of presenting himself to the Chancellor of another university to be hooded as a successful candidate for an earned Ph.D.

With Alan and a few other enthusiasts, I helped to found the Defence Studies Dining Club and thereby opened to myself opportunities to sit over my port listening to authoritative forecasts of impending doom expressed, almost always with urbanity and sometimes wittily, by generals, admirals and senior airmen (and once, with awesome dreariness by Edward Heath), to enjoy post-prandial gossip, on almost every topic except defence, and Laphroaig poured with a benevolent unparsimonious hand by mess-jacketed BSM Kent and Sergeant Murphy.

It was Derry Jeffares who introduced me to Philip James, the most eminent of the University's several eminent Professors of Law. I have always been attracted to lawyers; I envy them for their orderly minds and for the intellectual agility which allows them to argue with the passion of conviction either side in a case; and occasionally in the last forty years I have regretted that I did not stay for more than three weeks in a military hospital to complete, as then the only bearable alternatives to tatting and basket-weaving, my own studies for the Bar examinations, but never in all the years we have been friends have Philip and I discussed tort or malfeasance. Philip sustains by gruff voice and sardonic expression an austere front but behind that front there is a dancing intellect and such warmth as I have found in few academics – and there is Wybetty, his bubbling, affectionate and handsome Dutch wife.

I came in time to acquaintance with colleagues from other parts of the University that was closer than nodding, but only with Philip James to lasting friendship.

As earlier had Michael Flanders, so by his courage did John Younger persuade me to mock my own self-pity. At first my student and later my colleague, John went blind when already launched into a career, an almost unbearable blow for a painter. Instead of surrendering, as I with far less reason had so nearly surrendered, to vicious fate John had come to the University, took a First in English and was appointed to a lectureship. Every teaching day, with only his dog as companion, he took train from Halifax to Leeds and marched up from the city station to the School.

I was blessed, in the School of English we were all blessed, by two guardian angels, Audrey Stead, the ever-patient, indefatigable Administrative Assistant and our porter, Jim Dodd.

Dodd is one of those personalities, a character, whose presence gives life to an institution. So very Irish that at times it seemed as if he was speaking a foreign language, because we had both served in the War he selected me for especial care. He cosseted me as none other in the School, fed me with coffee and gossip and, he more widely-read than most of the professional experts in the School, honoured me with his opinions on books, politicians – and our fellows in the School and University.

For most of my time, the School of English was housed in a building designed by architects maniacally determined to make casual encounters impossible and other than with John Younger and those teaching American Literature I was seldom in close contact with any of my juniors (though one, Robert Welch, became a friend after he had moved on to a Chair in Northern Ireland). My peers were, with one notorious exception, all amiable colleagues and three of them – Derry Jeffares, Stewart

Sanderson and William Walsh – originals, endowed with sprightly intellects and humanity.

Stewart and his wife Alison are vociferously Scottish, both suffered the unendurable pangs of exile in a primitive land, but their charity to Kippe and to me, two aborigines, was unending and, as few others in Leeds, except the Jeffares and, I like to think, the Morpurgos – and often with the assistance of their closest friend, an Edinburgh professor but a Sassenach, the archaeologist Stewart Piggott, 'Stewart the Dig' – they made their home a club for students and staff, for visiting examiners and even for Englishmen. Though at times I showed insufficient respect for the discipline which he had pioneered for Leeds, Folk Life Studies, I have never suspected Stewart 'the Myth' of wearing the blinkers which condemned many around me to tunnel-vision. He published a perceptive critical study of Hemingway and he moved frequently and easily among writers and artists, if mostly in Edinburgh. Above all as aid to sociability he is worldly.

Worldliness was never the most evident of William Walsh's attributes. A shrewd administrator and, of all I observed at the byzantine business of University politics, both the most active and the most deft, he was even so given to occasional *naïvetés* – hard though I tried I could never persuade him that 'publisher' is not a synonym for 'gentleman' – but these lapses in sophistication added a softening touch of boyish innocence to a personality which might otherwise be awesome. There are,indeed,those who find William formidable, who are cowed by his fluency and verbal elegance, his erudition and his pungent wit but, for my part, had I gained nothing else from Leeds, the many hours I spent in his company would be recompense sufficient to justify the move from London.

University reputations are apt to be over-blown by university men and women. In truth,other than those self-assured television dons who pontificate over the media on every topic from the imminence of nuclear destruction to the price of cabbages, few academics are known to the citizenry of Budleigh Salterton or Thurso. I doubt that there was at Leeds more than a handful of scholars whose names would have won immediate recognition even on campuses outside Britain, let alone from an audience of informed readers. William is one of that handful. Those who are qualified to judge accept as seminal his *Use of Imagination* and his *Coleridge: The Work and the Relevance* is by them unanimously honoured. As for me, who in adolescence worshipped at Coleridge's portrait and have remained an unquestioning idolator ever since, any writer who can, as William, comprehend my unsaintly saint and can communicate his comprehension, merits and receives my gratitude.

William came to Leeds originally to be Professor of Education and he was one of the contributors to the 'Black Book' notable or notorious according to the political opinions of the commentator, but even when he was teaching teachers, literature was his compelling passion. (One of his graduate students reported to me that Professor Walsh's lectures on educa-

tion were the finest lectures on poetry he had ever heard.) Even while still
Chairman of the Education Department, William taught also in the School
of English and when, as one of those innovative exercises which at that
time made Leeds a leader among universities, the University established
Britain's first Chair of Commonwealth Literature, there could be only one
candidate for election: William Walsh.

In his undergraduate days a disciple of that arch-creator of disciples, F.
R. Leavis, thereafter he removed himself a step or so from the feet of his
Gamaliel, if never far enough to satisfy my anti-Leavisite prejudice, and
never so far as to make it impossible for him to write a book on Leavis.
(When *F. R. Leavis* appeared in 1981, I commented unkindly 'littler fleas
have littlest fleas'.) Never so exclusively obsessed with masterpieces as his
Cambridge mentor, without ever betraying the verities of criticism,
William used his critical energy on behalf of writers from English-speaking
countries other than the two great literary powers, Britain and the United
States, and, with no abatement of elegance, as readily for the worthy as for
the few indubitable masters. A critic of an older and nobler strain than is
the crabbed genus which commonly finds its habitat on university campuses
for him analysis is important but only as a means of enlightening and
enlivening readers.

I admire William's critical percipience and I envy his elegance, yet it is
not by his published works but by his company that he enriched my years
at Leeds.

In Senate I sat usually between William and Derry. Through hour after
hour of dreary and often pointless debate, I scribbled light verse, Derry
decorating the margins of his papers with drawings of vintage cars, William
drafting chapters for his next book. Derry and I allowed nothing to interrupt our absorbing activities but William was possessed of a sense not given
to us. Alerted by some heresy proclaimed on the far side of the Chamber,
he would stack his papers neatly, rise to his feet, catch the Vice-
Chancellor's eye and, with supporting gestures worthy of Martin Harvey,
launch himself into oratory, his every word selected from the vast closet of
his vocabulary with all the fastidiousness that a Regency buck gave to the
choice of a garment, his phrases fashioned as dexterously as Beau Brummell
tying a cravat. Excoriation completed and the offender dismayed into
nonentity, William would sit down and, without pause, return to the sentence he had been writing on Patrick White or R. K. Narayan.

Every morning in term when we were both free, he joined me for coffee. We talked of many things, 'of shoes, and ships, and sealing-wax. . .' of
cricket, poetry and the ineptitude of some of our colleagues. Often he
came to Cliff Cottage and there, standing in the centre of the sitting-room,
as extravagant gesture to make emphatic to a mesmerized audience the
weight of his orotund sentences, he tossed matches misspent on his
unlightable pipe in the general direction of the unlit fire.

But, in all the years when we were engaged in dialogue never once did

William allow me to finish a sentence.

Before my metamorphosis, I had been for a quarter-of-a-century a published author, but for most of that time authorship had been a profession subsidiary to other demanding activities and practised at week-ends or before breakfast. Now as don, and so duty-bound to research and publication, I could devote to writing all such time and energy as was not committed to teaching.

My years at Leeds added much to my bibliography. Not even the most captious commentator could dismiss as inconsistent with the remit of a Professor of American Literature an edition of an obscure novel by Fenimore Cooper, or a collection of the American writings of the most curmudgeonly and most articulate infantryman ever promoted to warrant-rank, not even though William Cobbett had vilified universities as 'dens of dunces'. My book on Benedict Arnold and John André, and my history of William and Mary could perhaps be faulted as acts of trespass across the demarcation-line into the province of the School of History but both, and notably *Their Majesties' Royall Colledge*, were obviously products of sturdy research and the history as heavily footnoted as any doctorial thesis. Two of the books published in those years, biographies of Barnes Wallis and Allen Lane, though both were founded on research thorough and more intractable than I had given to any other book (except perhaps the College's history), were both patently on topics foreign to the discipline in which my University title gave me authority and, even greater cause for raised eyebrows in the huge works-canteen which at Leeds passes as the Senior Common Room, both were serialized, *Barnes Wallis* in the *Sunday Times* and *Allen Lane: King Penguin* in the *Guardian*, and both were entered in what, with poetic licence, the popular press calls 'best-seller lists'. The academic fraternity is more charitable to colleagues whose sins are scarlet than ever it is to those whose books are read.

I had waited for almost half the allotted life-span for the fulfilment of Dr Swem's prophecy, that some day I would write the history of William and Mary, so long indeed that I had given up hope that the invitation would ever come. Even when, in 1970, I was asked to produce a plan, though I was flattered that the College should so honour its first British graduate, I was still far from confident that the book would ever come to print.

There were, during the first years when I was working on *Their Majesties' Royall Colledge: William and Mary in the Seventeenth and Eighteenth Cent-uries*, problems far more traumatic than any involved in the business of research and writing. The original intention that it be a collaborative effort proved impracticable and, to achieve publication as part of Virginia's contribution to the national celebration of the bicentenary of Independence, I was forced to risk estrangement from two much-loved old friends. The research assistant employed for me by the College was at first both keen and efficient but, after she had been sent to Leeds to work more closely with me, she took to pursuits more immediately pleasurable than delving through ancient documents and at the last, while I was in Australia, she deserted me without notice, leaving me to handle those tasks which call for good eye-sight: proof-reading, indexing and the choice of illustrations.

There were, however, many compensations. Kippe and I spent three Long Vacations in Williamsburg and, though in July and August Tidewater, Virginia is more humid than the Persian Gulf, those months as truly a resident revived in me that sense of belonging which had been mine as an undergraduate. As guest of the Rockefeller Foundation, I wrote the final draft of the text in surroundings more luxurious and more conducive to sustained authorship than any I had experienced previously: in a magnificently modernized thirteenth-century turret-room overlooking the two arms of Lake Como.

There were also compensations more trivial but no less satisfying. By taking into my hand the pre-history of the College which preceded the grant of a Royal Charter in 1693 and by mischievously using as trump-card evidence provided by its one vaunted senior, Harvard, I was able to play the game of priorities more sensationally than ever it had been played before, even by a college which is adept in this pastime. I proved, at least to my own satisfaction, that William and Mary need no longer cringe as America's second oldest college but has the right to boast that it is older than Harvard.

A lucky serendipitist, as twice before in my life (when discovering the Dunmore Papers and the unpublished letters of Thomas Gwatkin, the Tory William and Mary professor) when searching for evidence on something quite other in a London solicitor's office, I stumbled on the briefs and supporting documents, still tied with pink ribbon, relating to the case taken by the College after the Revolution in an impertinent, and deservedly unsuccessful, attempt to win back the income derived from the bequest of Robert Boyle which, properly, the British Government had denied to rebellious Colonials when they dared to call themselves independent.

It was of little significance to the History, but gratifying to me, that I also found an answer to a question which had perplexed me from the moment when first I began to be interested in Colonial America, but which I had never seen posed, let alone answered, by any of the recognized authorities. How could seventeenth and eighteenth century American Episcopalians take Communion when there was no bishop and therefore no Confirmation in any of the Thirteen Colonies? I wrote to ecclesiastical historians on both sides of the Atlantic, I consulted experts in Canon Law, and at last the explanation came from almost next door, from the man who had chaired the committee which had brought me to Leeds, from John Moorman, Bishop of Ripon. The mystery is resolved with mystical prescience by the qualifying clause to the last rubric in 'The Order of Confirmation': 'And there shall none be admitted to the holy

Communion, until such time as he be confirmed, *or be ready and desirous to be confirmed.*'

I delivered the typescript of the History by hand to the Washington D.C. publisher just before leaving for my first visit to Australasia. Back in England in time for the Long Vacation of 1975, I was yet again submitted to the ministrations of an ophthalmic surgeon and when the time came for us to fly out to the States so that I could sign the three hundred copies of the limited edition, I could not so much as see the legs of the air-hostess on the plane which took us to Washington. Even so, I was obstinately determined to use a calligraphic pen and, throughout most of the three days which was all I could spare from teaching, Kippe stood at my side tenderly removing from their slip-cases three hundred copies of a book printed on hand-made paper, leather-bound, lavishly embellished with gold leaf, both of us terrified lest I ruin with an ink-blot even one of a book priced at $250. Pride cleared my vision, I managed all without a blemish and, better still, I could see well enough to appreciate that. though against my not-so-mild protests, the designer had persisted with his pro-claimed intention to order the text in double-columns, (a format much favoured by Americans, which I abominate), whatever its literary or histor-ical shortcomings, he had made of my work, in both its limited and trade editions, a rarely elegant tribute to the College and to the memory of Dr Swem.

A few months later we were again in Williamsburg and, six years to the day after the College had added my name to its list of honorary doctors which had begun with Benjamin Franklin, on Charter Day, 8 February, in the year of America's Bicentennial, I stood again next to the President on the platform of Phi Beta Kappa Hall, this time to introduce *Their Majesties' Royall Colledge*.

No other of my books has given me so much satisfaction because no other, except *The Christ's Hospital Book*, was written to repay a debt and to The Christ's Hospital Book I contributed only one essay and a deal of edi-torial activity. I could but be gratified by the story that *Their Majesties' Royall Colledge* is unique in that it was presented, formally and with per-mission, to the Queen of England, the President of the United States and the President of the French Republic. Not one of the three has made any comment to me but the book was received favourably in many quarters – though the Richmond paper spelt my name incorrectly throughout a long review – and if I have any regret it is that, since the first outburst of hon-our and enthusiasm, the College appears to have forgotten that it has a published history.

There is an affliction of the spirit which is, I believe, endemic among authors and which I suffer most often and most severely when I am mid-way through a manuscript. It is then, as I look at the hundreds of blank pages waiting to be filled, that I ask myself what lunacy drove me to begin this book, why indeed I ever took to the lonely and frustrating business of authorship? Despondency in this kind is short-lived; long before the book is finished I am asking myself 'What next?'

It was so as I approached the final chapters of the College History, but of one thing I was determined, I would never again write the biography of a contemporary. For many hours in almost every day for five years I had stationed myself as an observer of the events and personalities of the seventeenth and eighteenth centuries, and this experience, coming as it did after three years of obsessive attention to Barnes Wallis, had convinced me that the historian who deals with times long past is more comfortably placed than his fellow whose business is his own times. He need not fear that what he writes will harm or hurt innocent protagonists, he has the support of predecessor commentators, and time has served as an efficient editor to guard him from a superfluity of evidence.

I considered a biography of Cobbett. Soldier turned writer, turned reforming politician, he seemed a subject nicely suited to my taste for working in the middle territory between Literature and History. Never more English than when he was living in the United States, when in England he had been among his contemporaries the best-informed and generally the most charitable commentator on America and so, it appeared, appropriate to such expertise as I possessed. As I had, so had he suffered for a while in the dreary wastes of New Brunswick.

I prepared a synopsis, my publisher was interested and then – another of those sorrows to which an author becomes accustomed but never hardened – we picked up the intelligence that another reputable writer was working on Cobbett. My ambitious plan was abandoned.

At that moment, no more than three weeks before I wrote the last paragraph of the College History, Bob Lusty suggested a life of Allen Lane and in the delights of some obligatory wrangling over a contract, I forgot my vow.

Once the agreement was signed, I woke to the full horror of the commitment. What was now before me was an ascent of Everest, the *Barnes Wallis* by comparison a stroll up Highgate Hill.

Barnes had been my friend but he had had little influence on my professional life and I none on his. Allen had been at times my Prospero and at others my Iago, he had fashioned and he had disrupted my career, my association with him had driven my family to the boundaries of disaster and had blessed it with benefits beyond measure. In the biography of Barnes Wallis I had made only one brief and anonymous appearance, but as Allen's chronicler I could allow myself no similar reticence for, as his fellow-grandfather and for such part as I had played in the Penguin story, I must allow to myself an occasional appearance front-stage. The history of our relationship was, to the best of my knowledge, the most vivid of all the many examples of conflict between malevolence and benevolence in Allen's complex character.

Before I began work on the biography of Barnes Wallis, I knew his wife but none of his children and none of those still living who had advanced or frustrated his work and, though I was determined to avoid causing distress unless it was unavoidable, I had no fear that I would be hampered in my quest for the truth by friendship or affection. In the event, it needed no strenuous exercise of discretion to present Wallis as a man of almost boring probity; not even the most eager panther could have scratched up from the evidence more than one tid-bit for the titillation of voyeurs and even that tiny chink in his moral armour I revealed only by a sly aside.

Allen had been alternately miserly and prodigal but I was convinced of his financial integrity. I had reason to believe that, though his reputation as Lothario was deserved, he himself spread it abroad in hyperbolic form in part to add the spice of danger to the delectable sauce of good looks and easy charm which he set before every woman he met, in part to add yet one more myth to the anthology of self-created fables in which he was hero or villain, and I had cause to suspect that he was by choice and activity a two-woman man.

I had known almost everyone closely associated with Allen, some, among them his widow and Ron Blass, his longest-serving collaborator at Penguin and his most ardent admirer, were my friends, his daughter Clare my much-cherished daughter-in-law.

I saw as a potential inhibition to objectivity even my one intervention in Penguin affairs after Allen's death, for I could never rid myself of the indignation inflamed by the brutish and callous treatment then meted out to Clare and, ever after, though as a passive if informed onlooker, I could never convince myself that the developments I observed in the firm were worthy of its former glories.

In the weeks after I committed myself, I saw also in front of me a practical problem which at the time seemed insuperable: three of the principal witnesses to the life and achievements of Allen Lane, his widow, his sister and his surviving brother, were all living in Australia. And I knew too that, as with my *Barnes Wallis*, I had in front of me the difficult passage through the mine-fields of oral history.

In 1945, at the time when the firm was celebrating its tenth birthday and Allen the mortification of the many false prophets who at its foundation had forecast, hopefully, that it would not last even for one year, I had asked Allen himself and six of his pioneering collaborators the identical question, 'Why the name Penguin?' and had been given seven different answers. Thirty years on and Allen dead, I put that question again to the six survivors. Back came six disparate replies, by now all well-rehearsed, and from four respondents a rider, in each case phrased according to the nature of the individual and yet all carrying similar meaning: 'No need to labour the point in your book but it could be useful to you to know that it was I who dreamed up the name Penguin.'

Ron Blass, Lettice and Clare all encouraged me. Allen merited a biography and I must be his biographer. The Australian National University offered me a Fellowship at its Humanities Research Centre, and by so doing not only made it feasible for me to interview Allen's three closest relatives in his own generation but also opened up to me the wondrous prospect of using six months of the first and only sabbatical year of my life for little else than research and writing.

Before we left for Canberra I called on the Vice Chancellor of Leeds.

Edward Boyle and I had met first thirty years earlier, at the last of Francis Hirst's house-parties, and in those thirty years time and time again we had tripped over each other's heels. He went to America with the Oxford Union debating-team which included also Anthony Wedgwood Benn: on my first lecture-tour, I followed the same itinerary and often we coincided on some distant campus. When he was Minister of Education, it was frequently my duty as Director of the NBL to visit his Curzon Street office to seek some benefit for books. He followed me as one of Allen Lane's chosen people. In my last year at the League he was Longman's Deputy Chairman. I went to Leeds; twelve months later he was appointed the University's Vice Chancellor. Familiarity, however, had bred only mutual wariness.

Boyle watched me suspiciously for signs of that same haughtiness towards him which undoubtedly had been evident when – he a precocious, pompous and ungainly undergraduate and I still dignified by uniform, rank-badges, medal-ribbons and a six-year tan – we had first come together as guests at the Cobden House and, with justice, he blamed me for the currency on the Leeds campus of stories (learnt from Mark Longman) about his Eton schooldays unflattering to his personality and unbecoming to the dignity of a Vice Chancellor.

That he was earnest in his care for the University I could not doubt, nor did I question that we were fortunate in having as nominal head a man who had spent most of his adult years shuffling up and down the corridors of power, but dignity was a word I could never associate with one so utterly bereft of social grace. His political past I might have honoured more had he not dragged into every conversation 'what we said in the Cabinet' but as it was, I, a right-wing Liberal, dismissed his lukewarm Conservatism as unprincipled, castigated as betrayal his opposition to independent and grammar schools, and dismissed as nothing better than currying popularity, the equivalent of baby-kissing, even his most trivial actions, as for example his abandoning the Vice Chancellor's official car in favour of the local buses.

Not all my reasons for mistrusting Boyle were trivial. I did not forget that in my time of crisis at the NBL he had not so much as acknowledged my plea for his support, nor did I forgive him for absenting himself from the meeting which had hustled me out of office. But even our mutually held enthusiasms, for cricket and for music, were marred by blemishes which denied empathy. I spurned his cricketing-lore on the grounds that it was only a zest for statistics and, though I could but accept that his knowledge of music was far greater than mine, I refused to recognize as comrade in music a man who chose as his most favoured composer my pet hate among musicians, Arnold Schoenberg.

I doubt that it ever troubled Edward Boyle that he could not come to terms with the Professor of American Literature, and nor was I much concerned that I could not summon up sufficient charity to shake off my habitual incapacity to tolerate neuters but, however deep the chasm between us, I had reason far more substantial than protocol for consulting the Vice Chancellor before I began work on the life of Allen Lane. In the year before Allen's death, when his dominion over the empire he had created was failing, Boyle had been his Deputy Chairman and in the months after Allen died, Boyle had been Acting Chairman of Penguins. I needed his evidence, even though I must regard him as potentially a hostile witness.

Only once in the years when we had been together at Leeds had Boyle admitted that he was aware of my long connection with Penguins, and then inadvertently, after I corrected a statement of his made in my presence at a University dinner when ex cathedra he had told the company of distinguished guests that the best of all Penguin series was the *History of England* 'edited by Jack Plumb'. Not even once had he referred to the fact that Allen's daughter was my daughter-in-law. But these were facts known to everyone connected with the firm and to most of our senior colleagues at Leeds. He knew them and he knew that I knew that he knew them. He could not be so obtuse that he did not know that I had been Clare's ally in her last desperate fight to thwart the plan of the Board over which he presided to subvert her father's wishes for the future of the firm, nor could he possibly believe that Clare would not have told me of the contemptuous and contemptible manner in which he had treated her.

Close to death, Allen had begged of Clare that she find a way to retain some family influence in Penguin; Clare turned to me for advice, and I found for her an adviser far more skilled than I. Peter Rosenwald, an experienced and hard-headed financier,accepted the role without thought for personal glory or personal gain but only because as David Roberts's son-in-law he recognized the obligations of long friendship between our two families. He gave to it all the finesse which had made him a success on both sides of the Atlantic. He enlisted the aid of Rothschilds and produced as alternative to the scheme envisaged by the Penguin Board a proposal which merited at very least scrupulous consideration and courtesy. It had been Boyle who, using the privilege of the Chair and the slim pretext that Peter was not a lawyer, had ruled that he could not accompany Clare to the meeting at the Carlton Club called ostensibly to discuss his plan, and it had been Boyle who had been of all the directors the most peremptory in dismissing the Rosenwald proposals.

I could not credit that Edward Boyle would look with favour or ease on the prospect of a biography of Allen Lane written by a survivor from Penguin's Golden Age who was also Clare's father-in-law.

In the event,when we met Boyle's interest was only a trifle more evident than it would have been had I told him that I was beginning work on a life of Thomas Jefferson. He offered to hand over to me what he described as 'a highly significant collection' of letters from Allen, a promise which, despite a dozen reminders, was never fulfilled and which, because I knew that Allen seldom wrote 'highly significant' letters, I had treated with some scepticism from the first. He agreed to allow me to cross-question him and that, again after many reminders, he did, but to little effect. Whenever I came close to some awkward matter, as is the custom of politicians, he answered a question I had not asked.

At the time, however, when Boyle received so casually my announcement that I had been commissioned to write Allen's biography I did wonder if I had misjudged him, if perhaps he was so earnest for the truth that he was prepared to accept it from wheresoever it came. Later, when the book was published and had been much lauded in the press, I revised my opinion. Boyle, I decided, was so certain of his own infallibility that he did not even notice comment that questioned his judgement, so convinced of his rectitude that he could not believe that his behaviour was ever other than impeccable. He did not thank me for the copy of the book I sent him and when, in part as consequence of the biography, the *Yorkshire Post* gave me its Special Literary Award, the Vice Chancellor stayed silent. (Perhaps in some obscure way he was offended by the sight of a Leeds professor being thus associated with Harold Macmillan, one of only two previous recipients of the honour and the one man who had publicly put down Edward Boyle.) In the years that followed he did not once mention to me the biography, Allen Lane, Penguins or my Clare.

16

Don on the Move

Australia is ill-served by many of its visible exports. In my youth I had gloried in the grace of Bradman and not even the paralysis that he wrought among the batsmen who were my heroes could nullify my admiration for Grimmett's cunning, but my stereotype Australians were the drunken street-brawling officers our convoy had left behind in Durban gaols and their beer-swilling younger countrymen on London's 'Cobber Row'. Within minutes of landing for the first time in Australia, I had reason to believe that the image of an Australian which I had for so long carried in my mind was fallacious; the Customs officer at the airport was the politest and most welcoming that ever I had encountered anywhere in the world; and in the next months, as with every successive visit, my affection for Australians and my respect for Australian culture grew.

It is true that I was peculiarly blessed, for the Australian National University is the best of all vantage-points from which to view that aspect of Australian life which contradicts the national reputation for uncouthness. Of all of the universities I knew, none, except perhaps the University of British Columbia, has a more gracious campus than ANU's, stretched along the mimosa shores of Lake Burley Griffin. Yet it was not the elegance of the setting which impressed me, but rather the unpretentious air of cultured commitment general among both staff and students. (Is there in all the world another university which boasts a living poet at work in a building named in his honour? Alec Hope's room was a few yards down the corridor from the office allotted to me in the A.D. Hope Building.)

Twentieth-century man shrieks protest at the chaos he himself has created in his cities but perversely is made uncomfortable by purity. The Australian capital is flagrantly modern and yet utterly free of the detritus of modernity – no bill-boards, no neon-signs, no pollution. I doubt that I could ever dare to love such a prim virgin. It was ANU and not Canberra which won my affection, which for a while tempted me to stay for the rest of my working life.

Something of the same vigour, something of the same freshness of enthusiasm which we found at ANU, we found in almost all the many universities we visited. And not only in the universities; in all the Australian cities the theatre truly lived, music and the visual arts flourished and everywhere there was interest in literature more active than shabby concern for examination set-books or best-sellers.

True, we moved often in rarefied circles, among academics, publishers, broadcasters, writers and painters, but it is not such as these who fill the startlingly magnificent Sydney Opera House or the arts complex in Adelaide, not such as these who have made possible for Melbourne one of the great art galleries, and certainly it was not such as these who sat with us as we watched a performance in-the-round of a new Australian play in a sociable little theatre on the outskirts of Perth, or roared approval for a Sydney production of *Two Gentlemen of Verona* played in Australian-Italian accents.

Nor was it by any means only this Australian enthusiasm for the arts which attracted me to the Commonwealth. In the mid-1970s Australia was as yet untouched by financial decay, yet paradoxically I was reminded of the United States as I had first known it at the tail-end of the Depression.

Others, and most vocal among them many Australians, have complained that Australia has fallen too readily for the American success-myth. There is force in the complaint but it was not the outward and visible signs, the two-car garages, the swimming-pools, the mink coats, which impressed upon me a sense of *déjà-vu* rather, awareness of some sensibilities reminiscent of that older and nobler America: unfeigned and yet unaggressive pride in community coupled with eagerness to accept and to cosset the stranger and, most surprising of all because it was contrary to all that we had been conditioned to expect, in the Australians even more evident than in the most patently Anglophile Americans, my own Virginians, affection, even admiration, for Britain.

Generalization about national attitudes are futile and almost always fatuous. My sampling of Australia and Australians was both wide and various but far from being scientific, and it could well be that my experience was atypical, but not once in three extensive visits did I see anything which even the most sensitive Englishman could describe as 'Pommie-bashing'. A little affectionate teasing, perhaps, of a kind not uncommon from a young adult to a much-respected and much older family friend. And none of that wistful sentimentality which gulled previous generations of Australians to talk of Britain as Home, but almost without exception the Australians I met thought and spoke of Britain as of no other country, as if its mores were part of their own unwaveringly independent national heritage, its sights, its way of life, its culture integral to their determined individualism.

This paradox of proprietorship in independence, of honour without subservience, was apparent in the universities; on every campus I listened to academics from all disciplines reminiscing about their student-days at Oxford, Cambridge, Manchester, Leeds, on every campus undergraduates consulted me about the possibilities of following the example of their teachers. Evidence of continuing affection for Britain was not confined to the educational élite. Every taxi-driver seemed eager to tell us of cousins in

Pontypool, aunts and uncles in Kirkcudbright or Penzance, and every taxi-driver knew more than we could boast about Pontypool, Penzance or Kirkcudbright. By our admittedly specious reckoning, half the barmaids, more than half the waitresses and all the actresses in Australia were saving money for the air-fare to London.

This magnetism, exercised by London in particular but also by Britain in general, is still for young Australians (and for young New Zealanders) a well-nigh irresistible force, so powerful that it is honoured as a national institution, is given by them a name, Overseas Experience, and treated to the familiarity of acronym. Young Australians (and young New Zealanders). especially it seems the sheilas, look upon OE as an almost inevitable part of the growing-up process. I have found them behind reception-desks in Toronto and Santiago, behind typewriters in Chicago and Stuttgart, at my bedside waiting to take my temperature when I came round from an anaesthetic. The NBL, like many another British institution or commercial organisation, could not have managed without a regular supply of Australian and New Zealand long-term temporaries and my home would have been less contented than it is had we not found our own New Zealander, Meg de Joux, whose OE we hope to make life-long. Though these antipodean envoys work their way into every part of the world, I have never yet met one who does not place Britain high on her itinerary. The magnet works, it seems, even for second generation New Australians. In a smart Melbourne restaurant (there are in Melbourne restaurants as smart as any in London, Paris or New York, and often serv-ing better food), an efficient but friendly waitress (and because of the national repugnance for tipping, Australian waitresses are generally more efficient and always more friendly than their peers elsewhere) gave to Kippe and me, to Eric Westbrook, then a Minister in the Government of Victoria and his painter-wife, and to Lettice Lane an excited exposé of her plan to work for a year in London and then, just as we were leaving, added almost as an afterthought, 'and, of course, I'm going to Thessaloniki, where my parents came from, I've scads of cousins in Greece'.

The most touching and in some ways the most revealing of all evidence to persisting congeniality was even so happily idiosyncratic. We were in Melbourne on the day when the news came through that some lunatic propagandist had vandalised the square at Headingley. Hearing our English accents, first a policeman in the street and then two strangers in an hotel-lounge came up to us to join in outrage at this vile act of sacrilege commit-ted in one of the most holy of all Anglo-Australian shrines.

The contradictions in the Australian attitude to Britain, identification with independence, interest without subservience, I came to regard as an essential element in the national spirit. I saw it everywhere and in all man-ner of Australians but nowhere was it more evident than in Penguins' Australian organisation.

Whenever I entered the Penguin headquarters on the outskirts of

Melbourne every instinct in me cried *déjà-vu*. This was not the modest little brick building on the Bath Road with its outcrop of Nissen huts that I
had known in 1945, and decidedly not either of the grandiose palaces built
latterly to house the masters of a great empire, but Harmondsworth in the
late 1950s, the same efficient and unostentatious design, the same brisk
colour-patterns. Just one addition and I would have been convinced that
Allen Lane's ghost had magicked Harmondsworth to Ringwood: the his-
torically deceitful group-portrait 'The Penguin Editors' which gloats over
the reception hall at Harmondsworth. (And so the staff at Ringwood are
spared the sight of caricatures of Allen, Bill Williams and Glover, of me as
a gargoyle hanging from one wall and glowering across a room in which
the Penguin Editors never met – they never met anywhere in the numbers
pretended by the picture – at a gargoyle of John Lehmann.)

The staff too were much as we had been twenty, thirty even forty years
earlier, most of them young, all of them enthusiastic, all of them evidently
convinced that in serving Penguins they were involved in an adventure,
that Penguin Books was subtly different and more significant than any
other publishing-house. Yet, whether emigré or native-born, every member of the Ringwood staff I came to know was insistent that this was an
Australian institution and even so, being as I perceived it typically
Australian went on to demonstrate loyalty to the Penguin tradition far
more openly than ever I have noticed – admittedly from a distance – in
their British coevals.

When first we went to Melbourne,we stayed with Richard Lane,
Allen's brother, with him (and brother John, killed in the War) co-founder
of the firm and my colleague in my earliest Penguin days. Dick was a marvellously generous host, a rich and willing source for information about
Allen's boyhood; about the time in the late 1920s and early 1930s when
he, John and Allen had made their flat in Talbot Square the headquarters
for a group of like-minded, frolicking young men and women; about their
term in Uncle John's decaying Bodley Head and the birth of Penguins. In
all,the Richard Lane I encountered in Melbourne was anything but 'that
moron Dick' Allen had made him out to be even to me, the most recent
recruit to the small upper-hierarchy at Harmondsworth. He was shrewd,
unfailingly loyal to Allen and yet in no way bemused by Allen's charisma.
He was as open with Allen's putative biographer as previously Barnes
Wallis had been with his. But Dick had long since severed all connection
with Penguin (Australia) and, though she too lived in Melbourne, he seldom saw Allen's widow.

Lettice Lane I had liked from our first meeting at the Silverbeck lunch-
table, but it was not easy for her to face an inquisition, even if the inter-
rogator was an old friend, her fellow-grandparent. The only time that I
ever knew Lettice to be timid was when she saw my tape-recorder. She
was, however, wondrously frank about a marriage which had often been
eccentric and seldom truly private, but over the years she had kept herself

generally aloof from Allen's public life – I do not remember seeing her even once in the offices at Harmondsworth, nor do I recall that she was ever present in the bar of the Peggy Bedford on the Bath Road where in the early days so many of the most vital matters of Penguin policy were discussed – and she had little or no contact with Penguins in Australia.

I do not know what nice judgement of protocol persuaded Trevor Glover, the Managing Director (himself a contented exile, though later returned to Britain to even more exalted rank) to select as our Australian mentor Rozanne Turner. I only knew that my kindlier gods were watching over him when he made the decision to send Rozanne to collect us from the Dick Lanes. Rozanne is what the Israelis call a *sabra*, an Australian by birth. At the time when she took us in hand she had never been to England but she exhibited, to an advanced degree, all those characteristics of dedication to the Penguin tradition and pride in its essentially Australian expression which I saw in so many of her colleagues and, being Australian, she was not content to treat the stranger to nothing more than efficient professional guidance. Immediately, and ever after, she opened to us her home in the hills above Melbourne. Rozanne is vibrant, in appearance as in spirit still an attractive girl,and I would find it even more difficult to accept that she is a grandmother than it is for me to comprehend that I am a great-grandfather were it not that I have seen her in Sassafras surrounded by children of all ages, and were it not that our homes in Leeds and in London have become staging-posts for wandering Turners.

We returned home from Australia, I with much of the research for the biography completed and some of the writing. I set myself to investigating the Penguin files.

Ron Blass did all that he could to make my task easy and Jim Rose, Boyle's successor and an old acquaintance from the days when he had been Ivor Brown's Assistant Literary Editor and I the Observer's humblest reviewer, gave me the freedom of the Chairman's office. Though I was sometimes accompanied to Harmondsworth by a former student, Elizabeth George, and she, contrary to all expectations raised by her traumatic undergraduate career, one of the most efficient aides I have ever encountered, I had no regular research assistants and Penguin's filing system was at that time shambolic.

I cannot tell why it is that publishers who, more than most professionals, should recognize the significance of archives and who, more often than businessmen in other trades, have in their possession priceless records, are most of them either incompetent or careless in the preservation of archives. In the three decades before I began my research, Penguin had been in correspondence with most of the great and small of English letters, with leading authors, scientists, archaeologists, historians, politicians and philosophers all over the world, but to uncover in the Augean stables that passed for Penguin archives even those letters which, from distant recollection or from more recent research, I knew had once existed, was a labour which would have daunted even Hercules and which was almost too much for a diminished Cyclops with only one eye. At the bottom of one drawer I found a bundle of postcards written to Allen over fourteen years by Bernard Shaw, the first eminent author who encouraged his lunatic six-penny-book venture, the first who wrote to a Penguin commission and the first to be honoured by a Penguin Million. In a cardboard-box with a nondescript collection of ephemera I discovered two mint copies of Hesketh Pearson's *The Whispering Gallery*, the book that the young Allen had forced upon his Bodley Head fellow-directors to publish and which immediately, before ever a copy reached the booksellers, they had been forced to withdraw by menace of an action for libel which must go against them. I came upon one cohesive and consequential series of correspondence, neatly filed but deposited in a cabinet which contained otherwise only records from a much later date, was perplexed because the style and the mode of argument seemed inconsistent with the evidence that the original of every outgoing letter had been signed by Allen himself and then, suddenly, a phrase triggered recollection of myself at my desk in the Nissen hut dictating to Irene Pierions. Every letter in that file had been composed by me for Allen's signature.

At last my work was done and the book ready for the printers. As is now habitual, but as seemed notably incongruous for the biography of a man who with the Penguin Specials had often harried authors, editors, designers and printers to race from signature of contract to publication in three months, I waited it seemed for years for proofs, and for still longer for my voucher-copies, and then pretended to no more interest in *Allen Lane: King Penguin*.

Clare, Lettice, Ron Blass, Bob Lusty: all were enthusiastic. Even the lady whose passionate interest in Allen I had treated with as much delicacy as was consonant with historicity wrote me a grateful and gracious letter.

Then came the reviews. I might have expected that many eminent critics would be eager to seize the opportunity to write on Allen Lane and the Paperback Revolution. I could not have anticipated that in the 'heavies' my book would be given the lead review, that even the popular press would notice it and I imagined myself to be too sophisticated in the ways of reviewers to hope for unanimous approval.

The first clipping I read heartened me; its author, Richard Hoggart, made no secret of the fact that he had himself harboured an ambition to write Allen's biography but he greeted my book with abundant generosity. The clippings poured in, their quantity and the variety of their sources unequalled by those which followed the publication of any other of my books except possibly *Barnes Wallis*. An Australian reviewer praised Allen's biographer for writing so objectively about his *father-in-law* but, with the exception of one antagonistic notice in an obscure journal (which deservedly ceased publication a few months later), all the reviews were laudatory. My publisher and I were deprived of the best of all publicity by an inconvenient strike in BBC Television, but there were broadcasts, personal appearances and friendly comments even in the gossip-columns. By almost every measure I had written a successful book but Allen had worked his magic too well, in these days best-sellerdom is rare without the aid of a paperback publisher. We could not hope that any paperback house other than Penguin would wish to issue a book devoted entirely to the career of the man who had created its one unassailable rival. We looked to Penguin.

Charles Clark, who had taken over from Bob Lusty at Hutchinson, was himself a former Penguin editor and he tried manfully to persuade the hierarchs on the Fulham Road to give to their Founder the credit of a biography in their list. From within Ron Blass worked on his fellow-directors, but there came back to Charles and to me only growling disclaimers. ('At Penguin we do not go in for ancestor-worship.')

Five years later, when Penguins were preparing for the firm's 50th Birthday, it was again proposed that the firm issue my biography of Allen and at the same time Ron Blass suggested that I be commissioned to organize the celebrations. Nothing came of either proposal but the commemorative volume published in 1985 paid a compliment to my work, if in a back-handed way, by following closely the lines of *Allen Lane: King Penguin* (though, of course, without any reference to events in the months after Allen's death). Peter Mayer, by then the Grand Vizier of an empire far larger than any dreamed of by Allen, most generously included me in all the jollifications, but even in 1985 it was only in Australia, and by Penguins at Ringwood that, as Allen's biographer and as almost the last survivor from the glorious days of the 1940s and 1950s, I was thrust forward as a spokesman and stellar performer. Characteristically Trevor Glover even gathered together a large number of his staff to listen to me telling them of their own ancient history. Typically these young Australians – many of whom were not even born when I commissioned Bindoff to write *Tudor England*, when Alan Glover contracted Rieu to translate *The Odyssey* – for an hour after my talk was ended kept me busy answering questions about Allen Lane, his methods and his aspirations, about Penguin policies and Penguin techniques as once they had been.

In the year of publication, however, honour did come to me from another intimate source. honour that is all the more precious to me because it was so gently conferred.

For many years I had been a member of the panel set up by the *Yorkshire Post* to award its Annual Literary Prizes. Judging between books of many kinds is an awkward task but there is much satisfaction for the juror when he sees hoisted a signal of recognition for some literary colleague. Little in all my career has given me so much pleasure as was mine when, sitting next to my old friend, Reggie Smith (the BBC's most skilful and most sensitive director of radio drama), and he for once not talking on his favourite topics – girls, booze, Communism, cricket, poetry and why did Kippe not return to the stage – we watched as his wife, Olivia Manning, went forward to collect the *Yorkshire Post* Book of the Year Prize.

Charles Clark and I were agreed that we must reject the suggestion, put to Hutchinson by Bernard Dineen, the *Post*'s omniscient Literary Editor, that for one year I withdraw from the jury so that Hutchinson could enter *Allen Lane: King Penguin* for the Prize. We argued that it would embarrass my fellow-jurors, all well-known to me, if they felt that they must prefer some other book to mine and that if they gave me their votes the whole world would cry 'nepotism!' My book was not offered as a candidate.

Two or three weeks before the prize-giving Bernard rang Kippe, asked her to ensure our presence at the luncheon in a Harrogate hotel, and begged her to keep his call secret from me.

As a juror I knew the names of the winners before they were announced to the public, and I was concentrating my limited attention on the resplendent hat worn by a large Yorkshire lady at the next table,when suddenly I heard Bernard speak my name. It was all reminiscent of that other sensational occasion, a half-century back, when Mr Fox had announced my Christ's Hospital 'scholarship' to my Islington school-mates.

'In recognition of a life-time of distinguished services to literature and publishing on both sides of the Atlantic. . .'. Harold Macmillan, Prime Minister, publisher, autobiographer and next only to Winston Churchill and Lloyd George the finest orator I ever heard, had been one of my two predecessors as recipient of the Special Literary Award; the other was Elizabeth Longford, biographer to the royal and the grand and wife to my one-time colleague, Frank Pakenham (whose many virtues were even in those days at the Foundation obvious, but for me thereafter not so memorable as that he came almost every day to Nuffield Lodge fresh from his morning battle with a so-called safety-razor, looking like a member of a swashbuckling Heidelberg student-corps). It was not so much the company in which I was placed, nor yet the rarity of the honour conferred on me,which set the *Post*'s Special Literary Award among my most prized possessions. I make no pretence to despising other symbols of recognition and I am proud of my Phi Beta Kappa key, my Alumni Gold Medal and my four honorary doctorates, but all those came to me from my second country, the United States. The *Yorkshire Post*'s Special Literary Award was a tribute from neighbours.

Coincidentally, but for reasons quite other than my services to literature and publishing, I was dignified by an even more intimate circle of friends, I became for a year President of the Amicable Society of Blues and I was elected Deputy Chairman of the Council of Almoners of Christ's Hospital.

The Amicables is the oldest of all Housey's societies, in all probability the oldest Old Boys' club in the world and one of London's oldest dining clubs (it has a continuous history dating back to 1629) and is unashamedly élitist. I doubt that the Brethren themselves, even on Audit Night when elections are held to fill vacancies in the forty-strong membership, could explain why some are chosen and some are never so much as advanced as candidates, but in the quarter-of-a-century when I have been an Amicable I have addressed as 'Brother' a President and a Vice-President of the Royal College of Surgeons, an Air Chief Marshal, a Permanent Secretary of the Ministry of Defence, the inventor of geodetic construction (my own Wallis), a Queen's Household Chaplain, the Editor of The Tatler (my own Youngman Carter), a captain of Essex and three other county cricketers, Oxford Professor of Poetry (my own Blunden), Cambridge's Kennedy Professor of Latin, an Ambassador, Secretaries of the MCC, the Bank of England, the Institute of Electrical Engineers and the Royal Institute of British Architects, the Director of the Chichester Festival Theatre, a Trustee of the British Museum, a Director-General of the BBC, the Deputy Director-General of the GPO, two England Rugby football Trial caps, a plethora of city tycoons, managing directors, actuaries and accountants sufficient to make St Matthew glad that he changed professions, the Warden of Radley College, three Treasurers, three Head Masters and four Clerks of Christ's Hospital, and even two publishers. But the dignity apparent in this resonant and varied roll-call is seldom evident at an Amicables Dinner. Then there is uproar ('brawling' according to our persisting usage, though perhaps the exchanges of wit are not so deft as they were two centuries back when the term was introduced into the Society's vocabulary). Then it is virtually de rigueur to court retribution by breaching some rule in the Society's arcane and catch-all Rule Book and, because the most awesome clause in our constitution decrees that in his year of office the President can do no wrong, then even he who looks to hide himself in the silent minority may find that he has offended against some lex non scripta, and accordingly be subject to a fine (still at the moment of sentence 'a bottle of port' but happily in payment now deflated to one pound).

Description thus cursory suggests that the society is a gaggle of doddering escapees from Who's Who playing at being juvenile delinquents, and so in a sense it is (and none the worse for that),but the fellowship is genuine and the ritualized mayhem but a slim disguise for conjoined activity in the interest of the Foundation.

Ladies have been entertained by the Society only four times in 360 years, but I have not known nor yet have I heard tell of a male guest of the Amicables who was not eager for a second invitation unless, perhaps, it was Charles Lamb. He, the most devoted and the most amicable of Blues but surprisingly not a Brother, being bidden to reply to the Toast to our Visitors, rose to his feet, stammered out the one word 'G-G-Gentlemen' and then, overcome by the awesomeness of his task, sat down, thereby adding to the annals of the Society the glory of the best, because the shortest, after-dinner speech of all time.

Coleridge, when still a school-boy, also came to our table but was not invited to speak or else the Brethren would have sat for three hours over their port, for once in 360 years awed into silence, enthralled as by the profundity, by the orotund sentences and inspired parentheses of that 'wondrous youth'. (S.T.C.: 'Charlie, I believe you never heard me preach.' C.L.: 'Sam, I never heard you do anything else.')

The Presidency moves inexorably from Brother to Brother according to seniority in the Society, and this automatic election may appear to strip the office of all distinction, but no Amicable will condemn as sin my pride in my term and all will forgive me for adding the boast that since the War there have been but two Brethren who were younger than I was at the moment of being invested with the President's gold medallion. (And I was 62 years old!)

The third and last dinner in every President's reign is set for the Anniversary of the Accession of Queen Elizabeth the First, 17 November. In the September before I stepped down, I went to Tennessee to serve for an academic year as Leeds Exchange Professor at Vanderbilt University so, because 'the President can do no wrong', I ordained that Good Queen Bess had come to the Throne on that very day in the year which, later, some who had been among her last and youngest subjects had selected as the day on which to offer thanks to the Almighty for the first harvest in New England. I flew home, ate the most expensive dinner of my life and was back on the Vanderbilt campus in time for my first class after the Thanksgiving week-end break.

The cost of a ticket Nashville-London-Nashville is a small price to pay for three hours of infallibility.

Solemnity is not necessarily the best fuel for serious purpose and in the two decades when I have been part of Christ's Hospital's recognized power-house, the Council of Almoners, I have wished often that its deliberations could be touched by the levity ever-present in the meetings of its rumbustious and unofficial auxiliary, the Amicable Society. Though there is a considerable coincidence in the membership of the two institutions, the imp of frivolousness seldom raises his mischievous head in the Council.

Until very recently, when the Hospital moved its Counting House from 'within blood-spurting distance of Tower Hill' to Horsham, the Council Chamber itself – the very room in which in 1929, had it not been for the intervention of the decorators, I would have faced the Grand Inquisitors – was against light-heartedness, sombre, darkly-panelled and burdened with acoustic properties which seemed to have been deliberately and malevolently devised to thwart the generally elderly ears around the ponderous and highly-polished tables, and the business before us was always too weighty to encourage light-heartedness. Always C.H. faced crisis or some seismic change, usually both at the same time.

To the delight of both biographer and subject, the fantastic commercial success of *Barnes Wallis: A Biography* had allowed me to fulfil a life-time ambition 'to enable others to enjoy the same advantages'. I became a Donation Governor and settled to the task, at once pleasurable and heartrending, of selecting from the hundreds of applications for a Presentation, the candidate who appeared to meet most closely the dual but often contradictory qualifications of need and potential. I look back upon my verdict with smugness born of after-knowledge; my choice, first, of Ian Shaw and, seven years later, of Nicholas King, establishes my perspicacity beyond all question.

17

Good News Yet to Hear

No sooner was I a Donation Governor than I was invited to serve as an Almoner. I sat at my first Council meeting next to another newcomer, my old friend and school-contemporary, Angus Ross, the two of us whispering together like awed new boys on their first day at school, but within comparatively short time we were both of us accepted as members of an unofficial inner cabinet and before the decade was out Angus was the Treasurer and I his Deputy.

As I was quick to point out to Angus, though he was now Worshipful, I as Deputy Chairman could boast one predecessor, Samuel Pepys, whose glory dimmed the fame of all the Treasurers since 1552.

Angus's term as Treasurer, and mine as his Deputy, was bedevilled by crises, financial, administrative and human which, certainly for those of us most intimately involved, made all previous turbulence seem no more sensational than a ripple on the Serpentine. So frequent and so regular were the telephone consultations between us that when of an evening the phone rang in Cliff Cottage, before ever I answered one or other of the students gathered there would say 'Angus Ross calling'. But this fraught period in our history was also the time when C.H. engineered one of the grandest developments in its history, more seminal even than the Great Migration of the boys from London to Sussex in 1902, the reunification of its Boys' and Girls' Schools.

I had been pleading the cause of co-education for many years. Before I was a Donation Governor, I had once goaded Barnes Wallis with the proposition that the time had come to bring together again our boys and our girls. Wallis's response was unequivocal, 'Over my dead body! Young men and young women these days jump into bed together readily enough without C.H. making the jumping easy.' Undeterred, and convinced that there are other advantages in co-education more persuasive than facility in the satisfaction of concupiscence, as a member of the Council and its Education Committee I continued to argue the case on educational, sociological and historical grounds. I was one of the very few members of the Council – in all probability the only one – who had himself experienced co-education, but I was far from being unique in my determination to re-unite our two Schools as one undivided and indivisible Christ's Hospital. Indeed, almost without exception those members of the Council who had any claim to call themselves educationalists were agreed that at some time in the near future we must move the Christ's Hospital Girls' School (the oldest girls' school in the world) from Hertford to Horsham, but I doubt that the re-unification would have been achieved in conscionable time had it not been that inflation threatened the very existence of the Foundation, for then it was that the financial experts among the Almoners were persuaded of the benefits that would flow from educating boys and girls in one place.

The logistical problems involved in the re-unification were complex and many, but I was mistaken when I forecast that none would cause so much debate and none so much anguish as the question of the girls' uniform. We were all agreed that we could not have our boys strutting as peacocks in their traditional and handsome uniforms and our girls still dressed as 'refugees from St Trinian's' (a description previously used by me in print which, even though it has given offence, I repeat because it is apt). I expected endless argument but, apart from some dissension created by Angus's outmoded conviction that no respectable lady will be seen in public without a hat, little came and not by any means the least contributor to the success of the re-unification has been the consonance with the boys' uniform of the dress devised for the girls. Within weeks of their arrival at Horsham it was difficult to remember that, except on certain public occasions, our boys and girls had been separated for more than three centuries.

When Angus died and the Kennedy Professor of Latin became Treasurer, it was inevitable that I quit the seat once occupied by Pepys. Ted Kenney and I considered ourselves 'regal dons' –

With hearts of gold and lungs of bronze,
Who shout and bang and brawl
The Absolute across the hall

– but dons, even 'Good Dons. . . Dons rooted, Dons that understand', in both of the Council's most senior offices: that was more than Christ's Hospital could stomach. Even so,for several years I continued to be a member of the inner circle.

Little in all my public life has caused me so much satisfaction as my work for the Foundation, and never have I given more willingly of my time, experience, knowledge and such wisdom as is mine than I did in those dozen or so years when I was part of the Cabal which directed the present and shaped the future of Christ's Hospital. It was, therefore, a blow almost beyond bearing when, suddenly and to me inexplicably, I was shut out of Housey's 'Cabinet'. My pride was shattered, my sense of justice outraged.

Time hath, my lord, a wallet at his back,
Wherein he puts alms for oblivion;
A great-sized monster of ingratitude;
Those scraps are good deeds past which are devoured
As soon as they are made, forgot as soon
As done.

I was tempted to flaunt off the C.H. stage, never to return.

Kippe counselled forbearance and, as ever when I am urged to discover in myself virtues which I hold in short supply, I rubbed open old wounds.

Three years earlier, from a sense of duty, I had accepted the task of revising and bringing up to date G.A.T. Allan's standard work on Christ's Hospital. I virtually rewrote the book and added several new chapters. The publisher paid no heed to the sheaves of corrections to the galleys sent to him by me and by David Young, the meticulous and scholarly Assistant Clerk. Even he added to the farrago some fictions of his own devising, inaccurate captions to illustrations I had not been shown. It was no consolation that my name was omitted from the title-page; there it was on the wrapper, and at all events 'everyone' knew that I was responsible for this, in all my professional career the most shameful and shaming episode.

I was determined to have good cause for self-pity and so, when Kippe insisted that my fellow-Almoners could not be held responsible for the slip-shod practices of a publishing-house, I shifted my ground from the specific to arrant generalization. All was symptomatic of disdain for obligations incurred, all condemned me to endure such years as were left to me as a miserable victim of ingratitude.

When debating with Kippe it is not possible to cling for long to abstractions. I was soon forced back to a particular. I turned my guns onto an easier target, the petty bureaucrats who administer universities' pension-schemes.

Early in the year when I was due to retire from Leeds I had received from one of those bureaucrats what purported to be the definitive statement of my pension-rights. I was shattered; seven-and-a-half years had been slashed from the period of calculable service as allowed to me by two earlier forecasts. My one year at King's, Newcastle, was disallowed and also – 'the most unkindest cut of all' because, as I exaggerated its implications, it demonstrated the ingratitude of the whole British nation – so were my six-and-a-half years in the Army.

I was dismayed. Because at the NBL I had left the control of my pension to Balleny and his minions, this pittance that was now promised me was virtually all that would come to me in my senescent years. But I was even more indignant, and with just cause. My total pension would be just a little more than one-third of that paid to some fat don who had passed the war years drinking his port in a comfortable common-room.

I hurled myself into a fury of telephone-calls and correspondence. I demanded to know why the Superannuation Scheme had reneged on its twice-repeated promise to honour my Army-service. Back – eventually – came the answer: War service qualified only if it was immediately preceded or immediately succeeded by at least one year in academic employment. Again I telephoned: I had served that year, at King's. Grudgingly, the haughty young man at the other end of the line promised to call me back and, when he did, his voice quivered with triumph. Yes, I had been at King's, the evidence could not be faulted, but most of my stipend had been paid by some foreign university. 'What of it?' I asked. 'But, Professor' (this use of the title was derogatory and he was so pleased with the inflection that he repeated it), 'But, Professor, that makes it overseas service.'

The revelation that the Elswick Road, Grey Street and Jesmond Dene were deemed to be 'overseas' so bemused me that I repeated myself. 'What of it?' He could no longer be patient with senility. 'Surely you see, Professor. Heaven knows the rubric is clear enough; at least one year in a British university, Professor. In 1938 and 1939, as already I have said and as you do not deny, you were in the employ of a foreign university. That makes it overseas service. Right?' 'Wrong', I interposed but he took no notice. 'Overseas service', he continued, 'counts as half. So, your time at King's was six months. Right?' I did not answer. 'Six months,' he repeated, 'and so from our point of view your Army service is irrelevant.'

I slammed down the telephone and began another letter of protest. I wrote more than eighty letters, President Graves of William and Mary intervened at length and indignantly on my behalf, so did three Members of Parliament, so did the University Registrar and so, eventually and to my surprise, did Edward Boyle and at the last, on appeal to all the Vice-Chancellors 'in stately conclave met', a verdict was given in my favour.

The news of my victory was passed to me first on the telephone by that same mean-spirited, minor mandarin who had battered me with the rubrics, and now he gushed. I must know, of course, that he had never wavered in his belief in the equity of my case but there were the regulations. What else could he do but follow where they led? I took this to be a rhetorical question and my silence goaded him. 'You are aware, Professor, that you have been very fortunate. We do not often allow exceptions.' That I could not allow to pass 'Not fortunate', I replied, 'and no exception. Just persistently devoted to an equitable interpretation of the regulations.' I was ready to end the conversation with some empty courtesy but he had more to say. 'Professor, a few years back we refused to credit the war-service of a member who had taken up his first academic appointment on the very day he was demobilized and had taught ever since in a *British* university and do you know why?' I ignored the emphasis on 'British' and mumbled that I did not know why. 'The regulation says', he spoke slowly as if convinced of my indifferent capacity for comprehension, 'that for his military service to be credited, the member must have served in the Forces of Her Majesty or His late Majesty. This member was an officer in the

Polish Air Force. Not acceptable!'

I remembered truck-loads of Poles singing their return to war as they passed through Iran on their way from Russian prison-camps to Egypt. I remembered the Poles at Cassino and the Polish Division on our right as we battered into the Gothic Line. I remembered Jan Kovslovski, an engineering student at King's who had gone back to Poland in September 1939 and returned to die as a fighter-pilot in the Battle of Britain. '"Never in the field of human conflict was so much owed by so many to so few"', I quoted. It was the best that my indignation would allow and again I crashed my phone into its cradle.

I sat staring at the wall. I saw the dreary sitting-room in Cockfosters, the tears streaming down my father's face and I heard again Neville Chamberlain's rasping voice.

It was for Poland that we had gone to war.

I had no intention of playing 'the lean and slipper'd pantaloon' after I retired, indeed the addition of the prefix Emeritus to my title presaged for me just one more in that succession of shifts in central role which had patterned my career, a return to free-lancing but, now that I had outfaced the machinations of the bureaucrats, I had one advantage, financial security, that had not been mine when, thirty years earlier, I had made a brief excursion into the open market. Before I left Leeds, I had already been invited into a world new to me but consonant with my experience and interests; I had agreed to serve as Consultant Director to a large travel organisation. Already Louie Attebery was conspiring to bring me for a second time to the lovely little campus of the College of Idaho close to the Sawtooth Mountains. There would be much for me to do and I might at last find time to write the two novels which had been forming in my mind for many years – one set in the time of the American Revolution, the others in the 1930s and 1940s of this century.

We were sad at leaving Leeds and sadder still at giving up our lovely house with its many rich associations, but I had seen too many elderly academics shuffling up and down the corridors begging for recognition and even for someone with whom to exchange gossip to condemn myself to spending the rest of my life above a shop in which I was no longer working. As so many entering on retirement, we played for a while with the notion of buying a country cottage but my near-blindness and Kippe's aversion to driving made isolation impracticable and the magnetism of London was powerful upon both of us.

It would not be the London of our earlier years, that we knew. I was no longer central to broadcasting and to the book-world. Most of those with whom I had been on Christian-name terms in the 1950s and 1960s had themselves retired, many were dead. I had grown to influence and reputation with a generation ten or even twenty years my senior, with such as Brogan, Gilbert Harding, Potter, Allen Lane and Alan Glover.

Their successors would either not know my name or else, when they heard it, be amazed that Jack Morpurgo was still alive. Several of those who were my then contemporaries – among them Arthur Thompson (Francis Clifford), and that wisest, wittiest and bravest of all my London friends, Michael Flanders, had died long-since. Even so, we were confident that only in London could we make for ourselves a new and stimulating life.

Our son Mark, a compulsive and skilful house-hunter, found for us a mews-house. By our customary expansive standards the house was small, but by brilliant logistical planning and with much generous assistance from Mr Dodd and my friend Sergeant Murphy of the University, we ferried to London from Leeds my most prized possession, my library of 30,000 books, and with the aid of an ingenious carpenter, made our home – we hope for the rest of our lives – in Hammersmith, a part of London remembered from occasional forays to The Doves with A. P. Herbert, but still not quite my own, if less foreign than those mysterious regions south of the River where all the streets lead in the wrong direction.

It was Leeds the city I was sorry to leave; the University I held still in affection, yet I quit with few pangs. Much of the stimulation of campus life had come to me from colleagues who had already moved on or were soon to retire and I recognized in myself symptoms of the disease which I fear above all others: boredom.

I was not bored with students, not even with teaching, but with repetition, with that inevitability which is forced on anyone who, because he must give to his students, in just one year and almost certainly for the only time in their lives, some knowledge of a literature whose masterpieces are few but indisputable, must return year after year to a virtually unchanged syllabus. I was sick of Natty Bumppo, wearied with Hester Prynne, and had I gone on for another two or three years, like Ishmael I would have felt 'a damp, drizzly November' in my soul and must have sunk Captain Ahab and all his crew before ever the *Pequod* left Nantucket. Retirement brought with it release from monotony.

There was, however, reason at once more subtle and more profound why I made my exit from academe without regret. From the moment when I had taken up my appointment, I had suspected that the University was stumbling in the dark, with the years that suspicion had grown to be a conviction, and by 1983 I was certain that not only Leeds but all British universities and perhaps all universities everywhere had mislaid their mission. (Still, romantically and loyally, I had hopes for the Australian National University and for William and Mary.)

I was by no means alone in arriving at this conclusion but most observers, and notably most observers within the universities, placed the blame unequivocally with Government, ascribing decline to the parsimony practised by governments all over the Western world in the 1970s and early 1980s.

There exists always some tension between governments and universities. Ministers and Civil Servants look upon universities as rivals, as potentially dangerous alternative centres of influence; universities watch governments warily, forever sensitive to threats to academic independence. I, who had so often protested against the academic world's prodigality in men and money, could only welcome the rationalization enforced by governmental retrenchment but I could not absolve government, all governments of whatever political colour, of most of the responsibility for the decline of the universities.

For two decades after the War, governments fostered the new universities and, even when that process was ended, still every government demanded an increase in the student-population. For almost four decades every government sought to reduce the status of universities, to make of them something little better than vocational training-schools. Margaret Thatcher's governments have merely been more strident and more insistent than their predecessors.

In all that concerns education I am an élitist, and so unashamed that I dare to regard the term when applied to me, not as synonymous with reactionary, not as a pejorative, but as a compliment to my wisdom. (So also was my hero, Thomas Jefferson, in this sense élitist; it was he, that most noble democrat, who said that only ten in every hundred of the population can benefit from a university education.) The pressure upon universities to cram in more and ever more students terrified me; many, I was convinced, would only be made miserable by higher education. *Unless* – and the qualification I found even more terrifying – *unless* we on the campuses capitulated to the Government's will to make the education given by us not higher education, but meaner than ever that had been which was offered by our predecessors; *unless* we accepted as our prime purpose 'the preparation of the young for the labour-market in a technological society'. I mistrusted (and events have shown that I was right to mistrust) Whitehall's occasional condescending nod to the Humanities, but it was not only for the future of my own favoured subjects that I feared. I held firmly to the belief that in all disciplines it is the all-pervasive responsibility of those who teach to communicate to those who are taught the delights of discovery, that we are in post to enliven the imagination of the young and to enhance their capacity for reasoning, that it is not our business to qualify them for careers.

Again I had powerful support and from one of this century's poets of technology. Barnes Wallis described the purposes of education thus: to encourage 'those qualities of mind and spirit of which we stand so sorely in need. . . to produce men of imagination, men capable of bold and original thought. . . .'

I lacked the influence, and perhaps also the brazenness, which might have allowed me to be an effective opponent to the drear developments which were bringing about the decay of the university but I was happy to be relieved of even the humblest involvement in their advancement.

My year at Vanderbilt – the penultimate year of my professorial career – had confirmed my suspicion that the phthisis I had diagnosed in the body corporate of Leeds was a disease not peculiar to my own university or to Britain. I had hoped for much from the campus which, in the early 1920s had fathered *The Fugitive* and Southern Agrarianism. It could be I looked also for some renaissance in myself of that piratical ebullience which had been mine when, for a few days forty-two years earlier, with Tim Hanson as colleague-advocate and Ora Kay Wisenbaker of Valdosta and the Georgia State Women's College as constant companion and charming ally, we had raided Nashville to win for William and Mary the prize of the next year's International Affairs Convention. I found all the flaws I had observed at Leeds – mechanistic dedication to the syllabus, indoctrination where there should have been enlivenment, indolence, intellectual sterility, an unbridgeable chasm between faculty and students – and at Vanderbilt most of them were writ large.

The ghosts of the Fugitives were indeed omnipresent, they appeared in almost every conversation so that long before the year was out I could have wished that Allen Tate, Robert Penn Warren, Marianne Moore, Laura Riding and Donald Davidson had been forbidden to put pen to paper but few of my colleagues – though notable among the few Dan Young the biographer of the Gamaliel to them all, John Crowe Ransom – showed much inclination to make these blessed spirits lively and useful to their successors as in my youth the shades of Coleridge and Lamb had been made lively and useful to me.

As for Ora Kay Wisenbaker, she had gone with the wind and with unrecoverable time back to Georgia and into mists of reminiscence.

That year in Tennessee also forced me to reconsider my claim to dual nationality. In the previous thirty-five years I had crossed and recrossed the Atlantic fifty times. Not once in all my visits had I felt myself to be an intruder, not once had I sensed that any American regarded me, as most visiting English writers were regarded, as a haughty and prying anthropologist come to dissect a primitive society. But since the War always I had been an itinerant, my roots in Britain, with a return-ticket in my pocket. In Tennessee, for the first time since 1936, I was truly a resident. Twelve months is somehow too long to be considered as 'passing through'. In Tennessee, for the first time since 1938, I lived, worked and relaxed in an exclusively American society.

In the four decades since first I had convinced myself that I was Anglo-American, I had changed. I had seen battle and death, I had known triumph and disaster, I had married and reared a family. The blood still pulsed but now on the prophylactic side of the lectern. The Southern co-eds in front of me looked and sounded remarkably like their mothers (or should it be their grandmothers?) but, even had I been tempted to use my English accent as some sort of aphrodisiac, my evident antiquity must have served as inhibitor.

It was not so much the changes in me, however, as the changes in America and Americans which made me doubt the persistence of my loyalty to the United States.

It was not a good time for an Englishman to be lost in provincial America. The motives which compelled Britain to send a task force to the Falklands were to most of my neighbours either incomprehensible or else interpreted as a vicious recrudescence of British imperialism. Press and radio reviled Britain and – more offensive to my sensitivity – even mocked the men who were fighting. (It was different in politically-sophisticated Washington and it was notable that it was Tim Hanson, of all my friends the least given to Anglophilia but a Washingtonian and as soldier well-nigh a professional, who was most sympathetic to the British cause and most vocal in admiration for British courage and British military dexterity.)

Resentment caused a rush of patriotic fervour to my brain, dulled my reason but made me more than ever before intolerant, more than ever before despising of the American propensity to the chauvinism which was now consuming me. It was not only in those tense weeks when, like true expatriates – or, as at the time I thought more apt, like the oppressed in Nazi-occupied Europe – we listened hourly to the BBC to find the truth that was denied to us by the American media, that I sensed decay in my love for the United States. Throughout that year I was living among foreigners who recognized no community of spirit with my countrymen. Not all were as devastatingly ignorant as the idiot co-ed who informed me, with all the authority of the voice from the burning bush, that of course England (again England!) was not a democracy. 'How could it be when you have all those lords and ladies? How could it be when you're ruled by a queen?' But my neighbours knew less of Britain than of Thailand and were less interested in British affairs than in Nicaraguan.

Since 1776 – in a primitive form since 1607 – twisting the Lion's tail has been for Americans a national sport and a sport made vicious by the green corpuscles in the American blood-stream whenever Ireland was in the news. The Lion was now *sans* claws, *sans* teeth, *sans* empire, the thrill had vanished and the sport became obsolescent. In Tennessee it was seldom played – though it did enjoy a brief revival in those weeks when suddenly the Lion remembered that it could roar. (During the Falklands affair, as if intent on provoking its one man-one woman audience, Nashville radio invariably called the islands the Malvinas.)

When the United States took over from Britain the leadership of the Western World the sport was eagerly adopted and adapted by Europeans and ever since, in its new form as tweaking the Eagle's beak, it has enjoyed international popularity.

Before that year in Nashville I had been mildly amused by American resentment of foreign criticism, by the refusal to accept tweaking the Eagle's beak as a game, but instead to regard it as *lèse-majesté*. Now I could no longer be indulgent; I was infuriated.

In those months of isolation I came dangerously close to losing my affection for the United States. Traits in the American character, quirks in the American manner, which hitherto I had regarded (superciliously) as no more vicious than the faults of a much-loved infant, I now saw as cancers that threatened the health of the whole world. I could no longer tolerate American worship of success, the pretensions of American provincial society, or the mawkishness of American patriotism. I could no longer accept as no more sinister than a schoolboy's pride in his own team the American conviction that democracy is an American product, stamped 'Made in USA' and exported only under an American licence.

My discontents were exacerbated by my immediate responsibilities. I was at Vanderbilt to display to American undergraduates some of the jewels of their own culture. But for more than forty years I had been persuaded that American and British cultural traditions are virtually inseparable, that all these treasures are also part of my heritage – as, indeed they are part of the heritage of every Briton – as for more than forty years I had held it as an article of faith that all that was noble in British culture belonged to every American. How then could I communicate the glories of the Declaration of Independence to an audience which had never heard of Magna Carta? How then (in literary-antique terms an even more intractable task) to reveal the magnificence of *Moby Dick* to young men and women who had never read *King Lear* or The Authorized Version?

Fortunately, for the most part I stayed silent but I seethed, *tu quoque* forever close to my lips. I wanted to say that the American was the shortest-lived empire in all history. I wanted to contrast American bumbling effort to free the Teheran hostages with the bold, efficient assault by the SAS on Iran's London Embassy. Even I found myself gloating over America's humiliation in Vietnam. I recognized the shoddiness of my reactions but could not suppress them whilst I was locked in a provincial prison.

Happily, even during that year, whenever I escaped I found again my own America and several later visits have persuaded me that the months of alienation were aberrant, that I can take again from the drawer in which for all that time it was locked, my American spiritual passport.

My love for America is now even more subjective than it was before my bout of disillusion – and no doubt even more sentimental – but it is also more assured. It no longer troubles me that there are American institutions which I find antipathetic, indeed I am no longer greatly concerned to consider institutions at all. My America is now a galaxy of individual Americans with whom I share not only some sense of the conjoined nature of our national histories and national cultures but also – and much more persuasive to mutual amity – a common past.

In Williamsburg with the Sands we talk of films, books and music and gossip about mutual friends; with the Rileys, of Colonial Virginia and the misdoings of our acquaintances; with the Walkers we leaven gossip with argument about the relative merits of Glenlivet and Wild Turkey whisky. In Maine, the Howards and I reminisced about Egypt and discussed music and poetry, the Kahrls added David Garrick as spice to en-liven our recounting of the more recent adventures of our two families. In Michigan with the Roblings, friendship was assured, again by familial closeness, but also by recall of the time when, John as central to American publishing as I to British, in the inextricably intertwined book-world of our two countries we first established a corps of mutually blessed friends and mutually disdained enemies.

Only with the Hansons, both of them unhesitatingly convinced that the United States is *sans reproche*, both of them hierophantic to the doctrine of Presidential infallibility (providing the President is a Republican), could there be any possibility that I might endanger our relationship by scepticism about the worthiness of American institutions or cynicism about American mores, but the risk is slight. From the first and through close on half a century, our concord had been based on the premise of disagreement. In Washington I have seldom voiced my more profound doubts and when I did my whisper was immediately made inaudible by Tim's roared *ipse dixit*. The oldest of my American friendships is still by me the most treasured of them all.

The gloom that shrouded my year in Nashville was lifted for a few times each week and for this relief, as for its miraculous consequence in establishing for me yet another new career, I owe a debt of gratitude to Vanderbilt.

Leeds had persistently disdained my experience; Vanderbilt invited me to give a course on the History and Practice of Publishing. The Department of English gathered together for my instruction a wondrously eccentric group of Juniors, Seniors and Graduate Students – only young men and women close to the borders of dementia would dare to register for a course as unprecedented and unpredictable as this – and for a whole academic year together we stumbled happily through a syllabus which I invented week by week.

Historians of literature and society have paid little heed to the part played by publishers as patrons to creators and as disseminators of ideas. There is, to my knowledge, only one book which even claims to be an authoritative and comprehensive history of the Book Trade and, for more substantial reason than that its few references to me are both mutually contradictory and inaccurate, that book I dismissed as inadequate for my purposes. In preparing my lectures I was forced to spend long hours dredging the generalized sources for occasional references to publishing – most of which I found inapposite or fallacious – and re-reading the smug househistories put out by publishers intent on glorifying their imprints. There are a few manuals which purport to instruct in the techniques of publishing but they are, most of them, as revealing as logarithm-tables and as enticing as a circular from the Inland Revenue.

I put forward my inability to produce a manageable reading-list to secure grace to excuse my group from the year-long torture by quiz and examination customarily inflicted by American schools and colleges, and was given leave to grade students on the evidence of term-papers on some relevant topic of their own choosing.

In all my teaching years, I never met a class as enthusiastic or as diligent as that collection of self-selected zanies and, without exception, the term-papers were a revelation of what students can do if they are challenged and intrigued. I, who had cause to boast knowledge of Colonial America more detailed and more profound than many acknowledged American experts, learnt from my students much about hitherto unnoticed eighteenth-century American bookseller-publishers. I, who had been active in every campaign since 'the Brophy penny' designed to secure for British authors some financial return for library-borrowings, discovered from one term-paper much of which previously I had been ignorant about Public Lending Right as implemented in Scandinavia and Australasia. A girl who had contributed little to class-room sessions, produced a carefully-researched and fascinating account of religious publishing in Tennessee, a boy a biography in no way 'potted' of the eighteenth century bookman William Daniell.

Early in the first semester one of my class, a little older than the rest and, as she told me without embarrassment, an unmarried mother, approached me with the request that in the place of the requisite term-paper she be allowed to submit a practical exercise. She was, she said, working her way through college as a compositor in a Nashville printery, and she was confident that she could persuade her employer to give to her effort the authority of page-proofs.

I knew of no reason for objecting to this proposal except that my own knowledge of typography was slim and all acquired by osmosis, by working for years close to Jan Tschischold, Hans Schmoller, Sean Jennett and John Frost, but I enlisted the support of the excellent typographer from the near-moribund University Press. I then wrote back to England for the file of my published occasional verse. By Christmas Judy had designed, set and printed a limited edition of *Verses Humorous and Post-Humorous* by J. E. Morpurgo, the traditional 'slim volume' of the poetaster but in appearance almost too elegant to serve for what in truth it was: a monument to the fallibility of those otherwise perspicacious editors who had originally accepted my hesitant versifying.

Early in the New Year Judy came to me again. Could I dream up for her second exercise some more complex and, though she did not say as much, some more worthy production-project. I remembered that when he died Pip Youngman Carter had left behind him an autobiography, unfinished and unpublished.

Pip's sister-in-law, Joyce Allingham, responded to my request that we be allowed to see what we could make of Pip's work with characteristic eagerness and generosity. Immediately she sent out the typescript and a selection of Pip's strong and sensitive portrait-drawings, she suggested that we fill some of the gaps in Pip's narrative with appropriate autobiographical fragments left by her sister Margery and, unprompted by me she offered to meet all the costs of publishing a limited edition and to donate all profits to the charitable Foundation associated with the Amicable Society of Blues.

I had our title for the book before ever we began work. *All I Did Was This*, the opening line of the text, was obvious and in all probability the title intended by the author. (Later, Bob Lusty claimed that he had suggested this title to Pip.)

One evening in every week Judy drove to our apartment nine miles out of town and there, while Kippe played her part as *locum tenens* grandmother to Judy's small son, the two of us worked through all the processes of publication – editing, captioning the illustrations, designing (this again with guidance from the typographer at the University Press), proof-correcting, selecting the binding-cloth – together we wrote, laid out and even addressed and mailed all that was required for a direct-sales campaign.

Most of the credit is Judy's for the distinguished appearance of *All I Did Was This* and for its success. In less than five months we covered Joyce's guarantees, we paid to the Amicable Foundation a not inconsiderable sum and I have left only my two file-copies – but I take as much pride from this small volume as from any publication with which I have been associated and not least because, immediately upon graduation, and on the strength of *Verses Humorous and Post-Humorous, All I Did Was This* and my deservedly warm recommendation, Judy Komisky was appointed to a senior production post in the only national publishing-house in Nashville, the publishing arm of Old Opry. So much for my protestations against turning universities into vocational training-schools!

For me, close to the last phase of my professorial career, the consequence of *All I Did Was This* was as seminal, perhaps even more seminal, than was this happy outcome for Judy Komisky. In the summer after I retired from Leeds we stayed, as was our annual custom, with John and Charlotte Robling in their apartment close to the lake in Chicago. John, too, was about to retire and one evening over dinner he remarked, apropos of very little, that it would be wonderful if we could find some venture in which we could collaborate. That very night, on impulse, I wrote to Joyce Allingham asking if there was any way in which we could help her in her work as executor for Marge and Pip. Back came an invitation to me to join the Board of P and M.Youngman Carter Ltd and the suggestion that, if it could be arranged amicably, John and I take over as Marge's literary agents, at least in the American market.

I have tried my hand at many activities in the service of the printed word. I have been author, editor, publisher, administrator, reviewer, Professor of Literature, chronicler of past achievement and, if only briefly, patron. It has never occurred to me that in the performance of any of these various tasks it was any part of my duty to stifle my prejudices or ignore my affections. I hope and believe that I have never allowed predilection to trap me into favouring the shoddy, or dislike for a person to sour my admiration for his work, but I neither deny nor regret that I have exercised such influence as is mine most strenuously and most consistently for writers, living or dead, whom I regarded as associates and, most of them, friends; for Blunden, Joyce Cary, Olivia Manning, Sydney Carter and Masefield, for Lamb, Coleridge, Leigh Hunt, Cobbett, even Keith Douglas.

So it was that I seized with delight upon the chance to work to enhance the fame of Margery Allingham. Marge was my friend, that was subjective, but objectively I held her to be the most important of the three *grandes dames* of English detective fiction, for her management of characterization and atmosphere more truly an artist than Dorothy L. Sayers and by every conceivable critical standard far superior to the far more popular Agatha Christie. I echoed, whole-heartedly and with all my intellect, Torquemada, that wizard of puzzlement. who wrote in the *Observer*, 'to [Allingham's] Albert Campion has fallen the honour of being the first detective to feature in a story which is by any standard a distinguished novel.'

Yet even when alive, Marge was too often regarded as the least of the magnificent three and after her death in 1966, though the faithful remained staunch, and an occasional reprint added new and younger readers to their number, there was not behind her *oeuvre* the kind of resolute, persistent and well-nigh frenetic advocacy which held Christie firm as the world's best-seller. There were signs, still distant but none the less undeniable, that if action was not taken immediately Margery Allingham might well slip into the list of authors affectionately remembered by fewer and ever fewer readers.

With all the zeal of revivalists preaching a return to the old and true religion, John and I hurled ourselves into the business of ensuring that Marge's popularity would endure at least to the end of the century – and we hoped long after, that her books would be available wherever the classics of crime-writing are cherished.

Six years later,we are justified by the record. With but two exceptions (her first and admittedly adolescent *Blackkerchief Dick* and one aberrant and somewhat hastily constructed novel, *Dance of the Years*) every one of her titles is now either in print or scheduled for reissue in both the British Commonwealth and the American markets. and twenty-three have been published in German translation (several of them for the first time). There are translations in Dutch, Italian, Portuguese. Of the major linguistic groups only the French have resisted our advances – obduracy in no way surprising to two as experienced as we two in the international literary market-place. Several books have been recorded as audio-cassettes, even one in Finnish. There have been dramatized adaptations on radio in Britain, Australia and Iceland. Fame is contagious and, although we cannot claim direct responsibility, we dare to hint that, had we not engineered this justifiable revival, it is unlikely that American publishers would have accepted for publication a detailed and scholarly bibliography and a biography, or that one British publisher would have contracted a rival life of Margery Allingham and another commissioned me to edit a volume of short stories, most of them hitherto uncollected and several hitherto unpublished.

Even when Marge and Pip still lived it had surprised me, as it had infuriated them, that with one unsatisfactory exception, an adaptation of *The Tiger in the Smoke,* none of Marge's books had ever been produced for cinema or television. Within a week of becoming a director of P. and M. Youngman Carter, I began the long and often frustrating process which ended when, early in 1989, the BBC screened the first episode of *Campion.* (American television is to follow, and so also the networks in many other countries.)

The story of this, perhaps the most sensational and, such is the power of television, assuredly the most potent of our triumphs, would in itself provide material for a novel.

I tried all my many contacts in British television, John his in Hollywood. One left-hand man to a movie-mogul flew from California to Chicago to talk to us, a junior impresario from the West Coast all the way to London to talk to me. All responded with encouragement and delay. All came back at last with some reason for rejection: Margery Allingham's work was too atmospheric to be translated to vision; it was too arcane; it would be beyond their budget; Miss Marples and Hercule Poirot filled the screen daily, there was no space left for Albert Campion.

Richard Armitage, son of Noel Gay and the impresario who had launched the highly successful London revival of his father's *Me and My Girl,* picked up from somewhere the gossip that I was touting Allingham round the market-place. He wrote to me and the letter reached me when we were again in Chicago, mourning with the Roblings the failure of all our efforts. He had long thought to produce Allingham for television; could we meet?

We met, and over tea-cups I voiced an error of judgement which, though it had no bearing on the business we were there to discuss, must have made Armitage question my reputation as an expert on things American. *In passim,* he told me that he was about to open *Me and My Girl* on Broadway. What did I give for its chances? I had seen the show in 1939, in the week before we went to war, and again in the early days of its return to London. Both times I had enjoyed its simplicity, its tunefulness and the brilliance of the performance but, with all the assurance that had been mine when advising Allen Lane not to publish Rieu's translation of *The Odyssey,* I told Armitage that a musical from another generation would never please an audience accustomed to Lloyd-Webber, that *Me and My Girl* was too resoundingly British to attract Americans, in fact that it could not last more than a few weeks on Broadway.

Five years later it is still showing to full houses.

Without comment, Armitage returned to the business that had brought us together. He would make the Campion films – if he could find a backer. He would write.

Three months later he wrote. He was, he said, still keen to bring Allingham to the screen but it would be an expensive undertaking and none of the men with big money shared his eagerness. Perhaps next year....

Within twelve months Armitage was dead and I had sold an option on the film-rights of eight Campion novels.

From the first, John and I had agreed that there was one producer whose sensitivity to the recent past made him an ideal candidate for adapting to film novels set in the two decades before the War, the War years and the first decades of peace but, for reasons which now seem foolish, because we thought him beyond the range of our ambitions and inevitably too involved with other major ventures, I had not approached the producer of *Upstairs, Downstairs*.

After Armitage had all but turned us down there was nothing else for it: I would try John Hawkesworth and if he spurned us, we would close our files.

Haughtily, though no doubt properly, Thames Television and the BBC refused to give me Hawkesworth's address. He was not listed in any of the obvious reference-books, so I went to the most obvious of all and wrote to the only John Hawkesworth in the London Telephone Directory. For all I knew the man I wanted lived in Moor Park or St George's, Weybridge, for all I knew the man to whom I addressed my three-page letter was a merchant banker, a fence or a dealer in erotica.

Two mornings later *the* John Hawkesworth phoned. For years, he told me, his wife had been nagging him to film the Campions. We must lunch together.

On the way to the restaurant I thought to ask my host if he was related to General Hawkesworth who had commanded 46 Division in some of the fiercest battles of the Italian Campaign. Questions of this order are usually futile – even when asked of a Morpurgo – and almost as fatuous as enquiring of a Bostonian if he knows a Patrick Kelly once met by the enquirer when on holiday in Florence and by him believed to live in Massachusetts – or was it Connecticut – but for a good thirty minutes before either of us so much as mentioned Albert Campion I reminisced about Ginger Hawkesworth, for a while during the War a fiery element in my life, who had died on his way back from Italy to take over an Army Corps. It was not planned; there was no way that I could have predicted the coincidence, but no doubt the fact that I had been in contact with his father for almost two years after John had seen him for the last time made less awkward than usual the first moves towards negotiation.

Even when John had reiterated his interest in the works of Margery

Allingham, the way forward was long and littered with anxieties. As at some time every author, however distinguished, however popular, I know the trauma of scrabbling through the morning mail for envelopes from editors. Early in my career I had suffered the despondency that comes with the sight of a rejection-slip and later the even deeper gloom that comes with reading one of those refusals, rejection-slips stretched out to the length of letters, which some editors write either because they are truly kindly or because they hope for a chance to publish the author's next work. As author I had experienced rejection, as editor I had often been responsible for the disappointment of others. Even I knew something of the byzantine behaviour of the movie-men. I had suffered in Hollywood and in London; three times I had sold an option to film my *Barnes Wallis* but the film had never been made. Even so, I was unprepared for what followed my lunch with Hawkesworth: long silences interspersed with bouts of urgent activity, anxiety alternating with excitement, euphoria with despair.

In the world of print a nod from an editor is close to being a guarantee that on some day (if in our sluggish times, on some day in a distant future) the mendicant author will receive his voucher copies. In the world of films, John's nod meant no more than that the responsibility for progress moved from my hands to his. There was still much for him to do – money to be found, the reactions of the British and American networks to be tested, treatments to be written – before ever we came to consider the first legal document. Even that was no more than an agreement to purchase an option to film and, until a definitive contract was signed, I waited, impotent to influence events, while script-writers were taken on, while John's company, Consolidated Productions, negotiated with the BBC in Britain and PBS in America. Nor was contract a remedy for worry; yet to come were scripts, locations, casting, direction and, at the last, after three years, the critics and the viewers.

That I rode all the ups, downs and troughs of those years with equanimity I owe to the confidence inspired by John Hawkesworth and to the heartening courtesy shown by him and by his colleagues to me as Marge's living *alter ego*. That I revelled in my neophyte status as entrepreneur I owe to the circumstance that collaboration brought us even closer to the Roblings, and to the unflagging support I received throughout from Joyce McLennan and Joyce Allingham.

Thirty years earlier, Francis Clifford had told me that in the moment when he sold *The Naked Runner* to Hollywood the moguls lost all interest in him. I had heard from many another author similar tales of how they had been courted by film-makers, captured and immediately disdained. If these sad histories typified the puny respect of cinema and television for the prime creator, Hawkesworth and his associates are atypical. I was kept informed about every step in the elaborate dance and whenever there was possibility that I (or through me Joyce Allingham) could contribute a detail unknown to the producer, I was consulted.

I have been throughout my career remarkably, and no doubt unde-servedly, fortunate in my closest colleagues. Except for a few months at Leeds, when I changed secretary four times, when nothing was done as I wanted it done and little done at all, I have been cossetted by secretaries and personal assistants, all of them efficient, all of them diligent and, a char-acteristic not entirely advantageous to an employer intent on keeping his mind on his work, most of them personable. Once I retired and so, for almost the first time in fifty years, found myself without the support of a large organisation and yet involved in activities even more diverse than ever before, I was in desperate need of the care of a good secretary. Ruth Thomas fitted that role magnificently and when she re-married and went into exile in Bristol, I was certain that she could never be replaced. Then came Joyce McLennan. Comparison is dangerous – several of my former secretaries watch over me still – but Joyce is as skilful as any of her prede-cessors, as dedicated to my work – and of them all the most handsome. And for expert knowledge of the Allingham *corpus* I would back her against Marge's bibliographer, her two biographers – and me.

I had known Joyce Allingham from the very first time I visited Tolleshunt D'Arcy but, until we began to work together, I had seen her only dimly through the blinding vividness of Marge and Pip, and had thought of her as the willing Martha to Marge's demanding Mary. In these last years I have come to appreciate that, though her devotion to her sister's work is intense and her determination to hold and enlarge public apprecia-tion of Margery Allingham unbounded, Joyce is no shadowy reflection of her sister's greatness but a personality in her own right, shrewd but gentle, determined but understanding, possessed of that kind of sophistication which is timeless and utterly without subservience to fashion. In all the vicissitudes that we have suffered in our attempt to bring about the Margery Allingham Renaissance, she has lifted me out of despondency, in all our triumphs her excitement has been for me a reward greater than any sense of achievement. And the greatest of all my rewards has been her friendship.

At a time in my life when so many of my closer acquaintances have gone to their graves or to living internment in a country cottage, the addi-tion of one new and stalwart friend to my sum of friendships is a miracle.

In the losing battle that the plot fights with the characters it often takes a cowardly revenge. Nearly all novels are fable at the end. . . because the plot requires to be wound up.

Thus E. M. Forster, wailing self-pity for the frustration of a writer of fiction but with no sympathy to spare for his fellow-craftsman, the auto-biographer who, alone among manufacturers of literary artefacts, is denied all possibility of designing his conclusion, who cannot tell whether the last chapter will be long or short, glorious or miserable.

Six years have passed since my sixty-fifth birthday signalled my statutory entry into senescence. I enjoy the petty privileges – half-price tickets for matinées and free travel on the London Underground – which a grudging society allows to those who have managed to survive into old age but, these apart, there is little superficial change in my condition. Still, as for the last forty-six years, I am chained to a desk littered with papers, books and cigarette-ash. My telephone shrills as often as ever it did in Albemarle Street, Harmondsworth or Leeds. Still there are students to advise and friends of distant acquaintances seeking help in placing their unplaceable manuscripts. Still I sign contracts. I neither feel nor covet that sense of release from activity of which the laureate of pensioners wrote when he retired from the East India House (and Elia was then only fifty and blessed with an annuity of £400 – a fortune by extrapolation to 1989!).

Yet actuarial calculation has forced upon me a subtle metamorphosis which has made me, in my seventies, close kin to the man I was in my twenties and no relation to the me of the intervening years.

Between 1939 and 1945 I dreamed and planned my future because only with optimistic practicality could I hold my mind against immediate terror, only by preparing for *après la guerre* could I persuade myself to discount the likelihood that I would never see peace. In 1989 I pretend to immortality, not because I am more than most men fearful of death but because without a view of the future the present would be worthless and insupportable.

The passage of the years has reduced, has well-nigh eliminated, that resilience which in my younger years made disappointment and distress ephemeral. I can no longer shrug off disaster and turn immediately to some new and intriguing endeavour, but age brings realism and has its own consolations, its own source of strength; pride in achievement. I need no longer nourish petty hurts; I see the boys and girls of Christ's Hospital re-united and I know that I contributed more than most to that happy conclusion. I read of the development of an omniscient and omnipotent Penguin empire, and I remember staff-meetings at Harmondsworth in the 1940s and 1950s, seven of us and I as vocal and as useful as any. In my years I have contributed something to understanding between my two countries, Britain and the United States. My bibliography is long, not without honour; I may yet add to it the edition of the Christ's Hospital Archives and I hope much more.

I have outlived the generation not truly my own which cossetted me to some reputation. I do not find it easy to accept that young editors either have never heard my name, or else greet it with that look of surprise which they might wear were they told that Christopher Marlowe was still writing plays, and I find hard to stomach the offer of some youthful producer to teach me microphone or camera technique. I console myself by recall of poor Wilfred Gibson, once the darling of the Georgians, in his last year waving under my nose the rejection-slip which was all that his own publisher deigned to enclose when returning a sheaf of his poems. At least I have not suffered similar humiliation – not yet.

I venture no balance-sheet for a life that has been long and varied, and, even if all that is left for debit or for credit is *requiescat in pace*, the task of completing my account I commit to some as yet unknown collaborator. But in all that has gone before I have allowed myself only occasional and passing reference to that element in my life which has given me most reason for contentment and most cause for pride. So, like some Victorian novelist confiding to his readers a summary of the post-dénouement circumstances of those of his characters who have survived the 'winding-up' of his plot, as I come close to the end of this chronicle, I enter into the record my family.

My children should have appeared on almost every page of the second half of this narrative, a loyal claque to my triumphs, an unflinching support in my times of adversity and, all of them, fascinating and warm-hearted companions, but in this unjustifiably curt codicil I write of my children as now they are.

Pieter and Michael have both followed where family tradition led and environment encouraged. Pieter, after a brief venture onto the stage, transferred to the service of the BBC the theatrical legacy he had inherited from both sides of his family, and has risen to be one of the Corporation's most trusted and most effective television-directors.

Michael, too, has followed family precedent, in his case into literary endeavour which I have attempted only once and his grandfather never: writing for children. (Emile Cammaerts did write what I hold to be the best of all critical books on Nonsense literature.) The pleasure he has given to his readers and the unanimous acclaim of commentators who do not share my cause for bias in his favour prove him to be one of the finest exponents of the genre currently writing in English. As for me, I can but confess that all my oft-boasted capacity for critical dispassion vanished, submerged by pride, even by a sort of personal vanity, when I sat in the audience at the Royal Première of the film-version of his book, *Why the Whales Came*.

It can hardly be said that Mark's career has been set by family tradition, though I suspect that his namesake, my father, is dancing delightedly in his grave when he looks out at a grandson now a tycoon in the life assurance industry, but it would not surprise me were Mark to announce that he is at work on a book.

The pleasure I take from the professional success of my three sons knows no limits and is, I hope, forgivable, yet it is not their eminence in their vocations which delights me and certainly not their prosperity, but rather their unwavering loyalty to us and to each other. And there is more, much more. I have three daughters-in-law who have made themselves intrinsic to the family sodality, grandchildren who, in fashion appropriate to their various ages, accept their grandparents as worthy companions and

– to me the most amazing and the most delectable of all my experiences –
I have a great-granddaughter.

No doubt it is because our familial relationships are generally comforting and so comfortable that the exception is, for us all, tragic and bitter. Our daughter married a Muslim, converted to Islam and separated herself and her children from the rest of the family.

Of us all, only Kippe has any right to be hurt by defection from the Established Church, but none of us can tolerate the intolerance of fundamentalist Mohammedanism and none of us can condone the illiberality of the social dogma now accepted without protest by a woman who was reared to liberal principles.

It is possible that I will not survive to fulfil the many ambitions which still possess me, that I may not add even one item to my bibliography, that I may never return to Australia or India, but if I knew how to pray there would be one prayer forever on my lips: that I be granted time and the capacity to recover for Kippe, for myself and for all the family, the affection of my daughter and my two Muslim grandchildren.

I began this exploration of memory with myself bemused, a castaway on an island made hideous by menace, lost between the familiar land of childhood and the enchanted continent of adolescence. Today, after six skirmishes with eye-surgeons, when I stand at the other end of the long, straight path down which sixty years ago my parents walked to the Christ's Hospital station I can scarcely make out even the outlines of the buildings once so awesome and yet so rich with promise.

The eye of the imagination cannot be dimmed by scalpels, there is before me another Centre Path. I do not know whither it leads. I lack the faith to believe that at its end I will find 'cloud-capp'd towers... gorgeous palaces... solemn temples' I expect only that some day, I know not when, I shall be dragged from its sure surface into the mud of oblivion. Meanwhile, for as long as I am able, I will walk that path looking forward, to right and to left, for new excitements. I do not covet an existence hereafter, for I cannot credit that the Deity is so scrupulously selective that He will allow to me the everlasting company of those who have been the benison of my earthly existence. All that I crave for my worldly future is Kippe by my side, her gently-guiding hand on my elbow. All that I fear is that eternity exists and I unable to single her out from its milliard population.

When that day comes when I am faded out of this 'insubstantial pageant', I hope that I will have courage left to console myself for my exclusion from mortality with the thought that in my lifetime I have contributed a few trifles to the happiness of my companions, and with the certain knowledge that there are others, some in my own family, whom I have helped to make competent to take up whatsoever I let slip from my grasp.

Index to Principal Persons